Praise for *Noble Ambitions*

"A compelling and fascinating look at the near demise of the country house."

—Ian Murray, executive director, The Royal Oak Foundation

"Rock stars, hippies, new money, and old money collide in this thrilling new exploration of the country house's tumultuous history after World War II, where demolition, aristocratic entrepreneurship, and the scrappy adolescence of country house tourism combined to enable the houses, if not their owners, to hold their own in contested times."

—Dr. Oliver Cox, University of Oxford

"The crisis of the country house in embattled twentieth-century Britain provides a metaphor of national decline and eventual renewal. . . . Nobody is better qualified to tell this tale of loss and transformation, in all its human complexity, than Adrian Tinniswood. A master of the sources, he brings the past to life through his vivid writing and seemingly bottomless fund of stories."

—Clive Aslet, author of *An Exuberant Catalogue of Dreams*

"By turns uproarious, scandalous, and occasionally melancholic, *Noble Ambitions* shows that the business of running a country house required vision and bravery, and the single-minded determination not to be 'the one to let it go.' From roaming lions to machine gun-toting footmen, this is a book that is full of stories much like the mansions that it so affectionately portrays."

—Ben Cowell, Historic Houses

"Delightful. Scrupulous research by Tinniswood, with telling details and poignant stories, makes this a compelling narrative of postwar Britain."

—Sandy Nairne CBE FSA, curator and writer

"Adrian Tinniswood's highly entertaining narrative of life in the postwar English country house is a refreshing antidote to the usual gloom-ridden accounts of debt and demolition. As this meticulously researched book reveals, not only was the country house alive and kicking, but it was at times quite literally a circus."

—Dr. Martin Postle, Paul Mellon Centre for Studies in British Art

"With pithy prose, witty asides, and great breadth and depth, Adrian Tinniswood tells the tale of the downfall and glorious rebirth of the English country house in the last half of the twentieth century. This entertaining book is that rarest of creatures: scholarly, fun, and hard to put down."

—Curt DiCamillo, fellow of the Royal Society of Arts

NOBLE

AMBITIONS

THE FALL AND RISE OF
THE ENGLISH COUNTRY HOUSE
AFTER WORLD WAR II

ADRIAN TINNISWOOD

BASIC BOOKS
NEW YORK

Basic Books
Hachette Book Group
1290 Avenue of the Americas, New York, NY 10104
www.basicbooks.com

Printed in the United States of America

First Edition: September 2021

Published by Basic Books, an imprint of Perseus Books, LLC, a subsidiary of Hachette Book Group, Inc. The Basic Books name and logo is a trademark of the Hachette Book Group.

The Hachette Speakers Bureau provides a wide range of authors for speaking events. To find out more, go to www.hachettespeakersbureau.com or call (866) 376-6591.

The publisher is not responsible for websites (or their content) that are not owned by the publisher.

Print book interior design by Trish Wilkinson.

Library of Congress Cataloging-in-Publication Data

Names: Tinniswood, Adrian, author.
Title: Noble ambitions : the fall and rise of the English country house after World
    War II / Adrian Tinniswood.
Other titles: Fall and rise of the English country house after World War II
Description: First edition. | New York : Basic Books, 2021. | Includes bibliographical
    references and index.
Identifiers: LCCN 2021009346 | ISBN 9781541617988 (hardcover) | ISBN
    9781541617995 (epub)
Subjects: LCSH: Manors—England—History—20th century. | Country homes—
    England—History—20th century. | Country life—England—History—20th
    century. | Social change—England—History—20th century. | England—Social
    conditions—20th century.
Classification: LCC DA566.4.G7 T56 2021 | DDC 942/.0855—dc23
LC record available at https://lccn.loc.gov/2021009346

ISBNs: 978-1-5416-1798-8 (hardcover), 978-1-5416-1799-5 (ebook)

LSC-C

Printing 1, 2021

For Felicity Bryan
1945–2020

Grandeur must be abandoned to be appreciated.

Blaise Pascal

CONTENTS

FOREWORD

In my beginning is my end. In succession
Houses rise and fall, crumble, are extended,
Are removed, destroyed, restored . . .

—T. S. ELIOT, "EAST COKER" (1940)

B Y THE OUTBREAK of the Second World War many of Britain's
country houses—whether ornate baroque palaces or picturesque Tudor manor houses, vast neoclassical mansions or battlemented Victorian follies—had been tottering for years under the
weight of rising taxes, a dwindling supply of domestic help, and
an uncomfortable sense that as a class their owners were surplus
to requirements, as anachronistic in twentieth-century Britain as
the rusting suits of armour that decorated their dusty halls. In 1939
the golden age of the country house, with its lavish entertaining
and its armies of servants, was a distant memory—and, in truth,
a memory that had been burnished by the passage of time until it
shone more brightly than it ever had in real life. But on one thing,
truth and memory were in agreement: the years since the end of
the First World War had been a disaster for the country house.
Estates had been broken up. Mansions had been emptied of their

1

contents and demolished. Families who had been at the heart of rural communities for generations had been forced to sell up and move away. The country house was in crisis.

It is hard to pinpoint just when the rot set in. Was it with the agricultural depressions of the 1870s and 1880s, or the advent of death duties in the 1890s? Was it due to the shortage of domestic servants after the First World War, the increase in land taxes, and the decline in land values? Or, less tangible but perhaps most significant of all, the growing sense in the 1920s and 1930s that the country house was a monument to an undemocratic past and a way of life that was neither viable nor socially desirable? Whatever the cause, by 1939 hundreds of estates had been broken up and the mansions which stood at the heart of those estates had been sold. In a single county, Northamptonshire, thirty of the seventy-two principal country houses standing in 1919 were sold over the next twenty years, several of them more than once.[1] And all too often, houses that couldn't find a buyer were simply demolished: in England alone, nearly 420 mansions were destroyed in the years between the wars. No wonder that in 1944, when Evelyn Waugh wrote *Brideshead Revisited*, that classic novel of loss, he was convinced, as he said later, "that the ancestral seats which were our chief national artistic achievement were doomed to decay and spoliation."[2]

They weren't alone in suffering hardships, of course. For most people in Britain, victory over the Axis powers was a bitter pill, bringing with it years of austerity. Around 750,000 new homes were needed in England and Wales alone in 1945, simply to house the existing population. Food shortages became so severe that the new Labour government which came to power in the summer of 1945 had to introduce temporary bread rationing and potato controls. The wartime rationing of many goods remained in force for years: petrol rationing only came to an end in 1950, and controls on meat and bacon would continue for another four years. Britain was poor and, with a per-person average daily intake of only 2,700 calories, it was hungry: there was a boom in the sale of weighing machines, and at golf's Open Championships at St Andrews in 1946 England's Henry Cotton blamed his poor performance on a lack of stamina caused by food rationing.

But whereas during the war an "all in it together" attitude had prevailed (on the surface, at least), the peace brought a renewal of class conflict, and faced with a future that didn't want them and a past that cost too much, country house owners grappled with difficult choices: Sell off a few farms, or that dusty little medieval book of hours in the library that no one had opened for centuries, or the Reynolds of Great-Great-Grandmother hanging on the stairs? Shut up the house for a while, move to somewhere more manageable on the edge of the estate and hope things would improve, or give up an ancestral seat which had been in the family for generations and bring in the demolition contractors to salvage what they could from a white elephant that no one wanted? In other words, stay or go?

Nevertheless, alongside this narrative of destruction and despair, the death duties and the dispersal of collections, and the demolition of country houses, there runs another, more complex story, and it is this alternative narrative that *Noble Ambitions* tries to unravel. Some great and less-great houses were abandoned by their owners, yes—but most were not. Some were demolished, yes; although again, most were not. Some became schools, or institutions, or National Trust showplaces. Most did not: they remained homes. For every impoverished country squire watching in horror as the taxman chipped away at the foundations of his ancestral seat, there was another who managed to carry on, writing angry letters to the *Times* about financial ruin and then ringing for his butler to take them to the post. And when country houses did come on the market, as they did in increasing numbers, there were new people ready to step in and buy themselves a piece of the past, ready to take their place in the community and able to compensate for the lack of a fat entry in *Debrett's* with a fat bank balance.

The English country house—like its comrades in Wales, Scotland, and Ireland, which put in occasional appearances in these pages—is a remarkably resilient beast. Predictions of its death came thick and fast in the twenty-nine years between the end of the war and the famous and enormously influential 1974 exhibition at the Victoria and Albert Museum which both proclaimed its destruction and ensured its survival and which ends my story, for the time being at least. Yet, even when the demolitions were at their height in the dark days of the 1950s, dozens of new country houses were going up, old ones were being reinvented, and old families were continuing to live in them. When new families took over old houses, they loved and cherished them every bit as much as their predecessors had. Life in the country house in the 1950s and 1960s was complicated. It was uncertain at times. But it was dynamic and exciting, and in spite of protestations to the contrary, it made an important contribution to British culture.

Noble Ambitions is my attempt to reconstruct and understand a way of life that was sometimes comic, sometimes fraught with anxiety and self-doubt, sometimes outrageous and glamorous. I have tried to understand a forgotten moment in the history of the English country house, a curiously intimate collaboration between members of the crumbling old order and of the rising new, as a rakish, raffish, yet aristocratic Swinging London came to interact with traditional rural values in the stately homes of Britain.

1

THIS IS WHY

T HE ANNUAL FLOWER show was an important event in the life of the little Wiltshire village of Corsley. Every August on bank holiday Monday people poured into Corsley to admire the floral displays and elaborate table decorations, the Madeira cakes and sultana scones and strawberry jams. Villagers vied with one another to win a prize in one of the 121 different categories, which ranged from best begonia in a pot and finest vegetable marrow to best boiled beetroot, best embroidered linen tray cloth, and the marvellously vague "something new from something old." A silver rose bowl was presented to the owner of the best flower exhibit, and there were egg-and-spoon races, a tug-of-war, and all kinds of sideshows, from darts and a bran tub to a coconut shy and a shooting gallery. The day ended with dancing in the village reading room to music from a local band. It was a very English affair.

The show was in hibernation during the Second World War, but it was revived again in August 1945 on the day when the *Enola Gay* loosed its load of 141 pounds of uranium-235 over Hiroshima. Proceeds from the fete went to the local Welcome Home Fund for returning servicemen and women. There weren't many entrants, but the organising committee nevertheless felt they had made "a most encouraging start towards a resumption of activities."[1]

The Marquess and Marchioness of Bath, 1949

They were right: the following year, 1946, saw interest return to prewar levels, with nearly five hundred entries assembled for the show on Monday, August 5. Corsley had been part of the Longleat estate for generations, and villagers were particularly keen to hear from their new landlord, Henry Thynne, who had succeeded his father as 6th Marquess of Bath two months earlier and who, as president of the Sports and Horticultural Society, was there to open the festivities. In his early forties, Lord Bath was "a handsome and youthful man with eyes like coals and little white teeth neatly arranged," according to one contemporary.[2] "Racily articulate, worldly-wise, quick to laughter," said another.[3]

There was no laughter this afternoon. Lord Bath stood up to speak at 3 p.m., and after offering the kind of congratulatory platitudes which were usually trotted out on these occasions—a thank-you to the organising committee, praise for the high standard of entries—he suddenly became very serious. "I should like to touch on a far more intimate and personal matter," he told the silent crowd. "For many years now we have been hearing of the changing face of Britain, and I regret to say that Corsley is about to play its part in this respect."[4] As he went on, the nature of the "intimate and personal matter" slowly dawned on his audience.

Lord Bath was selling their village.

As VISCOUNT WEYMOUTH (a traditional courtesy title for the Marquess of Bath's eldest son), Henry Thynne had been running the extensive family estates in Wiltshire, Somerset, Northamptonshire, and Shropshire since 1928. They were centred on Longleat House, the magnificent mansion which had been in his family since it was built by his ancestor, the entrepreneurial Sir John Thynne, back in the sixteenth century. Henry and his socialite wife, Daphne, didn't live at Longleat, however; they preferred Sturford Mead, a light and airy Regency villa just outside Corsley. There they gave libations of wine to a statue of Bacchus, originally intended for Longleat, which they had found in an outhouse. They entertained their bohemian friends, drank a lot (when they weren't pouring the drink over the marble feet of the god), and played jazz until all hours, safely out of earshot of Henry's widowed father, who remained in residence at Longleat House, kept company by his Great Dane, Stephen.

The old marquess had once lived in some style, keeping more than twenty indoor servants at Longleat and insisting that his footmen wear silk stockings, patent leather pumps, and cockade hats. But rising taxes and falling rents had taken their toll: he had been forced to sell off 8,600 acres of the Longleat estate between 1919 and 1921, and after his son took over the management of the estate there were further sales, the most significant of which came in 1939, when nearly 5,000 acres in Somerset went under the hammer, including dozens of farms and smallholdings. The sales largely involved land which the 5th Marquess had made over to Henry some years before. Death duties, introduced in 1894, two years before the old marquess succeeded to the title, had risen steadily until by the Second World War Henry was facing the prospect of having to pay 65 per cent of the value of his taxable estate when his father died; but gifts made more than three years before the death of the donor were exempt, and it was common practice for owners to hand over at least part of an estate during their lifetime.

But the Marquess of Bath held on to too much of his capital, and when he died at Longleat in June 1946, a few weeks before his eighty-fourth birthday, his son Henry found himself facing a bill from the Inland Revenue for more than £700,000—something in the region of £100 million in today's money. What was all the more galling to the new Lord Bath was that the Labour budget of April that year had raised estate duties from 65 per cent to 75 per cent: if his father had had the grace to die just before the budget, rather than just after it, Henry would have been £150,000 better off.

Now he felt he had no choice but to sell Corsley, along with other parts of the Longleat estate and the family's holdings in Northamptonshire and Shropshire, even though, he told his tenants, "to sell part of the Longleat estate is more than I can bear."[5]

In his speech to the stunned villagers of Corsley on that bank holiday Monday afternoon in 1946, Henry put the blame for his decision squarely on Clement Attlee's Labour government, which had come to power in a surprise election victory the previous year, and which was not only pushing through a programme of nationalising sectors of the British economy but also using taxation as a way of ironing out social inequalities, raising the rate of income tax to 97.5 per cent for the highest earners. "The days of the large estates are over," he said. "Tradition and inheritance are a thing of the past, and today it is the State—and the State only—that matters."[6] Personal initiative counted for nothing anymore; "the more money you earn, the more money is taken away from you." He had planned to modernise their homes, putting bathrooms, lavatories, and electric lights into every cottage and farmhouse, he told the villagers; now all that money must go towards death duties. "I hope you will bear me no malice in that which I have been forced to do."[7]

Henry offered Cley Hill, a local landmark in Corsley parish, to the National Trust, which, from its founding in 1895 as a small-holding charity dedicated to promoting "the permanent preservation for the benefit of the nation of lands and tenements (including buildings) of beauty or historic interest," had evolved into an articulate and sometimes strident advocate for the cause of the country house.[8] With a membership of 7,850 it was, however, still far from being the significant force in British culture that it would become by the end of the twentieth century. The trust accepted Cley in 1954. Henry may also have had informal discussions with the trust over the future of Longleat House itself; prewar legislation had altered the trust's charitable status so that if it accepted a house, the owner and his or her descendants would be allowed to stay on as tenants. "The advantage to the owner combines freedom from responsibility with the assurance that the connexion of his family with the family seat shall not be sharply and completely broken," an approving *Times* editorial declared.[9]

By 1946 the trust had been given eighteen country houses, and between 1946 and 1961 it would acquire another sixty. This represented a fraction of the whole but included many which are rightly regarded as among the very finest stately homes that Britain has to offer—Knole, Petworth, Stourhead. True, they tended to be presented as shrines at which only the cognoscenti were qualified to worship rather than as homes, making few concessions to the unlearned until well into the 1970s. "The classical columns supporting the entablature, carved by the mason William Griffin, are in the Renaissance vocabulary of Serlio's architectural treatises," declared the guidebook to Hardwick Hall in Derbyshire, while at Charlecote Park in Warwickshire, visitors were told that "the doorway, flanked by pairs of Ionic pilasters, carries on bold projecting consoles a superimposed order of coupled Corinthian columns."[10] Criticised in 1966 for a failure to cater to holiday makers and casual visitors, the National Trust's chairman, the Earl of Antrim, famously declared that the "trust's job is not to involve itself in the entertainment industry."[11]

The trust required a hefty capital sum from an owner as an endowment to pay for the future maintenance of a mansion, and anyway, Lord Bath was not prepared to give away a house which had been his family's home since the sixteenth century. He chose instead to sell off parts of the estate, and over the twelve months after the Corsley flower show, around 9,000 acres of land were put onto the market. First to go, in December 1946, was a farm at Church Stretton in Shropshire: at 280 acres it wasn't economically important, but it had some sentimental value because Sir John Thynne, founder of the family fortune and builder of Longleat, was born there in 1512. More significant was the 2,240-acre Norton Hall estate in Northamptonshire, "comprising practically the whole of the village of Norton and including the stately Gothic-style mansion and finely wooded park with lakes."[12] The stately Gothic-style mansion was stripped of its interior fittings by its new owner and blown up in 1952 by a unit of military engineers. The sale of "a large portion of the famous Longleat estate," including Corsley and several other villages and hamlets, 5,400 acres in all, took place at the Grand Cinema in Frome over two days in July 1947.[13] The cinema was crowded, and a cheer went up whenever existing tenants managed to buy their farms or homes. A village committee at Corsley acquired a piece of land for a war memorial playing field.

Henry wasn't asked to open the flower show that year.

Although Longleat House and its grounds were not for sale, he and Daphne had no intention of living there. The house was in any case still occupied by staff and pupils from the Royal School for Daughters of Officers of the Army, who had been evacuated there from Bath at the beginning of the war and had cohabited happily with Henry's father, who'd kept three rooms for himself and pottered around in a battered felt hat and a balding overcoat, followed always by his faithful Great Dane. Gradually he'd become part of school life. "In his room there would be a row of plates containing slices of the schoolgirls' birthday cakes," remembered Daphne.[14]

The idea of actually using Longleat as a home seemed absurd. There could be no return to its Edwardian heyday when Henry's grandmother had her loose change washed every day and the morning papers were toasted and ironed before appearing on the breakfast table. Henry hadn't lived at Longleat since his marriage to Daphne in 1927.

And he never would again.

2

THE TERRORS THAT
HAD BROKEN LOOSE

T HERE WERE NEWFOUND freedoms during the war. Henry
Thynne's viscountess, Daphne, enjoyed a simple life at
Sturford Mead, unencumbered by responsibilities and attended
by only a cook, Mrs Sims, and a housemaid. And a governess.
And a nanny for her four children. (The family butler, Marks,
had gone with Henry as his batman when Henry had joined the
Royal Wiltshire Yeomanry.) She made her own decisions for the
first time in her life, so that she "was never again able to feel as
dependent on other people as I had been before the war."[1] She
took in five evacuees from London, a fireman's wife and her four
children, whom she put in the servants' quarters in the basement.
She tried her hand at cheese making, armed with a pamphlet from
the Ministry of Agriculture. She hunted with the Mendip Farmers Hunt. She went on holiday with the children, driving them
down to Cornwall herself: "We lived on the beach, picking mus-
sels off the rocks to cook for supper [and] riding the huge waves
on surf-boards."[2]

But her war wasn't all sunshine and surf. When an American
military hospital was set up in the park at Longleat, she worked
there first as a telephone operator and then as the hospital librarian. And when she wasn't working at Longleat, she entertained

13

the troops. Nearby Warminster had become an important military centre, and old friends from before the war took to dropping in at Sturford Mead for an hour, a day, or a weekend. A cousin, Robin Wilson, who was stationed at Warminster with the Leicestershire Yeomanry, stabled his horse at Sturford Mead. The artist Rex Whistler, now a lieutenant in the Welsh Guards, played drawing games with Daphne's children in the schoolroom. Another regular visitor was Daphne's old friend the irascible Evelyn Waugh, who was stationed nearby, making a nuisance of himself with his superiors in the Special Service Brigade.

Sturford Mead remained what it had been before the war—a country house retreat, a home, a venue for weekend house parties. When the Guards Armoured Division was stationed at Warminster and various officers' wives played at camp followers, Daphne had them to stay. One weekend she played hostess to Debo Cavendish, Debo's two greyhounds, her husband, Andrew, and Andrew's older brother Billy, who were both in the Guards. One night, after everyone had gone to bed, a fire broke out in the drawing room, the result of carelessness rather than enemy action. Everyone woke, and what could have been a tragedy quickly degenerated into farce. Daphne ran to one telephone to call the fire brigade, and Andrew Cavendish picked up the other at the same time: both found themselves shouting not at the Warminster fire brigade but at each other. Then Daphne grabbed a fire extinguisher, lost control of it, and squirted Andrew full in the face, while Billy went outside and broke the drawing room window with a golf club, causing the fire to burn even more fiercely. Andrew crawled under the smoke on his stomach to rescue Daphne's most treasured possessions: her collection of dance records. The only one he managed to save was Irving Berlin's *I'm Playing with Fire*. "Meanwhile Debo collected her two greyhounds, calmly packed all her belongings, brought her suitcase down into the hall, and sat on top of it like Patience on a monument smiling at grief."[3]

In the midst of this, the police rang up to complain about the faulty blackout. "Do you realise you're showing a light?"[4]

LIFE WENT ON in the stately homes of England, war or no war. Maud Russell, one of London's most distinguished prewar society hostesses, welcomed an assortment of young evacuees to her Hampshire country house, Mottisfont Abbey, along with British, Canadian, and American soldiers and, in the lead-up to the Normandy landings, an entire military hospital. However, she also kept up weekend house parties throughout the war. Guests might include old friends like the collector and litterateur Eddie Marsh, the decorator and hostess Sibyl Colefax, political figures like Duff Cooper and Violet Bonham Carter, and figures from the world of the arts—the photographer and designer Cecil Beaton, the ballet dancer and choreographer Frederick Ashton, even the elderly novelist A. E. W. Mason, whose famous 1902 novel about courage and soldiering, *The Four Feathers*, held a particular resonance in the darkest days of the war.

People came and went at Mottisfont just as they had before the war. If the weather was good, they lay about in the gardens, reading and talking, or went walking in the woods. They came together for dinner and afterwards talked some more or played word games. Maud sometimes persuaded someone to read aloud to the company, although judging from the critical comments in her diary, she rarely chose well. "I made the mistake of asking Sibyl [Colefax] to read aloud forgetting one can never hear what she says when she talks," she wrote on one occasion.[5] On another, Duff Cooper read Tennyson's "Vision of Sin" "so badly and so indistinctly that it was grotesque and embarrassing."[6]

The Mottisfont household was a motley one in the war years. On a single weekend in June 1941, guests included Sibyl Colefax, Frederick Ashton, and the American socialite Alice Astor, who after having an affair in the late 1930s with Ashton (who was gay) was currently married to another gay Englishman. At the same time, five evacuee children, "a negro refugee from Southampton," and eight officers were living in the house.[7] In the stables there were two more evacuee children, another Southampton refugee, and eight batmen, who were presumably there to attend to the needs of the eight officers in the house. The Russells also kept an indoor staff of twelve during the war: Maud's lady's maid, Adele; Reeve, the butler, who lived with his wife over the stables; three housemaids, a cook and three kitchen maids, two footmen, and an odd man. "It was a strange feeling staying in this luxuriously appointed house," wrote Cecil Beaton, "so far and yet so near to all the terrors that had broken loose."[8]

THE DEBATE ABOUT the role of the country house after the war was already beginning while Cecil Beaton lazed in the sun and sketched the Mottisfont primroses, and it was a more complex debate than one might imagine. People like Maud Russell, whose considerable wealth came from investments rather than from the land and who wasn't encumbered with a large estate, hordes of dependent tenants, or centuries of tradition, saw no reason why their leisurely lifestyle shouldn't be prolonged indefinitely. Others hoped the war would boost the agricultural economy on which their fortunes rested, as the last war had—while all the time re-membering that the aftermath of that boom had been a cata-strophic collapse in land values.

Ever since its appearance in 1897, *Country Life* magazine had not only championed the cause of the country house but con-structed a vision of country house life as an elegant, arcadian para-dise, and throughout the Second World War it not only continued its influential series of weekly articles on individual homes but also published some intriguing speculative articles on the prospects for the postwar future of the country house, never doubting for a mo-ment that it had one. In October 1940, for example, the architec-tural critic and historian John Summerson wrote what purported to be a review of recent country house design but was in fact a plea for a new generation of architects to move away from "white walls, flat roofs and that air of sandal-clad priggishness which it is so deplorably easy for the new architecture to achieve."[9] When the time came to begin building again after the war, he wrote, there would be no room for experiments. Instead, we must have traditional design and traditional materials—good English bricks and sensible window openings. (Oddly enough, one of the houses chosen to illustrate his article was Raymond McGrath's modernist masterpiece of 1936, the Round House in Surrey, which with its white walls, flat roofs, and banks of curving windows seemed calculated to arouse the admiration of every sandal-clad prig in the country.) Summerson's article was followed over the next four years by a series in which *Country Life* occasionally invited architects to produce designs for country houses "which they feel will fit a world in which there are no longer any Hitlers, in which construction at last steals the headlines from destruction"—"castles-in-the-postwar-air," in fact.[10]

For the most part, the designs in the series were fairly modest, although they all contained provisions for servants, and one, by the team of Anthony Minoprio and Hugh Spenceley, was more substantial, with a domestic wing, a thirty-feet-by-seventeen-feet drawing room, and an impressive oval dining room. Minoprio and Spenceley took the optimistic view that after the war, "there will still be many people who can afford a country house and a small estate, just as there will still be women who prefer domestic service to work in a shop or factory."[11] Clough Williams-Ellis offered a project on the Welsh coast for a woman who planned to downsize from her current home to "a big sort of bungalow with some upstairs to it and two rooms large enough to take just the best pictures and furniture from the old house."[12] The idea was to start building the moment the war was over, and Williams-Ellis claimed he had already arranged to recycle squared granite from nearby military roadblocks. Frederick Gibberd, fresh from designing air-raid shelters in Hampstead, declared, "I am a modern architect" and proposed a small country house which looked rather like a garden shed. "This design may startle some who love the countryside and our architectural heritage," warned an uncertain *Country Life*.[13]

The most interesting contribution to the series came in July 1944, with a discussion between *Country Life*'s architectural editor, Christopher Hussey, and forty-three-year-old designer Robert Lutyens, whose father, Sir Edwin, doyen of twentieth-century country house architects, had died earlier that year. Asked by Hussey what would be wanted from a country house after the war, Wing Commander Lutyens showed he was his father's son by rejecting modernism as little more than a reflection of "a nervous instability in our social and economic life."[14] He suggested that a business executive just turned thirty, thinking of marrying and set on having a place in the country, should look for a site of around ten acres with paddocks for the children's ponies, an orchard, and perhaps a spinney and a stream. Essentials for a house to be built on that site included plenty of storage space, since "a family of any cultural pretentions accumulates vast quantities of papers, trunks, old clothes, linen, china, books, toys and whatnot." There must be day and night nurseries, a large living room with a windowed recess "for writing in," and proper domestic offices.[15]

In other ways, though, Robert Lutyens's postwar country house was less traditional. It had fewer rooms. Was there really any need for a dining room? Why not eat in the drawing room, or even the kitchen? (This was a step too far for Hussey, who complained that if this were the case, we should all spend the rest of our lives in "a perpetual picnic."[16]) Lutyens's point was that "if a house [was] designed in conformity with smug middle-class standards it [could] only approximate in miniature to the great houses, with their range of apartments, from which it [was] derived. But a multiplicity of rooms, all too small for satisfactory occupation, [were] a vexation of spirit and a waste of space."[17]

The starting point for all of these articles was the assumption that country houses would continue to be built after the war—in a modified form, perhaps, and on a smaller scale than the Longleats or even the Mottisfonts of this world. But the contributors had no doubt that there would still be a demand for Robert Lutyens's spacious place in the country with its orchard and paddocks for the children's ponies.

Others were less confident. "What country houses of any size," wondered Osbert Sitwell before the war, "can hope to survive the next fifty years?"[18] And Lord Lothian, proposing in 1934 that the National Trust should take on the running of the nation's more important country houses, predicted that within a generation, hardly any of those historic homes would be lived in by the families who had created them. That raised the question of whether a change of ownership might signal a change in fortunes for the better, of course; but by the early 1940s, with death duties running at 65 per cent, estates being broken up and sold to tenants or speculators, and the country houses which had once been the headquarters of those estates being abandoned, there were plenty of people who believed the stately homes of England were on the brink of catastrophe. The National Trust might be able to save a few of the more important ones, but what about the rest?

One answer seemed to be to find new uses for old buildings, as had happened after the First World War, when the public school system had stepped in to rescue Stowe, Prior Park, and a hundred less-distinguished mansions. In 1941 Viscount Esher, who chaired the National Trust's Historic Buildings Committee, suggested the future lay with the country club. Members could use the big house and its grounds for tennis, bathing, dancing, and the entertainment of weekend guests. "By such a plan the country house, and possibly its pictures and furniture, could finance itself, escape the slow but certain strangulation of taxation, and fill a different but not undignified place in the new life."[19]

A related idea was to turn mansions into maisonettes or service flats, with the main ground-floor state rooms used in common and the upstairs rooms converted into small apartments, each with a sitting room, three or four bedrooms, and a "small electrically equipped kitchenette, containing a refrigerator."[20] Christopher Hussey, who was an advocate of the idea, gave several examples of houses which had been successfully converted, including Lord Armstrong's Bamburgh Castle, on the Northumberland coast, and Escrick Park, an imposing Georgian house just outside York which was remodelled by John Carr of York in the 1760s and converted into eleven self-contained suites in 1930. Meals were served in the dining room, although tenants could choose to take them in their flat; other communal spaces included a ballroom and a fine library. There were attractive gardens, a hard tennis court, and a squash court on the site. The Escrick stables had been turned into heated garages with a "large car-wash with automatic washing-plant," and a riding stable on the grounds had become a laundry that served not only the flats but also the surrounding neighbourhood.[21]

The search for alternative uses for the country house continued throughout the war. The artist Hesketh Hubbard suggested that a large country mansion might be turned into homes for forty or fifty impoverished bachelors and widowers, with a manager and matron-housekeeper on-site. (What about the spinsters and widows, one wonders?) Another suggestion was to convert country houses into apartments for distinguished men *and* women who had served their country. "This would be a democratic and happy ending of the now out-of-date system of colossal houses for single families."[22] Others proposed similarly institutional uses: secondary schools or government offices. A country house in the Lake District was acquired by Liverpool Seamen's Welfare Centre as a rehabilitation centre for merchant sailors; Mottram Hall, near Macclesfield, was turned into a holiday home for employees of a big engineering firm in Manchester.

While these potential solutions were being bandied about, hundreds if not thousands of country houses were already functioning in a variety of nontraditional ways. In the lead-up to war, big companies had begun to buy or rent country houses as out-of-London accommodation in case worse came to worst and, as most people believed at the time, the capital was completely destroyed by German bombs within weeks of war breaking out. The Georgian Milton Hill House in Oxfordshire was transformed into Esso House; Chesterton Lodge, an enormous Italianate mansion outside Bicester, was bought by the Royal Exchange Assurance Corporation; and Lord Bearsted's Upton House in Warwickshire became the offices of his family bank, M. Samuel & Co., while Lord Bearsted himself became a colonel in the Intelligence Corps and helped to organise a British Resistance movement in case of invasion. Lord Astor offered part of the Cliveden estate in Buckinghamshire at a rent of a shilling a year to the Canadian Red Cross, which had been based there in the First World War. The Astors stored the contents of their St James's Square house in the stables at Cliveden for safety, which was just as well, because the London mansion was hit by incendiary bombs in October 1940.

Before war broke out, the Committee of Imperial Defence, a government body set up to coordinate defence strategy, had already tasked the Office of Works with drawing up a secret register of buildings that could be requisitioned for use in wartime. They included hotels, large schools, commercial premises—and country houses, which were meant to be reserved for the military or for evacuees and other refugees from the big cities. When war broke out, however, the canny owners of country houses did their best to forestall requisitioning by the military by offering their homes to boarding schools. The Duke of Devonshire invited the girls of Penrhos College in North Wales, whose buildings had been commandeered by the Ministry of Food, to take up residence at Chatsworth, reasoning that "if the house is full of schoolgirls the authorities will not allow soldiers anywhere near the place."[23] As we've seen, the aged Marquess of Bath made Longleat House available to the Royal School for Daughters of Officers of the Army, after *their* premises in Bath were taken over by the Admiralty. The Duke of Marlborough and his family moved into the east wing of Blenheim Palace in September 1939 to accommodate the arrival of four hundred boys and a hundred staff from Malvern College. The floors of the state rooms were hastily covered with linoleum, the damask curtains were protected with canvas covers, and the pictures and tapestries were covered with battens and boards. Brocket Hall in Hertfordshire, whose owner's enthusiasm for the Nazis was so great that one of the bedrooms was named after Joachim von Ribbentrop, was requisitioned as a maternity home.

By their nature—walled, gated, and usually at a discreet distance from other households—country houses also lent themselves to use by the various secret services which proliferated in wartime. So much so, in fact, that the Special Operations Executive, the SOE, was nicknamed "Stately 'Omes of England." Coleshill in the Vale of White Horse, an exquisite seventeenth-century house designed by Sir Roger Pratt, became the training headquarters for the so-called Auxiliary Units, saboteurs who were to form the core of the Resistance if the Germans invaded. The man in charge at Coleshill at one point was Lord Glanusk, a much-decorated war hero who arrived to take up his command in his Rolls-Royce accompanied by a new wife, a posse of Guards officers "with public school accents and double-barrelled names," and a string of racehorses.[24] He immediately placed his private wine cellar at the disposal of the officers' mess. Polish agents were trained at Audley End before being dropped behind enemy lines: one in three didn't come back.

As the war went on, some of the larger houses acquired a parade of tenants. Malvern College moved out of Blenheim Palace after only a year, and its place was taken by MI5, whose top-secret presence there was heralded by conductors on the bus route from Oxford to Woodstock, who used to call out as they reached the gates of Blenheim, "Anyone for MI5?"[25] And while the daughters of army officers were having lessons inside Longleat House, the American army was building a ninety-acre hospital in the park and the RAF was erecting what the 6th Lord Bath described as "lots of ugly corrugated iron sheds."[26] The neighbouring Stourhead estate fared a little better, but it was a close thing. The Air Ministry announced that, having acquired five thousand acres of land in Wiltshire, it intended to acquire one thousand more—including part of the Stourhead estate, which was to become a military aerodrome. "But is this not to be National Trust property?" asked one enraged MP, referring to Sir Henry Hoare's plan to hand over the house and half the estate to the trust. He was told by Sir Kingsley Wood, secretary of state for air, that in times like these the government had to put the needs of national defence first.[27] A few days later Sir Henry Hoare sent a stiff letter to Sir Kingsley: "If you compel me to sell you 300 acres of my estate so that you can build a training aerodrome, I shall immediately withdraw my offer to present the mansion house and 2,700 acres of the estate to the nation through the National Trust."[28] The Air Ministry backed down.

There were financial compensations for the upheaval caused by military occupation: the Compensation (Defence) Act of September 1, 1939, stated that an owner was entitled to "a sum equal to the rent which might reasonably be expected to be payable by a tenant in occupation of the land, during the period for which possession of the land is retained in the exercise of emergency powers." However, valuations, given by a district valuer or the military's own people, tended to be on the low side (or so country house owners maintained). The War Office, which used Bignor Manor in Sussex as a staging post for members of the Resistance before they were parachuted into France, paid its owner five pounds a week in rent and another two pounds a week in salary for looking after the agents. When the British government moved exiled Czechoslovakian president Edvard Beneš and his family (including his dog, an Alsatian named Toga) into Aston Abbotts

Abbey in Buckinghamshire, his staff were housed in neighbouring Wingrave Manor, whose owner, the Countess of Essex, received twenty pounds a week in rent.

The wanton vandalism carried out by soldiers, sailors, and airmen while they were billeted in country houses is the stuff of legend. Tales abound of jeeps driven down grand staircases, garden ornaments used for target practice by drunken troops, and family portraits turned into makeshift dartboards. James Lees-Milne, the gaunt, bisexual secretary of the National Trust's Country Houses Committee, whose passion for country houses and occasionally their owners made him a pioneering figure in the embryonic conservationist movement, was constantly remarking on the destruction he saw as he toured England on the trust's business. At Culverthorpe in Lincolnshire he found windows smashed and a great crack in the painted ceiling of the staircase hall. Castle Bromwich Hall, recently vacated by troops, was "in a filthy mess."[29] At Netley Park in Surrey he found that the "licentious soldiery" had smashed gilt-framed mirrors in the drawing room.[30]

Worse was the officially sanctioned destruction—the tank traps on the drive, the acres of Nissen huts in the park. And worst of all was the neglect. Leaking roofs were left unattended. Broken windows weren't repaired. At Castle Bromwich, Lees-Milne noted, dry rot was rampant; by the time Woburn Abbey was derequisitioned in 1946, the Georgian riding school, which had been used by a top-secret propaganda unit, was so badly decayed that it had to be demolished.

Sidney Herbert, eldest son of the 15th Earl of Pembroke, recorded in meticulous and heartrending detail the consequences of having his family seat, Wilton House, occupied by the army. After a brief period at the beginning of the war when Wilton played host to forty young evacuees from London, it was taken over as the headquarters of Southern Command, placing it at the heart of a huge complex of a vast military organisation. As some three million troops assembled in southern England in preparation for the

Normandy landings of 1944, it was Southern Command which had the responsibility of training and accommodating them, and it was Wilton which was the centre of operations.

Sidney's parents continued to use Wilton during the war, keeping four bedrooms for their own use and for family and guests, and living in the library on the west front. In the rest of the house the constant comings and goings of soldiers left their mark: the stone treads of a staircase installed by James Wyatt in the early years of the nineteenth century were chipped when an iron safe rolled down them and, more dramatically, the ceiling of the Wyatt staircase collapsed one morning "with a roar and a crash."[31]

But much more serious than the hard use was the neglect. Southern Command didn't leave Wilton until 1949, and one day in November 1947 the Countess of Pembroke mentioned to her son that paint was flaking off the ceiling in the Single Cube Room, part of the suite of state rooms designed in the mid-seventeenth century by Inigo Jones and John Webb.

The room was empty at the time, and Sidney went to take a look. He found that the ceiling was discoloured and large sections of brown fungus were growing through the carved cornice. He immediately fetched his father, and together they discovered that panelling in the Single Cube had split; when they touched it, large pieces crumbled into dust. "Yet none of the soldiers or civilians using this room for the past eight years had noticed anything wrong," he wrote.[32] On Monday morning he informed the camp commandant and telephoned the Ministry of Works and the War Office, both of which sent down officials to inspect the damage. It emerged that when the post office had installed telephones for the army in 1940, they had run the cables over the roof and down inside the rainwater gutters, blocking them: this had led to outbreaks of fungus and dry rot in the Single Cube Room, which had spread into the neighbouring Double Cube Room and affected stone and brick in other parts of the house. Whole sections of panelling and painted ceiling had to be cut away, and the walls were treated with fungicide. "Every brick and stone and piece of mortar [affected was] subjected to blow-lamps twice over, so that no infection could remain."[33]

The War Office, which had refused to allow the Earl of Pembroke's men to carry out any routine inspections of the structure while it was under military occupation, admitted responsibility for the damage. As Sidney said, "They could not do otherwise as the state rooms were still used by them."[34]

The repairs took years, and it was nearly half a century before the disruption caused by the War Office's carelessness was finally and completely made good. Other owners of country houses requisitioned by the military were less tenacious, or less fortunate. Their homes were never fit to live in again.

THE WAR AFFECTED the country house in ways more profound than smashed statues on the terrace or dry rot in the stables. In 1947 Debrett's published its "Final Roll of Honour," listing all the members of families in the *Peerage and Baronetage* who had been killed in action or had died of wounds while on active service in World War II. There were some 1,400 names on the list, from Sub-Lieutenant Michael Acheson, Royal Navy, nephew of the Earl of Gosford, to Captain William Young of the Royal Army Medical Corps, who died in Egypt in 1942, leaving behind a one-year-old son to inherit the family baronetcy. Mark Howard of Castle Howard was killed in Normandy in July 1944, aged twenty-six; his brother Christopher, a bomber pilot, was killed a few months later in a daylight raid over the Rhine. Castle Howard went to the sole surviving brother, George, who had himself been wounded in Burma in 1940. Sir Michael Gore-Booth of Lissadell, County Sligo, lost both of his brothers: Hugh died in Greece in 1943, and Brian drowned when his ship, HMS *Exmouth*, was torpedoed in the North Sea in 1940. Croome Park's 10th Earl of Coventry was lost at Dunkirk; his servants cried when they heard the news.

In September 1944 the 10th Duke of Devonshire's eldest son and heir, Billy, was walking ahead of his company outside the Belgian village of Heppen when he was shot through the heart by a German sniper. (One of his men wrote to the duke, saying how angry they had been: "We took no prisoners that day."[35]) The duke swore never to set foot in Chatsworth again. He wandered round the garden from time to time, but never the house. "The spirit of the place had gone," his daughter-in-law Deborah remembered. "Only an incurable optimist could guess it would ever return."[36]

The Howards' cousin Eric died in a Japanese prison camp in 1943. Alastair Windsor, 2nd Duke of Connaught and Strathearn, fell out of a window in Ottawa while he was drunk and died of hypothermia. Five peers were killed in air raids. The 1st Baron Stamp was killed when his house in Beckenham was hit by a bomb in 1941. His wife died with him, as did his oldest son and heir, who thus went into the record books as the man who held a peerage for the shortest length of time, since British law at the time held that when two persons died in circumstances in which it was uncertain which of them survived the other, such deaths should be presumed to have occurred in order of seniority. So when the 1st Baron Stamp's surviving son inherited the title, as 3rd Baron Stamp, he had to pay two sets of death duties on top of having lost his father, his mother, and his older brother.

As Viscount Weymouth, the 6th Marquess of Bath served as a major in the Royal Wiltshire Yeomanry during the war. He was wounded in the throat by a piece of shrapnel at El Alamein—not leading a tank charge, as his *Times* obituary later had it, but wandering around the battlefield on foot. "I was bored," he said later. "I had lost my tank and I had nothing to do."[37] Survivors like Bath were left with a sense of relief tempered with guilt. The Baths lost close friends: the writer Robert Byron, drowned when his ship was torpedoed off the Western Isles in 1941; the artist Rex Whistler, killed by a shell burst during his first battle in Normandy in 1944. Should they carry on trying to maintain a white elephant of a house like Longleat, people like the Baths asked themselves, in a world of rationing and housing shortages, a world which had no use for peers and palaces?

The troubled aesthete Brian Howard, an old friend of Henry and Daphne from the 1920s when they were all Bright Young Things together, and the prototype for the effete and affected Anthony Blanche in Evelyn Waugh's *Brideshead Revisited*, provided them with the answer in a poem he addressed to Daphne as she and her husband worried over how on earth they could keep Longleat:

Twenty years. The curtains drawn,
Windows sleeping, doors shut;
Here, the wasted, noble lawn,
There, trees cut.

Hymns to murder have been sung,
Robert, Rex have gone away.
Wandering these woods among,
Have we any right to May?

Yes. Remembering well these things;
What it was they cherished,
Why they met the torture kings,
Fought and won and perished.

Come, then. Stand on Heaven's Gate,
Lakes below and leaves above—
This, is why they found their fate.
Here, is where we feel their love.[38]

This was why they should carry on—not because of a debt to the ancient past, but because of a debt owed to dead friends. Because of why they died.

3

"I DON'T WANT TO BE
THE ONE TO LET IT GO"

I N 1950 THE *Illustrated London News* ran a feature on a dozen "stately homes of England that have passed to other hands."[1] It showed that the change-of-use ideas which *Country Life* had advocated during the war were now a reality. Houses were being turned into boarding schools and blocks of flats and youth hostels. Oxford University had bought Wroxton Abbey near Banbury, "a Tudor mansion on the foundations of an Augustinian priory." Madingley Hall, the sixteenth-century country house that Queen Victoria had rented for the Prince of Wales when he was a reluctant undergraduate at Cambridge in 1861, now belonged to that university, along with its village and 1,200 acres. Kingston Maurward, a particularly lovely Georgian mansion, had been acquired by Dorset County Council and was now a "farm institute"; Bradbourne in Kent, built in 1713 on the site of a Tudor house, was now used by a research institute for horticultural experiments. (It still is.)

"The private market for these many-roomed houses has long since vanished," claimed the anonymous author of the article, "and it is not unusual to find one of these old mansions in the hands of the demolition squad before the interested societies have had the opportunity of taking steps to preserve it."[2] In 1959 the

Birmingham Daily Post ran a profile of John Riley, a forty-nine-year-old Irish widower who for the past fifteen years had led a demolition team specialising in castles and country houses, and who was currently reducing to rubble Garnstone Castle in Herefordshire. Installed in one of the best rooms in the west wing, with a resident cook, Riley would live in state while the work was going on, hanging on until the last possible minute and then going into lodgings before moving on to the next stately home. "I do feel very sorry for some of the old family servants," he said. "For years the house and all it means has been their life. Then one day it all vanishes."[3]

An ignominious end for the stately homes of England had been predicted for decades, and the number of demolitions had been growing ever since the agricultural depressions of the 1870s and 1880s had been followed by the arrival of death duties in 1894, although at that stage fire, flood, and fortune's wheel were ruining more houses than taxation and a depressed rural economy. But after the end of the First World War the pace of demolitions picked up as estate taxes rose and rentals fell: more than 180 houses came down in the 1920s, and around 220 in the 1930s. Some were undistinguished; others were of national importance, like Thomas Wright's Nuthall Temple in Nottinghamshire, an exquisite little Palladian house filled with rococo plasterwork which was bought by a demolition contractor in 1928 and, once stripped of everything of value, deliberately burned down. Or the seventeenth-century Hamilton Palace in Lanarkshire, demolished in 1922 in what has been called "an act of vandalism that Scotland can never live down."[4] The solution that was usually rolled out was "Let the National Trust save it." But the trust was never going to be able to help more than a tiny minority of the thousands of country house owners who were struggling with an uncertain future.

THE LABOUR LANDSLIDE victory in the general election of July 1945 was, an appalled Evelyn Waugh recorded in his diary, "a prodigious surprise. . . . Practically all my friends are out."[5] At a postelection party held by press baron Lord Rothermere at the Dorchester, he found "a large, despondent crowd" which included a gaggle of society figures such as Sibyl Colefax, Emerald Cunard, and Nancy Mitford, who had all turned up to celebrate Churchill's victory only to be disappointed.

Maud Russell was there too. She had come up from her Hampshire country house, Mottisfont Abbey, to spend the night with her lover, the writer Ian Fleming, who was also sleeping with their host's wife, Ann Rothermere. Never one to take life too seriously, Maud thought the Conservative collapse was hilarious: "I couldn't resist laughing a good deal at the results and some of the long, foolish faces," she wrote at the time.[6] She proceeded to drown other people's sorrows in vodka, "real good vodka," leaving the predatory Fleming to wander round on his own, "but he kept on coming back to me."[7]

Others viewed the arrival of a socialist government with fear and loathing. "I am permanently depressed," wrote Osbert Sitwell. "The Government, I loathe. Even more than Winston."[8] The Labour Party's manifesto, *Let Us Face the Future*, promised to nationalise the fuel and power industries, iron and steel, transport—and land. "If a landlord cannot or will not provide proper facilities for his tenant farmers, the State should take over his land at a fair valuation."[9] The manifesto also argued for rent controls and for taxation "which bears less heavily on the lower-income groups."[10]

The prospect of a socialist utopia sent shivers through the more traditional country house–owning classes and reignited the wartime debate about the role of country houses in a world which seemed to have no more use for them. In November 1945 *Country Life* began another series of articles, "The Future of Great Country Houses," and declared that "without some form of relief or subvention, many of the more artistically and historically important [stately homes] cannot be maintained much longer, if at all, for their original purpose of a family home."[11]

The opening salvo in this latest campaign was fired by the Marchioness of Exeter, whose own country house, Burghley, was one of the greatest. After acknowledging that there were moves afoot to prevent arbitrary demolitions (the 1944 Town and Country Planning Act had given a measure of protection to buildings of special architectural merit or historic interest), the marchioness asked what the nation wanted from its historic houses. Should they be preserved "as national institutions, or museums, or public schools and hospitals; or as living, warm, family homes in which every picture, or tapestry or piece of furniture has a story to tell"? (There are no prizes for guessing on which side of the argument she came down.) The problem was, she couldn't find the staff, and "neither the Ministry of Labour nor the Employment Exchanges are willing to help."[12]

As we shall see, the notion that country houses, especially the larger ones with important collections, could only fulfil their true purpose if they continued to function as homes, was regularly trotted out as an argument for some form of state aid to private owners, in spite of the fact that the Baths and the Devonshires of the world chose *not* to live in their ancestral seats. Perhaps the most famous statement of the way in which life in the country house breathed life *into* the country house came from Vita Sackville-West in 1941:

> Museums? A museum is a dead thing; a house which is still the home of men and women is a living thing which has not lost its soul. The soul of a house, the atmosphere of a house, are as much part of the house as the architecture of that house or as the furnishings within it. Divorced from life, it dies. But if it keeps its life it means that the kitchen still provides food for the inhabitants: makes jam, puts fruit into bottles, stores the honey, dries the herbs, and carries on in the same tradition as has always obtained in the country. Useful things, practical things, keeping a number of people going throughout the year.[13]

The problem was to establish exactly what kind of life was appropriate, or even possible, for the country house in the postwar world. When the Marchioness of Exeter went to live at Burghley as a young bride before the First World War, she found herself reigning as chatelaine over a small army of domestic servants—thirty-four, to be exact. She had a lady's maid to dress her and a sewing maid to help; two chauffeurs to drive her around; a butler, underbutler, and two footmen to wait on her at table. As her family grew, she employed a governess, nurse, undernurse, and schoolroom maid to look after her three children. Her husband's private secretary was a baronet. Now, she complained, "the modern generation fight shy of any form of domestic employment." If the nation wanted its treasure houses to be maintained "by their traditional and rightful guardians, not as museums but as homes with a soul and atmosphere," then the nation must provide the staff.[14]

The second of four articles in the series came from the 4th Baron Methuen, owner of Corsham Court in Wiltshire. Starting, as the Marchioness of Exeter had, from the assumption that the country house required some form of state aid if it was to survive in postwar Britain, Methuen gave a more measured (and more farsighted) series of proposals, which boiled down to the suggestion that Parliament might provide enough money to cover perhaps 50 per cent of the maintenance costs of historic houses which had been placed on a Ministry of Works schedule. Owners could choose to opt in, and in return, "if the whole of the house, including the interior and possibly the grounds, is included in the schedule, the owner should agree to giving the public access, say during thirty-six days in the year"—a solution which was to be adopted, albeit in a less generous form, with the advent of Historic Buildings Councils in the 1950s.[15]

In the third article H. D. Walston, an expert on farming and agricultural reform (he became director of agriculture in the British Zone of Germany in 1946), airily dismissed the problems faced by the Methuens and Exeters of this world—if the National Trust

33

wouldn't take their stately mansions, they could hand them over to become "schools, research institutes, or something of that sort."[16] Walston, the owner of a modest country house in Somerset, was concerned with the plight of smaller places like his own, "those of no great history and even of no great architectural merit."[17] He claimed that their problems were more pressing just because there were so many more of them—they made up the vast majority of country houses—and his solution was for owners to take over the management of house and estate themselves rather than relying on agents and managers:

> Some part of the house should be devoted entirely to the running of the estate: the stableyard and some of the garages—almost always too big for modern needs—could become a small estate yard. One or two of the downstairs rooms in the house would be the offices, and some of the surplus bedrooms could house the office staff and perhaps some of the unmarried estate workers. There might also be some pupils, as there always seems to be a large number of young men who want to spend a year on a small estate to learn the practical problems of management at first hand.[18]

One of the larger rooms in the house could be turned over to the villagers for their meetings, dances, and whist drives; the kitchen garden could replace the village allotments while the pleasure gardens could be used as communal tennis courts and for "outdoor meetings of the Women's Institute on summer evenings."[19]

The final article in the series was by Christopher Hussey, and he had quite a radical proposal: that the state should take over the running of the larger country houses with significant collections and open them to the public. The owner would retain what he called "titular possession" and would keep a reasonable portion of the house and grounds for his or her private use. The owner would also have the right to use the state rooms when the house was closed. The state would provide all the staff and would shoulder the full cost of maintenance and repair in return for the income from entrance fees. In that way the nation's treasure houses would remain homes—a central tenet in discussions about the future of the country house—while being maintained for the public benefit.

In his 1946 budget the Labour chancellor of the exchequer, Hugh Dalton, announced that he was setting up a National Land Fund to acquire places of beauty for the nation, arguing that they should be dedicated "to the memory of the men who had died for their country in war."[20] Administered by the Treasury and given an initial budget of £50 million, which was raised from the sale of surplus war materials, one of the fund's purposes was to deal with land transferred to the state in lieu of death duties and to compensate the Inland Revenue for the duties lost. The Finance Act which brought the fund contained a clause which said: "The Treasury may direct that all or any of the property [so acquired] shall, on such conditions as they may direct, be transferred to, or to trustees for, any body of persons not established or conducted for profit and having as its object, or one of its objects, the provision, improvement or preservation of amenities enjoyed, or to be enjoyed, by the public or the acquisition of land to be used by the public."[21]

In plain English, that meant the Treasury could accept property in lieu of death duties and hand it over to a charitable body to manage. So in the first twelve months of the fund's existence, the Youth Hostels Association was given a modern seaside house on the North Cornish coast near Padstow because it was "suited to be used as a hostel for the enjoyment of young people with not much money to spend."[22] Bala Lake in North Wales, part of the Glan-llyn estate of the late Sir Watkin Williams-Wynn, was taken into public ownership, eventually becoming part of Snowdonia National Park. And the Earl of Mount Edgcumbe's Cotehele in Cornwall went to the National Trust, the first of more than a dozen country houses to do so under the scheme over the next thirty years.

When it was set up, the fund wasn't allowed to accept furniture or works of art, only land and buildings, but in 1953 its remit was widened to include objects associated with a particular building "where it appears to the Treasury desirable for the objects to remain associated with the building."[23] That meant that a house and its important contents could be accepted in lieu as a single entity.

This was a lifeline for a few, but it was never going to be an answer for the majority. The Treasury (and, for that matter, the National Trust) might be interested in an historic house like Cotehele, but they were never going to consider a run-down Georgian pile surrounded by creeping suburbs, or a turreted and castellated Edwardian monster with no decent furniture and precious little history. The number of country houses accepted in lieu and handed to the National Trust was only a tiny fraction of the total number of houses at risk. Three times as many came to the trust as gifts from donors who were high-minded or at the end of their tether, or sometimes both. And even here, the path to a successful transfer was fraught with uncertainties on both sides. In 1949 Conservative Party politician Ronald Tree announced that because of high taxation, he was selling Ditchley, one of the finest Palladian mansions in the country, and moving to New York. The house, designed by James Gibbs and restored by Tree and his first wife, Nancy, in the 1930s, was bought by the Earl of Wilton, who told James Lees-Milne over dinner one evening that once the sale had gone through, he intended to make it over to the National Trust. That was an alluring prospect to the secretary of the trust's Country Houses Committee: Lees-Milne was a huge fan of Ditchley, describing it simply as "perfection" and vowing after his first visit there that "I have never seen better taste."[24] But he refused to get excited. "I shall not believe it until it has happened," he confided to his diary, "having had other disappointments of this nature before."[25] And he was wise to be sceptical:

Wilton changed his mind and sold Ditchley on to the philanthropist Sir David Wills.

Also in 1949, the Labour politician Tom Driberg, having announced that he was leaving his lovely Georgian house to the trust in his will, suddenly announced that he wasn't. He was hard up, and he was going to have to sell it instead. In the event, the gay Driberg made a *mariage blanc* with a hospital administrator named Ena Binfield, telling friends that he needed someone to run the house, Bradwell Lodge in Essex. He kept Bradwell for another twenty years, although he did try to persuade the trust to take it on and allow him to continue living in it; but the question of an endowment always got in the way and eventually, in 1971, he sold it.

A second government initiative to tackle the country house problem also came from Clement Attlee's Labour administration. On December 10, 1948, Sir Stafford Cripps, who had succeeded Hugh Dalton as chancellor of the exchequer the previous year, announced the appointment of a committee to consider "what general arrangements might be made by the Government for the preservation, maintenance, and use of houses of outstanding historical or architectural interest."[26] The seven-person committee, which began meeting in early 1949, was made up of the usual mix of experts and public figures. Ava Anderson, the only woman in the group, was a prominent society hostess and the wife of Sir John Anderson, chancellor of the exchequer in Churchill's wartime cabinet. Her conservative outlook was balanced by that of John Little, a well-known trade union official and a past president of the Amalgamated Engineering Union. Architecture was represented by septuagenarian William Ansell, a past president of the Royal Institute of British Architects and the designer of several undistinguished country houses. Art historian Anthony Blunt was surveyor of the Queen's pictures, the director of the Courtauld Institute of Art, and a recently retired Soviet spy. Since the committee's terms of reference included Wales and Scotland as well as England (the Northern Ireland Parliament was involved in its own version of legislation to protect historic houses), Wales was represented by the archaeologist Sir Cyril Fox, the president of the Society of Antiquaries, who was just embarking on his monumental study of Monmouthshire houses of the fifteenth to seventeenth centuries. Scotland had the prominent Edinburgh accountant Sir John Imrie.

The most intriguing member of the committee (if one excepts Anthony Blunt) was its chair. Sir Ernest Gowers had just retired from a successful forty-five-year career in the civil service and was embarking on a second career as the chairman of a string of difficult commissions and enquiries on subjects ranging from foot-and-mouth disease to capital punishment (which turned him into a convinced abolitionist). He was also a tireless crusader for plain English, and his recent book *Plain Words: A Guide to the Use of English*, which he had written at the request of the permanent secretary to the treasury as part of a campaign to raise the standard of official writing, was already proving to be a surprise bestseller. Gowers was a tall, courteous man with no particular interest in the country house but with a friendly face, an ability to grasp an issue with clarity, and, as his obituarist said, "the patience and power to slog away until he found an answer that satisfied him."[27]

For the next eighteen months he and his colleagues slogged away. They took evidence from thirty-four government departments and public authorities, from the town clerk of Bexley on the outskirts of London, representatives from the Ministry of Works, and the Lord Lyon King of Arms; from eighteen voluntary associations, including the National Trust and the National Trust for Scotland, the Georgian Group and the Yorkshire Archaeological and Historical Society; from fifty-seven individuals, including four dukes, three marquesses, three earls, and a countess. They visited twenty-six historic houses, from the fourteenth-century Penshurst Place in Kent to the Edwardian Hill of Tarvit in Fife. At Knole, Lord Sackville, "distinguished and patrician in a tidy blue suit and yellow waistcoat," showed the committee round himself.[28] The Duke of Wellington appeared before the committee in person to claim that "the English country house is the greatest contribution made by England to the visual arts."[29] *Country Life's* Christopher Hussey also stood in the fine early-Georgian room which the Treasury had put at the committee's disposal and argued that country houses were "a living element in the social fabric of the nation, uniting visibly the present with national history."[30] For the grant-giving Pilgrim Trust, Lords Macmillan and Kilmaine made the familiar argument that country houses were best preserved as family homes. "These houses are always and have been the homes of their owners, constructed for family life. . . . They are not merely beautiful structures, but possess an indefinable atmosphere. . . . To convert them into mere 'show-places' or to institutionalise them as museums, Government offices, hospitals, or schools would deprive them of their intrinsic character and rob them of their 'soul.'"[31]

Throughout 1949 the Gowers committee deliberated. No one was quite sure what proposals it would come up with—not even its members. Four days after Cripps made his announcement setting up the committee, Lady Anderson lunched alone with James Lees-Milne and confided that she had no idea what the terms of reference were. She thought the committee was basically a socialist plot to confiscate the National Trust's country houses. The trust and others suspected that Attlee's government wanted a wholesale nationalisation of the country house, or that the Ministry of Works would cherry-pick the best houses and leave the others to go to ruin. The Labour politician Herbert Morrison, on the other hand, warned Cripps that he would end up with a scheme "to relieve the idle rich at the expense of the taxpayer"—as indeed he did.[32]

HM Treasury's *Report of the Committee on Houses of Outstanding Historic or Architectural Interest*, to give the Gowers report its proper title, appeared on June 23, 1950. Its opening lines made clear that it had accepted the case for preservation. "What our terms of reference require us to consider is not whether houses of outstanding historical or architectural interest should be preserved, but how this is to be done."[33] The nation was facing a disaster comparable to the dissolution of the monasteries. And it was equally clear where the threat came from. "Taxation is primarily responsible for this impending catastrophe."[34] According to the Inland Revenue's own figures, high rates of income tax and surtax meant that hardly any private individuals, no matter how much their gross income or whatever its source, could be left with much more than £5,000 a year; and a big country house might require twice that in annual upkeep simply to prevent it from falling down.

The other factors identified by the committee were the shortage and expense of getting staff, both indoor and outdoor—"The owner of one great house told us that he had found one look at it to be enough to drive a prospective employee away"—and the rising costs of repair and maintenance.[35] Familiar arguments, but the situation was compounded by planning restrictions brought about by the 1947 Town and Country Planning Act, which made it harder for country house owners to sell off outlying parcels of land for development, and by the nationalisation of the coal industry in the same year, which meant that they could no longer look to coal royalties to supplement their income. The outlook was bleak:

> The resource to which an owner then naturally turns is the sale of the contents of the house piece by piece. But this only delays the inevitable end, at the cost perhaps of the dispersal of fine collections of works of art. Sooner or later the house becomes decrepit and the garden runs wild; the park timber is cut down and the beauty of the setting destroyed. Eventually the house itself is sold (if a purchaser can be found) and it may either be put to a use that ruins its remaining features of interest, or broken up for the sake of the lead, timber and fittings of value it contains.[36]

The committee's recommendation was to set up Historic Buildings Councils for England and Wales, and Scotland, with wide-ranging powers to give grants and loans, to designate country houses and their contents as particularly important, and even to acquire designated houses through compulsory purchase and "to hold and manage properties so acquired until some suitable use can be found by which they can be preserved."[37]

But the Gowers report went much further than this. Accepting as a basic premise that a private owner, especially one whose family had been in residence for generations, was the best person to look after a country house, the committee proposed a whole series of tax exemptions for owner-occupiers, in addition to any award of grants by the new Historic Buildings Councils. The quid pro quo was that owner-occupiers must agree to give some public access to their homes, the solution advocated by Lord Methuen back in 1945.

The Gowers report was the first official statement about the cultural importance of the country house in the life of the nation, and this, coupled with the acknowledgment that the nation needed to preserve it and the assertion that this was best done by maintaining it in private hands, by keeping it as a home rather than a museum, meant, in its crudest form, state aid for the landed classes. This wasn't at all what Stafford Cripps had been expecting. "It amounts to creating 2000 pensioner families in perpetuity who—whatever their qualities and their way of life—are to be kept by the State in large houses with gardens," he complained when he first saw the report. "We must devise a better way."[38]

It wasn't a good time to suggest that country house owners should be given state handouts and tax breaks so that they could maintain what many regarded, rightly or wrongly, as a privileged lifestyle. Hugh Dalton, now Labour's minister for planning, sought to separate stately homes from their occupants. "The national interest is in the houses, contents and amenity lands; not in their present owners," he said.[39] Dalton, like several of his cabinet colleagues, reckoned it would be far better to make it easier for important houses to pass to the National Trust "and other public bodies."[40] But ideological qualms meant that the Labour government did nothing to implement the Gowers report.

The Conservatives' ascension to power in October 1951 raised hopes that the new administration, which was traditionally supportive of the landed classes, would look after its own. Those hopes were promptly dashed by ministers who saw in Gowers yet another example of Soviet-style planning, another instance of unwarranted state interference in the life of the individual. David Eccles, the new minister of works, declared, "We cannot choose to live as our ancestors and it is unhealthy to try too hard to do so"; while Harold Macmillan, the minister of planning, simply said, "The fact must be faced that the mode of life for which these notable houses stood [is] doomed."[41] The government might be persuaded to save a small selection of the very best country houses "as symbols of a former civilisation," but that was as far as state intervention should go.[42]

But campaigners, lobby groups, and country house owners kept up the pressure on government. In September 1952 the National Trust made an urgent appeal for action to save "buildings on which our greatest architects, sculptors, and painters have lavished their genius [and which] are today literally falling down."[43] In Parliament, the lords—many of whom had a personal interest in the outcome—debated the demolition of historic houses and called for the implementation of the Gowers proposals. Eventually, in February 1953, Eccles relented and announced the creation of Historic Buildings Councils for England, Wales, and Scotland. (The first chair of the English HBC was Sir Alan "Tommy" Lascelles, who had just retired as private secretary to Elizabeth II: Eccles told him he had been chosen because he knew "nothing about architects and [had] not got long hair."[44]) These HBCs were watered-down versions of the bodies proposed by Gowers, with reduced powers and less money at their disposal. They couldn't make grants themselves, for example, but only recommend them to the minister of works; and their budget, £250,000 a year, was only half of what the report had recommended. But it was a start, and throughout the 1950s and 1960s a steady stream of repair grants were given to the National Trust, to institutions, and to around 230 private owners, on the understanding that they would open their houses to the public for twenty or thirty days a year and would contribute half of the money themselves.

Some owners were refused grants because they were just too rich. A few turned down the offer of money because they couldn't bear to open their homes to the public. Most were grateful for the help. Some wanted more. Awarded £15,470 towards the cost of repairs to Ragley Hall in 1963, the young Marquess of Hertford, who ran his own PR firm, told the HBC—and the public—that unless he received more money he would abandon Ragley and de-molish it. "I know that it would be an act of vandalism," he told the press. "I know that it would be an irreparable loss. I doubt if I should ever be happy again, having done it."[45] But he would still do it. The HBC capitulated and paid for the whole cost of the re-pairs, and even gave him £2,000 a year for five years "to contribute towards the cost of upkeep."[46]

The Marquess of Bath happily bit the hand that fed him. He declared, "I dislike grants, I think they are iniquitous, and I think all forms of subsidies ought to be abolished. If you cannot look after your own property . . . then you should get rid of it."[47] Which was a bit rich, considering that he had just accepted £40,000 to-wards the eradication of the deathwatch beetle that was eating up Longleat.

The Gowers report was a significant landmark in the twentieth-century history of the country house, and, with different names and in slightly different guises, the three Historic Buildings Councils survive today, along with a fourth, for Northern Ireland, which was created in 1972. Throughout the 1950s and 1960s the councils provided lifelines which kept some owners afloat when they would otherwise certainly have gone under.

But it was never going to be enough, and Harold Macmillan's conviction that "the mode of life for which these notable houses stood was doomed" was borne out by the bleak statistics of loss.

In England alone, well over four hundred country houses were demolished in the 1950s and nearly three hundred more in the 1960s, matching the total number of losses from the first half of the twentieth century. The country house was indeed in crisis, and a sporadic and selective system of grant-giving wasn't going to save it.

THIS RATHER DRY narrative of taxation and legislation and royal commissions obscures the human side of things: the sons and daughters trying to cope with the knowledge that a centuries-old connection with a community was coming to an end on their watch; the families for whom death, bad luck, and bad financial advice spelled ruin. One wouldn't want to overplay this—there were plenty of owners who breathed a huge sigh of relief and dreamed of life in a quiet little Georgian rectory somewhere as they slammed the nailed portal shut behind them and threw the keys at the bank. And there were plenty more whose connection with their not-so-stately home stretched back for only a decade or two, men and women who would sell without a qualm and buy another place somewhere else when the stock market picked up again.

But there were those for whom connection with the past was everything and selling up was a personal failure. "Chatsworth may not go on as a family home," the 11th Duke of Devonshire told his wife as they wrestled with the prospect of maintaining that vast pile in the early 1950s. "But I don't want to be the one to let it go."[48] Michael Saunders Watson, who in 1967 gave up a promising naval career to take on Rockingham Castle in Northamptonshire, a rambling pile which had been in his family since the sixteenth century, immediately set himself the target of passing on the estate to his children in as good a condition as when he received it. He, too, didn't want to be the one to let it go.

The Devonshires were victims of bad timing. On November 26, 1950, the 10th Duke of Devonshire, "Eddy" to his family, was indulging in his favourite pastime of chopping wood in an out-house at Compton Place, his early eighteenth-century mansion in Eastbourne, when he suffered sudden chest pains. He managed to reach the hall of the house before he collapsed and died.

Eddy was only fifty-five, and his death was not just a blow to his family; it was a disaster for the Devonshire fortunes. He had transferred a large part of his assets to a trust, the Chatsworth Settlement, but when he died the statutory period between the date of the gift and the owner's death still had fourteen weeks left to run. That gap of just under one hundred days meant that the entire estate was taxable at the maximum rate of 80 per cent. It meant that Eddy's son and heir, Andrew, was faced with a tax bill of £4.72 million. That is somewhere in the region of half a billion pounds in today's money.

Andrew's elderly grandmother Evelyn, the Dowager Duchess of Devonshire, was distraught, and not only because of the loss of her son. "I still feel numb and bewildered so cannot realise either our personal loss or the catastrophe to the family fortunes," she wrote. "It seems cruel after Eddy had taken such trouble and made such sacrifices of personal ownership and control."[49] Andrew's mother, Eddy's widow, was sympathetic, but she had no grasp of financial matters.

Ironically, the one member of the immediate family who *did* have a sound business head was Andrew's wife, Deborah, the youngest and most capable of the six Mitford sisters; but as a woman, and one who had married in, Debo was routinely excluded from discussions about the future. She was reduced to sneaking a glance at lawyers' letters that her husband had left lying around at breakfast if she wanted to find out what was happening to the estate.

Andrew's initial response to the crisis was to sell whatever could be sold. The contents of Compton Place went, and the house itself was let to a language school. The family's town house in Berkeley Square went, along with twelve thousand acres of agricultural land in Scotland and forty-two thousand acres in Derbyshire. And Andrew began to consider the possibility of handing over Chatsworth to the nation, a plan which gave rise to some wonderfully bad verse in the *Manchester Guardian*:

> *The Chatsworth estate to avoid confiscation*
> *May shortly be offered, a gift to the nation:*
> *This priceless collection of manifold beauties*
> *May pass to the State to discharge the death duties.*
>
> *Though heirlooms must piecemeal be put up for sale, if*
> *The Treasury decides to send in the bum-bailiff,*
> *The Chancellor, deploring litigious battles,*
> *In lieu of cash payment may settle for chattels.*
>
> *It therefore may seem an attractive solution*
> *To make the doomed mansion a State institution—*
> *But treasures of old to the nation entrusted*
> *Have mildewed and mouldered and rotted and rusted.*
>
> *The art-loving public with gloom universal*
> *May mourn every instance of sale and dispersal,*
> *But if they can't keep it in good preservation,*
> *Should Chatsworth be made a bequest to the Nation?*[50]

There were letters to the *Times* lamenting that Chatsworth's collections might be dispersed. The *Daily Mail* reckoned that the Devonshires' tax bill would put two shillings (ten pence) in one wage packet for every workingman, and raged, "A pint of beer and five cigarettes—and bang goes Chatsworth!"[51] On the other side of the political divide, the left-leaning *Daily Herald* railed against "the arrogance of a dominant few and the grovelling of a subservient multitude," and exulted in the thought that "soon, Chatsworth will belong to us."[52]

The Devonshires, meanwhile, were living in the agent's house in the estate village of Edensor, a mile from Chatsworth, with "an extraordinary number of domestic staff," recalled Debo, "and a frightening butler who would tell anyone who would listen that he had known better places."[53] They had been there since 1946 and they had no plans to move into the big house, which was looked after by the comptroller, W. K. Shimwell, and was open to the public, as it had been before the war. Andrew's plan that Chatsworth should go to the Treasury to help pay the death duties—at one point there was a notion that the house and collection would be kept intact and turned into the Victoria and Albert Museum of the north—meant the family would be able to hold on to their other Derbyshire house, Hardwick Hall.* Famous as the home of Bess of Hardwick and one of the most magnificent Elizabethan mansions in the country, Hardwick was open to the public at two shillings a head; in recent years it had been occupied on and off by Andrew's grandmother Evelyn as a kind of dower house.

Negotiations with the Treasury took time. A lot of time. In 1952, two years after his father's death, Andrew, now the 11th Duke, sent a proposal to Rab Butler, who had become chancellor of the exchequer in the Conservative government which Churchill had formed the previous year. The duke was prepared to sell a large proportion of the Chatsworth art collection and lease the house itself to the Ministry of Education, keeping a private apartment that he would maintain at his own expense. There was disagreement over what this deal was worth, over who would pay for what, and

---

*The Devonshires had quite a collection of mansions. As well as Chatsworth, Hardwick Hall, and Compton Place, they owned Bolton Abbey in North Yorkshire, Lismore Castle in County Waterford, and a smattering of smaller country houses strewn around their estates. The 9th Duke had sold Devonshire House in Piccadilly, their London residence, in 1920, and their Chiswick House estate, including the famous Palladian masterpiece built for the Earl of Burlington, in 1929. They were men (and women) of property.

over how the revenue from visitors would be shared. At the same time Andrew was growing uneasy at the thought of giving up his ancestral seat, and in March 1953 the Treasury was told that "the duke feels he is not morally justified in giving the whole of Chatsworth to the nation; he ought to retain at least a part for the sake of his predecessors who created the house and its collection and for his successors."[54] *I don't want to be the one to let it go.*

The negotiations dragged on, with interest on the debt growing at what seems a frightening rate of £1,400 a week. However, the duke's financial advisers had pointed out to him that while interest was 2 per cent, it was possible to invest his capital at a much higher rate. It was to his advantage to pay as slowly as possible. Then one day in August 1955, while his London-bound train was halted at Bedford station, the duke had an idea which he described as "not quite St Paul on the road to Damascus" but still a "revelation."[55] Why not keep Chatsworth and offer Hardwick Hall to the Treasury instead?

The Treasury didn't reject the idea out of hand. Instead it referred the duke's new proposal to the Ministry of Works, and an official there, F. J. Root, suggested three options. Hardwick could be accepted in lieu of the death duties and handed over to the National Trust, but Root didn't think the trust was up to managing such an important house. It could be managed by the Victoria and Albert Museum, but the V&A had recently taken over the management of two important country houses, Ham House in Richmond and Osterley Park in Middlesex, and the Treasury was worried that it might overextend itself. Or Hardwick could be managed directly by the state, in the shape of the Ministry of Works, which already looked after the seventeenth-century Audley End in Essex. This was the most sensible option, said Root.

But senior officials at the ministry disagreed with Root's analysis, and slowly the idea of handing Hardwick over to the National Trust emerged as the favoured option. The duke said that he would be happy with this, so long as his grandmother was given a life tenancy (she would die in 1960, in her ninetieth year) and the trust wouldn't expect him to fork out for an endowment.

It was all complicated by, as the columnist Kenneth Rose noted in his diary, "the fact that he must negotiate with his uncle."[56] Harold Macmillan, who was married to Andrew's aunt, became chancellor of the exchequer at Christmas 1955. Whether that proved a help or a hindrance is hard to say, but in 1956 the Treasury, the Ministry of Works, and the duke at last agreed on a way forwards. Hardwick, its principal contents, and three thousand acres of surrounding farmland would go to the National Trust (although the ruinous Old Hall, which stood close by, would be in the guardianship of the Ministry of Works), and nine important pieces from Chatsworth would be transferred to the Treasury and displayed in various national museums.

It still wasn't enough. Christie's held sales of books, silver, furniture, and paintings from Chatsworth in 1958. The final payment of death duties wasn't made until 1967, and even then, the Devonshires were paying off the interest for another seven years.

IN 1957, WITH the future of Chatsworth no longer hanging in the balance, Andrew Devonshire made the decision to move back to the house that he hadn't lived in for decades. He was giving in to pressure from his librarian, Francis Thompson, who was concerned that the contents of the library were being neglected; from his land agent, Hugh Read, who was concerned that the house was being neglected; and from his wife, who thought she was being neglected. Debo had been keen to live in the house since her father-in-law's death in 1950. The couple would walk in the park and she would tease the duke, saying, "Oh, look at that lovely house. I wonder who lives there?"—only for him to tell her to shut up. Thompson, Read, and Debo were all convinced that without a family presence, the house would become nothing more than a museum, "as arid and lifeless as so many others."[57] Andrew's financial advisers warned him against the idea, but in the end, he said,

"I decided that I was more frightened of my wife than my advisers; so the decision was taken to return."[58]

The notion that there was a fundamental, intangible, almost mystical difference between an institution and a home was powerful in the postwar years and is still powerful today. It informed much public discussion about the future of the country house and set up the private, lived-in home as an ideal, infinitely preferable to the publicly owned house. In a 1952 article on stately homes which were opening to the public, one popular magazine declared that private houses "differ from the publicly owned mansions in that they are still homes and sometimes in going round you will see lying about an opened book, a newspaper, a letter or something else which tells you that when the public have gone, the room will be lived in again by people who regard it just as home and not as a museum."[59]

The practicalities of making a vast baroque pile like Chatsworth suitable for twentieth-century family living (when the decision was made, the Devonshires had two teenage children and a new baby) were formidable. The state rooms were open to the public four days a week from Easter until the beginning of October; in any case, they weren't suitable for the family, and Debo, who was left to make most of the arrangements, chose bedrooms on the west front and a suite of drawing room and dining room on the south front, with a kitchen and pantry on the floor below and guest bedrooms and nurseries scattered around the house. A service lift was installed in an old stairwell to bring the food up from the kitchen, although the new dining room's only possible access to the lift was blocked by a Lely portrait of George Monck, the man who had restored Charles II to the throne. That carried no weight with Debo, who ordered him to be cut in half. "When the door was opened the old soldier's legs swung round, startling the diners, but when it was shut General Monck appeared complete, legs and all."[60]

Seventeen new bathrooms and central heating were installed, and six staff flats were created. Telephones replaced the old bell system that had been used to summon the servants. Pieces of furniture were brought in from other Devonshire houses. The artist Lucian Freud was invited to stay and to paint a mural in one of the new bathrooms; sadly, he got bored with Derbyshire after only five days and went back to London with the mural still incomplete.

Debo personally supervised all the redecoration, choosing colours and carpets, arranging paintings and furniture. "I was too mean to pay for something I could do myself," she recalled, "and cannot imagine living surrounded by someone else's taste."[61] She was delighted when Nancy Lancaster, inventor of the Georgian country house style and owner of the interior decorators Colefax and Fowler, came to stay soon after the house was finished and said to Andrew, "My God, you're lucky. If I had done this house for you, you would have had to sell it to pay me."[62]

Andrew and Debo moved into Chatsworth in November 1959, nearly two years after their decision to make it their home. "Chatsworth House, Derbyshire, has become a home again after being unoccupied for twenty-one years," reported the local paper. "The Duke and Duchess of Devonshire, with their three children, have moved into a modernised suite of twenty rooms on its first floor."[63] "As soon as I arrived," Debo remembered later without a hint of irony, "I felt Chatsworth was home, and a perfectly ordinary home at that."[64]

The Duchess of Devonshire in the Chatsworth chapel with her children, 1952

4

KEEPING UP APPEARANCES

L UNCH WAS A frugal meal served by a sinister-looking butler
in a uniform that didn't fit. The two guests suspected he had
been hired for the occasion.

Afterwards, their host showed them over the house. With
childlike enthusiasm he pointed out one piece of furniture after
another. Each time he told them that yes, it was true that this
chair or that side table was broken, but he was just about to have it
repaired. When they reached the state bedroom, the hand-painted
Chinese wallpaper was peeling away from the walls. The state bed
itself, an early eighteenth-century masterpiece with a full canopy
and hangings of embroidered silk, held three basins and a chamber
pot to collect the rainwater that dripped from the ceiling above.

This was Erddig Hall in the early 1950s. The finest country
house in Wales and its precious collection of Georgian furniture
were caught in a combination of circumstances that threatened
catastrophe. Simon Yorke, Erddig's owner, was eccentric and impoverished, desperately keeping the world at bay and refusing all
offers of help. In fact his guests that day, the 7th Marquess of
Anglesey and Sir Grismond Philipps, chairman of the Historic
Buildings Council for Wales, were lucky to be there at all. Curious
to find out if the rumours were true and Erddig really was falling
down around Yorke's ears, they had invited themselves for lunch,

and their reclusive but well-mannered host hadn't been able to think of a good reason to put them off. It was rare now for anyone to penetrate beyond Erddig's front door. Visitors were usually turned away. There was no telephone—Yorke had had it taken out. The postman had been ordered to leave mail at the lodge. When the hunt met at Erddig, they were never allowed inside. If members dared to ask if they might use the lavatory, they were directed to the bushes.

But no one could help noticing the broken windows, the saplings growing from the walls, the derelict outbuildings. And all the

An upstairs passage at Erddig in the early 1970s

time a brutally insensitive National Coal Board allowed mining directly underneath this architectural masterpiece, so that its back broke and its roofs lay at crazy angles, funnelling water into the attics and the state rooms instead of channelling it away to the gutters. Erddig was indeed falling down.

Erddig's plight was extreme but not unique. And Yorke's refusal to accept that after more than two centuries of ownership it might be his family who had to let it go, was something he had in common with hundreds of country house owners in the decade after the Second World War. Erddig was one of the lucky ones: after Yorke's death in 1966, his brother Philip, who inherited the estate, was determined to save it, and it was eventually gifted to the National Trust.

But determination wasn't always enough. In June 1945 Viscount Cranley succeeded his father as the 6th Earl of Onslow, and a short time later he and his countess moved into the family seat, Clandon Park in Surrey. Lord Onslow had had a hard war: he had been awarded the Military Cross for an action in the Western Desert in 1941 when he'd led two troops of tanks into battle standing up in his scout car and waving them on with his handkerchief, and three years later he'd taken part in the Normandy landings and ended up in a prisoner-of-war camp in Germany.

Clandon Park had had an easier time of it. During the war it had functioned as an outstation of the Public Record Office, occupied only by a vast quantity of documents and the archivist Noel Blakiston, his wife, Giana, and their two young daughters. But it still suffered from the familiar maintenance backlog. James Lees-Milne, who was friendly with the Blakistons and used to visit them at Clandon from time to time, described the house as "dirty and in decay,"[1] with piles of paper filling the state rooms and the lead on the roof in need of replacing. "I was depressed by the soullessness of this house," he wrote on another occasion. "The Onslows can have no taste whatever."[2]

Like so many other owners in the aftermath of war, the On-slows moved back into their ancestral seat with some trepidation. Clandon had a claim to be the coldest country house in England—"Even on a hot June day the marble-floored hall and saloon strike one as chill rather than cool," wrote *Country Life*'s architectural editor, John Cornforth.[3] That marble-floored hall was a forty-foot cube, and together with the saloon it filled the central section of the house, with equally impressive state rooms on each side making up the rest of the main floor. As Cornforth also said, "Its very grand conception makes it difficult to adapt for modern life."[4] The Blakistons used to eat in the servants' quarters in the basement.

The Onslows were in their early thirties and had a seven-year-old son and a five-year-old daughter. At the beginning of the war, when Lord Onslow's parents still occupied the house (and his father was writing to the papers to say that peacocks were the answer to food shortages—they made "excellent eating"*), there was a small army of servants at Clandon.[5] Now, though, domestic help on that scale was out of the question. The couple set up a produce business, supplying fresh fruit and vegetables to customers in the London area. (The earl's cabbages won prizes at the local farming club's annual show.) They had a pedigree herd of cattle; they bred and sold Irish terriers. They auctioned off the nursery furniture, along with rather a lot of their own, including Chippendale dining chairs and a satinwood commode and dressing table "probably executed to the design of Adam."[6] A Chippendale "cock-fighting" table fetched £200. Meanwhile, the Countess of Onslow was dyeing American army blankets and turning them into curtains for Clandon's saloon.

---

*The supply of peacocks must have run out by 1941, when Lady Onslow was fined five pounds by Guildford magistrates for obtaining twice the household's ration of meat from her local butcher.

They kept up appearances. The grounds of Clandon were the scene of a Red Cross Youth fair in May 1947 ("The fete will include a large-scale firework display").[7] The following year the Surrey Agricultural Show was held there: the earl was president of the agricultural association and took the chair at the annual dinner while his wife distributed the trophies won at the show. A ball was held at Clandon in aid of the Soldiers', Sailors', and Airmen's Families Association, raising a healthy profit of £950 10s.

But after four years of keeping up appearances the couple decided they had had enough. They couldn't afford to live at Clandon Park any longer. So at the end of 1949 they began negotiations to hand over the place to the National Trust. James Lees-Milne, who hadn't set foot at Clandon since visiting the Blakistons during

The Onslows at Clandon, March 1951

the war, abruptly revised his opinion of the house and its owners' taste. Now, he wrote in his diary, the state rooms were all "splendid, with some of the best Palladian ceilings in England."[8] The Onslows offered the house and garden and said they would loan the contents of the state rooms. But they couldn't raise the endowment that the trust needed, and for the time being the negotiations foundered. The Onslows moved to a small modern house on the main street of the village of West Clandon and installed a curator-cum-caretaker and his wife in a flat on the top floor of Clandon Park.

AT THE OTHER end of the stately scale were families whose country houses were smaller, whose roots may have been a little shallower, but whose battles to hold on to the past in a changing world were no less determined. Minor gentry, they would have been called before the war. Country squires, before that. Now they were the new poor, struggling to keep up appearances.

Ronald Pearson's father had bought Baynton House in Wiltshire, an attractive seventeenth-century mansion remodelled by the Georgians, during the First World War. Ronald came back from the Second to find his brother and sister preparing to sell this "little sister to those mansions which are known as the Stately Homes of England."[9] He couldn't bear to see the place go and scratched around for ways to hold on to it. Immediately after the war his sister had taken in paying guests, mainly officers and their wives—"furnished rooms to let, four guineas a week, food and lighting included"—and he took his cue from her, opening the family seat as Baynton Guest House and Country Club.[10] He reclaimed neglected hard tennis courts and turned a sludge of a lake into a swimming pool, installed a bar and renamed the drawing room "the lounge."

Pearson tried everything to make the country club work. He advertised "Old-fashioned Christmas and New Year House Parties."[11] He announced that dogs were welcome. He pestered contacts at the British Council, suggesting that they should send visiting foreign dignitaries to Baynton: "Their cultural relations with this country would be raised to new heights by experience of our manners and customs"; and he offered to give them personal tours of Stonehenge, Salisbury Cathedral, and the Roman baths at Bath.[12]

None of it was enough. Baynton Guest House and Country Club closed in 1948, two years after it opened, and Pearson went into the business of growing watercress. That proved more successful, but even so, the struggle to keep up the house proved too much, and Baynton was sold in the early 1960s.

There was yet another important group of country house owners: people who managed, people who were reasonably well-off but not rich, who worked to supplement their income, who lived happily in a house in the country rather than a country house, who socialised with the traditional landed elite but never really belonged to it. Typical of this group were Ralph and Frances Partridge, the middle-aged Bloomsburyites who lived in quiet contentment at Ham Spray, a small Regency country house in north Wiltshire. Their staff consisted of Mrs Chant, a daily help from the village who frequently failed to turn up, sending the liberal Partridges into paroxysms of guilt as they realised how dependent they were on servants. They went up to London sometimes, but they stayed in hotels or with friends rather than keeping a flat or a house of their own. Those friends were mostly upper middle class and arty, like them, although their circle also included minor aristocrats, members of the old gentry, and a few fabulously wealthy members of the nouveaux riches. They entertained weekend guests; they were entertained in the country houses of others.

In October 1949, for example, the Partridges were invited to spend the weekend at Long Crichel House in Dorset, a Georgian rectory presided over by a group of gay friends who had shared it since 1945. There was music critic Desmond Shawe-Taylor; Eardley Knollys, art critic and regional manager for the National Trust; and Edward Sackville-West, whose father had just handed over the ancestral seat, Knole, to the National Trust, much to the dismay of Eddy's cousin Vita. "I hate that beastly Nat. Trust symbol," she wrote to her husband, Harold Nicolson, furious at her family and at society's outmoded dependence on male primogeniture. "Knole should have been mine, mine, mine. We were meant for each other."[13] "Eardley, Desmond and Eddy lead a highly civilised life here," wrote an envious James Lees-Milne, a close friend and colleague of Knollys's and a frequent visitor to Long Crichel. "Comfortable house, pretty things, good food."[14]

The Partridges were equally delighted with Long Crichel, which Frances described as a "marquetry box of coloured, complicated, patterned comforts" and "this most hospitable of country houses."[15] They would be regular guests there throughout the 1950s, although on this first visit they were rather daunted by the determined brilliance of their hosts, and also by the fact that they were put in separate bedrooms. Shawe-Taylor, Knollys, and Sackville-West had recently been joined by literary critic Raymond Mortimer, who was in a long-term relationship with Vita Sackville-West's husband (and James Lees-Milne's ex-lover) Harold Nicolson, and the tone was easy, urbane, and determinedly queer: Frances was naively puzzled to see from the visitors' book that women rarely visited Long Crichel and to hear marriage talked of only in terms of convenience. On a later visit, she was shocked that the "Crichelois," as she called them, didn't bat an eye at the relationship between two dinner guests, Michael and Sonia Pitt-Rivers, who had recently married, treating "this marriage between a lifelong homosexual and a neurotic forty-year-old woman as if it was perfectly normal."[16]

Frances's astonishment is surprising considering that the Partridges were themselves no strangers to complicated relationships, having survived their own more famous *ménage à quatre*. In 1924 the writer Lytton Strachey, who was in love with Ralph Partridge, had bought Ham Spray House, which was, according to the estate agent's particulars, a "very charming country house" on the border between Wiltshire and Berkshire.[17] Ralph was then married to the painter Dora Carrington, who was herself in love with Strachey, while Ralph had begun a sexual relationship with Frances, whom he had met while she was working at the writer and publisher David Garnett's bookshop in London. For a time the four Bloomsbury-ites lived uncomfortably together at Ham Spray, on and off, but two months after Strachey's death from stomach cancer in 1932, Dora Carrington borrowed a shotgun from her friend and neighbour, the poet and novelist Bryan Guinness, and on the morning of March 11, 1932, while there was no one else at Ham Spray, she put on Strachey's yellow silk dressing gown and, facing a mirror so that she could see exactly what she was doing, she rested the butt of the 12-bore on the floor, placed the muzzle against her side, and pulled the trigger with her toe. She died six hours later. Ralph and Frances married the following year and, in spite of the memories, remained at Ham Spray until Ralph's death in 1960.

The Partridges were pacifists and socialists. In 1948, Frances lamented that while during the war "it had seemed as though the relation between master and man . . . was suffering a sea-change," after only a few years of peace "the gentry had reassumed their right to the privileges and support that money gives."[18] When they spent a weekend at Maud Russell's Mottisfont Abbey in April 1955 (where they slept in "the softest bed and the smoothest sheets"), Frances felt uncomfortable at being waited on by an elderly grey-haired maid, who, simply by cosseting her and making sure she had everything she needed, unwittingly manoeuvred her into becoming a member of a privileged class.

Yet for all their egalitarian principles, the Partridges lived guilt-ily but habitually in that world where bohemian late Bloomsbury overlapped with the traditional landed classes—a world where country house life continued oblivious to royal commissions and negotiations with the Treasury. One moment they were dining at Bryan Guinness's exquisite William and Mary country house, Biddesden, where they threw themselves into music-making with

Laurie Lee, a fellow dinner guest who played daughter Fiona Guinness's Amati while Bryan Guinness sang and Frances accompanied them on the piano. The next they were spending the weekend at Hilton Hall, the early seventeenth-century country house in Cambridgeshire owned by David Garnett and his second wife, Angelica. (Garnett had been married to Frances's sister Ray, who had died in 1940; Angelica was the daughter of Vanessa Bell and Duncan Grant, who had been Garnett's lover. Sometimes one feels one needs a chart.) Hilton was beautiful, with a magnificent staircase, panelled walls, kilim rugs on the flagstone floors, and works by most of the Bloomsbury artists on the walls. And life there was pleasantly informal: visitors usually entered by the back door and walked straight into the kitchen, where Siamese cats would be wandering round and wailing. But it was freezing—"the coldest house I have ever spent a night in," wrote Frances later, "and I used to smuggle an extra eiderdown in the back of the car to help suppress its penetrating chill."[19]

IN SEPTEMBER 1955 the Partridges, by now firm friends with Eddy Sackville-West, went to stay with him at Coolville, a pleasant, apricot-coloured country house in County Tipperary where Eddy could live in a way that was all but impossible for someone of his means in England. The drawing room was papered red with huge white roses; the carpets were red; Eddy's four maids wore red uniforms; and he changed into a red velvet dinner jacket for dinner. The house was, as Frances said, "a beautifully constructed, smoothly working toy."[20] And there were interesting people to meet. The novelist Elizabeth Bowen came to dinner, "horse-faced, with big hands and a clumsy body in a short black evening dress and flashing diamond corsage."[21] The Partridges took to her immediately, in spite of Frances's uncomplimentary description, and they were delighted when she invited everyone back a couple of nights later to dine with her at Bowen's Court, the Georgian mansion forty miles west in County Cork which was built by her ancestors and so lovingly described in her book of the same name as "an island—and like an island, a world."[22] They ate "at a candle-lit table in a vast room full of shadows, servants waiting, and Elizabeth in a white evening dress and emeralds."[23] It seemed for a moment as though, in Ireland at least, where labour was quite cheap and servants were easy to find, it was still possible to live in style.

Yet not even Ireland could keep reality at bay for long: four years later, after being brought to the edge of a nervous breakdown in her desperate attempts to maintain Bowen's Court, Elizabeth Bowen sold her family home to a farmer, who demolished it. "It was a clean end," she wrote from her new home in Oxford in 1963. "Bowen's Court never lived to be a ruin."[24]

Keeping up appearances had been the norm for the owners of Irish country houses ever since independence in 1922, although few did it quite as flamboyantly as Eddy Sackville-West. By the 1950s the burnings of Anglo-Irish mansions and the breakup of estates by the Irish Land Commission, which had characterised the war of independence and its aftermath, were things of the past. At Mount Stewart in County Down, the widowed Marchioness of Londonderry still kept thirty-five indoor servants, although she wasn't afraid of hard work herself. In her seventies, she was often found on her knees in the gardens at Mount Stewart, which had been her life's work and arguably her greatest achievement. There is a story that once, when she was in her gardening trousers and bent over in the foliage, some visitors came and asked for Lady Londonderry. "I'll tell her," she said, and then went into the house, put on a dress and some jewellery, and came back out to greet them. They had no idea she was the same person.

Some owners even dared to modernise their homes: when Sheila Plunkett spent money hauling the limited plumbing of Dunsany Castle in County Meath into the twentieth century, her father-in-law, Lord Dunsany, complained that there were now so many bathrooms in the place that the castle should be rechristened

"The Lavatories." And Ireland suffered none of the rationing that continued in the United Kingdom until the summer of 1954. The historian Antonia Fraser, daughter of the Labour peer Frank Longford, remembered the gluttonous sense of liberation she felt as a teenager in the 1940s on spending holidays with her Irish relatives at Dunsany and at the family seat, Pakenham Hall in County Westmeath. "At Dunsany there were four large meals a day," she remembered, "the tea alone encompassing more food than breakfast and lunch together at 8 Chad [8 Chadlington Road, her North Oxford home]." At Pakenham Hall, it was enough to say that "uncle Edward was known, not without reason, as the Fattest Man in Ireland."[25] But there was also poverty (although poverty is a relative term), and there were the same discreet sales of land and books and paintings that afflicted the traditional country house–owning classes in Britain. One day Edward, the younger brother of the 5th Lord Longford, was dining at his club when he noticed a large silver table decoration which seemed strangely familiar. "There used to be a piece just like that at Pakenham when I was a boy," he said to the club secretary. "That *is* the piece that was at Pakenham when you were a boy," replied the secretary. "Your nephew sold it to us."[26]

THE PARTRIDGES' FAVOURITE Irish country house was Luggala, an absurdly pretty Strawberry Hill Gothic confection nestled in a valley high in the Wicklow Mountains.

Luggala was already something of a legend in postwar high society when the couple stayed there for a night at the end of another visit to Ireland in August 1952. So was its owner, Oonagh, Lady Oranmore and Browne. Born in 1910, the youngest daughter of the brewing magnate Ernest Guinness, Oonagh was given Luggala by her father in 1937 as a present on her second marriage, to Dominick, 4th Lord Oranmore and Browne. Her first, to Philip Kindersley, had ended in divorce after six years; and after this second marriage went the same way in 1950, when she was forty, this beautiful, slightly remote society hostess began to entertain at Luggala in earnest. Louche writers and painters, intellectuals and peers of the realm, professional drunks and young married couples who weren't married to each other were all drawn to Luggala in the 1950s and 1960s. The little lodge in the Wicklow Mountains became celebrated, in the words of its chronicler, Robert O'Byrne, as somewhere guests were invited for drinks or dinner, "only to emerge several days later blinking in the harsh light of the ordinary world, aware that during that lost period of time they had enjoyed themselves immensely without necessarily being clear about the details of how, or why, or even with whom."[27]

Clear or not, reminiscences of visits to Luggala—most of them involving excessive drinking—fill memoirs and autobiographies of luminaries in the 1950s and 1960s. The journalist Lord Kilbracken remembered a night in 1952 when the entire house party of around a dozen decamped to a housewarming in the next county. Actually, "remembered" is putting it too strongly: he had a hazy memory of dancing with the wife of the film director John Huston and being sick in the garden, but that was about it. Viscount Gormanston, on the other hand, remembered his first visit to Luggala all too clearly. He drove up from Dublin with Brendan Behan, another regular guest, but Behan insisted on stopping at so many pubs on the way that by the time they arrived, "I was legless," said the young Anglo-Irish peer.[28] Oonagh's butler, Patrick Cummins, had to drag Gormanston to the kitchen and force black coffee down him before he was fit to make an appearance abovestairs.

Filmmaker Michael Luke described how a guest at Luggala might see Erskine Childers talking to Sean O'Casey while Claud Cockburn lay full-length on the drawing room carpet "after an exhilarating morning of informed discussion spent not far from the brandy decanter."[29] And through it all floated their serene hostess, supported by the faithful Cummins, a gentle Irish Jeeves. The British politician Woodrow Wyatt, who stayed at Luggala in December 1957, said Oonagh was "as lovely as the angel on the Christmas tree," an image which cropped up again and again in contemporary descriptions of her. Anjelica Huston, who frequently stayed at Luggala in the early 1950s with her father, John, said Oonagh was "an Alice-in-Wonderland figure . . . forever in the guise of a little girl."[30] Luke remembered her as a more complex character, remote, vulnerable, "half witch, half goddess, [yet] nevertheless 'real' in a very unusual, disturbing and exhilarating way."[31]

Ralph and Frances Partridge began their first visit to Luggala by meeting their fellow houseguests in Dublin, where they were treated to a bohemian rhapsody of sorts. There was the journalist and historian Robert Kee, an old friend of the Partridges, who was currently carrying on a hectic affair with Oonagh. The painter Lucian Freud was there. So was Freud's wife, Kitty, the daughter of sculptor Jacob Epstein, although she was shortly to leave Freud because he was sleeping with Oonagh's beautiful young niece Caroline Blackwood. Literary critic Cyril Connolly was in the party, "tall, dark, ugly and animated."[32] Daphne Thynne, the Marchioness of Bath, was there as well. Her marriage to Henry Thynne was breaking up, and the following year she would leave Longleat forever and marry the travel writer and war hero Xan Fielding.

Already drunk, this motley crew was eager to tell the Partridges about their latest adventure. It was the week of the Dublin Horse Show, and the previous night the entire party had been invited to a grand coming-out dance that Lord and Lady Powerscourt were holding for their daughter in the newly decorated ballroom at the Gresham Hotel on O'Connell Street. Before they arrived at the hotel, they had been drinking quite heavily and there had been a fight; three of them had black eyes. Worst of all, Lucian Freud was wearing tartan trousers. The doorman at the Gresham refused to let him in. When they demanded to see Lord Powerscourt, the peer told them he wasn't having any drunks at his daughter's party. Daphne Thynne, who had a slight stammer, flounced out, saying, "Thank you for the most b-b-beastly party I've ever b-b-been to in my life." To which Lord Powerscourt replied, "I'm so glad you didn't enjoy it."[33]

The *Tatler* paid fulsome tribute to the success of the dance— "an extremely good party which everyone enjoyed immensely"— before going through the distinguished company name by titled name.[34] There was no mention of the Luggala party.

After telling the Partridges the story of their exploits at the Gresham Hotel at some length, the guests piled into cars and drove in convoy out to Luggala, some twenty-five miles away. As they approached the house, the Partridges began to come under its peculiar spell. "Incredible beauty lay before us as we climbed the last ridge before dipping into the valley," Frances wrote in her diary. "Range upon range of mountains spread around us with their tops still golden in the setting sun, and the deep, green, lost valley below."[35] As they arrived the front door opened and they were ushered into the hall, which doubled as a dining room and boasted a huge oval table laid for dinner. And in the drawing room, waiting to greet them, was Oonagh, Lady Oranmore and Browne, "with her hair down her back and in her short diaphanous dress looking exactly like the fairy off a Christmas tree."[36]

Luggala was a far cry from the Onslows and their ilk, who were struggling and failing to hold on to their homes, or the Devonshires, who were reeling from wartime losses and trying to decide what to do with their string of country houses. But it demonstrates that the orthodox narrative which sets the postwar country house in the midst of decline and desperation, although accurate enough in itself, is only part of the story. Luggala and the other great party houses of the 1950s and 1960s belong to a parallel narrative, one in which privileged and wealthy members of the jet set (a term first coined in 1949) and their 1960s successors, *Vogue*'s "beautiful people," could, if they chose, entertain lavishly without giving a damn about what people thought of them. Those with roots in Great Britain or Ireland still saw the possession of a country house as an essential adjunct, something that went along with the apartments in Paris and New York, the villas in Menton and the Bahamas.

And there is no doubt that for those who looked on in wonder and amazement and just a little envy, it was a seductive lifestyle. "What can all those servants feel about the indulgent, selfish display of their masters' goings-on?" Frances Partridge asked when she was back in the more predictable surroundings of Wiltshire and struggling to reconcile her enjoyment of Luggala and its joy in living with her puritanical socialism.[37] The answers she received were conventionally disapproving. Her friend Julia, Lytton Strachey's niece, said "the output of such lives was *nil.*" Julia's partner, the artist Lawrence Gowing, thought the servants must feel both pride and pity for Oonagh and her set. And yet in spite of themselves the Partridges confessed that they were bowled over by Luggala and its "material splendour, recklessness, dash and style"—all of which, as Frances admitted ruefully to herself, were "supported on things none of us approves of."[38]

AROUND 4 A.M. on January 25, 1956, a fire broke out at Luggala. Caused by faulty wiring, it started in the room of sixteen-year-old Garech, Oonagh's eldest son with Lord Oranmore and Browne. Gay Kindersley, her twenty-five-year-old son by her first marriage, organised family and servants to form a human chain bringing buckets of water from a stream behind the house, while butler Patrick Cummins and other members of the staff rescued furniture and paintings. "Disregarding the explosions from dozens of stored champagne bottles (Veuve Clicquot, 1947)," claimed Lord Kilbracken, Cummins "rescued those sentimental objects—photograph albums, family pictures, the visitors' book—which no amount of insurance money could ever have replaced."[39] Three local fire brigades were summoned with difficulty, since the local telephone exchange closed at 10 p.m. Heavy snow delayed their arrival, and when the engines did reach the steep drive, they skidded on ice and had to be dug out. The farce continued as the firemen finally trained a hose on the blaze only to find no water was coming out—they had forgotten to connect it to the pump on the fire engine. Robert Kee stood as though hypnotised, watching the fire, until he suddenly remembered that all his belongings and money were still in the house, and he pitched in to help with the rescue work. And in the midst of all the shouting and the roaring of the flames and the chaos, Oonagh herself, a mink coat flung over her nightdress, sat on a dining chair in front of the house calmly directing operations.

Luggala was ruined. But, unlike so many country house owners in the 1950s, Oonagh Oranmore and Browne had both the will and the resources to rebuild. The lodge was insured, and her insurers offered £18,941. Her surveyor reckoned the real cost of rebuilding would be £25,358, and Oonagh was happy to meet the shortfall. She engaged the Dublin architect Alan Hope, who was told that "the house should be reinstated exactly as it was formerly and as soon as possible."[40] The task of redecorating Luggala went to John Hill of the London firm of Green and Abbott. Hill, the older brother of artist Derek Hill, produced a curious—and, at the time, unfashionable—vaguely early Victorian scheme, with chintzes and, in the drawing room, a reproduction of Pugin's "Gothic Lily" wallpaper, which had been originally designed for the House of Lords. But there were also more modern touches: bright colours, wallpaper by Edward Bawden, and wall-to-wall carpets throughout. Interior decorator David Mlinaric, who visited in the 1960s, was impressed, noting with approval that "there was always an element of a refreshing colour palette that wasn't necessarily historically accurate."[41]

One day in the spring of 1956, Lord Kilbracken took an American friend to see the ruins of Luggala and regaled her as they drove into the Wicklow Mountains with stories about all-night parties, "about the night the marquis collapsed."[42] The house had been deserted and abandoned since the fire, he told her—it wouldn't reopen until the following year—and Oonagh would be away, but at least they could see the ruins. In the late-afternoon light they pulled up at what had once been the front door and stared in silence at the melancholy debris—rubble, broken bricks, scorched wallpaper. And as they looked, they heard the sound of footsteps coming through the ruins towards them. A moment later, Patrick Cummins appeared, immaculate in a spotless white jacket and perfectly creased trousers. "Good evening, m'lord," he said. "Did you wish to see her ladyship?" Oonagh had flown over from Paris for the day to take her youngest son, Tara, out of school.

"They are at present taking tea in one of the cow-sheds," Patrick stated. "It has been converted for the occasion. Would you care to join them?"

Lord Kilbracken would. "Very, very good, m'lord. Will you just step this way?"[43]

Now that's keeping up appearances.

5

REDUCING MANSIONS

"THE PRESENT PROBLEM of inhabiting country houses has been aggravated in numberless instances by the hospitable enlargements made in the prosperous century between Waterloo and Mons," declared *Country Life* in a 1953 editorial entitled "Reducing Mansions," "and in a number of recent instances has been resolved by their removal."[1]

Reducing mansions—an elegant phrase which disguised the inelegant demolition of those parts of a country house which were now surplus to requirements—enjoyed something of a vogue in the years after the war. Knowsley Hall, seat of the Earls of Derby, was one of a number of country houses to lose their servants' wing in the 1950s. So was the Mountbattens' Broadlands in Hampshire. The owners of Leyswood in Sussex, Richard Norman Shaw's magnificent fifteen-bedroom composition in his Old English style, all gables and towers and tall chimneys, took the opposite view and demolished the main house in 1955, leaving only the servants' wing and a gatehouse, which were used, in the words of the estate agents' particulars, "as a more manageable family home and company offices."[2] Tackley Park in Oxfordshire was demolished in 1959, all except for the service range, which was converted into a house, and some outbuildings, which were turned into flats. "If you need to dynamite a country house, do it early on a Monday

71

morning," said the Marquess of Normanby, who took down the servants' wing at Mulgrave Castle in Yorkshire.[3] In the 1960s the Jacobethan Hodnet Hall in Shropshire was severely reduced by the Heber-Percy family, who had lived at different houses on the site since the thirteenth century. It lost an entire upper storey; the kitchens were converted into garages; and the great hall, once filled "with a terrifying array of stuffed animals" ranging from the heads of stags and foxes to lions, zebras, and even a baboon, was completely dismantled.[4] Not a great loss, one feels.

Something similar happened at Eridge Park in Sussex, a house with a restless past. Between 1790 and 1830 the 2nd Earl of Abergavenny turned a derelict Tudor manor house into a vast, flamboyant, and supremely impractical Gothic castle, all high machicolated towers and battlemented turrets. In 1938 the 4th Marquess of Abergavenny inherited the castle and quickly decided it was too run-down and too impractical. He knocked the whole thing down and built an entirely new house in a plain neo-Georgian style to the designs of the prolific Brighton architect John Denman. This new Eridge was still big, with a self-contained, three-storey servants' wing, a separate family wing, and a sprawling range of reception rooms and guest accommodations. And by 1954, when the 5th Marquess succeeded his father, it was too big. Lord Abergavenny let one half of the house to the pioneering fashion historian Doris Langley Moore, who opened a museum of costume at Eridge in 1955 before eventually gifting her collection to Bath, where it formed the core of the city's Fashion Museum.

In 1958, after consulting with Denman, the marquess decided to demolish the servants' wing and most of the main block, even though they were barely twenty years old, leaving only the two-storey family wing, and even there some of the surviving rooms were partitioned to make more convenient spaces. A swimming pool took the place of the demolished guest wing.

Woburn Abbey in Bedfordshire presented a more complicated set of problems. The 12th Duke of Bedford inherited it in 1940, when Woburn was occupied by a secret black propaganda unit which was later joined by members of the Women's Royal Naval Service who were working at nearby Bletchley Park. The duke's pro-Nazi sympathies were well known: for example, in 1941 he published *A Personal Statement*, in which he maintained that Hitler wasn't all that bad and that reports of German atrocities were wildly exaggerated. "Research has shown me that on occasions when Hitler has been criticised for bad faith he has received provocation of a kind which his critics have been careful to underestimate or to conceal entirely."[5] As a result the duke was encouraged to spend the war as far away from his ancestral seat as possible. For most of it he stayed at his Scottish shooting lodge, Cairnsmore, with occasional visits to the House of Lords, where he earned himself no friends with his claims that the war "represents an attempt by the money-lending financiers, currency speculators and big business monopolists to destroy the relatively sane financial system of the Axis Powers."[6]

After Woburn was derequisitioned in 1946, the duke came south and settled in one of his estate houses in the village while he struggled to repair the damage caused to the abbey by years of neglect. His son and heir was fruit-farming in South Africa, but the duke was assisted by an old friend, an ex–boarding house landlady named Ada Osborne Samuel who acted as resident caretaker at Woburn, keeping an eye on the paintings and furniture stored in one wing of the house during its occupation by the military. She was referred to as his personal agent. The duke also brought in a surveyor from the real estate consultancy Knight Frank & Rutley, William Cunningham.

There was a lot to be done before Woburn could be made habitable again. The product of different building periods, it was essentially mid-Georgian, a vast quadrangular palace with corner pavilions, facing an equally vast detached range containing an indoor riding school and an indoor tennis court, flanked by two stable blocks. Cunningham and his firm advised the duke to demolish this range, even though it was considered to be one of architect Henry Holland's finest works. A regrettable decision, but there was worse to come. The entire east range of the abbey facing Holland's riding house was suffering badly from dry rot. It must also go. And so it did, along with about a third of the abbey's north and south ranges, opening up the old quadrangle and transforming the palatial courtyard house into a truncated U. Albert Richardson, an old friend of the duke's father and a professor of architecture at University College London, was brought in to tidy up what was left while the duke, his personal agent, and his surveyor organised repairs to houses on the estate and two of Holland's buildings in the abbey grounds, the Chinese Dairy of 1787 and an orangery of 1788, now called the Sculpture Gallery.

It was at this point that the duke fell afoul of the formidable bureaucratic machine that was the Ministry of Works. In 1941, as part of a whole raft of regulations intended to ensure that all available materials and labour were directed towards the war effort, the government had passed legislation requiring anyone who wanted to spend more than £100 on building or repairing a property to obtain a licence from the ministry. Everyone expected the Control of Building Operations Order, as it was called, to be lifted when the war ended, but instead the Labour government renewed it annually, seeing it as an opportunity to do just what the name of the order suggested and keep control of building operations. As the minister of works, George Brown, pointed out during an acrimonious parliamentary debate on the 1951 renewal of the order, it no longer had anything to do with the war or war conditions; now it was about "the fact that the essential building programme on which we are embarking—housing, power stations, factories, industrial buildings, and the defence programme—is of such an order than unless we take some steps to control the less essential work . . . we shall not get the vital, essential part of the building programme done."[7]

Licences for repairs to country houses that were directly at-tributable to war damage were usually easy to obtain, but licences for alterations, renovations, and decoration were a different mat-ter. For a class which had been accustomed for centuries to be-ing in control not only of its own destiny but of the destinies of others, bureaucratic constraints by the men from the minis-try were not only irksome; they were incomprehensible. It was with an increasing sense of frustration that owners tried to nego-tiate the labyrinthine ways of local housing committees, alloca-tion committees, licencing subcommittees, regional offices, and ministerial inspectors—the panoply of what the architect Clough Williams-Ellis described as the "penny-wise pound-foolishness of the government building programmes."[8] The legislation was much too rigid: it seemed ridiculous that the control order stipulated that exactly the same amount could be spent in a year on all resi-dential properties, whether a one-room flat or a mansion contain-ing a hundred rooms. And the penalties for noncompliance were severe, even though it was easy to break the law unintentionally: a licence was obtained on the basis of a budget which was bound to double or treble before the work was finished. If one went over the licenced budget, one could end up in court.

There was something unsavoury about the whole business, too, however well intentioned it may have been. Local authorities put up posters asking people to give information about unlicenced building work in spite of complaints that it was "degrading and contrary to the British tradition" to encourage them to inform on their neighbours.[9] One London council took to plastering build-ing sites where licences hadn't been obtained with bright yellow notices proclaiming "Black Market Building" in bold letters.[10] In the West Country a man from the ministry whose job it was to investigate reports of unlicenced building work was jailed for six months after being secretly recorded asking for a bribe in return for keeping quiet about infringements.

Most country house owners did the necessary paperwork and obtained their licences. Some did not. Victor Roden, the owner of the Meaford Hall estate in Staffordshire, was prosecuted for exceeding the £100 limit while making unauthorised repairs to one of his lodges. In spite of pleading that he had used salvaged materials from the recently reduced Jacobethan mansion and that he didn't think these materials counted towards the total cost of the work, he was fined a total of thirty pounds. The chair of the magistrates rubbed salt in Roden's wounds by pointing out that had he applied for a licence in the prescribed way, he would have got one. "However, we are very glad you made a good job of the house." There was laughter in the court.[11]

That was in 1949. No one laughed the following year when the 2nd Earl of Peel was prosecuted for carrying out work at his home, Hyning Hall in Lancashire, which exceeded the sum stipulated in his building licence by a whopping £17,000. The work included fitting an antique staircase and chimneypieces, refurbishing bedrooms, and installing antique panelling worth £5,000 in the dining room. Brought before Liverpool assizes, Peel claimed that he didn't see what was going on in the upper part of the house because he had an artificial leg and therefore couldn't ascend to the top floor. He also said he needed a house that was appropriate for his status as lord lieutenant of the county, somewhere he could entertain visiting dignitaries, even royalty perhaps. Counsel for his architects, Thomas Jones and Edgar Middleton, who were in the dock beside him, argued rather inconsequentially that Hyning was not a Chatsworth or a Blenheim. "It was not a particularly beautiful house," the King's Counsel told the court.[12]

None of the arguments washed with the judge. Mr Justice Lynskey told Peel that he had narrowly escaped a jail sentence. Instead he was fined £25,000. Jones and Middleton were fined £1,500 each. There was no likelihood of a royal visit after that. Days later Lord Peel resigned as lord lieutenant.

It was the control of building order that caught out the Duke of Bedford. Altogether the repairs to the abbey, including the demolitions, were estimated to cost £150,000, and the Ministry of Works granted licences for work at a rate of £10,000 to £12,000 a year. But Ada Samuel (and, presumably, her employer) took a rather relaxed view of what was and was not included in those licences, and in addition, unauthorised work to the value of £2,000 was carried out at Mrs Samuel's own home and that of her daughter, both in the estate village of Eversholt. In March 1953 Mrs Samuel, the duke's management company, London and Devon Estates Ltd. (of which Mrs Samuel was a director), and the surveyor William Cunningham were summonsed to appear at Bedford magistrates' court, which charged that between February 1, 1948, and the end of 1951 they had carried out unlicenced work for more than £2,783 on the Chinese Dairy and the Sculpture Gallery at the abbey, and that they had also exceeded the work licenced at properties on the estate, including the Eversholt homes of Mrs Samuel and her daughter. Altogether the three defendants were accused of carrying out around £9,500 of unauthorised building work. They pleaded not guilty. Defence counsel asked the magistrates to come and see the abbey for themselves, which they did—and then sent the defendants for trial at Bedfordshire assizes.

At the assize on May 6, 1953, they changed their plea to guilty. Mr Justice Cassels gave a pretty fair summary of the whole affair when he said he didn't think the charges had been incurred deliberately. "Everybody concerned was most anxious to comply with the regulations, but the great misfortune was that nobody did and each person concerned thought somebody else was doing it."[13] He fined Ada Samuel fifty pounds. William Cunningham, whose involvement had been limited to the Chinese Dairy, was given an absolute discharge. The duke's management company was fined £5,000.

In 1955 THE 8th Marquis of Lansdowne (unlike his ancestors, he preferred to use the French spelling of his title) demolished, not an unneeded Victorian servants' wing or an indoor riding school, but pretty much his entire house, leaving only the stables and the family's private apartments.

The marquis had unexpectedly come into possession of Bowood House in Wiltshire in 1945, when he was thirty-two. Until then George Mercer Nairne, as he then was, had had little prospect of inheriting the family title and the estates that went with it. His uncle, the 6th Marquess, had fathered three healthy boys, any one of whom stood to inherit the title and the estates that went with it before George would be called on to step in. But in 1933 the eldest, nineteen-year-old Henry, threw himself in front of a train at the Regent's Park tube station. This meant that the second son, Charles, inherited as 7th Marquess upon his father's death in 1936. When war broke out Charles and his younger brother, Ned, both joined up. Neither had married. Ned was killed in Normandy in August 1944, and one week later Charles went missing at Cassino while serving with the Royal Armoured Corps.

George Mercer Nairne, meanwhile, fought in North Africa with the Free French Forces before being dropped behind enemy lines to work with the French Resistance in preparation for the Normandy landings, earning himself the Croix de Guerre and the Légion d'Honneur. After the liberation of Paris in August 1944, he was appointed private secretary to the new British ambassador there, Duff Cooper.

On January 5, 1945, he opened the embassy's diplomatic bag to read in the previous day's *Times* that he was now the 8th Marquis of Lansdowne. "Although the available evidence cannot be said to be complete, and has not been officially confirmed by the War Office, reports have been received by Lord Lansdowne's family which point to the conclusion that he has been killed in action," he read. "Lord Lansdowne, who was unmarried, is succeeded by his first cousin, Captain George John Charles Mercer Nairne."[14] He was stunned.

Lansdowne House, the family's legendary mansion on Berkeley Square, had been given up in 1929; a Robert Adam drawing room from it ended up in the Philadelphia Museum of Art, and the beautiful dining room, also by Adam and with a ceiling by the plasterer Joseph Rose, was bought by the Metropolitan Museum of Art in New York. But the new marquis's inheritance was still considerable, including property in Hampshire, a ninety-five-thousand-acre estate in County Kerry called Derreen, and Bowood, the family's principal seat.

The 8th Marquis was no stranger to grand houses. He already lived with his American wife, Barbara, and their two children at Meikleour, a lumbering nineteenth-century château in Perthshire, and he continued to regard Meikleour as his home for the rest of his life. His mother, who had lost Mercer Nairne's father in the early months of the First World War, had remarried; her second husband was John Jacob Astor V, and the Astors divided their time between their London home in Carlton House Terrace and Hever in Kent, the romantic castle where Henry VIII had wooed Anne Boleyn (and which had been made a good deal more romantic by John Jacob's father, William Waldorf Astor). One of the marquis's aunts was the Duchess of St Albans, who lived in a substantial but plain Georgian mansion in County Tipperary; another was the Dowager Duchess of Devonshire, who had presided over Chatsworth before the war and who now lived in Hardwick Hall, the greatest dower house in England.

Bowood could stand with the best of them. "Some people have mistaken it for a small town," commented John Britton in his early nineteenth-century *Beauties of Wiltshire*.[15] It was vast (that was its problem) and boasted a building history that read like a who's who of great British architects. The hundred-room main block, always known as the Big House, was designed in 1755 by Henry

Keene, surveyor to the fabric of Westminster Abbey, along with two courtyards containing the stables and other offices. In the 1760s, Robert Adam was brought in to complete Keene's work and created a magnificent set of interiors including the Great Room, which became the dining room. Joseph Rose, Adam's favourite plasterworker, executed the decoration. Adam also designed a long range, known as the Diocletian Wing, which hid Keene's courtyards from the gardens. In the course of the nineteenth century the architects George Dance the Younger, C. R. Cockerell, and Sir Charles Barry, who designed the Houses of Parliament, were all employed to make various additions and amendments to the eighteenth-century house. The result was complicated, "an irregular and diversifed mass of architectural parts," as *Country Life* put it in 1904.[16] It was also quite beautiful.

But Bowood was an unwieldy and expensive thing, and by the 1920s the family had retreated to what they called the Little House—the Diocletian Wing and the two courts, which by then housed their private apartments. The Big House, with its huge and exquisite Adam state rooms, was only opened up on special occasions. It was here that the ill-fated 7th Marquess had celebrated his coming of age in 1938, with a ball for four hundred guests.

During the war, the Big House found a purpose when it was occupied first by Westonbirt School for Girls and then by the Air Ministry, which used it as a rather grand hostel for VIPs flying in and out of the RAF aerodrome at nearby Lyneham. But when the marquis arrived to survey his inheritance in 1945, the Air Ministry had gone and his cousin, Lady Kitty, sister to the three dead boys, was living in the Little House with her husband, Edward Bigham, and their sons. The Big House was empty and suffering from dry rot. The gardens were neglected. Farms and cottages needed repairs. And while the 8th Marquis wasn't exactly impoverished, he hadn't the resources to revive the ailing estate.

Things were further complicated by the fact that although the Lansdowne estates went with the title, the 7th Marquess had left most of Bowood's contents to Lady Kitty, with the exception of as-yet-unspecified heirlooms which were to stay with the house because of their historical significance. As trustees of the 7th Marquess's will, Lady Kitty and her husband were left to decide what was an heirloom; the rest was theirs to keep or to sell.

Wisely, one feels, the new marquis and his wife opted to stay at Buckhill, the Bowood agent's house, while they took stock of things and began negotiations with the Bighams, who had a lease on the Little House until 1951. What could they do? Selling up was the obvious course, but in the bleak economic climate of the late 1940s, who would want to buy what the marquis himself described as "a huge Palladian palace badly infected with dry rot, stripped of furniture and badly battered by its war service"?[17] In any case, he didn't want to be the one to end the Lansdownes' connection with Bowood, feeling, as the 13th Duke of Bedford said of Woburn Abbey in similar circumstances, that if he disposed of the house, "something would have gone out of the family, and indeed the history of England, which could never possibly be replaced."[18]

Another option was to let the Big House to some institution. In 1947 the Lansdownes were introduced to the architect Philip Tilden through Sir John Carew Pole, whose Cornish country house, Antony House, Tilden was remodelling and reducing in size. Tilden visited Bowood, and Lansdowne later recalled that their "discussions revolved round ways and means of isolating the Big House entirely from the Little House."[19] The marquis approached several school authorities with the suggestion that they might like to take on the Big House. But nothing came of it.

By 1952 the Bighams had left the Little House, having reached an accommodation with the marquis and marchioness whereby many of the paintings and the best furniture remained at Bowood and, in return, they took over the Lansdownes' Irish estate in Kerry. Still the marquis searched for an economically viable solution to the problem of Bowood's future while he and his wife divided their time between Meikleour and their London home, only visiting Wiltshire for a few weeks in the spring and autumn and staying either at Buckhill or in the nursery wing of the Little House. Farms were sold; a group of cottages in need of repair were offered to the National Trust (which refused them on the familiar grounds that the gift required a bigger endowment than Lansdowne was prepared to offer). The walled garden at Bowood was let as a market garden, and there was the occasional discreet sale of paintings and porcelain and furniture.

And then, after years of hesitation, the marquis came to a decision. He was convinced that, paradoxically, the only way to save Bowood as a family home was to demolish it—most of it, anyway. In September 1952 the Ministry of Works granted him a licence for a demolition contract, and the following February he showed members of the Ministry of Housing's new Advisory Committee on Buildings of Special Architectural or Historic Interest round the mansion to convince them that the only alternative to his abandoning Bowood as a lived-in family home was to demolish the Big House. He consulted the Georgian Group, whose chairman, Lord Rosse, agreed that "only worse alternatives existed."[20] Lansdowne commissioned a local demolition contractor and employed the architect F. Sortain Samuels, who was advising the Earl of Derby on the best way of reducing his own monstrous pile, Knowsley Hall, to convert the Little House and Adam's Diocletian Wing into something workable.

The news of the demolition finally broke in June 1955 with the announcement that there was to be a sale of fixtures and fittings at the house at the end of the month, after which the demolition of the Big House would begin. Lansdowne had been careful to get his ducks in a row; in his more elegant words, "Both officially and unofficially, men and women of great taste and expert in architectural matters, who have been kind enough to study the details of the problem thoroughly with me, have accepted my decision."[21] As a result, there was remarkably little protest—in itself a telling indication of the despair which everyone was feeling over the future of the country house by the mid-1950s. That year, 1955, forty-eight country houses were lost, nearly one a week. Even *Country Life*, while calling Lansdowne's decision "deplorable" and arguing for alternative uses to be found for large houses, reluctantly agreed that the Advisory Committee on Buildings of Special Architectural or Historic Interest had acted for the best "by sanctioning amputation."[22] Most people agreed with the *Sphere*, which concluded a lavishly illustrated feature on Bowood's interiors by saying that "all lovers of the English heritage will sympathise with Lord Lansdowne in the hard decision he has had to take."[23]

The Bowood sale "of antique fixtures, fittings and architectural features" was widely reported: it raised more than £18,000.[24] The dining room—marble mantelpiece and fireplaces, ceiling, wall panel, lamps, and doors—went for £5,000 and was installed in the new Lloyd's building which was going up on Lime Street in the City.* Two carved marble mantelpieces designed by Adam and executed by Thomas Carter fetched £1,250 and £1,100 respectively; a pine staircase complete with balustrade, newel posts, and handrail went for a mere £3. The Adam portico on the west front of the house sold for £110. Another portico, this time from the south front, was bought by a Welsh undertaker; it still adorns his family's funeral parlour in Cardiff.

Although the general reaction remained one of regretful sympathy, the flurry of publicity surrounding the auction led Lansdowne to write a rather defensive letter to the *Times*, arguing that what would remain after demolition would be "a perfectly balanced architectural entity" consisting of Adam's Diocletian Wing, five flats for estate employees in one of Keene's two courtyards, and private family apartments in the other (which was the smaller, as he was careful to point out).[25] This led to a furious response from James Lees-Milne, one of very few experts to disagree in public with

---

*It was reinstalled in the new Lloyd's building designed by Richard Rogers and completed in 1986.

Lansdowne's plans. Blaming Lansdowne's advisers, Lees-Milne raged that "the block about to be destroyed contain[ed] a number of apartments as masterly and perfect as any Robert Adam created."[26] The fact that guardian bodies like the Advisory Committee on Buildings of Special Architectural or Historic Interest and the Georgian Group were happy to go along with the demolition seemed "both feeble and shocking," he said.[27] Couldn't they at least have suggested some alternative use for the Big House? He ended by claiming that in France and Italy, Bowood would be a classified monument. "The fate that now awaits it would not be tolerated in these two countries for a moment."[28]

But Lees-Milne's was a voice crying in the architectural wilderness. His attack provoked huffy responses from William Holford, chair of the Buildings of Special Architectural or Historic Interest Committee and a distinguished architect in his own right, and from the Georgian Group's Lord Rosse. There were no letters of support. The demolition of the Big House went ahead that summer and F. Sortain Samuels's modernisation of the Little House followed. "A house has been formed that can be readily adapted according to the number of people who are in it and, what is equally important, according to the number of people who are available to run it," claimed John Cornforth when he wrote up the house for *Country Life* in 1972. "Much of great interest and value has been preserved."[29] And much of great interest and value had been lost.

THE NOTION THAT the stately homes of England were glittering dinosaurs, doomed to extinction in a drab utilitarian world of council houses and bumbling bureaucrats, was gaining ground in the early 1950s, while the statutory protections promised by the 1947 Town and Planning Act wouldn't really kick in until the mid-1960s, leaving the owners of country houses to lament their fate, blame successive governments, and demolish large sections of their historic mansions in hopeless attempts to turn them into something that, in spite of Cornforth's optimism, they could never be—modern, convenient, servantless homes.

Lord Lansdowne's dramatic reduction of Bowood was not the most extraordinary example of downsizing short of total demolition. There are two contenders for that doubtful honour. One is Bury Hill House, an enormous eighteenth-century mansion remodelled in the nineteenth by Decimus Burton. Bury Hill consisted, conventionally, of a porticoed central block flanked by two pavilions. For most of its life it belonged to a wealthy family of brewers, the Barclays. But they sold it in 1952, and shortly afterwards, while it was being converted into maisonettes, a fire damaged the central section. This was pulled down, but the two pavilions were kept and turned into apartments. That left a gap where the main house used to be. The result was very odd.

But not as odd as Stratton Park in Hampshire. The Stratton estate was bought in 1801 by Sir Francis Baring of the Baring banking family, who brought in George Dance the Younger to give them a fashionable neoclassical mansion with a huge Doric portico. At the time it was "a great subject of conversation among the resident gentry, and . . . praises [were] bestowed upon its classical properties."[30] That had changed by 1960, when John Baring bought the house from the family firm. It was in a poor state of repair and suffering from dry rot: "People today just cannot afford to keep up the great houses which are merely showpieces," said the banker.[31]

"Basher Baring," as the press dubbed him, promptly demolished almost all of Dance's work. He commissioned the architects Stephen Gardiner and Christopher Knight to design a startling modern country house, all glass and right angles. But most startling of all was the fact that Basher and his architects decided to retain Dance's Doric portico as the focus of the new composition, hoping that the new house would be "integrated with a fragment of the old," as the modernist architect Michael Webb put it in a 1967 article for *Country Life*, citing the example of Basil Spence's new Coventry Cathedral and its relationship to the ruins of the old.[32]

In an indication of how little the great neoclassical country houses of the early nineteenth century were valued in the 1960s, Webb dismissed the old Stratton as "never a distinguished building" and claimed rather optimistically that the new house, which a twenty-first-century critic might describe as a cross between a secondary school and an office building in an industrial park, blended effortlessly into its rural setting.[33] The new Stratton was, said Webb, exactly what the landowning family of the mid-twentieth century needed: "a spacious yet easily maintained house that respects the spirit of tradition without being cramped by it."[34]

Perhaps it did meet a need. It was spacious, and no doubt it was easily maintained. But respect for tradition involves rather more than demolishing most of the past and making do with the fragment that remains.

6

FIT FOR A QUEEN

IN MAY 1947, even before Buckingham Palace formally announced that the twenty-one-year-old Princess Elizabeth was to marry Lieutenant Philip Mountbatten, rumours started to circulate about where the couple were going to live. Their official London residence was to be Clarence House, next door to St James's Palace, which had been built in 1825 for the Duke of Clarence, the future William IV; but with building controls in place and no exemptions for royalty, the renovations there took much longer than expected, and the newlyweds spent the first eighteen months of their marriage in Elizabeth's former apartments at Buckingham Palace, eventually moving to Clarence House in the summer of 1949.

Everyone assumed they would also want a country house of their own, somewhere not too far from London, where they could relax on weekends. Bagshot Park in Surrey, a monster of a house built in 1879 and used for sixty years as the principal residence of the Duke of Connaught, one of Queen Victoria's children, was one suggestion. Another was Fort Belvedere in Windsor Great Park, a battlemented and turreted folly where Elizabeth's uncle, Edward VIII, had committed follies of his own until that morning in December 1936 when, watched by his brothers and the world, he sat at his desk in Belvedere's octagonal drawing room, signed the Instrument of Abdication, and left for a life of exile and might-have-been dreams.

Not a happy place for the heir to the throne to start her married life. The royal family's memories of that crisis year ran deep: the Queen Mother once told Deborah Devonshire the reason she always refused invitations to visit Chatsworth was that she and her husband had been staying there in 1936 on the eve of the abdication, and the associations were still too painful.

Princess Elizabeth's choice of a country house was pretty much devoid of associations, unhappy or otherwise. Sunninghill Park, a twenty-five-room Georgian mansion on 670 acres on the edge of Windsor Great Park, had a quietly attractive pedimented exterior. Remodelled and extended by architect James Wyatt in about 1770, it had belonged in the 1930s to a business tycoon named Philip Hill, who had bought it for £150,000 and spent another £100,000 on improvements, including a marble bathroom which was reputed to have cost £20,000. After Hill's death in 1944 the Commissioners of Crown Lands bought it with a view to providing a country seat for Princess Elizabeth when she came of age.

Sunninghill had been requisitioned by the military during World War II, but in the summer of 1947 the RAF moved out and the business of clearing temporary huts from the grounds began. Windsor Council said they would like the huts. So did squatters, whose threats to move in were taken so seriously the main entrances were guarded by police and motorcycle police patrolled the perimeter of the park. After a standoff, George VI gave permission for twelve large huts on the grounds to be used for temporary housing, while the remaining hundred huts were dismantled and re-erected on one of the council's housing sites near Ascot.

On August 14, 1947, Buckingham Palace officially announced that the King "has been graciously pleased to grant Sunninghill Park to Princess Elizabeth as a grace and favour residence."[1] The royal wedding was set for November 20 that year, and workmen moved in immediately to begin repairing and redecorating the house. Just how the bride and groom were going to deal with social housing on the lawn of their new mansion wasn't clear. But as things turned out, they didn't have to deal with it. Around midnight on August 29 a keeper in Windsor Forest saw flames coming from the house and called the fire brigade. Seventy-five firemen with ten pumps and a turntable ladder fought until dawn to contain the blaze, but the fire travelled through the roof void, so that as they put it out in one place it erupted in another. By morning, the house was almost completely destroyed.

Press and police muttered darkly about socialists and squatters and politically motivated arson. But forensic investigators swiftly discovered that the cause of Sunninghill's destruction was a cigarette end dropped by one of the workmen in the newly timbered library. While the fire brigade was still damping down the ashes, speculation started up about where the Princess and her Greek prince were going to live now. George VI was at Balmoral, and the deputy ranger of Windsor Great Park travelled up to Scotland to discuss the possibilities. Henry III Tower at Windsor Castle was mooted; so was Frogmore Cottage in the private grounds of Windsor Castle, where George V and Queen Mary had lived when they were Prince and Princess of Wales. Two days after the fire, the press confidently reported that Bagshot Park "has been chosen as Princess Elizabeth's new home."[2] Rumours and denials followed each other in quick succession until at the beginning of January, three weeks after the royal couple had returned from their honeymoon (spent first in a lodge at Broadlands, the estate owned by Earl Mountbatten, and then at Birkhall, a 1715 house near Balmoral owned by the King), the announcement came that they had taken a two-year lease on a country house in Surrey called Windlesham Moor.

Windlesham was more modern than Sunninghill Park and nowhere near as grand. With white, creeper-covered walls, French windows, and an arched, roofed sun loggia, it was designed by a minor Edwardian country house architect, Percy Newton, and completed in 1914, just in time to be requisitioned as a military hospital, which meant that the final touches to the gardens were delayed until the early 1920s. By coincidence, the house and about fifty acres now belonged to the widow of Philip Hill, who had sold Sunninghill to the Crown commissioners; she had remarried and was spending most of her time in South Africa, so she was very happy to lease the house.

The fact that Windlesham Moor was only thirty-three years old had its advantages. It was relatively small, with four reception rooms and seven main bedrooms, but there were also seven bathrooms, and the house offered thermostatically controlled central heating, mains electricity, and garaging for half a dozen cars. There was sensible staff accommodation for a housekeeper, a butler, and a few indoor servants, and the gardens boasted a nine-hole golf course and a tennis court, which the Duke of Edinburgh, as he had become on the eve of his wedding, converted into a cricket pitch. When he was home on weekends, he roped in the servants to come and practise with him. "So far they have broken only two windows," said one newspaper report, which also gave the generally accepted verdict on Windlesham: "a pleasant house, if unimpressive."[3]

The house was let partly furnished, and before the Duke and Duchess of Edinburgh moved in at the end of January 1948, they installed a combined radio and record player and other furniture of their own, much of it drawn from the 2,500 wedding presents that had arrived at St James's Palace from all over the world. They also installed an inspector from Scotland Yard who was the Princess's personal bodyguard; her two corgis; a terrier called Rummy who was jointly owned by the couple; and a Siamese kitten called Tibs.

Windlesham Moor was hardly palatial. Compared to the King's private country houses, Sandringham House and Balmoral Castle, it was tiny. But Sandringham and Balmoral had both been acquired nearly a century before, and George VI's postwar Britain was a world away from the regal splendours of his great-grandmother

Victoria's travelling court. In any case, the Surrey house was a temporary home—the idea was that once Sunninghill was rebuilt the royal couple would move there as originally planned, although since they were given no special priority for labour or materials, it was going to be a slow process. Windlesham was also intended, like Sunninghill, as a weekend retreat rather than a full-time home. The couple lived at Clarence House during the week, and Princess Elizabeth had an office in Buckingham Palace. Philip was posted to the Royal Naval Staff College at Greenwich. When duties and public engagements permitted, they drove down to Windlesham on Friday evenings, returning to London on Sunday after lunch.

And in a pattern which would be repeated throughout their early married life, Philip sometimes went down to Windlesham during the week. Having telephoned ahead to warn the servants, he would roar up the drive in his open-top MG accompanied by a good-looking, well-spoken young woman. A woman who wasn't named but who clearly wasn't his wife. The couple would talk and laugh together over beef sandwiches and gin and orange. "We gossiped as staff do," a footman remembered years later, "and jokingly referred to her as his fancy woman, or lady friend—even though I never saw them kiss or canoodle."[4]

Princess Elizabeth began to spend more time at Windlesham Moor in the summer of 1948, after she ceased to fulfil public engagements and began to prepare for the birth of her first baby that November. Charles was born at Buckingham Palace, but it was at Windlesham eight months later that the Duke and Duchess of Edinburgh invited a British Newsreel Association cameraman attached to the royal household to film them with their new baby. Sitting on a rug spread out on the lawn in the sunshine, the future heir apparent gazed into the camera, oblivious of his parents' attempts to interest him in a rubber duck given by Queen Mary. The short film was informal, a sign of things to come in the new Elizabethan age: the Duke wore a blazer and slacks as he played with his son; his wife, in a loose, summery twinset, waved a teddy bear in the baby's general direction and beamed. The three of them looked for all the world like an ordinary upper-middle-class family—prosperous, certainly, but no more than that. He, some kind of professional in the City and a stalwart of the local golf club; she, a homemaker who discussed dinner party menus with the cook and played an average hand of bridge a couple of afternoons a week. And in austerity Britain, perhaps that was the point.

The lease on Windlesham Moor ran out at the end of 1949, by which time the idea of rebuilding Sunninghill Park had been abandoned, or at least postponed indefinitely. The Edinburghs now had their refurbished apartment at Clarence House, and that autumn Philip was posted to the Mediterranean fleet, based at Malta. Over the next couple of years Elizabeth joined him for quite lengthy stays. There was no need for another country house. By July 1951, when they returned from Malta for good, the King was already ill with lung cancer, and for the rest of the year Elizabeth was called on to stand in for him at various royal functions. In February 1952, while she and Philip were in Kenya on the first leg of a state visit to Australia and New Zealand which George VI had had to give up because of his poor health, the King died in his sleep at Sandringham. And suddenly Queen Elizabeth II found herself possessed of, along with a throne and a dwindling empire, more country houses than she could possibly need.

EVEN IN A grey postwar Britain dominated by class conflict, ration books, and building controls, the world in which royalty moved was a world of big houses, some of which were very big indeed. Elizabeth II had at her disposal the two principal royal residences: Buckingham Palace, which contained 775 rooms covering an area of just over nineteen acres, with another forty acres of gardens; and Windsor Castle, the oldest and largest occupied castle in the world, where a suite of private apartments was modernised so that she and her husband could use the place as a weekend retreat. The changes at Windsor included nurseries for the royal couple's growing family (Princess Anne had been born in August 1950) and a kitchen equipped with all the latest labour-saving devices. The Duke of Edinburgh loved gadgets—according to his valet he often brought home the latest appliances, such as an electric food mixer, oblivious to the fact that they were intended primarily to ease the lives of servantless couples.

The Queen also now owned Sandringham and Balmoral in her own right. Osborne House, the Italianate palace on the Isle of Wight built by Queen Victoria and Prince Albert, had been given to the state by their son Edward VII, who hated the place; and Hampton Court Palace hadn't been lived in by a monarch since the time of George II, although there were still a number of grace-and-favour apartments there, given to retired courtiers and other household officials as a reward for good service to the Crown. There was also a string of substantial mansions in various royal parks, administered by the Crown commissioners but still within the gift of the Queen. Fort Belvedere had stood empty since the war: in 1956 it was let on a ninety-nine-year lease to the Queen's cousin, Gerald Lascelles, the younger son of Mary, the Princess Royal, daughter of George V. Cumberland Lodge, also in Windsor Great Park, was let to a charitable foundation. Another Windsor Great Park residence, Royal Lodge, at the end of the Long Walk, was used by the Queen's mother as an occasional retreat. White Lodge in Richmond Park, briefly the home of the Queen's parents in 1924–1925, had been let to a succession of private tenants; after the death in 1954 of the last of these, Colonel James Veitch, it was granted to the Sadler's Wells Ballet School: today it is still the home of what has now become the Royal Ballet School.

The Queen's mother also had a country house of her own. In June 1952, four months after the sudden death of her husband, Queen Elizabeth the Queen Mother went up to Balmoral. But after a week, she found the memories too hard. "We spent so many happy hours here," she told her mother-in-law, Queen Mary. "Life seems incredibly meaningless without him."[5] So she went to stay with old friends at Caithness in the far north of Scotland. Clare Vyner and his wife, Doris, had an Edwardian shooting lodge, the romantically named House of the Northern Gate, on Dunnet Head, the most northerly point on the mainland of the United Kingdom. The area was wild and remote and a perfect spot for the Queen Mother to begin to come to terms with her grief. The Vyners took her out for drives along the stark and deserted coastline, and it was on one of these drives that they came across Barrogill, a battered castle down by the sea. It was deserted and in a bad state, and when she made enquiries the next day, the Queen Mother heard that it was about to be demolished. "I thought this would be a terrible pity," she remembered later. "One had seen so much destruction in one's life."[6] The owner, Frederic Imbert-Terry, offered to give her the place for nothing, but they agreed on £100 and she decided to revert to Barrogill's earlier name, the Castle of Mey.

It was the start of a long love affair with Mey, the only house the Queen Mother owned in her long life. It was built in the sixteenth century by the 4th Earl of Caithness as a base for his second son, who, in one of those little squabbles that characterised family life at that time in that part of Scotland, was strangled by his older brother (who was in turn starved to death by their father). After passing to a surviving son, the tall, forbidding tower house was extended in 1819 by the Scottish architect William Burn for the 12th Earl. Although it was never grand or palatial, Mey was undeniably romantic, a turreted sanctuary on the wild northern shore.

With help from the Vyners, the Queen Mother brought electricity to the castle. Furniture and furnishings came from local sales—in the 1950s a number of houses in the area suffered the fate that so nearly befell Mey—or from Lenygon & Morant, which had held a royal warrant to supply George VI (and Edward VIII, George V, and Edward VII, come to that), or from Miss Miller Calder's antique shop in Thurso, where Doris Vyner would hunt out suitable pieces.

The Queen Mother at the Castle of Mey, 1955

From 1956 onwards the Queen Mother took to visiting the castle every August for a week or so. At first she lived there quietly, seeing only the Vyners, but in 1959 she began to entertain friends and relations, and the local gentry took to making sure they were in Caithness in August, staging luncheons and dinner parties in the hope that their new neighbour might be persuaded to visit with them. Local interest was further roused by the appearance of the Queen, who, from 1955 onwards, made a habit of stopping each summer at Scrabster, the local harbour, in the royal yacht *Britannia* for a brief visit to her mother at Mey. The Queen Mother's private secretary, Martin Gilliat, liked to take a party of guests to Orkney in a small ferry boat, fighting across the Pentland Firth, the point where the North Sea meets the Atlantic and a stretch of water said to be the most dangerous in the country. "Really terrifying" was the verdict of Elizabeth Basset, one of the Queen Mother's ladies-in-waiting. "Ships passing to and fro seem hardly to be moving against the waves and the little bays are filled with foam whipped from the waves."[7]

Not everybody liked Mey's bleak remoteness. For years, Princess Margaret refused to stay there, saying it was far too draughty. When she finally did pay a visit, she told her mother, "I can't think why you have such a horrible place as the Castle of Mey." To which the Queen Mother replied icily, "Well, darling, you needn't come again."[8]

Uniquely among the royal family in the 1950s and 1960s, Princess Margaret had no country house of her own, but she was an inveterate weekend guest. In 1949, for example, when she was still only eighteen, she spent a weekend at Badminton with the hunting-mad Duke of Beaufort. On Saturday he took her to a meeting of the Berkeley Hunt; on Sunday, after attending a Mothering Sunday service at the local church, she was walked to the kennels to see the Badminton foxhounds.

Margaret was a notoriously demanding houseguest. For a private weekend visit to a country house, she brought her lady-in-waiting, Lady Elizabeth Cavendish; her secretary, Rose Gordon; and her personal detective, Detective Inspector Fred Crocker. That was to be expected. But her hosts were required to submit the names of her fellow guests to Lady Elizabeth in advance, together with a file on each one, and Margaret exercised her veto on anyone she didn't expect to find congenial. At dinner, she was always served first, and no one was allowed to speak to her unless she spoke to them first.

Yet she loved the well-heeled bohemian circles into which photographer Antony Armstrong-Jones, whom she married in 1960, introduced her, and she could be surprisingly casual when the mood took her. One afternoon she and Tony arrived, unannounced and by helicopter, on the lawn of the journalist and travel writer Quentin Crewe's newly acquired country house, Wootton in Bedfordshire. The couple had come to see how Crewe and his wife, the journalist and writer Angela Huth, were settling in, and within moments they were cheerfully stripping wallpaper off the drawing room walls, without even being offered a cup of tea: the Crewes hadn't yet unpacked the crockery.

The problem was that no one could be sure of the Princess's reactions. Another writer and journalist, Polly Devlin, remembered being invited for dinner at the flat of her boyfriend, later husband, Andy Garnett, where the other guests were Garnett's old friend Tony Armstrong-Jones—and Tony's wife. Devlin didn't know she was expected to curtsey and immediately earned herself a black mark. Margaret ate little, smoked a lot, and was rude about everything, Devlin remembered. But after dinner was over, the Princess rolled up her sleeves and got on with the washing up.

Queen Elizabeth and her family were all frequent houseguests. A single weekend in November 1958 saw the Queen Mother staying with her brother, David Bowes-Lyon, at her childhood home, St Paul's Walden Bury in Hertfordshire; Princess Margaret as a guest of the Earl of Scarborough at his Palladian mansion, Sandbeck Park near Sheffield; and the Queen, the Duke of Edinburgh, and Princess Anne all visiting the Duke's uncle, Earl Mountbatten, at Broadlands, the spectacular Georgian house in Hampshire that had come to his wife, Edwina, in 1939 on the death of her father, Lord Mount Temple. It was Prince Charles's tenth birthday weekend, and on Sunday morning the Duke drove over to fetch him from Cheam, his prep school in Berkshire.

Princess Margaret's weekend in Yorkshire was a by-product of her public duties. She had spent that Friday in Huddersfield, opening a new school, having lunch with the mayor, and carrying out various engagements in the town. Her host at Sandbeck, an hour to the south, was not only lord lieutenant of the West Riding of Yorkshire; he was also lord chamberlain of her sister's household and thus one of the most important members of the Queen's court, and Margaret was a regular visitor to Sandbeck when she was in the north of England (as was her sister, who found it a convenient place to have lunch when the Doncaster Races were on). The earl usually organised a house party of a dozen or so young people to entertain the then still-single Princess: "The Earl and Countess of Scarborough will have their only son, the 20-year-old Viscount Lumley, at home," noted a hopeful *Yorkshire Post* on one occasion.[9]

The Queen's own social circle was small. During the 1950s and 1960s she and the Duke of Edinburgh developed a ritual of spending a weekend privately with the Mountbattens once a year, as close as possible to their wedding anniversary on November 20. Broadlands was a couple of hours from Buckingham Palace—the Duke often drove them himself—and it was both private and palatial. Lady Mountbatten once told a visiting journalist that the bowls of water placed at strategic points around the place were there for her Sealyham, Snippett. "The house is so big that he simply could not walk all the way down to the kitchen for a drink."[10]

But throughout the 1950s and into the 1960s, the private country house which the Queen and Prince Philip* used most consistently as a retreat from their formal duties was Uckfield House in Sussex. An unassuming Regency villa which had been renovated in an easy neo-Georgian style in the late 1930s by the Brighton architect John Denman, it was the home of Lord Rupert Nevill, second son of the 4th Marquess of Abergavenny and a wealthy businessman in his own right, and his wife, Camilla, daughter of the 9th Earl of Portsmouth. Nevill's connection with the royal family began during the war, when as an officer in the Life Guards he belonged to a unit which provided a personal bodyguard to George VI, tasked with whisking the King away to safety in the event of a German invasion. The Queen was godmother to the

---

*As he became on February 22, 1957, when it was announced that he was now "His Royal Highness The Prince Philip, Duke of Edinburgh."

Nevills' son Guy; in 1970 Lord Rupert was appointed treasurer of the Duke's household, and six years later he became his private secretary, holding both posts until his early death in 1982 at the age of fifty-eight.

A royal visit could be quite a nerve-racking experience. When the Queen Mother lunched at Sissinghurst in 1954, her hosts, Harold Nicolson and Vita Sackville-West, went to enormous effort to lay on an impressive spread, with their best flatware and crockery, fine wines and liqueurs, flowers. Afterwards, the Queen Mother told Tommy Lascelles how much she had enjoyed the day. "What I particularly liked was that the Nicolsons had gone to no special trouble for me," she said. "It was just like a cottage meal."[11]

The level of formality surrounding a private visit by royalty to a country house was not quite what it had been before the war, when Queen Mary would arrive with two dressers, one footman, one page, two chauffeurs, one lady-in-waiting, a maid for the lady-in-waiting, and a detective—and was preceded by a list of requirements that included having fresh barley water placed in her bedroom every two hours throughout the day. She brought her own sheets and pillowcases. The Duke of Edinburgh didn't even bring his own pyjamas. When a valet at one weekend house party remarked that the palace had failed to pack them, he quickly corrected him. "Never wear the things," he told the man.[12] When Princess Margaret and Lord Snowdon went away for the weekend, their under-butler, Richard Wood, who valeted for Snowdon, and Margaret's maid packed for them and then clambered with the luggage into a small Volkswagen; Richard drove to their destination, and he and the maid unpacked and hung the couple's clothes, ready for their arrival. In the evening, Richard helped serve at their hosts' dinner table.[13]

With the Nevills, a weekend at Uckfield was an opportunity for the Queen to set aside the rituals of life at court. Most of them, anyway. All members of the royal family seemed to adhere to Edward VII's approach to life: he was, said one of his court-iers, "always ready to forget his rank, as long as everyone else re-member[ed] it."[14] But weekends with the Nevills were probably as close as the Queen and Prince Philip came to shrugging off the shackles. They stayed at Uckfield two or three times a year. The Duke usually drove, although on at least one occasion he ar-rived on the front lawn in a helicopter, which he had just piloted onto the flight deck of an aircraft carrier moored at Portsmouth for a royal inspection visit. Sometimes there was a small house party, sometimes just the Nevills. And sometimes private and public overlapped. On one occasion they all drove over to Cow-dray Park, where the Duke played polo and the Queen watched, hatless and wearing sunglasses and "a green two-piece suit with black accessories."[15]

Even a visit without any official engagements was scarcely pri-vate. A fixed point in a weekend at Uckfield, or indeed at any of the private country houses where they stayed, was Sunday service at the local church. The first time the Queen and Prince Philip visited the Nevills after Elizabeth's accession to the throne was in March 1953, and the congregation was taken by surprise. Puzzled by the presence of uniformed police and plainclothes detectives as they arrived for matins, worshippers were told who was going to join them only a few moments before the service was due to begin. Then two cars, the first driven by the Duke of Edinburgh and the second by Lord Rupert, pulled up at the lych-gate and the royal party strolled in, escorted by the rector, who led them to roped-off pews at the front of the church. By the end of the service, which was rounded off with the singing of the national anthem, word had got round and crowds had gathered outside to catch a glimpse of the royal couple.

The following year Prince Charles and Princess Anne, aged five and three respectively, visited the Nevills accompanied only by their nanny, Helen Lightbody. No one knew they were there, and when they were taken by car to watch the local hunt set off from the local inn, hardly anyone recognised them, only a fourteen-year-old local girl whose family refused to believe her when she went home that day and told them. But when the Queen came to Uckfield in the spring of 1955, the press was ready. News of her stay appeared in Saturday's newspapers, and when she arrived at Holy Cross on Sunday morning she was met by hordes of local people lining the streets, eighteen press photographers at the lych-gate, and an unknown number of reporters, all jostling for pole position. Pictures appeared on the BBC's television news that evening.

There was more to come. Later that year, on Friday, October 28, 1955, when press speculation and public prurience were at their height over the prospect of Princess Margaret's marriage to Group Captain Peter Townsend, a divorced man and a commoner to boot, a car took Margaret out of the rear entrance of Clarence House, while a crowd of three hundred people waited at the front gate, and drove her down to Uckfield. A little later a big, chauffeur-driven car left the Knightsbridge flat belonging to Lord Rupert Nevill's brother, the Marquess of Abergavenny. In the back seat was Townsend, who had been staying with the Abergavennys. Lady Nevill sat beside him.

Unknown to almost everyone except the Archbishop of Canterbury, who had been informed the previous day, Margaret and Townsend had already decided there was no future for them. On Monday evening the BBC interrupted its TV and radio schedules to make Margaret's famous statement beginning, "I would like it to be known that I have decided not to marry Group Captain Peter Townsend. . . . Mindful of the Church's teachings that Christian marriage is indissoluble, and conscious of my duty to the Commonwealth, I have resolved to put these considerations before others."[16]

But the couple wanted one more weekend together, and the Nevills had offered them Uckfield House. Unfortunately for them, word of their visit got out: by Saturday, November 5, the newspapers were announcing that Margaret was staying with the Nevills.

A paparazzi long shot of Princess Margaret and Peter Townsend at Uckfield, October 1955

Undeterred by deliberately false reports that Townsend was spending the weekend ten miles away at the Abergavennys' Eridge Park,
the crowds began to gather. "Police and their dogs patrolled," recalled Townsend, "reporters perched in trees or hid in ditches; the
Princess and I could neither come nor go. We could only walk
in the grounds, sniped at occasionally by long-range lenses."[17] On
Sunday they did just that while they were being denounced from
pulpits across the country. The Roman Catholic Bishop of Brent-
wood sent a pastoral letter to be read in every church in his diocese,
condemning the fact that "even in the highest quarters" the holiness
of marriage was being disregarded. "If Princess Margaret married
Group Captain Townsend she will deliberately be sinning against
the express command of Our Lord," declared the Anglican vicar of
Andover.[18] Meanwhile, cheated of a sight of Princess Margaret at
church—she had wisely decided to give morning service a miss that
week—crowds gathered at the end of the quarter-mile lane leading to the main entrance to the mansion, held back by uniformed

police. At one time there were more than sixty cars parked along the nearby road, while their occupants brought out picnic baskets and camp stoves. Reporters who tried to come through the fields and onto the grounds of Uckfield were turned back by plainclothes detectives. And in a move which prefigured the late twentieth century's relentless pursuit of the royal family, one national newspaper hired a helicopter which hovered over Uckfield House throughout the Sunday afternoon while a photographer tried to snap the unhappy couple, as the miserable end of their private affair was played out in public against a backdrop of terraces and lawns.

7

IDEAL HOMES

I N JANUARY 1951, *Country Life*'s annual roundup of the previous year's property market was headlined, "Downward Trend." In 1952 it was "Downward Trend Confirmed." In 1953 it was back to "Downward Trend."[1]

When it came to country houses, it was hard to sell anything that was too far off the beaten track, or inconveniently large, or lacking modern conveniences. If the asking price didn't reflect the cost of modernising a place, it was virtually impossible. Houses remained on the market for years.

"Exceptional small Georgian residence, completely modernised and easily run" went an advertisement for Cromlyn in County Westmeath, adding optimistically that the house, on 230 acres, was "wired for main electricity expected shortly."[2] Phrases like "small country house" and "moderate size" figured prominently in agents' particulars, as did references to modern conveniences. Houses had to be easy to maintain and fitted with efficient heating systems and proper bathrooms before a buyer would look seriously at them.

A supply of domestic staff was also a deciding factor. "A house near a village, close to a good bus route, or on the outskirts of a country town usually scores over a more remote property," reported estate agents Strutt & Parker in 1958, "however attractive it may be architecturally."[3]

What counted as "large" was being revised downward, too. Something that before the war had been considered a medium-size country house, with perhaps ten principal bedrooms, was now seen by potential purchasers as a huge country mansion that was difficult to staff and uneconomical to run. The real estate services company Jackson-Stops, looking back at the trends of 1950, had to admit that "in many cases it is to demolition contractors that an unfortunate owner must turn if he wishes to rid himself of what is often an onerous burden."[4]

In many cases, yes. But not in most. Most houses found buyers. Elsing Hall, a beautiful late-medieval moated manor house with thirty acres in a remote corner of Norfolk, came on the market for the first time in its six-hundred-year history in 1955, with an asking price of £8,500. It took three years to sell, and the undisclosed price was almost certainly less than that, but it still sold. For comparison, around the same time my own parents bought a small semidetached house in a Derby suburb for £2,500.

Sometimes a modest house sold quite quickly. Frances Partridge, whose husband Ralph died in November 1960, put Ham Spray on the market five months later with an asking price of £9,500. Within days she was swamped with viewers who wandered round enthusiastically or haggled over the price or disparaged the house, to her intense irritation. A "pale schoolmistress" didn't bat an eye at the price tag, but then she didn't put in an offer, either.[5] One wonders how many who came to view were more interested in Bloomsbury, ghoulishly seizing the opportunity to see the house in which Lytton Strachey died of cancer and Dora Carrington shot herself. Three lots of viewers came in a single rainy afternoon and trudged round in mackintoshes and gum boots, after which one put in an offer of £8,000, which Frances turned down flat. Another day, two loud young men wandered round finding fault, "till it seemed as though only a lunatic could want to take over this Paradise from me." They offered £6,750. No one would want the house, they told Frances, only its location. "A fierce desire to keep it came over me, resentment of their coarse male violation," she wrote in her diary.[6] A week later a nice couple called Elwes turned up and made appreciative noises, endearing themselves to Frances enough for her to offer them a glass of sherry. They met the asking price and bought the house. It had been on the market for less than a month.

Ham Spray was quite manageable, with eight bedrooms and three reception rooms. The bigger the house, the harder it was to sell. The early-Georgian Himley Hall in Staffordshire ("fine hall, suite of six reception rooms, ballroom, fifteen principal bedrooms, nine bathrooms, swimming bath, squash court"), ancestral seat of the Earls of Dudley and the place where the Duke and Duchess of Kent spent their honeymoon, couldn't find a private buyer when it came onto the market in 1946: it eventually went to the West Midlands Coal Board for use as their headquarters.[7] Cobham Hall in Kent, one of the country's great country houses and the home of the Darnley family for nearly 250 years, couldn't find a private buyer either. Described rather confusingly by the agent as "a splendid example of Tudor architecture generally ascribed to Inigo Jones" when it came on the market in 1956, it was bought that year by the Ministry of Works, which carried out a programme of repairs before handing it over to a girls' boarding school in the early 1960s.[8]

With so many country houses in search of a purpose, it was a buyer's market. At almost any point in the 1950s and 1960s a person who yearned for a place in the country could take their pick from mansions and manor houses of all shapes and sizes and periods, in any corner of England, Scotland, Wales, or Ireland, with or without large gardens and parkland, extensive outbuildings, or agricultural estates.

So why build? Because that is what a number of people did. Between 1945 and 1974, well over one hundred country houses were built in the British Isles, ranging from modest rural villas to Palladian palaces. Hundreds more were remodelled or restored or dramatically extended, just at a time when others were being reduced or demolished.

The reasons for this new work were as varied as the houses themselves. Some owners, not content with pulling down an inconvenient Victorian servants' wing or a rickety clock tower, preferred to do away with their ancestral seat entirely and replace it with a modern home equipped with all the necessities of postwar life—a sensible suite of reception rooms, central heating and plenty of bathrooms, a kitchen placed next to the dining room rather than several hundred feet away down a succession of dark corridors. Others couldn't bring themselves to demolish the seat but opted to move to a more modest purpose-built house in the park. Some bought small and elderly country homes but soon found they needed more—a light and spacious drawing room, perhaps, or space for a growing family—and opted for a sensitive, or sometimes insensitive, extension. And others still bought an agricultural estate, found the house at its heart wasn't to their liking, and replaced it with something new which they could claim as their own creation.

The architects who specialised in country houses in the 1950s and 1960s were a select band. Architecture in Britain after the war was an ideological business, and many of the younger generation were intent on building a brave new world for workers rather than shoring up the past. Sir Edwin Lutyens was dead, his ashes interred in the crypt of St Paul's Cathedral, his reputation as the leading country house architect of the first half of the twentieth century secured by the four hefty, hagiographic *Lutyens Memorial Volumes* celebrating his work and life. But a prewar generation of country house architects, most of whom had been born back in the 1880s, was still picking up commissions here and there. Philip Tilden, who had earned his credentials with houses like Sir Philip Sassoon's Port Lympne and Winston Churchill's Chartwell, confined himself to advising on a number of judicious (and in some cases injudicious) partial demolitions before suffering a stroke in 1951. He spent the last five years of his life writing his unreliable but entertaining memoirs, *True Remembrances*. Sir Albert Richardson, long regarded by younger architects as a hopeless reactionary, confirmed their view by becoming a pillar of the establishment— Knight Commander of the Royal Victorian Order, president of the Royal Academy of Arts, holder of a string of honorary degrees. In 1945 he went into partnership with his son-in-law Eric Houfe, and together they combined commercial work with historic conservation, the repair of war-damaged buildings in the City, and the occasional country house commission.

Trenwith Wills, whose productive prewar partnership with Gerald Wellesley came to an end in 1943 when the latter became the 7th Duke of Wellington, went into practice with his wife, Simonne Jinsenn, after the war. Like Richardson & Houfe, Trenwith Wills & Wills found work restoring or adding to existing houses. They turned a squash court into a top-lit picture gallery to show off Lord Bearsted's collection of paintings at Upton House in Warwickshire, repaired Castle Howard's fire-damaged dome, and carried out a number of projects at Stratfield Saye in Hampshire, the home of Trenwith's ducal ex-partner, including a monument to Gerry Wellington designed in the duke's lifetime (both men died the same year, 1972). Its centrepiece was an antique porphyry urn: Gerry insisted it be lined with lead so as not to crack if his ashes were still hot when they were placed inside.[9] Trenwith Wills & Wills also produced a couple of brand-new country houses: at Buckminster Park in Leicestershire, where a large late eighteenth-century mansion had been demolished after the war, they created a more manageable neo-Georgian replacement in 1964–1965; and at Fonthill in Wiltshire they replaced an inconveniently large house (by Arts and Crafts architect Detmar Blow, and nearly twenty years younger than Trenwith Wills) with another piece of restrained neo-Georgian in 1972.

The couple's masterpiece during this period was a re-creation of one of Trenwith Wills's prewar country houses, Hinton Ampner in Hampshire. In the 1930s Wills and Wellesley had transformed an ugly Victorian monster on the side of a valley in Hampshire into an elegant faux-Regency mansion for its owner, a dilettante collector and neo-Georgian enthusiast named Ralph Dutton. The house was begun in 1935, although the war meant it wasn't finished and furnished and filled with Dutton's possessions until the late 1940s. One Sunday afternoon in April 1960 Dutton was out walking on the estate when he noticed a plume of smoke rising from the roof. He found out later that a spark from a log fire in the library had landed on a sofa. By the time he reached home, the local fire brigade was in action, struggling to tackle a blaze which was moving from room to room with terrifying force. The main part of the house was destroyed, along with most of Dutton's furniture, paintings, and books. But within twenty-four hours Trenwith and Simonne were at Hinton discussing plans to repair and improve the house. They all agreed it should have the same Georgian character as the earlier version: "Had I been young, perhaps a house in contemporary idiom would have shown more enterprise," said Dutton afterwards. "But I was not young, and a Georgian fabric was essential as a setting for the furniture and objects which I had every intention of collecting to replace all I had lost."[10] The result, which took three years to complete, was a stunningly beautiful piece of neo-Regency inside and out. It remains one of the greatest of all postwar country houses.

The most durable member of the earlier generation of country house architects was the redoubtable Clough Williams-Ellis, whose career began when Edward VII was on the throne and who was still designing country houses when he was in his eighties. Much more than just an architect, Williams-Ellis was a persuasive polemicist and a pioneering conservationist, a William Morris with a lightness of touch to mediate his campaigning ardour. *England and the Octopus*, his 1928 plea for a more sensitive approach to development, paved the way—a meandering, tree-lined way without advertising billboards or neon signs—for British town and country planning strategy in the midcentury. His belief in the moral power of beauty and its opposite, the degrading nature of ugliness, informed everything he did, from Portmeirion—the absurd and wonderful Italianate village he created in North Wales, which Lewis Mumford described in 1964 as "a fantastic collection of architectural relics and impish modern fantasies . . . a gay, deliberately irresponsible reaction against the dull sterilities of so much that passes as modern architecture"—to his commitment to the National Trust.[11] In *On Trust for the Nation*, his 1947 review of the National Trust's first half century, Williams-Ellis made an eloquent plea for the preservation of historic buildings:

> Trees will grow again if the seed be sown, so will men. Not so a Wren church, not so an ancient City Hall, nor an Augustan mansion, nor even the elegant little bow-fronted Regency house that had a fan light like the half of a spider's web, canopied and lace-like balconies and a delicate stair that spiraled up as gracefully as those shells in which one listened to the sea. All that beauty which is gone is lost to the world for ever—it is just that much the more desolate.[12]

His attitude toward country houses might be described as one of passionate pragmatism. He believed, along with the rest of the conservationist movement after the war, that where possible private ownership of a country house was the preferred option: "An old house that is actually lived in by its traditional family or by a thoroughly understanding owner has unquestionably a bloom upon it and a human interest that the same place under purely official guardianship must definitely lack."[13] But he recognized that this wasn't always possible and that it was better to have a great house put to institutional use if the alternative was demolition. (Williams-Ellis had been instrumental in saving Stowe from destruction in the 1920s, when it was turned into a public school, and he was Stowe School's first consulting architect.) He also recognized that it was impossible to save everything. "It is quality, not bulk, that has survival value, as the unintelligent brontosaurus found to its cost."[14]

Williams-Ellis had an established reputation as an architect and a planner long before the Second World War broke out, with a string of good country houses to his name as well as an eclectic mix of buildings, from rectories, cottages, and garden temples to Battersea Dogs' Home. When peace came, he resumed his architectural practice, in spite of being in his midsixties and in spite of suffering the perennial curse of the long-lived architect: seeing his earlier houses demolished. Three were lost, and at least one was pulled down by a developer who had wind of a plan to preserve it. One of the more notable losses was Caversham Place, a pedimented twelve-bedroomed house near Reading which he built in 1924 for the explorer George Pereira and which was replaced by a housing development in the 1950s.

But the destruction with which Clough was most intimately connected was that of his own family home, Plas Brondanw in Gwynedd. In 1908 his father had handed over to him a romantic seventeenth-century house in the wild Welsh mountains which had been deserted by the family a couple of generations earlier and was now home to seven families, including a celebrated salmon poacher who used the great chimney in the brewhouse for smoking and curing his ill-gotten fish. Over the years, Williams-Ellis gradually took back possession of parts of the house as tenants left or died, and restored them for his own family's use.

Early one morning in December 1951, the architect and his wife, Amabel, woke to a smell of smoke. A fire had broken out in the library below and, fanned by strong winds, it spread through the house. "From miles away," Williams-Ellis later wrote, "the fire-brigade saw the old Plas lit up in all its windows against the night sky and its dark hillside as though for some great festivity."[15]

The main four-storey block was completely destroyed, and the Williams-Ellises lost almost everything, including their diaries and engagement books, so that they were forced to place a notice in the *Times* apologising "should [they] fail to keep any fixtures made but not remembered."[16] They lost most of their belongings; the house wasn't properly insured; materials were scarce; and any restoration work would be subject to the building licences still in force. Both were past middle age. They might be forgiven for calling it a day.

But Williams-Ellis responded as only an architect could. "So much needed doing in the way of internal improvements and modernisation and I so much enjoyed the opportunity of at last carrying out my long-cherished ideas," he wrote later, that "I might well have been suspected of arson."[17] Using his own gang of estate workers under his personal supervision, materials from a local school that he bought and demolished, and a truckload of Georgian doors and mantelpieces bought from a London architectural salvage firm, he had Plas Brondanw rebuilt within two years. A mound of debris was left facing the house and a monument placed on it with the inscription, "This flaming urn raised on the ashes of their home by Clough and Amabel Williams-Ellis celebrates the rebuilding of Plas Brondanw 1953 two years from its burning."[18]

In 1958, when Williams-Ellis was seventy-five, a letter came out of the blue from a wealthy banker, Sir Vivyan Naylor-Holland, asking to meet with "a view to discussing a project that I have in mind where I think your advice would be helpful."[19] Naylor-Holland had just inherited a baronetcy and the enormous house that went with it, Nantclwyd Hall in Denbighshire. He wanted to knock it down, and he wanted Williams-Ellis to design him a new house elsewhere on the estate.

Nantclwyd, which had a claim to fame as the place where lawn tennis was first played, at Christmas 1873, consisted of a muddle of additions and extensions and outbuildings—laundries, garages, kennels, and a huge redbrick-and-cast-iron water tower. "It really all looked just about as welcoming as a railway marshalling yard," recalled Williams-Ellis. But at its heart there was a late seventeenth-century wing, and the architect persuaded his client to keep this as the centrepiece of the new house, creating an impressive classical house in a landscape of terraces and temples.

The relationship between architect and client, which went on for nearly two decades, was a rocky one. Naylor-Holland was subject to whims and had, to borrow Williams-Ellis's description of another client, a whim of iron. He insisted on two heated swimming pools, one indoor and one outdoor, which Williams-Ellis thought excessive. And the pair battled for years over the location of a new billiard room. It travelled to the top of the house and down again to the bottom of it, said Williams-Ellis, "each time with the necessary strengthening of the floor and the dismantling and reassembling of the table itself," before being housed somewhere else entirely.[20] Eventually the architect had to tell his client that he was too old for all these changes of mind. But the end result of their collaboration was a thing of beauty on a scale that was rare indeed in the 1960s. Williams-Ellis's new south front is limewashed, low, and plain, with deep modillioned eaves and a Dutch gable as its off-centre centrepiece, simultaneously harking back to Nantclwyd's seventeenth-century roots and reminding visitors that the house is an organic creation which has grown over time, fitting perfectly into the classical landscape that surrounds it. Nantclwyd is not only Williams-Ellis's masterpiece; it is one of the great houses of the later twentieth century, a delightful piece of good-natured and Elysian classicism.

Williams-Ellis wasn't done yet. In 1968, having finally decided to retire at the age of eighty-five, he was approached by "a spirited but perplexed young couple," the Mason-Hornbys, who had inherited an estate in Cumbria. It came with "a monstrously overgrown and incoherent mansion," said Williams-Ellis, "that could only have been comfortable but never convenient . . . and that neither employer nor employed would willingly even attempt to run today."[21] Dalton Hall, a big, Georgian mansion which had been heavily remodelled by the Victorians, boasted a Doric porte cochère which opened into a vast, glass-domed staircase hall and what Williams-Ellis described as "a succession of bleak reception rooms."[22] Worse, it was riddled with dry rot, and Williams-Ellis had no hesitation in recommending that the couple demolish it and build a new house on the site. By a stroke of irony, this advice from one of Britain's leading pioneers of the conservation movement aroused the ire of local people, who campaigned hard to save their local country house.

But the old Dalton Hall went, to be replaced by Clough Williams-Ellis's last country house, a plain building of nine bays, symmetrical on all four fronts, with pilastered pediments front and back. His relations with the Mason-Hornbys were extremely happy: they agreed to Williams-Ellis's conditions, that a car should be sent to fetch him from his North Wales home whenever

Clough Williams-Ellis, age ninety, up a ladder at Dalton Hall

he was needed on-site and that a local architect should be hired to act as clerk of works. The only time architect and clients came near to falling out was when the young couple lit a fire in their new drawing room and the room swiftly filled with smoke. It turned out that a sheet of brown paper from the first attempt to light the fire had floated up the flue like a message to Father Christmas and lodged itself against the grill that was in place over the chimney to prevent birds from nesting there.

"It is very warming to have ended my long building career with so satisfying a last fling," wrote Williams-Ellis in 1978, the year of his death, "and to find that I was still effectively operational, even to the extent of climbing ladders quite confidently!"[23]

AMONG THE YOUNGER generation of architects, those who had been born around the time of the First World War and whose careers were interrupted before they began by the Second, the most notable country house specialists were Martyn Beckett, Francis Johnson, and Claud Phillimore, who between them built upwards of eighty new houses.

They form a disparate group. Beckett, a charming man (and an accomplished jazz pianist), was happy to give a client just what they wanted, unlike some of his more dogmatic contemporaries in and out of the country house world. The results, as his obituarist kindly put it, could be "uneven."[24] The house he designed for himself near Helmsley in North Yorkshire was praised by architectural historian Mark Girouard as "a modern country house in which it is possible to lead a civilised existence without the accompaniment of sash-windows and sub-Adam fireplaces"; although today it reminds one rather too much of a 1960s health centre.[25]

On the other hand, he was capable of flights of fancy, one of which produced perhaps the most unlikely country house of the postwar years. In 1961 the 5th Earl Granville bought the island of North Uist in the Outer Hebrides. It was an impossibly wild and remote spot on the edge of the world, but Granville decided for some reason that he and his young family were going to live there. He invited Beckett to the island, took him to the northern shore, and, in a gale so strong that the two men could hardly stand upright, announced, "I would like to build a house here."[26] Ready to oblige, Beckett took inspiration from Round Square, the seventeenth-century circular building designed around a courtyard at Gordonstoun School, where he had acted as consultant architect from 1954 to 1958. A single storey of battered concrete walls two feet thick with double-glazed windows respected the fierce climate, and in a nod to vernacular tradition the gatehouse leading into the courtyard was marked by a crowstepped gable, while an answering gable directly opposite, with the earl's arms, marked the entrance into the house itself. A mansion which pretends to be a converted stable, was the *Buildings of Scotland*'s rather harsh verdict; Callernish is in fact an innovative solution to the site, inward-looking for shelter and outward-looking for the spectacular views of the savage Atlantic only feet away from its windows.

In his relaxed approach to style, Martyn Beckett was unusual among his contemporaries in the country house world. If there was no dominant figure, no Lutyens to define the era, there was certainly a dominant style, one involving pediments and porticos and cut-down piano nobiles, which was variously called English Palladianism, neo-Georgian, neo-Regency, and, towards the end of the period, modern classicism, progressive classicism, and intellectual classicism. The style—if so many different responses to the idea of the classical can really be called a style—was a reaction to modernism, an attempt to reclaim the past. It was conservative, reactionary even, a determined attempt to redefine modernity and to put aesthetics before function. And it produced some beautiful country houses.

Francis Johnson, one of classicism's leading exponents in a career which spanned more than half a century and involved the remodelling or restoration of dozens of country houses and the design of at least five brand-new ones, voiced the views of many postwar country house architects when he declared that "I have always been a Classicist at heart, albeit an omnivorous one. I love clarity and forms which seem timeless."[27] Operating chiefly in his native Yorkshire, Johnson catered to a clientele of traditionally minded landed squires and nobles. One of his finest new houses came about as the result of a fire. In November 1940, Sunderlandwick Hall near Driffield, described at the time as "one of the most imposing Elizabethan mansions in the north of England," burned to the ground.[28] Although there were proposals to clear the site and build new housing after the war, nothing seems to have happened, and the only survivor, a big early-Victorian stable block, was kept and converted into two houses. In 1956 Sir Thomas Ferens bought Sunderlandwick for the land, and in 1961, largely at the instigation of his wife, Jessie, he invited Johnson to build them a new house on the site. They wanted something light, elegant, traditional, and manageable; something that wasn't dwarfed by the classical stable block, which still survived. And the dimensions of the rooms had to suit their collection of oriental carpets.

Johnson's solution was to design an L-shaped house with arms facing southwest and southeast, and an entrance court hidden in the angle. The effect was to make the house look much more substantial than it really is. Inside everything was as light, elegant, and traditional as the Ferens could have possibly wanted, culminating in a spectacular staircase hall with the most sinuous of curving staircases. Johnson considered it to be one of his greatest successes, and the house was given a statutory listing as a building of special interest in 1998, three years after his death: the listing text described it as "a skilful and imaginative recreation of a late Georgian house."[29] But that's not quite accurate. Writing about the house in 1984, John Cornforth noted that the artfully simple architectural detail continued "the deliberately simplified Classicism of the late 1920s and early '30s rather than reusing full Renaissance or eighteenth-century mouldings."[30] Sunderlandwick is no piece of Georgian pastiche: it could never be anything but a twentieth-century creation.

It was to their credit that most postwar country house architects managed to work within the classical tradition without descending into mere mimicry. The period's most productive designer, if not perhaps the most innovative, was Claud Phillimore, who specialised in a quiet neo-Regency style. The grandson of an eminent High Court judge, Phillimore had just launched his architectural practice when the Second World War broke out. He spent six years in the army before returning to architecture in 1945, and almost immediately he was invited up to Northumberland by Sir Stephen Middleton, who had decided that his ancestral seat, a grand Greek Revival mansion called Belsay Hall, was just too grand. He wasn't prepared to demolish Belsay, but he wanted to move to a more modest eighteenth-century house on the edge of the park, and in 1950 he asked Phillimore to convert it for his use. The project was delayed when Middleton had a little trouble with the law—he was fined £500 for carrying out work on an estate cottage without the necessary building permissions, a second offence, and his agent was sent to jail for six months on the same charge. When the scheme began again it was to a smaller scale than that originally envisaged by Middleton and Phillimore, and the reduction led to some rather odd results: a single-storey wing containing a porch and a certain lack of symmetry which led to criticism from *Country Life*'s Christopher Hussey: "I feel that these little drawbacks could have been avoided," he wrote, which was the Hussey equivalent of frenzied condemnation.[31]

Phillimore's first really big country house project, Knowsley Hall in Lancashire, is an example of how difficult the aristocracy found it to make the transition to life in postwar Britain. Knowsley's owner, Edward Stanley, 18th Earl of Derby, inherited the mansion along with the title from his grandfather in 1938, when he was twenty years old. It was a vast accretion of work from different periods, and until the beginning of the twentieth century it looked very peculiar indeed, its turrets and battlements mingling unhappily with elegant Regency colonnades. The architect W. H. Romaine-Walker had made a valiant attempt to pull the house together in 1908 for the 17th Earl, and the result was a Wrenaissance garden front and some nice neo-Georgian interiors. But there was still much to do, and Knowsley's sprawling labyrinth of impractical Victorian additions were neither beautiful nor useful in 1950s Lancashire.

In 1951 the earl was appointed lord lieutenant of the county in place of the one-legged Earl Peel, who had narrowly escaped jail for carrying out work at Hyning Hall without a building licence. He may have begun to think about scaling down Knowsley at this point, but his thoughts on the future of the place were focused the following year when Knowsley was the scene of a dreadful crime.

On the evening of October 9, 1952, without any warning, a nineteen-year-old trainee footman ran amok in the house with a German submachine gun he had bought from a friend for three pounds and a pair of trousers. Lady Derby was dining alone in front of the television when the servant, Harold Winstanley, walked in unannounced and unsummoned. He was smoking a cigarette. "That aroused my suspicion at once," the countess said later.[32] Even more suspicious was the fact that he was brandishing a Schmeisser machine pistol. He told her to stand up and then shot her, wounding her in the neck. When the Derbys' butler and under-butler came to investigate, he shot them both dead. He went on to wound the earl's valet in the hand and pistol-whip Knowsley's chef before going to the pub for a beer. Then he dialled 999 from a local phone box and turned himself in.

No motive was ever discovered, and everyone, the footman included, was keen to emphasise that the Derbys' relations with their staff were perfectly amicable and there were no tensions belowstairs. Winstanley offered no explanation for his actions other than to say that he panicked. He was found to be guilty of murder but insane and sent to Broadmoor Hospital.

The episode left scars, emotional as well as physical, and it may be that it was this, coupled with the knowledge that as lord lieutenant the earl was poised to welcome Queen Elizabeth II and the Duke of Edinburgh to Knowsley when they made their first state visit to the county in Lancashire in 1954, that led him to ask Phillimore to embark on a drastic remodelling. In public, the earl merely said it was because half the house was unused. "You can't just shut off forty rooms and forget about them," he went on. "You have to keep them, heat them and so on, because, if they are left, you may get dry rot or something like that which would spread right through the house."[33] So over a fifteen-month period in 1953–1954 Phillimore demolished more than an acre of floor space, about a third of the whole. By April 1954 an entire wing had gone, apart from a fragment which housed the boiler house, electricity plant, and water tanks. "We finally decided it was probably better to leave it as it is," said the earl.[34] A library wing was demolished, but most of the state rooms were retained and redecorated and the domestic offices were replanned, on a remarkably ambitious scale for the time. There were a new kitchen, sculleries, and pantries; a laundry; a servants' hall and steward's room; a butler's pantry, housekeeper's room, and accommodation for footmen and housemaids. This was, as the architectural historian John Martin Robinson has pointed out, the last time in England that provision was made for servants on this scale.[35]

By 1963 the earl's determination to carry on country house life as though the twentieth century hadn't happened was on the wane. He decided to build a new house, a quarter of a mile away, and let Knowsley to the police, retaining the estate offices, library, and state rooms. "I am taking this opportunity of building a modern house so that future generations of my family can go on living at Knowsley despite death duties and rising costs," he announced.

Phillimore, who was commissioned to build the new house, was equally keen to stress its modernity. "The rooms will not be large and are designed for living in this modern age," he said. "They will be suitable for intimate and modest entertaining."[36]

"Intimate" and "modest" are relative terms. Although the house was a plain two-storey rectangular block in Phillimore's neo-Regency style, it was still ninety feet by eighty feet, excluding an adjoining wing for garages and staff quarters. Rooms had twelve-foot ceilings on the ground floor and nine-foot ceilings on the first; there were eight guest bedrooms as well as separate bedrooms for the earl and his countess; and staff accommodation included bedrooms for six maids and four menservants, a staff sitting room, and a staff dining room, as well as the usual offices—pantry, larder, china room, kitchen, and so on.

STRADDLING THE GAP between the two generations of country house architects who were operating in the 1950s and 1960s, late-Victorians like Sir Albert Richardson and Trenwith Wills and their younger compatriots, Phillimore, Beckett, and Johnson, was Raymond Erith. And Erith was greater than any of them.

Born in 1904, he opened his first practice in Westminster in 1928. A shy, modest man (he once described himself ruefully as "a bad salesman"), he designed a handful of buildings—small houses, shops, a church—before retreating to rural Essex in 1940 and taking up farming.[37] After the war he returned to architecture, which gave him a living but not much in the way of glittering prizes. "I get dozens of odd jobs, bathrooms, smoking chimneys, leaky roofs and the rest," he wrote in 1949. "I am a real market-town architect."[38] His passionate advocacy of classicism didn't help. It was more than simply a stylistic preference with him; it was an ideological position, and one which was distinctly unfashionable. "The very few architects who still adhere to the classical tradition," he said in a lecture to the Suffolk Society of Architects in 1953, "are looked upon, quite kindly and not without sympathy, as people who through some impediment in their mental make-up are quite incapable of clear or reasoned thought."[39]

Nevertheless, he continued to adhere to the classical tradition in its various forms—Soane and the English eighteenth century, or Alberti and Palladio in the Italian Renaissance—but always looking to build on his influences and mould them into something both beautiful and contemporary. In the later 1950s more prestigious commissions began to come in: new provost's lodgings at Queen's College, Oxford (1958–1960) and a fellows' library at Lady Margaret Hall, Oxford (1959–1961); the reconstruction of 10, 11, and 12 Downing Street. In 1962 Quinlan Terry joined the practice as Erith's assistant, becoming his partner five years later.

Erith wasn't a country house architect in the same way that Francis Johnson and Claud Phillimore were. His practice was always more varied than that, taking in farm buildings, factories, city offices, even a quite extraordinary Georgian Gothic pub, Jack Straw's Castle in Hampstead (1963–1964), all weatherboarding and battlements, which was described by Erith himself as "the ugliest building in Hampstead."[40] But the handful of country houses which he did design stand out as some of the finest to appear in the second half of the twentieth century. With The Pediment, an exquisitely small country house at Aynho in Northamptonshire, he told his client, Elizabeth Watt, that he wanted to create more than a house; he wanted to create a piece of architecture. "I think a house with a pediment would fill the bill very well indeed," he wrote.[41] A carved inscription on the drawing room fireplace reads, "The significance of the dwelling is in the dweller."[42] At Morley Hall in Hertfordshire, which he remodelled and extended in 1955–1957, he explained to his clients, Mr and Mrs Buxton, just what it was he was aiming for: "What I want is the quality of Palladio's simpler country houses which were built for the landowner to go to in the summer, to see the harvest got in: unambitious country architecture which *is* architecture all the same. It is of course a most ambitious idea, but by some odd fluke I have got near."[43]

Wivenhoe New Park in Essex (1962–1964), a contemporary take on the sixteenth- and seventeenth-century villas of the Veneto, was praised by *Country Life* as "a free rendering of the Palladian villa," which looked to Italy rather than to English Palladianism. "Unlike many of the neo-Georgian houses built in recent years, Wivenhoe New Park really does seem to evoke the past, while being entirely suited to modern living."[44] So it is—Italianate and arcadian rather than austere and cold like so many Georgian classical country houses, it contrives to be both domestic and grand at the same time.

Erith's last and largest country house, and his masterpiece, was King's Walden Bury in Hertfordshire. In 1967 Erith was approached by Sir Thomas and Lady Pilkington, who wanted to replace their nineteenth-century Elizabethan Revival mansion at King's Walden with something more practical. Practical, but still big enough by mid-twentieth-century standards: the main rooms were all to be well over fourteen feet high, because the Pilkingtons had a pair of chandeliers that measured seven feet six inches from top to bottom, and they stipulated that their new drawing room must be big enough that the chandeliers didn't dangle dangerously close to passing scalps.

As with Palladio's own villas, measurement and proportion were everything. Erith opted to use the Venetian foot of fourteen inches as a module, not only because it harked back to the progenitors of King's Walden on the Veneto but also because it gave a greater sense of space. The measurements of the doors to the main rooms, for example, are in the proportion two-to-one, which makes them six Venetian feet high by three wide—eighty-four inches by forty-two, instead of the more conventional seventy-two by thirty-six.

The wings are quite plain, with most of the architectural detail reserved for the five bays that make up the centre of the house:

a recessed double portico, Doric below and Ionic above, on the south front; and arched windows and an elaborate pediment on the entrance front, part stone and part wood. Inside, the detailing is muted: mouldings borrowed from Palladio and restrained decoration. John Cornforth, who described the house in September 1973, two months before Raymond Erith's sudden death from a heart attack at the age of sixty-nine, was ecstatic: not only was it "an admirable solution to the problem of living in a spacious house in domestically uncertain times," he wrote, but it was "the most handsome country house built in England since the war."[45]

Quinlan Terry, who worked closely with Erith on the design, reckoned King's Walden was more baroque than anything, the design having acquired a life of its own: "The truth is that while classical architecture is a principle, its style evolves; its strength is that it can adapt itself to change without sacrificing its principle."[46] And that is the key to the success of King's Walden Bury—it draws on the late-Renaissance classicism of Palladio, but it takes it and moulds it and transforms it into something which works beautifully and is entirely of its time. That is what the best country houses of the period did: they took the old and made it new.

8

MODERN MOVEMENTS

W HEN THE DESIGNS for the 5th Duke of Westminster's new Eaton Hall were published in 1970, the Duke of Bedford wrote to the press to say that "one of the virtues of the Grosvenor family is that they frequently demolish their stately home. I trust future generations will continue this tradition."[1]

Westminster's startling modernist creation sent shock waves through the conservative world of country house connoisseurship. The previous Eaton Hall, a magnificent Gothic folly designed for the 1st Duke by Alfred Waterhouse in the 1870s, was described by an awestruck Nikolaus Pevsner a century later as a "Wagnerian palace [and] the most ambitious instance of Gothic Revival domestic architecture anywhere in the country."[2] But it had been demolished in 1961–1962 after the War Office, which took a ninety-nine-year lease on the hall after the war, handed it back: at that point the 3rd Duke decided (mistakenly, as it turned out) that his family was unlikely ever to live there again and that the cost of restoration and repairs were too much for the estate to bear.

There had been attempts before the war to design country houses in a contemporary idiom: modernist masterpieces like Amyas Connell's 1931 High and Over in Buckinghamshire, a flat-roofed, Y-plan house of reinforced concrete and cement render on the outside and chrome, jade-green cellulose, and concealed lighting on the inside; or Oliver Hill's Art Deco Joldwynds in Surrey (1931–1933), with its glass staircase tower and an ivory-coloured entrance hall inlaid with coral and jade. Such experiments were always in a minority, and reactions among the self-appointed arbiters of country house taste ranged from bewildered fascination to outright hostility. "People are finding their conceptions of beauty being strangely changed by all the new shapes and materials around them," wrote an uncertain Christopher Hussey in 1934.[3] And in a prewar Britain riddled with antisemitism, modernism's associations with Jewish exiles from Hitler's Germany like Erich Mendelsohn made it doubly suspect: "Fascism will not tolerate aliens practising their trade or profession within Britain or the Empire," warned a group of fascist architects after Mendelsohn and Serge Chermayeff (a British citizen) won a competition to design a new seaside pavilion for Earl De La Warr at Bexhill-on-Sea in 1934.[4]

After the war, a generation of younger architects put the past behind them and focused on creating a brave new world of urban utopias, planned towns, and high-rise housing. Building big houses for rich people seemed not only anachronistic but also politically incorrect. Nevertheless, exciting modernist houses *were* built in the country in the decades after the war: fiercely horizontal boxes in dramatic rural settings with flat roofs, open-plan interiors, and lots and lots of glass. The house which architect and planner Derek Lovejoy built for himself on a Surrey hillside in 1960 (and called, in a clear statement of intent, "New England") was one such: its centrepiece was a forty-foot-long living room with two frameless glass walls opposite each other, "making this part of the house as transparent as an empty aquarium," said *Country Life's* H. Dalton Clifford in a generally approving article written shortly after the house was finished.[5] New England made use of the latest technology: time switches and thermostats, seventy-five flush-fitted ceiling lights, sound-absorbent rubber flooring, and an eight-foot-wide serving hatch between kitchen and dining room with a flap that dropped down to form a cocktail bar. "Presumably

Mrs Lovejoy does not mind her guests sitting at the bar with their apéritifs and watching her, through the super-cinemascope-shaped opening, while she puts the finishing touches to a meal."[6]

Cray Clearing, built in 1963–1964 by the architect Francis Pollen for his parents, was another successful attempt to combine contemporary style and the taste for a rural idyll. Long, low, and very Frank Lloyd Wright, it stood (until it was unhappily demolished in 1995) in beech woods above Henley: flat-roofed and single-storeyed like New England, it had floor-to-ceiling windows and matching wireless and television sets at opposite sides of the drawing room fireplace, fitted into specially designed cases of African teak and pigskin, with stereophonic grids built into a bookcase at the end of the room.

NOT SURPRISINGLY, NEW technology and the most modern of modern conveniences usually found their way into modernist houses. "Oil-fired heating is the modern method with no equal for comfort and convenience," ran a 1957 Shell-Mex advertisement in *Country Life*. The ad was illustrated with a Felix Kelly painting of Oldany House in Suffolk, a modern country house on seven acres overlooking Aldeburgh golf course, and it was accompanied by an endorsement from Oldany's owner, a Mr C. J. Penhouse, who "enjoys exactly the temperature he wants for as long as he wants. He merely makes the required setting on a dial, and his oil-fired heating system does the rest."[7]

Panels backed with foil insulation and aluminium foil suspended in cavity walls were appearing in the 1950s, and a few architects were already designing for solar gain and making use of heat pumps and exchangers to maintain constant temperatures. "Heat [from the sun] builds up inside the house—a phenomenon known as 'greenhouse effect,'" wrote one awed commentator in 1963.[8] Two years earlier, Admiral Sir Reginald Plunkett-Ernle-Erle-Drax, an octagenarian campaigner for solar power, had used solar panels to take the chill off his outdoor swimming pool.

New technology wasn't the exclusive preserve of the moderns. But it was the futuristic country house that really lent itself to the wholehearted adoption of new technology. Having already cut themselves adrift from tradition, the owners of such houses had no compunction about installing the latest gadgets in their homes of steel and glass and reinforced concrete. The department store owner Gerald Bentall was just such a man. In 1954 he bought Witley Park in Surrey, a thousand-acre estate near Godalming.

Witley was famous. At the heart of the estate was a fifteen-bedroomed half-timbered mansion built at the end of the nineteenth century for an immensely rich company promoter, James Whitaker Wright. Wright was something of a fantasist: he created a glass-ceilinged billiard room under an artificial lake in the park, a "submerged fairy-room" thirty feet high and equipped with settees and chairs, palm trees and little tables. "Outside the clear crystal glass is a curtain of green water," wrote a journalist in 1903, "and goldfish come and press their noses against the glass."[9] This submerged fairy-room alone was said to have cost Wright £20,000, money which didn't belong to him. His fantasies caught up with him the following year, when he was sentenced to seven years' penal servitude for fraud; while he was at the courthouse waiting to be moved to Brixton Prison to start his sentence, he lit a cigar, took some cyanide, and died, in one of Edwardian England's most talked-about causes célèbres.*

By the time Gerald Bentall bought Witley Park the house was in a poor state, having been damaged by fire at some point. He worked the estate (a keen farmer and cattle breeder, he listed his recreation in *Who's Who* as "agriculture") but did nothing with the house until his third marriage in 1959, which spurred him to build a brand-new house on a more open site in a different corner of the park. His choice of architect was Patrick Gwynne, one of

---

* After his death he was found to be carrying a loaded revolver. Security was not tight at the Edwardian Old Bailey.

Britain's most distinguished modernists. Gwynne had designed a string of smaller houses in the years after the war, although none, perhaps, to match The Holmewood, the house he'd designed in Esher for his parents in 1938. Clearly influenced by Le Corbusier's Villa Savoye, The Holmewood was perched on stilts, with all the main rooms up on the first floor to make the most of the views; having seen it (Gwynne lived and worked there, his parents having both died in 1942), Bentall decided he wanted something similar for Witley. What he got was one of postwar Britain's most remarkable houses—not a white box but a complex structure based on hexagonal shapes and 120-degree angles. The big, southwest-facing room was a hexagon; the stilts supporting the upper storey were hexagonal; even the flower beds were hexagonal.

And technology was everywhere. Push-button electric motors opened and closed the windows and drew the blinds. The wireless, television, and gramophone were all built in, with concealed stereo speakers. So was a film projector; its built-in screen could be made to descend in front of one of the big picture windows. A rotating drinks cupboard with its own refrigerator could be replenished from the kitchen servery before revolving silently into view in the living room. The house needed only James Bond or the Man from U.N.C.L.E. to make it complete.

WITLEY PARK WAS Patrick Gwynne's biggest private house commission. Yet it only had four bedrooms and a small service flat. It was, as Mark Girouard noted in his 1963 *Country Life* article on the house (an article entitled "A Change from Neo-Georgian"), "a country house adapted to present-day conditions, scaled down in size and capable of being run with the help of a single living-in couple and a daily help."[10] And with Witley and so many of its comrades, the problem of definition raises its head in a tiresome way. They, and dozens like them, are all houses in the country. But to what extent can they be called "country houses"? The idea that Mrs Lovejoy should be cooking dinner in the kitchen at New

England while her guests sip their sidecars and manhattans and carry on a conversation with her through the cinemascope-sized serving hatch, seems a world away from the formalities of prewar ducal dining at Chatsworth or Blenheim Palace.

The days when a country house was the headquarters of a large agricultural estate, serviced by a small army of domestic servants and outdoor staff, were already passing by the time of the First World War, and by 1945 it was quite usual for a country house, no matter how big it might be, to function purely as a weekend retreat, somewhere to escape to on a Saturday and to escape from on a Monday morning. While owners were busy demolishing an inconveniently large servants' wing or sparing the servants' wing and demolishing the inconveniently large mansion that went with it, it isn't surprising that those who chose contemporary taste also wanted the convenience of a service flat and a serving hatch.

There were still some modernist mansions, though—steel-framed, glass-clad, flat-roofed pavilions whose scale and size demanded that they be allowed to take their place among the stately homes of England. For all its idiosyncracies, Basher Baring's Stratton Park was one such. Another was Upper Exbury, the country house built by James Dunbar-Nasmith for his old friend Leopold de Rothschild in 1964–1965. Rothschild's father and brother spent their lives laying out the famous specialist gardens at Exbury in Hampshire; the house at the heart of the gardens, rebuilt in 1919, had been requisitioned by the Royal Navy during the war for use in the D-Day landings, and although it was eventually returned to the family in 1955, they chose not to occupy it. Instead, Leopold took over the kitchen garden, which looked south to the Solent and the Isle of Wight, and built himself a substantial country house which made good use of the views. Leopold was passionately fond of music—for years, he sang with the Bach Choir in London, and he was actively involved with Glyndebourne, the English Chamber Orchestra, and English National Opera. So although it was meant as a weekend place, Upper Exbury, as the new house was known, had to be big enough to accommodate musical performances: Leopold told Dunbar-Nasmith that he wanted to be able to give chamber music concerts for up to fifty people. The music room, which formed the heart of the house, doubled as a drawing room and was equipped with two grand pianos, a clavichord, and a hi-fi installation. It had four levels: a seating area; a concert platform large enough for those two grand pianos and a string quartet; a breakfast area which gave onto a terrace; and a gallery. They were all connected by stairs which wound round a central chimney. A smaller sitting room next door had a sliding wall which could be opened up to give additional seating space for Rothschild's concerts. All the main rooms faced south, towards the sea; a service wing to the north held the kitchen and a staff sitting room, with staff bedrooms above.

If size is what matters in defining the twentieth-century country house, Exbury qualifies. In 1967 Pevsner reckoned it was one of the largest private houses to be built since the war. Its modernity was not quite modernism, in that there were pitched roofs covered with slates and walls of buff-coloured brick. But it represented an interesting attempt to design a fully fledged country house in a nontraditional idiom.

Which brings us back to Eaton Hall. The 3rd Duke of Westminster's decision in March 1960 to demolish the Victorian house, the fourth at least on the site since the Grosvenor family had begun occupying this particular corner of Cheshire in the 1440s, was met with regret but a certain resignation. No one thought it conceivable that the Grosvenors could ever live there again; only a few Victorian Society stalwarts asked whether another use couldn't have been found for it. "No" was the answer: the duke, a semi-invalid whose main interest in life was breeding pedigree ducks, was facing a bill for death duties of £8.5 million on his estates in Cheshire and North Wales alone, with his Mayfair and Belgravia properties still waiting valuations from the estate duty office, and spending money on a run-down Gothic monster wasn't high on his list of priorities. The fixtures and fittings went at a five-day sale on the premises—everything from mahogany, oak, pine, and walnut panelling to iron downpipes, floorboards, and the plate glass in the windows. A pair of limed oak vestibule doors went to the as-yet-unbuilt Roman Catholic cathedral in Liverpool; 475 guineas were paid for a white Carrara marble chimneypiece brought from Rome by the 1st Duke in 1869, with a square-faced clock designed by Waterhouse set into it. An elephant's head went for seven guineas.

By the summer of 1962 the hall had been taken down, with the exception of the Victorian clock tower, chapel, and stables, which were to be kept, and the brick and stone were being sold off as hardcore. However, the 3rd Duke died unmarried the following year, leaving a cousin to inherit the title and the Grosvenor estates. The 4th Duke was already living happily in Saighton Grange, a sensibly sized country house on the Eaton Hall estate in Cheshire, and he saw no reason to move—not that there was anywhere to move to.

But the 4th Duke's tenure was short-lived. In 1967 he died without children, and the Westminster title and estates passed for the third time in four years. The 5th Duke was his brother Robert, a professional soldier who lived with his family on an island in the middle of Lough Erne in County Fermanagh. It was Robert who decided to build a new Eaton Hall, and Robert's choice of architect was John Dennys, who was married to his wife's sister.

Family connections aside, Dennys wasn't an obvious choice to design the most ambitious modern house in England; his career as an architect up to that point included an old people's home in Holland Park, a North London primary school, and parts of Corby New Town. But he had also remodelled Saighton Grange for the Grosvenors in a safe neo-Georgian style, and he was a distinguished teacher at the Architectural Association School of Architecture, serving as president of the AA in 1970–1971. His career was cut short in 1973 when he died in an accident whilst on holiday in Greece, at only fifty-one, before his new creation at Eaton Hall was completed. "He was up to date in all things," said his *Times* obituarist, "but retained many of the qualities now brushed aside as old-fashioned."[11]

With walls clad in travertine marble chippings, which gleamed white in the sun and the rain, and with the main rooms raised up over a games room and a heated swimming pool, the new Eaton Hall was built on a ducal scale: a two-storey central living hall and three big reception rooms on the main floor, and on the floor above, twelve bedrooms, two private sitting rooms, and seven bathrooms. There was plenty of room for servants, and there were more bedrooms in the stable block for those really big house parties.

It being the early 1970s, the construction of Eaton Hall was plagued by labour disputes. The contractor, Bovis, dismissed twelve men "for constantly walking off the site." The dispute was all about bonuses, claimed the duke, although a union official said it stemmed from resentment at having to build such a luxurious place for a duke when millions of people were without a decent home. "The men can see tons of money being poured into the job."[12]

When it was finally completed, in 1973, Dennys's Eaton Hall didn't exactly meet with universal approval. It was compared to a university campus building. The Duke of Bedford called it "a fine office block for a factory on a by-pass," and it seems that the Grosvenor family soon came to share his opinion. The 5th Duke spent only a couple of years at Eaton, where the carillon in Waterhouse's clock tower played "Home, Sweet Home" whenever he arrived, before he retreated to his island home in Fermanagh. His son, who inherited in 1979, announced in 1988 that he had decided to take "a long hard look at the design of the house in order to achieve greater harmony with its surroundings." "The building is an eyesore," said a spokesman for the estate, with rather more directness.[13] The Cardiff-based Percy Thomas Partnership was brought in to build a new gabled roof, to replace the white marble cladding with local red sandstone, and to redesign the interiors with advice from Hugh Casson "in a manner more in keeping with the lifestyle of the landed gentry."[14] The result looks oddly like a French château set in the middle of the Cheshire countryside. More in keeping with the lifestyle of the landed gentry it might be, but I can't help feeling that something was lost when its gleaming white predecessor disappeared.

PERHAPS THE MOST remarkable, and certainly the most curious, attempt to design a country house in an entirely contemporary idiom took place in Derbyshire in the early 1970s. The venue for this experiment was Stainsby House, an imposing eighteenth-and-nineteenth-century mansion on the edge of the village of Horsley Woodhouse. Stainsby had fallen on hard times after the Second World War. After a period as a Roman Catholic boys' boarding school, it was taken over in the 1950s as a poultry farm, its new owners retreating to an apartment in a corner of the house and leaving the chickens to rule the roost until the stench brought in the medical officer of health.

In 1972 Stainsby was bought by a local businessman who demolished the decrepit mansion and commissioned a big new country house on the eighteen-acre site from Nottingham architect David Shelley, an enthusiastic modernist. Shelley's work already included the 1970 Coward House, a steel-framed structure built into a low hillside in the heart of Sherwood Forest, with walls of glass, terrazzo floors, and that compulsory component of every midcentury modern home, an integrated cocktail bar.

His client at Stainsby was Robert Morley, owner of a local packaging company. Morley may have wanted something like the Coward House, striking enough among the lines of terraced housing that made up the little mining villages on the Derbyshire-Nottinghamshire border, but if so, he was destined to be disappointed. Known locally as "the house of a hundred curves," Shelley's Stainsby House looked like the set of a science fiction film—an English country house as imagined by the makers of *2001: A Space Odyssey*. White and sinuous—the aim was to create a house with as few straight lines and flat walls as possible— Shelley's Stainsby was a fabulous jumble of sweeping rooflines, arched window openings, and battered walls. At fifteen thousand square feet, the house was big—as big as fifteen miners' houses, noted one socially aware critic—and it had a helicopter pad, a bowed drive, marble floors, and early solar panels. It cost about £250,000, over £3.3 million in today's money.

The interior was just as futuristic as the exterior: a kidney-shaped indoor swimming pool, circular sunken baths, asymmetrical granite chimneypieces. Even the kitchen counter and the serving hatch were curved. The only incongruous note was struck by the study, which was given a beamed ceiling beneath which stood a billiards table, a traditional kneehole desk, and a heavy buttoned-leather settee. The desire for tradition clearly died hard, even in Derbyshire's own space odyssey. And that odyssey was short-lived: the owner moved to the Channel Islands the year after Stainsby was finished, and after languishing on the market for two years, the house was sold in 1977 for only £150,000.

Modernity was a niche market, as indeed it still is, with designs that depart from the familiar in a dramatic fashion winning plaudits from the professionals but not praise from the public. Which is a shame. The country house world would be a greyer place without its Stainsbys and its Eaton Halls.

9

THE AMERICAN DREAM

I T COULD BE a screenplay for one of those gentle comedies that British film studios used to do so well. In 1924, a young American from Portland, Maine, was on vacation in England and strolling down the Strand when a coloured engraving in a shop window caught his eye. It showed a glimpse into the courtyard of a romantic fourteenth-century manor house, Ightham Mote in Kent, and something about it intrigued him.

Some years later the same young man, whose name was Charles Henry Robinson, was holidaying in England again when he recognised a photograph of that courtyard in a copy of *Country Life.**
Ightham's owner, Sir Thomas Colyer Colyer-Fergusson, opened the house to the public on Friday afternoons at a shilling a head, and Sevenoaks, the nearest railway station, was only seventy minutes from Victoria. With time on his hands, Robinson decided to go down and see if the reality measured up to the romance.

It did. Ightham Mote was the stuff of fairy tales. "Like its brethren of romance," gushed a late-Victorian guide to Kent, "the Ightham Mote–house lies sleeping in the midst of thick woods, which you may re-people at will with such marvels as Sir Tristram

---

*Robinson later remembered this happening in 1927 or 1928; in fact, the article in question appeared in 1932.

or Sir Percival was wont to encounter."[1] A dream of a place, and it was no coincidence that Ightham was one of the first houses to be featured in *Country Life*. In 1897, the new magazine carried an article on "the quaintest house imaginable": "England has grander places, places where the clang of the mailed heel would seem to have rung louder, statelier places where satin-coated gentlemen and powdered dames might have been more at home, perhaps; but the country possesses few houses quite comparable to Ightham Mote."[2]

Charles Robinson was enchanted, haunted by its charm. Ightham was, he told himself, "the only house in England that I should ever care to own."[3] And he was rich enough to buy it. But Sir Thomas Colyer Colyer-Fergusson, who was of an antiquarian turn of mind—his favourite pastime was transcribing parish registers—had no intention of selling.

Fast forward to the 1950s. Sir Thomas was dead and his grandson and heir had moved quickly to sell the estate. Most of Ightham's contents went in a three-day sale in October 1951, but the house itself failed to make its reserve price at auction, in spite of the estate agents' best efforts: "One of the finest remaining Old English Moated Manors. Possessing original Architectural Features varying from Edward III to Tudor. Blended suitably by careful Craftsmanship and mellowed by nature."[4] (Which made it sound rather like a whiskey.) In a last-ditch attempt to save the house, three local businessmen—a builder, a farmer, and a chemist—formed a syndicate to buy Ightham and thirty-seven acres, paying around £5,500 for the freehold, with the intention of keeping it safe until a suitable buyer could be found. But there was no sign of a saviour. Unoccupied, the house began to deteriorate. By the summer of 1952 *Country Life* was convinced it was doomed.[5]

Cue Charles Henry Robinson. Robinson hadn't forgotten his prewar visit to Ightham Mote, or the fact that it was "the only house in England that I should ever care to own." In the spring of 1953, on another of his regular visits to Britain, he went down to see what had become of the place, and he was appalled at what he saw. "[I] found it sinister and cynical, crumbling into its moat," he wrote later. "It was like some old person, abandoned and embittered, that needed a little affection, care and security."[6] He harangued the National Trust to step in and save it, something they couldn't and wouldn't do without the necessary endowment. So he met with the members of the syndicate and suggested he might buy it himself.

But what would he do with it? Robinson was a bachelor in his early fifties, and his business interests lay in America. It would cost a small fortune to put Ightham Mote right, and he would have to do it from the other side of the Atlantic. Sailing home on the *Queen Mary* a week later he had second thoughts about his romantic but impulsive gesture, and he wrote from aboard ship to tell the syndicate the deal was off. But when he went to post his letter, the liner was approaching New York and the library, which served as the ship's post office, was locked. The letter was never sent. Instead, Robinson talked things over with his relatives when he got home, and they all urged him to buy the house. "I would like to see you spend some money," said one nephew, "because you know if we kids get it we'll spend it anyway."[7]

So Robinson bought Ightham Mote and saved it and filled it with his own collection of period furniture; when he retired he moved in, declaring that "a house like the Mote belongs to the ages. One does not possess it, rather the opposite: one acts as a temporary protector or guardian."[8]

God bless America.

ROBINSON'S INVOLVEMENT WITH Ightham Mote stemmed from two time-honoured traditions which had been pursued by prosperous white Americans for years: stately home tourism and a desire to acquire a piece of the Old Country. Americans have always come to Britain as sightseers, marvelling at its culture, complaining about its cuisine, staring in disbelief at its primitive sanitation.

"I have not the least doubt," declared literary critic Edmund Wilson after a visit to Europe in 1954, "that I have derived a good deal more benefit of the civilizing as well as of the inspirational kind from the admirable American bathroom than I have from the cathedrals of Europe."[9] In the 1840s hundreds of American tourists trekked up to Abbotsford in Roxburghshire to pay homage to the ghost of Sir Walter Scott, while a mandatory visit to Stratford often took in the Lucy family's Charlecote Park, where Shakespeare was reputed to have been flogged for poaching a deer.

Antiquity was also worthy of attention for its own sake. In the 1870s Henry James visited the early-medieval Stokesay Castle in Shropshire after a fellow American told him that "Edward IV and Elizabeth are still hanging about there."[10] James also fell in love with Haddon Hall, its ancient walls and its romantic associations, in spite of the fact that that particular corner of Derbyshire was, as he noted ruefully, "infested by Americans."[11] (The Peak District was easily reached from Liverpool, which was then the main port of entry for American travellers.) And he was overwhelmed by Warwick Castle and Blenheim Palace. "When I think of an English mansion, I shall think only of Warwick," he wrote in 1872, "and when I think of an English park, only of Blenheim."[12] By the 1920s, Sulgrave Manor in Northamptonshire was on the list of must-see country houses: the ancestral home of the Washington family was purchased by public subscription and opened to the public in June 1921 to commemorate the signing of the 1814 Treaty of Ghent, which ended the War of 1812 between the two nations. The opening was originally intended to celebrate the treaty's centenary, but the First World War delayed things rather.

The 1950s saw increasing numbers of American tourists coming to the British Isles. They were drawn to Europe by cheaper air travel and a desire on the part of veterans to revisit wartime haunts, and to Britain in particular by the comforting prospect of a common(ish) language. In 1950 127,830 US civilians visited the

United Kingdom, an annual figure that by the end of the decade had risen to 356,540. Altogether Britain in the 1950s saw 2.25 million US civilians. (By way of comparison, there are now around 3.9 million visits by Americans every year.) This was in addition to the quarter of a million US servicepeople and their families who were stationed in the UK at some point in the decade.[13]

The British patronised their American guests, stereotyping them and constantly reminding them that theirs was an inferior culture. "It has been said by the Americans that we act with a superiority to them and treat them like kids," wrote one correspondent to a popular magazine in 1952. "In my opinion, we *are* superior to them. The vast majority of people in these islands do not wish to live the American way of life, which includes jiving, jitterbugging, bebop, the wearing of silly looking clothes and weird haircuts."[14]

But Britain needed the tourism dollars. Helpful guidebooks to the country and its quaint little ways began to appear, catering to the new visitors. "Iced water . . . is out of the question," announced one American writer, Ruth McKenney, in *Here's England*, a handbook produced for her fellow citizens in the early 1950s. "Do not ask for it."[15] Her advice was comprehensive and copious. "Cricket is not dull," she declared, barely concealing her air of desperation. Avoid coach tours at all costs, she said: "A smart crack over the back of the neck with a heavy blunt instrument can produce (and much more cheaply) the same sensation as a day in the company of thirty-six fellow victims, seeing Stratford, Warwick, Kenilworth, Broadway, and Tewkesbury Abbey—tomorrow Chester and the Lake District. One of the most pitiful sights of an English summertime is the bus-load of tourists descending in the twilight at a dreary commercial hotel."[16]

History and heritage were the obvious focus for inbound tourism. "Fifteenth-century coaching inn with historical associations . . . of appeal to American visitors," ran a 1957 sale advertisement for a country hotel in the Home Counties.[17] And the nascent stately home industry was eager to cash in, relentlessly courting Americans and directing its marketing efforts towards America. By the early 1970s half of all visitors to Warwick Castle were from abroad, and three-quarters of those were from North America, having made a beeline for Shakespeare country. Woburn Abbey's Duke of Bedford, who once offered the services of his surprisingly compliant butler as a prize in a US competition, advertised "Dinner with a Duke" in American magazines. Soon after Beaulieu opened to the public, Lord Montagu went on a lecture tour of America, travelling twelve thousand miles, speaking in twenty-two states, and making fourteen radio and TV broadcasts. "I also sent my family coronation robes on a separate tour," he wrote in 1968. "They appeared in shop windows all over the States and earned me and Britain two thousand dollars."[18] Rather later, the Duchess of Devonshire lectured on Chatsworth in New York, and seized the opportunity while she was in America to make a personal pilgrimage to Graceland, the home of one of her great heroes. Debo was a huge Elvis fan.

CHARLES HENRY ROBINSON'S desire to actually live in a country house was also part of a bigger picture. From Consuelo Vanderbilt's *The Glitter and the Gold* to Julian Fellowes's *Downton Abbey*, the story of British nobility and its undignified scramble to marry American money has become part of the folklore of Edwardian landed society. But mid-Atlantic romance continued long after bartered brides turned into cultural clichés.

In postwar Britain the most famous Anglo-American love affair remained the marriage of the Duke of Windsor and Wallis Simpson, which had taken place at the Château de Candé in the Loire Valley on June 3, 1937. But a glance through the 1947 edition of *Debrett's* shows that of the 901 Lords Temporal who were alive then, forty-five—or almost one in twenty—were married to or had been married to American citizens.* In fact, one or two had been wedded to several: the 8th Earl of Carrick, having married Marion Caher Donoghue of Philadelphia in 1930, married Margaret Power of Montana eight years later, while at the same time Marion became the wife of the 4th Lord Chesham. Nor was she the only American bride to exchange one lord for another. Helen Zimmerman of Cincinnati, who was a duchess for more than thirty years through her marriage to the 9th Duke of Manchester, exchanged that title for another when she became Countess of Kintore, giving up her first husband's three country houses— Kimbolton Castle and Brampton Park in Huntingdonshire and Tandragee Castle in County Armagh—for the remote fastness of her second husband's ancestral seat of Keith Hall in the far north of Scotland. Such swapping of partners was perhaps one reason why the editors of *Debrett's* were moved to remind contributors that they were unable to omit material dates and details "which in the nature of things cannot possibly have altered since they were recorded" from new editions of the *Peerage.*[19]

By 1973, when the heraldic standard-bearing lions which once adorned the cover of *Debrett's* had been replaced by an advertisement for Rothmans, "blenders of fine tobaccos through six reigns," the number of peers with American wives or ex-wives had risen still further, as had the number of ex-partners generally: the Duke of Leinster and Lord Strabolgi were both on their fourth marriages, for example, while the 7th Baron Lilford was on his fifth. The 2nd Earl Beatty was also on his fourth marriage, the first three brides having all been American. Beatty's first wife,

---

*Although America was easily the most popular source of brides for the British aristocracy, the empire yielded up its share: Canada, Australia, New Zealand, Kenya, Rhodesia, India, and Hong Kong were all represented. So were France, Argentina, Sweden, Denmark, Norway, Belgium, Chile, Serbia, Hungary, Latvia, Poland, and Austria. The midcentury nobility were a cosmopolitan lot.

Dorothy Power, went on to become the second of three wives of Perry Cust, Lord Brownlow; Brownlow was Dorothy's fifth husband. What had been seen as an indissoluble union at the beginning of the twentieth century was clearly becoming soluble by the early 1970s: fifty peers of the realm had between them managed to amass fifty-four American wives, out of an awe-inspiring total of eighty-four wives of all nationalities.

One can make too much of this particular manifestation of the Special Relationship, and it is in any case just an unscientific snapshot of a class which was steadily loosening its ties to the country house and was changing its shape quite dramatically. For instance, by the early 1970s the peerage had expanded to include several hundred life peers and peeresses whose backgrounds, politics, and economic status often militated against their acquisition of a country house. But the snapshot does suggest that one of the legacies of the great migration of American heiresses in the early part of the century was that America was woven quite deeply into the culture of British landed society.

Just as significant were the handful of Americans who established another tradition by settling in Britain and buying country houses of their own. William Waldorf Astor, who moved from New York in 1891, became a British citizen in 1899, and bought Hever Castle in Kent four years later, is one early example. Astor became so British that he ended up in the House of Lords. Then there was his son Waldorf Astor and Waldorf's wife, Nancy, who met on an Atlantic liner on the way to England in 1905 and married the following year; Waldorf's father gave them Cliveden as a wedding present. Anglo-American Ronald Tree also met his wife-to-be Nancy during an Atlantic crossing; the couple were married in 1920, settled in England, and rented two Northamptonshire country houses, Cottesbrooke Hall and Kelmarsh Hall, before buying Ditchley Park in Oxfordshire in 1933 and changing the face of English interior design. Another Anglo-American was Olive Paget, the daughter of Almeric Paget, who was a grandson of the Marquess of Anglesey, and New York heiress Pauline Payne Whitney: born in the United States in 1899, Olive moved to England when she was a child. After a short-lived marriage to Charles Winn, the second son of Nostell Priory's Lord St Oswald, she married big-game hunter Arthur Wilson-Filmer. Together they bought the outrageously romantic Leeds Castle in Kent, and although the marriage didn't last, Olive's love affair with Leeds did: she remained its chatelaine until her death in 1974, having married and divorced a third husband, Sir Adrian Baillie.

The list of American émigrés who played a significant role in country house life before the Second World War is a long one. There was Lawrence Johnston, a keen amateur gardener whose mother married a Winthrop and bought her son the estate of Hidcote Manor in the Cotswolds; Huttleston Broughton, whose British father married the daughter of an American oil tycoon and who presided over Anglesey Abbey in Cambridgeshire from 1926 until his death forty years later; Chicagoan Henry "Chips" Channon, whose marriage to heiress Honor Guinness enabled him to buy Kelvedon Hall in Essex in 1938. "So now I am a Squire of Essex and shall probably gravitate more and more towards a country life," Chips confided to his diary.[20]

A number of these émigrés and their country houses were still going strong in postwar Britain, including Waldorf and Nancy Astor, Olive Baillie, Huttleston Broughton, Nancy Lancaster, and Chips Channon. To what extent did they have an impact on country house life? They had no wish to import American cultural values. Quite the reverse, in fact. They were eager to adopt British mores, eager to be accepted. Lawrence Johnston took British citizenship in 1900, when he was twenty-nine, so that he could fight for his adopted country in the Boer War. Ronald Tree was master of the Pytchley Hunt. Huttleston Broughton sat in the House of Lords as Lord Fairhaven. So did William Waldorf Astor, as the 1st Viscount Astor. His second son, John Jacob, who was born in Manhattan, was raised to the peerage as Baron Astor of Hever in

1956, having owned that most British of British institutions, the *Times*, for more than thirty years. John Jacob's brother Waldorf was an MP before taking his seat as 2nd Viscount Astor, at which point Nancy Astor took over her husband's parliamentary seat, becoming the first woman to sit in the House of Commons. Chips Channon was an MP from 1935 until his death in 1958. He may not have found the peerage he longed for—and how he longed for it—but he at least received a knighthood from Macmillan's government in 1957. (Channon, who famously described himself as "riveted by lust, furniture, glamour, and society and jewels," was so anglicised that even his male lover was described as "a classic English queen."[21])

So we shouldn't look for the Americanisation of the stately home, for cultural clichés like ketchup bottles at dinner and Stetsons in the gun room, or the Stars and Stripes fluttering over the battlements. By the 1950s most of the Americans and Anglo-Americans who had acquired country houses before the Second World War were more English than the English.

Chips Channon, who was a houseguest at Leeds Castle during the war—"We sunbathed, overate, drank champagne, gossiped all day," he wrote in his diary after a visit in August 1943, as though the war were no business of his—was present at one of Lady Baillie's summer balls at her London home, Lowndes House, in 1950, when French interior designer Stéphane Boudin transformed the garden into a magical ballroom edged with floodlit herbaceous borders. The nineteen-year-old Princess Margaret was guest of honour and stayed until 4:30 a.m. Frank Sinatra sang. Neither pleased Channon, who could be extraordinarily sour. Princess Margaret looked "very small and a wee bit Mongolian," while Sinatra's crooning provoked nothing but intense boredom. "I consider all cabaret stunts bores; we fashionable fools prefer our own banal chatter."[22]

Lady Baillie's houseguests at Leeds Castle, where she spent every weekend when she was in England, were drawn from a wide circle of admirers and professional hangers-on, film stars and nobles and politicians. There was the odd duchess—the Duchesses of Argyll and Roxburghe were both her guests at one time or another—and smart characters who turned up in Aston Martins and whose sources of income weren't altogether clear. There was even a princess: not Princess Margaret but Princess Jorjadze, a chorus girl who after marrying two English lords—Ashley and Stanley—and two movie stars—Douglas Fairbanks and Clark Gable—finally settled down in 1954 with a racing driver and racehorse breeder from Tbilisi, Prince Dimitri Aleksandrovich Jorjadze. Then there was Olive's entourage. Chief courtier was David Margesson, a Conservative politician who was elevated to the peerage as Viscount Margesson in 1965 and who was thought to be her lover. He had his own rooms at Leeds. So did her other favourite, Geoffrey Lloyd, another Conservative politician who held various ministerial posts, including that of minister for education in Macmillan's government. There was no competition for Olive's affections: Lloyd was, as the family euphemistically put it, "a confirmed bachelor."

So were rather a lot of her retinue—another instance, perhaps, of Lady Baillie's cosmopolitan roots. There was the American John Galliher, "Johnny G.," who had no obvious means of support but was known as "a good man to have around" and specialised in befriending wealthy women; Bert Whitley, a very minor film actor from New York; and Mickey Renshaw, a man with a savage wit who was described by James Lees-Milne as "a social gadfly of ill-defined occupation."[23]

This was the set that surrounded Olive Baillie at Leeds Castle until her death in 1974. They reassured her, they entertained her, they spent her money. And they helped to confirm her status in a society which was changing fast but which was still a little uncertain about rich Anglo-Americans like her. Not that she was afraid to make use of her connections when she wanted to get her way. She was an enthusiastic collector of exotic birds, many of whose descendants still flap and waddle around the grounds of Leeds

Castle today, and she wasn't too fussy about their provenance. Once, after a clandestine meeting at an old mill outside Düsseldorf where she bought (for hard cash) a quantity of rare parakeets, she found that officials at the airport insisted her purchases be flown to England as freight. "I'm afraid that is out of the question," she announced, and telephoned the vice chairman of the British Overseas Airways Corporation, who happened to be a close friend. He immediately arranged for seats to be removed from the aircraft so that Olive and her estate manager, John Money, could fly home with the boxes of parakeets at their feet.

Like many very wealthy people, Lady Baillie kept a careful eye on her money. Her grandson Anthony Russell, who spent much of his childhood at Leeds with "Granny B.," recalled that "if a guest at one of her houses expected to get away with surreptitious and extravagant use of the telephone provided in each bedroom, Borrett [her butler] would discreetly place an itemised bill there before departure."[24]

J. PAUL GETTY, the richest man in America and quite possibly the world, wasn't content to leave his telephone bills to chance and the discretion of his guests. He had locks fitted to the dials of the half-dozen or so telephones scattered around his magnificent Tudor mansion, Sutton Place in Surrey. He and a few select members of staff had keys; everyone else had to use the coin-operated phone he'd installed in a ground-floor cubby hole. It had a big enamel sign on the door which read PUBLIC TELEPHONE.

Getty first saw Sutton Place when he was in England in the summer of 1951. On June 26 he noted in his diary that he "drove alone to Sutton Place, another stately home. There are some rooms over one hundred feet long. . . . There is a fine Holbein in the drawing room."[25] Eight years and one day later, on June 27, 1959, he was invited to dinner by the owners, the Duke and Duchess of Sutherland, and over dinner the duke mentioned that he was putting Sutton up for sale. It was a big, beautiful, and important

Tudor mansion, with everything one might expect from a house which had stood on that spot since Sir Richard Weston, one of Henry VIII's courtiers, built it in the years after the Field of Cloth of Gold, the extravagantly appointed meeting between the kings of England and France in 1520: terra-cotta decoration which is some of the earliest Renaissance detailing in Britain; a great hall whose windows were filled with the original heraldic painted glass; a spectacular (if Victorian) long gallery; and accommodation which included thirty-four bedrooms and plentiful staff quarters, all in 750 acres of wooded parkland.

Getty decided to buy it. Sutherland wanted £400,000, but the oil tycoon's offer of £300,000 was accepted, and by the end of 1959 the sale had gone through, and, as Getty wrote in his auto-biography, "the Getty companies took possession of what was to become their Eastern Hemisphere liaison centre. Executives and businessmen would thereafter meet here, compare notes and dis-cuss economic problems and trends and a thousand other matters in a quiet, congenial—and luxurious—atmosphere conducive to constructive thinking."[26]

Although the richest American didn't intend to make Sutton his permanent home, that is what it turned out to be. At the end of 1959 he hadn't been back to America since coming over to Europe on a business trip in 1951, and although he kept promising himself he would return, he never did, and he lived at Sutton Place until his death in 1976.

Stories of Getty's meanness and his obsession with privacy were legion. There was the pay phone, although he always main-tained that it and the locking dials were only installed as tempo-rary measures after his estate manager, Albert Thurgood, pointed out that guests, businesspeople, and even tradesmen were making use of the direct outside lines to call family and friends all over the world. (Charges for one call came to £101.) He was compared to the notoriously reclusive Howard Hughes: a magazine article from the early 1970s said that he lived alone, "sadness and loneliness

dominating his reclining years. . . . His wealth has brought him
. . . solitude."[27]

In fact, during his time at Sutton Place Getty surrounded
himself with friends and lovers. He attended literary lunches and
crowned the local May Queen, gave out the cups at the local tennis
tournament, lent Sutton Place to the St John Ambulance Brigade
for their annual charity ball. He threw Christmas parties for children from the local orphanage, wearing a Beatles wig or a funny
party hat. Especially in the early years of his time at Sutton Place,
the house was opened to the public in aid of the National Society
for the Prevention of Cruelty to Children or the Red Cross, and
the gardens were sometimes opened separately in aid of various
charities. That was hardly the behaviour of a recluse.

The housewarming party he threw in July 1960 was one of the
most dazzling social events of the year. It doubled as a coming-
out ball for Jeanette Constable-Maxwell, daughter of Getty's
great friend Ian Constable-Maxwell, one of the founders of the
Clermont Club, and some 2,500 guests turned up, only half of
whom had actually been invited, according to Getty. Three or-
chestras played, and there was dancing in the great hall, the long
gallery, and the gardens, where a dance floor had been set up beside the swimming pool. One of the forty invited journalists and
reporters either fell or was pushed into the pool quite early in the
proceedings, which carried on until dawn. Getty supplied a hot
dog van and a milk bar complete with a Guernsey cow, who was
there purely as decoration and who at one stage ambled into the
great hall.

It was all too much for Betty Kenward, social diarist for *Queen*
magazine. For one thing, the place was far too crowded, she wrote
later. The stalls with milkshakes and soft drinks made the garden
look like a market. Worst of all, "the ladies' cloakroom was in an
empty bedroom, and next door in another empty room was a row
of creosoted loos in creosoted huts such as you had at point-to-
points in the old days, which the ladies in their often very pale silks

A housewarming party at Sutton Place, July 1960

and satins were asked to use, as Mr Getty had had all the luxurious bathrooms locked."[28]

Other guests included Prince William of Gloucester, the Duke of Rutland, and a horde of American and British bankers, business tycoons, politicians, and diplomats. Getty held a dinner for fifty-four before the festivities began: the wife of the Venezuelan ambassador was placed on his right and the Duchess of Roxburghe on his left. David and Lady Pamela Mountbatten Hicks ate at Getty's table, as did Earl Beatty and his fourth countess. Guests marvelled over Getty's pictures. They ate his lobster and caviar. They drank his champagne. At 6:15 a.m. the band was still playing in the long gallery and a crooner was still singing as fifty or so couples swayed round the floor. The last guests, who departed at 7:50 a.m., had left their Mini's lights on. Two of Getty's servants had to push them down the drive.

Throwing a party on that scale was not the act of a brooding recluse, which is how the press liked to portray Getty. But it was the act of a man who knew the value of everything, as he made clear in his autobiography. "The cost of the 'house-warming' was high (and, I should make clear, borne by me personally)," he wrote, "but the great amount of worldwide publicity that resulted proved highly beneficial to all the Getty companies and their stockholders."[29] A friend told him he'd gotten a fantastic bargain. "It would have cost your companies fifty million dollars at the very least to buy the same amount of advertising space."[30]

J. Paul Getty died at Sutton Place on June 6, 1976, at the age of eighty-three. The subsequent and convoluted history of this most precious Tudor mansion involves new American owners and gives a hint of how complicated things could become when global corporate moguls wanted to buy an English country house in a rapidly rising market under a byzantine tax regime. Sutton Place was never owned by Getty himself, for example. Instead, it belonged to the Sutton Place Property Company, a subsidiary of the Pacific Western Oil Corporation, which was in turn a subsidiary of the Getty Oil Company. In 1980, after a legal wrangle in which a British development company tried and failed to halt the sale of the house on the grounds that it had an agreement to buy the shares of the Sutton Place Property Company, the estate was sold for £7.75 million, which at the time was the highest price ever paid for a property in Britain. The new owner was the Eagle Trust and Management Company of Houston, Texas, which transferred its ownership to the Anglo Texas Property Company, which leased the house and 330 acres to a wealthy Wisconsin art collector, Stanley J. Seeger.

The heir to an oil and timber fortune, Seeger had amassed an eclectic mix of art objects and curiosities, ranging from Orson Welles's personal shooting script for *Citizen Kane* and Winston Churchill's armchair to eighty-eight Picassos and Francis Bacon's triptych *Studies from the Human Body*, which he hung in the great hall at Sutton Place. "It caused a scandal," recalled Seeger's partner, Christopher Cone. "You didn't do things like that in a Grade I Tudor mansion."[31]

Seeger transferred his lease to the Sutton Place Heritage Trust, which he set up to maintain the house and his collection. In the meantime, Eagle Trust sold off sixty-six acres of the estate to Sainsbury's for £6 million so the retailer could build a superstore, and Anglo Texas sold the freehold to a Jersey-based company, Shieldberg Investments. In 1986, having rarely spent a night at the house, Seeger announced that the Sutton Place Heritage Trust was to give up its lease: maintaining the house had proved to be too expensive, even for his deep pockets. The estate came on the market again, with the agent, Strutt & Parker, looking for offers over £8 million. It was bought by another American collector, Frederick R. Koch, who hung his own collection on its walls but never lived there. Koch's Sutton Place Foundation spent £12 million on a ten-year restoration programme before putting the whole estate up for sale. It was bought in 1999 for £32 million and quickly put back on the market, a commodity to be bought and sold by corporations.

10

A RICH INTERIOR LIFE

T HE BLEAK AUSTERITIES of the late 1940s and early 1950s didn't augur well for interior design in the country house. Building controls, high taxes, and a feeling that spending thousands of pounds on wallpaper was just the sort of thing that the landed classes *would* do and the sooner the revolution came the better, combined with countless struggles simply to save the stately homes of England from demolition, meant that tarting up the Blue Drawing Room was the last thing on the minds of most owners. Although for those who were in a position to brighten up the old mansion, the thriving trade in architectural salvage meant that it was possible to buy an entire Blue Drawing Room—decorative plasterwork, painted ceiling, Adam chimneypiece, doors, windows, floors, and all. And furnishing it from the myriad antique shops that had sprung up all over the country wouldn't be a problem, either.

By the end of the war, many of the great prewar society decorators who had defined country house taste in the 1920s and 1930s were either dead or getting ready to retire. Ethel Bethell, the legendary proprietrix of Elden Ltd, had died in 1932. Syrie Maugham was nearing seventy, struggling with tuberculosis, and carrying on her business in New York, using her apartment in the Dakota as a showroom. Sibyl Colefax, the endearingly archetypal lion-hunting, social-climbing socialite and the woman who had turned obtaining commissions from her friends into a fine art, was in poor health and slightly straitened circumstances, although these things are relative and she was good at keeping up appearances, presiding over lunches at the Dorchester and sending her guests a bill for their food afterwards. John Fowler, her partner and chief decorator in the firm of Colefax and Fowler, spent most of the war as an air-raid protection warden in London while working one day a week to keep Colefax and Fowler afloat by doing whatever work came his way.

Country house commissions were few and far between. Ronald Fleming, a champion of Regency style before the war, went into business with another prewar stalwart, Dolly Mann: advertisements for the Mann and Fleming showrooms in Mount Street, Mayfair, declared their business to be "Antiques: Decoration," but antique dealing seems to have been their main occupation. Fleming's only important country house work came in 1960, after Hinton Ampner, Ralph Dutton's Regency Revival villa in Hampshire, burned down. Fleming had decorated Dutton's Belgravia flat in the 1930s, and now he helped his friend to decorate the rebuilt Hinton Ampner, with Mann and Fleming supplying many of the fabrics and wallpapers. He was advising the Eyston family on the restoration of Mapledurham House when he died in 1968.

Fleming lived at 20 Thurloe Square, an address he shared in the 1940s and '50s with a group of distinguished figures from the country house world. The great architectural historian John Harris lived in the basement; James Lees-Milne lived on the top floor with his new wife, Alvilde. Fleming had the ground-floor flat, which he filled with conventional showroom pieces—Regency furniture, Egyptian statues, and a few modern pictures. The occupant of the first-floor flat, and the landlord of the building, was Geoffrey Houghton Brown, antique dealer, decorator, and serial buyer of historic houses. (He owned twelve at one time or another, including Sir Christopher Wren's Winslow Hall in Buckinghamshire, which he bought in 1948 and saved from demolition, and Philip Webb's Clouds in Wiltshire.) Houghton Brown's flat, recalled John Harris nearly half a century later, was filled with "glinting Boulle, gilt tables and stands, lacquer, Louis XIV porphyry with ormolu mounts, tapestries, an Aubusson carpet and . . . porcelain in glazed cabinets."[1] Everything had a price.

When Houghton Brown decided to have the Thurloe Square house redecorated in 1946, he didn't do it himself. Nor did he go to Fleming in the ground-floor flat. Instead he asked someone referred to in Lees-Milne's diary simply as "that horrible H."[2] We don't know what was horrible about him, but it is pretty certain that "H." was forty-year-old Felix Harbord, who was poised to become one of the period's leading decorators.

After he trained as an architect in the office of Albert Richardson and studied painting at the Slade School of Fine Art at University College London, Harbord's career as a designer began to take off in the late 1930s: in addition to designing sets and costumes for the theatre and taking on a stint as art keeper to the Bute Collection at Mount Stuart, he created a flamboyantly rococo orangery at Godmersham Park in Kent for the Tritton family and a scholarly William Kent entrance hall for Kingston Russell House in Dorset. Then came the war. He changed his name from Cyril to Felix, joined the Royal Engineers, and, in March 1945, became one of the Monuments Men, rescuing works of art and other cultural artefacts that had been squirrelled away by the Nazis. Goring "looted with great taste," he said.[3]

He also managed to squirrel away a few items of his own, it seems. In 2015 some awkward questions were asked about the provenance of a chandelier now in the first minister of Scotland's official residence in Edinburgh, which, according to the Simon Wiesenthal Centre, Harbord had packed in empty munitions boxes, possibly while it was at the main British collection point in Saxony, and sent home to Britain. Harbord had claimed at the time that he had found it in a German street.

Returning to England, Harbord became known as a "decor expert." Rather a vague term, but then interior decorators in the mid-twentieth century had to be prepared to turn their hands to many things. Some, like Ronald Fleming, became antique dealers and shopkeepers, selling wallpapers and textiles, paintings and furniture. Harbord was certainly a dealer-collector, buying and selling pictures and antiques for himself, sometimes selling them on to other dealers, sometimes acquiring pieces for loyal clients. He "nursed rooms and houses," said John Cornforth, who might have added that he nursed customers, too.[4] His eye for fine things influenced a younger generation of antique dealers, notably Christopher Gibbs, friend of the Rolling Stones and the man who is credited with inventing the phrase "Swinging London" (and, less happily, with being the first to wear flared trousers). Harbord also dabbled in theatre design—he did the sets and costumes for the Sandy Wilson musical *Call It Love* in 1960, for example, and designed the sets for the stately home comedy *The Grass Is Greener*—and created the floral displays at the 1954 show at Carlton House Terrace by the Incorporated Society of London Fashion Designers, a precursor of London Fashion Week: "Even the wrought-iron lift cage [was] transformed into a orangery, with evergreens and real oranges."[5] He was in demand as a fashionable party decorator, creating spectacular settings for debutante balls and intimate supper dances. And he took on the occasional country house commission.

"Not a man for simple things or the simple life," in John Cornforth's assessment, Harbord went for the quirky, for the grand manner, sometimes for both.[6] There was no doubting his scholarship, but like the best interior decorators, he never considered himself bound by it. At Cecil Beaton's Reddish House in Wiltshire, "a small architectural jewel of the Charles II period," enthused one magazine, ignoring the fact that it actually dates from the early eighteenth century, he installed grey marble columns in the entrance-hall-cum-dining-room and a frankly peculiar sunroom which, according to the ever-diplomatic Christopher Hussey, "illustrates the simple but decorative potentialities of split cane."[7] He also designed interiors at Beaton's London home, 8 Pelham Place, although it isn't clear whether it was Harbord or Beaton who came up with the idea of walls lined with black velvet trimmed with gold and silver filigree. Beaton called him "the most talented decorator since William Kent."[8]

At Oving, a seventeenth-and-eighteenth-century house overlooking the Vale of Aylesbury where he worked in 1954–1955 for Michael Berry, chairman and editor-in-chief of the *Daily Telegraph*, Harbord created a series of stunning "Georgian" interiors, importing both motifs and actual architectural fragments from other houses and mixing plasterwork and stucco from the 1740s with his own designs so well that even seasoned architectural historians admitted that the new work "was of a style and quality hard to distinguish from the original decoration."[9] Never one for skimping with his clients' money, Harbord designed the carpets himself and had them woven at the Real Fábrica de Tapices factory in Madrid: the carpet in the entrance hall was "richly scattered with birds," noted Mark Girouard, "among which are some very endearing bats."[10] Harbord also decorated Berry's Westminster house with a fabulous scheme involving rococo frames surrounding capriccios of London churches.

Harbord's masterpiece was Aileen Plunket's Luttrellstown Castle in County Dublin, an enormous Gothic pile with a complex history on 570 acres. Built originally by the Luttrells in the fourteenth century and heavily remodelled in the late eighteenth and nineteenth centuries, it had a notorious local reputation as a stronghold of the Anglo-Irish ascendancy and "was held in such odium," reported the *Leinster Leader* in 1941, that "the very birds shunned the trees which grew within its walls and the rooks were never known to build their nest among the branches."[11] Aileen's indulgent father had bought it as a present soon after her marriage in 1927 to socialite and racehorse-breeder Brinsley Sheridan Plunket, and Aileen and Brinny, as her husband was known, regularly entertained film stars and aristocrats at Luttrellstown, a glittering couple whose faces and parties were familiar in the gossip columns and the society pages. In 1940, like so many glittering couples then and now, they divorced. Aileen went off to America, letting Luttrellstown to a succession of Italian diplomats. Brinny joined the Royal Air Force and died in a dogfight over Sudan in 1941.

At the end of the war Aileen came back to Ireland and began to entertain in some style at Luttrellstown. There was a ball to mark the start of the Dublin Horse Show each summer, a New Year's Eve dance, and any number of big house parties. "Everyone looks forward to the parties at Luttrellstown and they are never disappointed," declared one gossip columnist in 1948, after a particularly successful dance where the guests included the American ambassador, the Earl and Countess of Rosse (Antony Armstrong-Jones's stepfather and mother), military men, racing trainers, and a host of British and Irish aristocrats and socialites.[12]

Aileen was convinced she was ruined in 1949 when she was presented with a large tax bill after the death of her father, Ernest Guinness, who had made over vast sums to his three girls and then inconveniently died before the end of the statutory period which would have exempted the gifts from tax; but that didn't have much effect on her entertaining. Nor did her marriage in 1956 to Yugoslavian American designer Valerian Stux-Rybar, whose clients included Christine Onassis and who was known as the world's most expensive interior decorator. For the nine years they were married, she moved back and forth across the Atlantic, dividing her time between Luttrellstown Castle and her new husband's Manhattan apartment on East 72nd Street, where "the beauty of the dining room, drawing room and bedrooms are beyond my powers of description," said the *Tatler*'s Jennifer, unhelpfully.[13]

Luttrellstown Castle's occupation by Italian diplomats during the Emergency, as the Second World War was called in neutral Ireland, had left it in need of a face-lift, and in June 1946 Felix

Harbord's name first appeared in the Luttrellstown visitor's book. Described by Aileen as her architect, he would stay there a total of sixty times over the next twenty-five years, creating what have been described as some of "the most elaborate interiors formed in the British Isles since the Second World War."[14] Because Harbord was involved in the redecoration over such a long period, his scheme evolved steadily rather than being imposed on the house in a moment. He installed some fine Georgian chimneypieces, along with plasterwork which looked for all the world as though it had been taken from eighteenth-century moulds but was in fact designed by him. Tapestries were found in Dublin; years after the fabulous staircase hall had to all intents and purposes been completed, he introduced a ceiling painting from about 1730 which was said to be by Sir James Thornhill and to have come from a country house in Suffolk, although John Cornforth, who wrote about Harbord's Luttrellstown in 1984, three years after the decorator's death in Paris and one year after Aileen was forced to sell up and retire to England, disputed both the attribution and the provenance. It didn't matter: the painting looked as though it had been in the castle forever.

In the 1960s a series of historical portraits which had hung in the ballroom were moved to the staircase hall after a set of hunting scenes was found to replace them. Harbord brought in Franco-Dutch paintings, gilded reliefs, and painted furniture. When he found something that he thought might be right for the house, he would introduce it—with Aileen Plunket's approval, of course, and with her money. A carpet in the ballroom was woven in 1835 and came from the Russian Imperial Manufactory; a set of chairs in the same room originally stood in the Château de Maintenon in the Eure-et-Loir. The overall effect is opulent, certainly, and there is a curious and indefinable sense of fun about the whole thing. But one of Harbord's great strengths was his ability to control his theatricality, rarely descending into mere flamboyance. The state rooms at Luttrellstown never look like a stage set or a showroom.

Instead, they give the impression that men and women of taste had lived in the castle for centuries. Cornforth summed up Harbord's precious blend of scholarship and theatricality: "The element of make-believe influenced almost all his architectural decoration, but it could flourish more fully in the freer, headier Irish atmosphere of Luttrellstown. There is often an element of exaggeration in Irish houses . . . and with it a more infectious spirit that makes parties gayer: Luttrellstown evidently epitomises that tradition."[15]

Sadly, the long and vital relationship between client and decorator turned sour in 1972, when there was a little misunderstanding over the whereabouts of eight paintings belonging to Aileen Plunket. It isn't clear exactly what happened, but she took Harbord to the High Court and won a battle to get the pictures back. He was told to pay the costs of the action and to give £1,400 in damages to the dealers to whom he had sold them. After that, there were no more visits to Luttrellstown Castle.

PERHAPS BECAUSE OF his fall from grace and because his later life was a series of financial crises, the name of Felix Harbord has been all but forgotten, a footnote in the history of the postwar country house. In contrast, the firm that dominated the market throughout the period, towering over all others, was Colefax and Fowler, and its two leading lights, Nancy Lancaster and John Fowler, were without doubt the most influential figures in country house interior design.

American by birth, Nancy Perkins, to use her maiden name, was accustomed to life in the English country house. In 1926 she and her second husband, Ronald Tree, moved to England, renting Cottesbrooke Hall, a lovely early eighteenth-century house designed by Francis Smith of Warwick. They almost bought it outright, but Nancy didn't like the way the owner had restored some of the rooms, "in a sort of fake Adam," she said.[16] So instead they took a lease on a nearby house, Kelmarsh Hall, built by James Gibbs in the late 1720s and virtually untouched since then. The owner, Claude Lancaster, offered it to them rent-free on the understanding that they would modernise it—a project they decided to direct themselves.

Nancy fell in love with Kelmarsh. Working with architect Paul Phipps—"the most dashing young man of his year," according to her—and a Mr Kick, a contract housepainter who did work for Phipps, she and Ronnie transformed the dull, rather forbidding interiors—"mostly navy blue and maroon, and stuffed with all sorts of horrible furniture"—into light, airy, and elegant spaces, helped by Ethel Bethell, who was particularly knowledgeable about eighteenth-century textiles.[17] Nancy also fell in love with Kelmarsh's owner, carrying on an affair with Claude Lancaster for nearly twenty years and eventually marrying him in 1948, after she and Tree divorced. (The Lancaster marriage was not a success: friends said she only married him to get her hands on Kelmarsh, and when they divorced five years later, Claude had to cut off the electricity before she would move out.)

In the meantime, in 1933 Nancy and Ronnie bought Ditchley Park in Oxfordshire, another Gibbs house, and here they developed a style of country house decoration which has lasted for nearly a century. Mixing opulent and sometimes deliberately faded silks and satins and velvets with muted wall colourings, antique furniture, and old pictures, they created a sense of slightly shabby comfort, an impression that Ditchley was neither brash nor dilapidated but had grown old with dignity and love. Everything was subordinated to the overall effect. Ronnie wanted to buy a red lacquer desk for one of the rooms: Nancy vetoed it as "too eye-catching." She once caught sight of a painting in the saleroom at Christie's and burst out, "I do want that picture; it's exactly the colour I want. It matches my curtains."[18] It was a Van Dyck.

This was the rather convoluted background to Nancy Tree's involvement with Colefax and Fowler. By the end of the Second World War, when Sibyl Colefax was in poor health and looking to sell her business, the Trees were in the middle of their divorce.

Ronnie bought the business and the lease on Colefax and Fowler's premises at 39 Brook Street in Mayfair for £15,000 and presented both to Nancy, a parting gift.

Colefax and Fowler's chief designer, the abrasive and temperamental John Fowler, came with the firm. Nancy didn't take the business too seriously, breezing in and out of Brook Street as the mood took her, hiring a car and a driver to go on buying expeditions with Fowler and coming back with her prizes—a pair of terra-cotta jars, a piece of faded mahogany—which were just as likely to end up in her own house as in the showroom. They drove together to big country house sales in the Cotswolds or Dorset or Cambridgeshire. The contents of Ashburnham Place in Sussex, home of the Ashburnham family since before the Norman Conquest, were auctioned by Sotheby's on the death of the last Ashburnham in 1953. As the couple rummaged through the attics, they found three travel commodes made of pretty china with crimson leather seats. "We found three sizes—one for the father, one for the mother and one for the children—just like the three bears. We bought them all."[19]

Country dealers would hold antiques back for them. Sometimes country house owners telephoned out of the blue. "I hear you like beautiful things; I have some here for sale."[20] During those early years the firm operated as more of an antique shop than a decorating business: *Harper's Bazaar* marvelled that the ballroom at Brook Street, "in which everything is for sale, looks like the fabulous emporiums in eighteenth-century Venetian pictures."[21]

Fowler was a difficult man. James Lees-Milne, who first met him when they shared an Anderson shelter in Chelsea during the war, reckoned he was always a poor boy with a chip on his shoulder. "At heart he despised the affluent aristocracy," Lees-Milne claimed. He "voted Labour at every general election and was ready to join any protest march against the establishment."[22] In fact Fowler was raised in a solidly middle-class household, not prosperous but not so poor either. The family home was a Norman

Shaw house in the fashionable artistic community of Bedford Park, and Fowler was sent to Felsted, a traditional boarding school in Essex. But if Lees-Milne's remarks about his sensitivity over his background were true, they couldn't have been helped by Nancy, who used to claim he had never seen a proper bathroom until he met her. The business partners fought like cats and dogs throughout their fifteen-year partnership. Nancy Astor, who was Nancy's aunt, used to say they were the unhappiest unmarried couple she had ever met, and their quarrels, which often played out in front of clients, were legendary. On one occasion, when the Duke of Norfolk had invited them down to advise on the decoration of Arundel Park, the house that Claud Phillimore had designed on the grounds of Arundel Castle, he was bewildered to watch as they contradicted each other with increasing violence.

"I don't like that colour."

"That sofa can't go there."

"You don't know what you're doing."[23]

John Fowler in the 1950s

Their partnership was at its best when it came to decorating Nancy Lancaster's own home. After being ejected from Kelmarsh in 1953, she set about finding herself another country house. Her standards were high: It had to be something from the long eighteenth century—nothing earlier than Charles II or later than George III. She didn't like Adam. She didn't like "beams and things." It had to be a place she could make her own. "I want to get a house with just the bones," she said. "I want to put the fat on it myself."[24] By her own count she looked at around 150 houses, from A la Ronde, the curious little sixteen-sided folly near Exmouth, to a string of massive mansions that had been offered to the National Trust and rejected. Eventually, one Sunday in June 1954, she was with her two sons driving in search of Tythrop Park, recommended to her by the Duke of Grafton, when she came across Haseley Court in Oxfordshire, a lovely eighteenth-century house of silver stone. The core was Queen Anne, although there was a medieval heart in there somewhere; a Gothic wing had been added towards the end of the eighteenth century. She called her estate agent from the village that afternoon and bought Haseley and fifty acres for £3,000, without even bothering to have a survey.

That showed faith, because Haseley was in a terrible state. The previous owner, a Conservative MP, had shot himself in his bedroom in 1939. (Nancy used to refer to that particular bedroom as the Shooting Gallery.) Haseley had been requisitioned during the war and deserted ever since: the only attention it had received since the military left was twice-yearly visits from a local gardener, who came to clip the topiary hedges. Windows were boarded up; stucco was peeling from the walls. "It would have been cheaper if I'd bought Versailles," said Nancy.[25] But together with Fowler and decorative painter George Oakes, who would eventually become design director of Colefax and Fowler, she began to put the fat on the bones. Fowler painted the entrance hall in soft white; blue silk covered the walls of the drawing room, with plaster details picked out by Fowler in gold. Her own bedroom, a vast space in the

Gothic wing which was described in 1968 as "less like a bedroom than a cross between a private oratory, an inspired operatic hunting lodge, and an ark, or galleon, floating high above the garden's sea of flowers," was painted pumpkin orange, a reference to the saloon at Ditchley, where before the war Nancy had scraped the panelling with a coin and found that colour.[26] Pieces that had been at Ditchley or Kelmarsh were retrieved from storage in London. Others came from the country house sales that Nancy and John Fowler used to haunt—a spectacular Waterford chandelier from Clumber Park, a pair of carved-wood stag trophies from Brympton d'Evercy. She bought painted pelmets and some Chippendale carvings from Ditchley's new owner, Lord Wilton. The feel was Georgian, as it was with all of Nancy's houses and most of Fowler's interiors, but there was no attempt at faux authenticity. Haseley was a product of the 1950s, and it could never be anything else.

The business partners still fought. Imogen Taylor, Fowler's assistant, regularly swore she'd never work for Nancy again. (She remained at Colefax and Fowler until her retirement decades later.) At one stage, Nancy was furious when she returned from a trip to America after instructing Fowler that she wanted trompe l'oeil Gothic decoration in her bedroom rather than plasterwork: "Damn John. . . . He's gone ahead and done exactly what I told him not to." It was only when she took a second look that she realised he and Oakes had done just what she asked. "That's how convincing their trompe l'oeil was."[27] Her only lasting complaint about Fowler's work was that on a painted overmantel panel, Diana the Huntress's breasts were far too big. "I used to threaten to expose myself to teach them."[28]

NANCY LANCASTER LIVED well at Haseley. She kept a butler, Spencer; an odd-job man; a chef, and his wife who helped him in the kitchen; a couple of housemaids; and Winnie, her lady's maid. When her son Michael put Mereworth Castle in Kent, another John Fowler project, up for sale in 1966 and brought his wife and two children to live at Haseley for a year, he came with a nurse, a maid, and another butler. The formidable Nancy Astor used to turn up whenever she felt like it, arriving in her Rolls-Royce with a footman to help out with the entertaining and her long-suffering maid Rose Harrison. (Nancy used to slip her temperance-mad aunt the occasional glass of Dubonnet, telling her it wasn't alcoholic.)

Until 1971, Nancy lived at Haseley much as she had at Ditchley before the war. "A woman of great character," Cecil Beaton confided to his diary after a weekend there in the spring of 1959. "And the fact that she is rich makes everything seem so much more easy and agreeable."[29] She entertained regularly, coming down from London every Friday to make sure the house and the staff were ready to receive visitors. She breezed into Colefax and Fowler when the mood took her or when she was in search of a particular item for one of Haseley's bedrooms. She proffered advice to Fowler and his team, whether they wanted it or not—and they usually didn't. But with her money—she claimed later that she lost around £8,000 a year on Colefax and Fowler—and her social networking skills, she helped the firm to grow into something of an institution.

The real work, though, was done by John Fowler. If Nancy was a dilettante, Fowler was not. He depended for a living on his taste, and that taste, essentially Georgian with the occasional flight of fancy but always in keeping with the history of a house, a room, a chimneypiece, meant his reputation soared throughout the 1950s and 1960s, until by the time of his death from cancer in 1977 he was widely regarded as, in the Duchess of Devonshire's memorable phrase, "the prince of decorators."[30] And although he decorated plenty of fashionable flats and town houses in Belgravia and Mayfair, it was his country house practice that earned him that title. He advised the National Trust on the decoration of twenty-five of its country houses between 1956, when he was called in to give his thoughts on new colour schemes for Claydon House in Buckinghamshire, and 1977, the year of his death, when he was working at Dyrham Park in Gloucestershire. His role with the trust began informally but turned into an official position (with a retainer of £1,000 a year) after he decided to step back from his job at Colefax and Fowler in 1969, and some of the trust's finest country houses were given the Fowler look, from Mount Stewart and Montacute to Erddig and Uppark. Millions of people every year wander through Fowler interiors without ever realising it or recognising the enormous impact he had on the country house in the third quarter of the twentieth century. Chintzes and Brussels weave carpets, festoon curtains in heavy silk damask, strong colours and elegant flock wallpapers—one of Fowler's great gifts was the ability to create neo-Georgian interiors that rivalled and occasionally outshone their eighteenth-century forebears.

In addition to his work for the trust, Fowler worked on thirty-seven private country houses, ranging from major stately homes like Alnwick, Ragley, and Wilton to supremely attractive minor-gentry houses: the Georgian Radbourne Hall in Derbyshire, for example, where he decorated the main rooms in 1958–1960 after the owner, Major John Chandos-Pole, pulled down part of the house and carried out a thorough restoration of the remainder; or Blithfield Hall in Staffordshire, home of the Bagot family since the fourteenth century. Lord and Lady Bagot called in Fowler in 1953 to look at their early nineteenth-century Gothic great hall because the Queen Mother was coming to lunch. She was opening Blithfield Reservoir, and the water board asked to use the hall: the Bagots agreed on condition that the board paid for it to be re-decorated. They were expecting an expensive makeover, but when Fowler arrived he asked them for a scrubbing brush and a bucket of water, gave a section of battleship-grey wall a scrub, and announced that all it needed was a good wash with scouring powder. Lady Bagot, who was a relative newcomer to Blithfield, later recalled, "We spent the rest of the day exploring the old house from cellar to attic, rushing about opening cupboards, looking into chests, like two excited children."[31] It was the start of a beautiful friendship: although Fowler never made another visit, when the Bagots were in a position to redecorate more rooms a couple of years later, they went back to him for advice—and were astonished to find he remembered every detail of every room.

Dealing with Fowler could be daunting. Anyone who telephoned the Brook Street showroom first had to satisfy his assistant, Imogen Taylor, and her copy of *Burke's Landed Gentry*. If they managed to negotiate these obstacles, they might be invited for an audience, and if Fowler liked the look of them—or, more importantly, the look of the project—he and Taylor would go down for a day visit. As his biographer, Martin Wood, put it, "John's basic philosophy was always 'to do right by the house'; what the client wanted was a secondary consideration and what was good for the firm's profitability didn't figure in the scheme of things."[32] He would produce a report, rough floor plans, and sketches for curtain designs, none of which he charged for. The profit, such as it was, came from the markup on fabrics and curtains. Taylor remembered later that at any one time he might have as many as fifteen jobs on the go, two or three of which were substantial.

He had his strategies for getting his own way. He was often able to bully private customers, but with National Trust committees he needed to be more subtle. The Duchess of Devonshire, who watched him in action a number of times, described his approach:

> He had a clever way of making sure the right stuff or the right colour was chosen for covering furniture and making curtains for a National Trust house where a committee was meant to do the choosing. Knowing that he was the one who knew, he was determined, rightly, to make the decision, and he bowed to the committee like this: he produced several patterns and laid them out side by side. Picking up the first he said, "I expect you think that blue is too pale," the second, "I'm sure you think that blue is not right for the date," and the third, which he had already chosen, he would grasp in his hand and say with a note of triumph

in his voice, "And you, darling you, with your unerring eye, will say this one is perfect."[33]

He was a master at bringing out the best in any space. The ceiling of the Palladio Room at Clandon Park was given extraordinary depth by being painted in five subtle shades of white. At the Duke of Northumberland's Syon House, he used *twelve* different whites in his treatment of Robert Adam's magnificent marble hall, highlighting the architectural detail in the most astonishing way. Hardy Amies, whose Savile Row shop was decorated by Fowler in a mere three whites, was careful to maintain the scheme while the decorator was alive, but as soon as he was dead Amies had it painted plain white. "Having it three whites," he said, "never sold another fucking frock."[34]

There was no historical precedent for decorating methods like this, and while Fowler always respected history, it was the spirit rather than the letter that interested him, so while he blended scholarship and invention, it was not always in equal measure. That didn't matter too much with private clients who, after all, wanted nice rooms to live in and entertain in rather than historically accurate museums. But when it came to the National Trust, the desire for an ultimately unattainable authenticity was much greater, and Fowler sometimes fell afoul of the past.

A perfect example of this, and of the way that ex-owners of historic houses found it hard to relinquish control of their ancestral seats, came in 1971, when the National Trust opened Sudbury Hall in Derbyshire to the public for the first time. Built between 1659 and 1691 for George Vernon, a local squire whose judicious choice of wives—three of them—financed his new house, it was given to the Treasury along with the principal contents in settlement of death duties after the death in 1963 of George's descendant, the 9th Lord Vernon. Those contents were rather sparse—the house had been tenanted in the nineteenth century, and there were sales in the twentieth—and after the Treasury handed everything over to the National Trust in line with the 1953 Finance Act, the trust's experts decided to focus on the spectacular seventeenth-century carving and plasterwork as a way of making up for the lack of furniture. John Fowler was brought in, and under his guidance the plasterwork was picked out in different shades of white, and some of the nineteenth-century colour schemes were kept while others were jettisoned in favour of treatments which were part seventeenth century, part pure Fowler. The long gallery had been used as a library; now the bookcases were taken out to reveal the original seventeenth-century wainscoting, but the nineteenth-century colouring was retained, while the chimneypieces and doorcases were marbled.

Most dramatic of all was the treatment of Sudbury's magnificent Great Staircase, with its elaborate balustrade. Carved by Edward Pierce, who worked with Sir Christopher Wren on the rebuilding of St Paul's Cathedral, it was one of the finest staircases still in situ in any country house. At the time the Vernon family gave up Sudbury, it was painted dark brown, as were the doorcases leading off the staircase hall; the walls were off-white. Having taken scrapes which showed that at one point the balustrade had been white, the trust decided to reinstate that colour and stripped the treads of the stairs down to the wood before painting. Following Fowler's advice, they painted the walls a rather startling bright yellow.*

John Cornforth, a tireless advocate for Fowler's work, claimed that while it came as a bit of a shock to begin with, the new colour scheme quickly settled down, "and now when one stands at the foot of the stairs one can enjoy an excitement extremely rare in a Charles II country house."[35] For others, though, it was entirely the wrong kind of excitement. The Duchess of Devonshire, who came to review the progress of the restoration work as a member of the National Trust's regional committee, recalled later how members

---

* The colour is known today as "Sudbury Yellow." You can buy it from Farrow & Ball.

had arrived at the house to find Pierce's staircase had been painted white and the walls bright yellow. "This huge step had never been mentioned, let alone discussed at a meeting. Jaws dropped."[36]

The 10th Lord Vernon, who had handed over the house and who had remained, perhaps unwisely, in the village of Sudbury in a house built for him in 1965 by Martyn Beckett, did more than drop his jaw. After Cornforth's defensive piece on Fowler's Sudbury appeared in *Country Life* in June 1971, Vernon responded by complaining loudly that the trust had gone to quite unnecessary expense to ruin his erstwhile family seat. His criticisms, which were picked up and published in the *Times* under the headline "National Trust 'Destroying Stately Home Character,'" included the fact that the trust had dismantled the library in the long gallery, stripped varnish from floors to reveal bare boards, and, worst of all, wrecked the staircase by painting it in two shades of white.[37]

Vernon announced that he wasn't going to attend the opening. John Cornforth, whose article had kicked off the controversy, pointed out politely that Sudbury hadn't been a gift from Lord Vernon but simply "the subject of a financial transaction involving the Treasury."[38] What happened to it now was none of Vernon's business, in other words. Moreover, the underfurnished look which had led the trust to focus on the decoration had been increased when Vernon moved out, "taking many of the smaller things with him."[39] And when Robin Fedden, the National Trust's deputy director-general, told Vernon in print in so many words that he didn't know what he was talking about ("He would seem to have been misinformed") and that the trust was merely working with historical precedents, others rallied to Vernon's defence.[40] Fowler's personal taste was what now dominated Sudbury, said one. "The clock has not been turned back to 1671; it has been set at '1971: Period of National Trust Redecoration.'"[41] George Seymour, the owner of another nice seventeenth-century staircase, this one at Thrumpton Hall in Nottinghamshire, questioned the trust's wisdom "in employing an interior decorator rather than drawing upon the advice of owners of similar houses and, where possible, the previous owner."[42] (One of Lord Vernon's beefs was that the trust hadn't consulted him at all on the new work.)

Seymour also raised the familiar point that "what people want most to see is a house which appears lived in," even when it isn't, before he criticised the trust for spending too lavishly on redecoration. With less money they could, he argued, achieve results "which would afford more pleasure to members of the public."[43]

The row eventually died down, and Sudbury Hall quietly opened to the public. But the controversy had thrown into stark relief the tension between aesthetics and authenticity. As some decorators adopted an ever-more scientific approach to the reconstruction of historic interiors in the 1980s and 1990s, the drive for "correct" period colours and furnishings came to dominate the world of historic house museums and Fowler's approach fell out of favour, along with much of his more dramatic work for the National Trust, which is steadily being erased. A sad loss, one feels, as the past becomes fifty shades of grey.

In 1966 young David Mlinaric, described at the time as the "Architect of Swinging London," confessed to having a recurring nightmare in which travellers to the moon took with them copies of eighteenth-century French furniture instead of good contemporary designs.[44] Looking back at the work of Felix Harbord and Ronald Fleming, of Nancy Lancaster and John Fowler, it seems as if the long eighteenth century was the only possible choice when it came to the postwar country house interior. The New Elizabethans were Georgians at heart, and they wanted rooms that evoked that particular image of the past, what John Cornforth characterised as a "humble elegance," although in truth there was little that was humble about all those dragged and grained walls, gilded plaster swags, and swathes of opulent, sun-faded silks trimmed with gold fringe and tassels.

But there were influential dissidents in the country house world, designers who sought out the modern, never rejecting history completely but combining old and new in a way that was entirely modern. Chief among them was David Hicks, whose interiors became a byword for sixties style in historic settings. Born in 1929, Hicks began his career almost by chance in 1954 when, as a junior advertising executive with J. Walter Thompson, he decorated his mother's flat in Belgravia. The bright colours he chose—mauves and oranges and greens—and the marked absence of Colefax and Fowler chintz, were photographed by *House and Garden*, and he was taken up by Leslie Benson, ex-wife of Condé Nast, who told him, "I've had Syrie Maugham and John Fowler; I want something new."[45] Two years later he went into partnership with antique dealer Tom Parr, and the pair opened their own shop, Hicks and Parr, on Lowndes Street, off Belgrave Square. They split up in 1959: Parr joined Colefax and Fowler, ending up as head of the firm; and Hicks opened a shop of his own, David Hicks Ltd.

Forthright to the point of arrogance—"The *nouveaux riches* have no taste—they merely ape pathetically the conventional ideas of the seedy aristocrat" was one of his aphorisms—Hicks claimed his big break came in 1963, when he decorated a music room in Hampstead for the young and cool Alistair Vane-Tempest-Stewart, 9th Marquess of Londonderry, and his even cooler marchioness, Nicolette, known to everyone as Nico.[46] Friends dated it to 1960, when Hicks married Lady Pamela Mountbatten, daughter of Earl Mountbatten, much to everyone's surprise, since his homosexuality was an open secret.* Nicky Haslam, who knew Hicks well, described him and his partner, Norman Prouting, as "the hot young gay couple in London" in the 1950s. The wedding reception, with

---

*When Hicks's grand engagement was announced, his friend Antony Armstrong-Jones said, "Oh, I don't call that grand." A few months later the world found out what he meant.

1,200 guests, was held at Broadlands, Mountbatten's Hampshire country house; those who posed with the bride and groom for the wedding photos by Tom Hustler, "darling of the debs," included the Queen Mother, Prince Philip, the Prince of Wales, Princess Anne (who was a bridesmaid), Princess Margaret, the Duchess of Gloucester, the Duchess of Kent, Princess Alexandra, and the Queen of Sweden.[47]

The newlyweds bought Britwell Salome, a beautiful early eighteenth-century country house in Oxfordshire, and Hicks set about redecorating it as a showcase for his ideas while making the most of his new social network. At first he adopted a conventional approach to the plain Georgian interiors, but he soon began to experiment with bold colour schemes and a mix of contemporary and traditional objects. "Period houses treated in a modern manner can be exciting," he declared, and he didn't scruple to introduce bright scarlets, aubergines, and bronze-browns. The staircase hall was papered in blue and white, a large-scale design taken from a fragment of seventeenth-century Portuguese cotton damask, and Hicks filled the space with a camel-hair rug from Addis Ababa, a Georgian reading desk, and an assortment of found objects and bowls of potpourri. The entrance hall was given curtains of brown tweed. (Lady Pamela claimed that he discovered his penchant for dark browns when she threw a glass of Coca-Cola at his head and it smashed on the wall behind him. Theirs was a tempestuous relationship.) The walls of the oval dining room, a Catholic chapel in the days when Britwell was a recusant stronghold, were painted dark claret, with the doorcases picked out in white and gold. The drawing room was given a textured contemporary carpet in beige; painted Louis XVI furniture rubbed shoulders with low, modern sofas and fabrics; and the Gibbsian chimneypiece was crowned with an enormous, frameless abstract by Bruce Tippett which had been painted specially for the room. Architectural historian Gervase Jackson-Stops, who saw Britwell in the early 1970s, when Hicks had completed the transformation of the house, was enormously impressed. "What [Hicks and his wife] have achieved," he wrote in *Country Life*, "is likely to be recognised by future generations not only as one of the most important phases in its history, but also as the epitome of a 1960s response to the past, a response that is in large part of David Hicks's own creation."[48] The twenty-first century is less enthusiastic about aubergine and beige.

Hicks was brash and egotistical. "I'm very famous and clever," he once said, "and I'm married to a very rich lady."[49] It was a combination that appealed to the rich and famous, and his career blossomed in the 1960s. He designed the interiors for a chain of restaurants; a black-and-chrome salon for society hairdresser Vidal Sassoon; a living room with purple tweed walls and Victorian furniture upholstered in magenta leather for beauty entrepreneur Helena Rubinstein; a nightclub on Cunard's new *Queen Elizabeth 2*, done in grey flannel with silver; the sets for the quirky 1968 film *Petulia*, which starred Julie Christie and featured a soundtrack showcasing Janis Joplin and the Grateful Dead.

His country house output was relatively small, although it always had impact. There was an unusually chintzy bedroom at Kelvedon Hall in Essex in the early 1960s for Chips Channon's son Paul and some bright interiors for Nico Londonderry at her husband's country house, Wynyard Park in Country Durham. At Easton Neston in Northamptonshire he was asked by Lady Hesketh to design a library "in the manner of [Nicholas] Hawksmoor," who had designed the house; in an unlikely partnership with conservation architect Roderick Gradidge, a traditionalist if ever there was one, Hicks created a monumental set of bookcases based loosely on Hawksmoor's work at the Codrington Library at All Souls College, Oxford, and painted them a dark olive green. "The dark colour of the paintwork stands out dramatically against the white cornice and panelling," he wrote in his 1968 book on design, modestly titled *David Hicks on Living—with Taste*.[50]

At Baronscourt in County Tyrone in the mid-1970s, Hicks managed what was, after Britwell Salome, his finest country house commission. The seat of the Dukes of Abercorn, Baronscourt had quite the architectural pedigree. It was built by the Scottish neo-classicist George Steuart in 1779–1782, enlarged by Sir John Soane ten years later, and remodelled by the distinguished Irish father-and-son team of Richard Morrison and William Vitruvius Morrison in 1837–1841. But it was impractically big, and when the duke made over the house in 1970 to his son, the Marquess of Abercorn, the family was on the brink of demolishing part of it. Instead, the west wing was turned into a self-contained unit for the duke and duchess while the rest of the house was converted for the use of the marquess and marchioness and their young family. Hicks was brought in to redecorate the house, and the masculine Morrison interiors made a perfect fit with his bold colours: deep-red lacquer on the walls of the staircase hall, and reds, purples, and yellows in the library, where he recycled purple velvet curtains from the dining room in the east wing and applied them as wall coverings.

The large dining room itself was converted into a family room, and the uncompromising collision between past and present showed Hicks at his best. Keeping the nineteenth-century plaster-work ceiling, pedimented doorcases, and scagliola pilasters, he inserted a modern kitchen at one end, a storeroom at the other, and between them, a modern living and eating space with low sofas and tubular steel Bauhaus chairs. Tall, unornamented green cupboards, which Hicks called "modern island skyscrapers," helped to define the spaces without damaging the earlier decoration.[51] "They will surely interest future generations as an example of a 1970s approach to the problems of country-house life," said *Country Life*.[52]

11

COUNTRY PURSUITS

I N DECEMBER 1963 the *Tatler*'s Angela Ince had some words of wisdom for those who were spending the weekend with friends in the country. Never agree to participate in any sport, she warned. If your host says casually after dinner on Friday, "Thought I might try for a pheasant in the morning," and invites you to join him, don't do it. You'll have to get up at dawn. There will only be one gun, and any suggestion that you might have a go will be greeted by him with alarm. You'll be deafened by occasional shots ("the bark of a shotgun, so picturesque across 400 yards, so perturbing at two"). And your sole contribution to the morning's "sport" will be when you are sent "a sycophantic but ill-trained Labrador, to pick up a bundle which you are not absolutely certain is dead."[1]

Even less enthralling, cautioned Ince, was an invitation to follow the hunt. You turn up to find your host and hostess are mounted "and wearing dashingly becoming clothes." You have to stand very close to hear what they're saying to you, which means you're hit by the horse's head every time it moves. "Jolly men will be carrying trays of port and sherry, none of it for you. Other jolly men will be suggesting you follow on foot, a simple phrase which gives no indication of the desolation and panic involved."[2] If you are lucky enough to see a fox, you will very likely be turning it and bringing down the wrath of the entire hunt on your head. "You will end up feeling pretty much like an under-privileged peasant."[3]

Field sports were an integral part of country house life, and as the divide between urban and rural values deepened after the war—helped by a Labour government which was wrongly but widely perceived to be only concerned with the interests of an urban working class—they assumed a new significance. Like the country house itself, shooting and hunting with hounds became symbols of a cultural conservatism, of old rural traditions, of a way of life that was threatened by outsiders who just didn't understand.

The threats came from different directions. Until the early twentieth century, even the most elaborate shooting party was a social occasion, with a landowner inviting six or seven friends and neighbours, who brought along their wives, their valets, and their wives' lady's maids. (With very few exceptions, shooting was an exclusively male activity.) It was often an extended house party, with guests arriving on Monday, shooting on Tuesday, Wednesday, and Thursday, and leaving on Friday. The women joined the guns for lunch, perhaps staying on to watch for the afternoon, and everyone gathered for a formal dinner at eight. But maintaining a shoot was an expensive business, and after the First World War a landowner might lay off some of the costs by letting one or two guns to friends. From there it was a short step to letting the entire shoot to a syndicate. It was good estate management, and it helped to plug the growing gap between the costs involved in running an agricultural estate and the income derived from agricultural rents. By the 1950s there were probably more syndicated shoots than there were shoots run by an owner to entertain friends. A typical advertisement might read, "Guns available in pheasant shoot in Home Counties. Shooting Saturdays. 10 days guaranteed. 3,000 birds reared. £800 a gun."[4]

Syndicates saved shooting. But at the same time, they introduced into the field the kind of prosperous businessman (and they had to be prosperous to afford £80 for a day's sport) who might have learned to handle a gun at a shooting school but who, to put it politely, wasn't familiar with the ways of the country. "They do not know country manners, and they think that money will buy anything," wrote the exasperated owner of one shoot in 1952.[5] They wore the wrong clothes; they encroached on a neighbour's stand; they brought along badly behaved or untrained dogs; they were rude or patronising to keepers and beaters. And they were sometimes downright dangerous, peppering beaters, dogs, and their fellow guns with shot. One *Country Life* commentary read, "It is worth taking a definite line with dangerous shots, greedy shots and insufferable bores, for all three are a source of trouble. Hard drinkers and inveterate gamblers are equally pestilential. The first are seldom amusing and usually manage to keep everyone up far too late the night before shooting, and the second are a menace."[6]

The same commentator, the right-wing reactionary and ardent field sports enthusiast Jim Wentworth Day, had similarly forthright views on women with guns: "The woman who wants to come out for no other reason than to have herself photographed is a pest. I have a vivid recollection of two trusting young females who spread fear and consternation through two separate shoots. Each came with the latest Mayfair 'country creation,' complete with cartridge-belts, brand new 20-bores and cocky little hats adorned with jays' feathers. One shot her host in the hip, luckily at sixty yards range, and the other only just failed to get me."[7]

The inappropriately dressed shooter made frequent appearances in comic literature, from the legions of Norfolk-jacketed, bandolier-wearing Birmingham businessmen who popped up in *Punch* to Rupert Pilimore, who turned up at a shoot in a grey lounge suit, a pink shirt, and a Balliol tie in J. K. Stanford's sporting classic of 1944, *The Twelfth*. It comes as no surprise that the postwar years saw an explosion of sartorial advice for the nervous new gun. On no account wear a loud tweed—it would scare the birds. So would brass buttons. Veldtschoen shoes and boots would make sure the feet stayed dry. A hat was de rigueur, because you were far less likely to be seen by the birds if you were wearing one. If you were determined to wear a waistcoat, you should make sure it was loose-fitting and quiet, like tweed, since raising the gun exposed the waistcoat. At the same time it was important to look stylish: "There is really no excuse to greet one's host looking as though dressed in ex-government surplus stock," declared the *Tatler*, which helpfully provided a list of old, established tailors. "For mitten or glove wearers I suggest Swaine, Adeney, Brigg & Sons. Their shooting gloves of suede-backed Tan Cape leather with knitted woollen wrists (50s.) are magnificent."[8]

More serious were the attempts to instil good manners into the city professional who, having paid through the nose for his shooting, was determined to get value for money, no matter what the cost. Some sporting writers felt it necessary to set out the most basic dos and don'ts:

1. Don't shoot if you only *think* a shot is safe, you must *know* it is.
2. Never shoot or even carry a gun, loaded, between drives, unless you are definitely asked to do so by the manager of the shoot.
3. Never shoot at a pheasant which will pass over the head of one of your neighbouring guns.
4. If you are in any doubt as to whether a bird passing between you and your neighbour is yours or his, say "Yours" at the earliest moment possible and leave it to him. If he says "Yours" before you can do so, shoot, but be sorry you were slow to call out.[9]

Most serious of all was the sense of disquiet at the sight of a country pursuit taken over by people who had no connection to the land. "North Lancashire: 4,500-acre pheasant shoot to let on lease to single private tenant (no syndicates)" read one advertisement in 1962.[10] Syndicates often paid scant attention to the rearing of birds. They put so much pressure on keepers to ensure a good bag—quantity rather than quality—that those keepers filled the coverts with hand-reared, virtually tame birds, or even resorted to using release pens on shooting days. That wasn't sport. And as outsiders, the members of syndicates often failed to understand local sensitivities. They upset tenant farmers over whose land they shot and were peremptory with farm workers, showing little inter-est in the land and those who earned their living from the land. "It is perhaps difficult for the paying gun to identify himself with the locality and its rather parochial affairs," admitted Richard Wells, the author of a 1968 *Country Life* article on the right approach to syndicate shooting (and *Country Life* was compulsory reading, not only for those who belonged in the country, but for those who yearned to belong). "But if there is to be a future for shooting it must be through co-operation and mutual understanding be-tween all the parties." Syndicate members had to take time to get to know the people over whose land they shot, and those who helped them to have a day's sport. "Visits out of season to see how the countryside is looking and the birds are doing, with time to talk to anybody with a familiar face—and with the ability to put the correct name to the familiar face—will be time well spent."[11]

"THESE SHOOTING SYNDICATES are now becoming so numerous . . . that they're becoming a menace to Saturday hunting for the better part of the season," grumbled one hunter in 1959 after a fox led the hounds into the middle of a shooting party.[12]

Before the war, 189 packs hunted in England and Wales alone, and another 15 or so in Scotland and Northern Ireland. During the war their activities declined dramatically: hunting was seen as a distraction from and an impediment to the real business of the countryside, the production of food, although a few of the more enthusiastic hunters complained. One bemoaned the fact that there were now more planes in the air on hunting days, so that "owing to the noise, it is difficult to know what the hounds are doing, or even their whereabouts."[13] Others muttered about the appearance of women as grooms and whippers-in after the men had been called up to fight. Some packs were put down. *Country Life* even ran an article (by none other than the artist Lionel Edwards, the twentieth century's great chronicler of hunting) entitled "Foxes Make Playful Pets."[14] But the 1945 election that propelled Clement Attlee's Labour Party into government and seemed to herald an attack on traditional aristocratic values led to a defiant entrenchment and a growth in the popularity of hunting. Threatened, as *Country Life* put it in 1948, by "town-dwelling cranks and also certain Left-wing political elements," the number of packs increased over prewar levels. By the early 1960s, if one includes those with foxhounds, staghounds, otterhounds, bloodhounds, harriers, and beagles, there were 337 hunts in England and Wales. By then tens of thousands of people mounted were attending hunts every week, split half and half between the sexes. "Hunting flourishes as never before," declared the *Times* in 1960. "Each year there are more packs seeking recognition by the Masters of Foxhounds Association. This is the remarkable truth."[15]

The popularity of the horse was reckoned to be one reason for hunting's rise, along with the Pony Club, founded back in 1929 to encourage children to start riding and now an important vehicle for teaching youngsters the principles of foxhunting. And talking of important vehicles, the rise in car ownership also played its part, despite the fact that older members of the hunt routinely cursed the petrol engine for the way its fumes confused the hounds. Take this description of a hunt from 1962:

Doors slammed and engines roared, and to left and right swarms of cars whizzed off in search of vantage points on the flanks of hounds. . . . As I listened to the whirr of the engines I thought of the horror the noise would have brought to the ears of an M.F.H. [Master of Fox Hounds] of a former generation. Yet the modern Master recognises it as basically a healthy sound, however great its potential for frustration and however teasing the problem it poses. For it speaks of the following, wider than ever before, that fox-hunting has today. I have seen more cars than horses move off behind a pack of hounds.[16]

Followers might be on the increase, but the hunters themselves were an exclusive set, despite protestations to the contrary, and there was a flood of advice designed to help newcomers to negotiate the formidably esoteric web of rituals and conventions attached to hunting. Much of that advice was sartorial. Men wore black coats in the field until the master of foxhounds (the MFH), who was in charge of the hunt, its members, and its staff, invited them to wear red or scarlet, but not pink—"hunting pink" was considered an old-fashioned term by the 1950s. This honour came to them either as a result of a long-held commitment to the hunt or because they had stumped up a sufficiently large sum as a subscription. Women did not wear scarlet in the field, but at the master's invitation they could add colours to their collar and replace the black buttons on their coat with brass. A white hunting stock should be worn, with a horizontal, plain gold stock pin; the vertical pin was reserved for the master, the huntsman, and the whips. The type and number of buttons on one's coat varied according to status and role. Hat ribbons were worn down by masters and hunt staff but tucked up or stitched under by everyone else.

Then there was the language. Anyone who followed the hounds on a horse and didn't subscribe to the hunt wasn't asked by the secretary to pay for their day's enjoyment; they were "capped." To see a fox was to "view" it, and the sight of a fox was a "view." The pack consisted of hounds, never dogs. And, as one helpful manual on hunting etiquette for beginners pointed out, "You must never refer to two hounds or three hounds, but always to a *couple of hounds* or *one and a half couple*, as the case may be, and *three and a half couple* and so on."[17] But one hound all by itself was not a "half couple"; it was one hound. And the right way to refer to two or three foxes was as a "brace" or a "brace and a half." Of course it was.

Who were the hunters? One theory is that many were towns-people who, having moved to the country in search of Eden, were keen to espouse rural values and traditions in the belief that they would help them to fit into established social hierarchies. It wasn't just a case of turning up on a winter's morning for a hard ride. There were social activities for members, too: the hunt ball, the annual point-to-point, summer dances at members' country houses.

Apologists for the hunt often claimed that far from being an elitist activity, it was enjoyed by all classes, citing examples such as the Banwen Miners Hunt, formed in the little Welsh colliery village of Banwen in 1962, and arguing that enthusiasm for fox-hunting cut across class boundaries and involved people from many walks of life. To a certain extent that was true, in that hunt followers were drawn from all sections of rural life and cross-class bonding was strengthened in the face of growing opposition in the 1960s to the idea of foxhunting. But the sheer expense of riding to hounds—subscriptions, caps, equipment, and livery costs—excluded most people, never mind their inability to take time off work two or three or four days a week from early November until March or April. As one commentator pointed out in 1964, "If you imagined three quarters of the regular hunters in this country to be men and women living off their property or their shares you probably wouldn't be far out."[18]

There were some low-key farmers' hunts without the prestige or the prohibitive costs. There were middle-ranking, squirearchical hunts with masters—or joint masters, since there was a tendency after the war to split the role of master of foxhounds into two, three, or even four positions in order to ease the economic burden placed on masters—who lived in middle-ranking country houses. A glance through back issues of the *Tatler* shows that the majority of masters and joint masters who strolled through its pages in the 1950s and 1960s, caught in cigarette-wreathed conversation at a hunt ball or trotting earnestly along a muddy lane, lived uncomfortably or otherwise in modest Georgian piles or turreted Victorian mansions. But the older hunts had aristocratic or at least gentry connections, and strong associations with the country houses that went with them. The Duke of Rutland owned the Belvoir hounds, which were kennelled at Belvoir Castle. The hunt was known both as the Belvoir and as the Duke of Rutland's Hounds, and the joint master was Lieutenant Colonel James Hanbury, who lived at Burley-on-the-Hill, the biggest country house in Rutland. (A surprising number of masters and joint masters were ex–army men: *Baily's Hunting Directory*, the bible of the foxhunting fraternity, was littered with colonels and majors and the occasional captain.) The Fitzwilliam Hunt's eighteenth-century kennels at the Earl of Fitzwilliam's Milton Park, near Peterborough, built in the form of a medieval gatehouse, were said to be the oldest still in service in the world. The masters and staff of the Berkeley Hunt in Gloucestershire wore yellow coats with green collars, matching the outdoor livery of the Berkeley family of Berkeley Castle, while the women's colours of navy and maroon matched the indoor livery.

Even where the links between nobility and the hunt had loosened, the associations with the country house remained strong. Old press photographs show hunts gathered in front of one mansion after another: the Meynell at Sudbury Hall, Rolleston Hall, Snelston Hall, Osmaston Manor; the Quorn at Quenby Hall or Prestwold Hall; the Belvoir at Belton House and, of course, Belvoir Castle.

One of the most famous hunts was the Beaufort, ruled over from Badminton House for sixty years by the 10th Duke of Beaufort, whose car licence plate number was simply MFH1. The Beauforts had hunted Gloucestershire and Wiltshire for generations: one of the children of the 8th Duke recalled, "We are not allowed to hunt more than three times a week, till we are five years old."[19] The 10th Duke, known simply as "Master," rode to hounds six

Prince Charles hunting with the Beaufort, 1976

days a week. "Not the broad acres of the Badminton estate alone," wrote one fawning journalist in what was a startling claim in the mid-twentieth century, "but the whole of 'the Duke's country,' is a standing witness to the benefits of feudalism as against its democratic substitutes."[20] Prince Charles and Princess Anne both rode with the Beaufort; so did Anne's first husband, Mark Phillips. Country houses for sale or to let were advertised as being "in Beaufort country."

These long-lineaged hunts sometimes brought the occasional architectural legacies. The Duke of Richmond's kennels at Goodwood, said in the 1790s to have cost the staggering sum of £10,000 (well over a million pounds in today's money), were designed by James Wyatt; kept warm by stoves, their occupants lived in more comfort than the duke's houseguests. At Hamilton Palace in Lanarkshire, William Adam (father of Robert) designed a colossal hunting lodge for the 5th Duke of Hamilton in about 1732. Originally named, rather endearingly, "The Wham" and then called Chatelherault after a French dukedom to which the Hamiltons were laying claim, it boasted a facade 280 feet long, towers, and pavilions; kennels, a dog yard, and accommodation for hunt staff; a banqueting hall and elaborately stuccoed apartments for the duke. Adam clearly had his tongue in his cheek when he referred to Chatelherault in his *Vitruvius Scoticus* simply as "the Dogg Kennell."[21]

There were Gothic kennels, castellated kennels, Italianate kennels, even a design by the Regency architect Thomas Frederick Hunt for some Tudoresque kennels. These last remained unbuilt, as far as I know, but perhaps that is just as well: one twentieth-century writer said of Hunt's design that "the result, half-timbered and thatched, is theoretically sound but, alas, resembles the pavilion of a superior suburban bowls club."[22] Most of the grandest country house kennels had been converted to other uses by the 1950s, as packs were moved or disbanded and huntsmen opted for more utilitarian buildings. Wyatt's Goodwood kennels were turned into a clubhouse for golfers; Chatelherault is now the centrepiece of a country park, with a visitor centre, a café, and conference and wedding facilities. Some kennels were demolished. A few, like Milton and Belvoir and Berkeley, remained in use throughout the postwar period.

OPPOSITION TO HUNTING was nothing new in the mid-twentieth century, although in the past it had focused on the moral harm it did to the pursuer rather than the physical harm it did to the pursued. Most of it was led by the League for the Prohibition of Cruel Sports, founded in 1925, and the National Society for the

Abolition of Cruel Sports, founded by a splinter group from the league in 1932. One might have expected the Royal Society for the Prevention of Cruelty to Animals to take a lead as the oldest and largest animal welfare organisation in the country, but for much of its history, those who ran the RSPCA were active participants in field sports. In 1926, for example, there was a stir when the group turned down a bequest of £10,000 which was offered on the condition that it declared its opposition to all sports involving the death of birds, animals, or fish. Lord Banbury, a member of the RSPCA's council, explained why they felt unable to accept the money:

> Lord Lambourne is Chairman of the Council. Lord Lambourne hunts and shoots, and therefore it would be impossible to accept the bequest unless we got rid of him. I hunt and shoot, General Colvin [another member of the council] hunts and shoots. . . . The King is patron of this Society, and his Majesty shoots. The Prince of Wales is the President, and he hunts—in fact he says it is the finest sport in the world. Are we to get rid of the King, the Prince of Wales, Lord Lambourne, General Colvin . . . and last but least, myself?[23]

With enemies like this, it might seem that foxhunting didn't need friends. But tentative moves in Parliament to introduce anti–field sports bills in the 1920s mobilised the hunting fraternity, which decided it needed a lobbying group of its own, and on December 4, 1930, the first meeting of the new British Field Sports Society was held in London. The Duke of Beaufort was its president, and its fifteen vice presidents included two more dukes, another eleven peers of the realm, one MP who was about to be elevated to the peerage, and Edward Exton Barclay, a master of the foxhounds who listed his career in *Who's Who* as "Lord of the Manor." All were substantial landowners with country houses of their own.

The aims of the BFSS were simple: to organise an articulate opposition to the antihunting lobby. Whenever a letter appeared in the press attacking field sports—and it was made clear that the society intended to appeal to shooting and fishing enthusiasts as well as hunters—a representative should reply giving counter-arguments. Parliamentary candidates should be made to understand that by supporting anti–field sport legislation they would lose votes. Speakers at the first meeting of the society denounced opposition to field sports as somehow unpatriotic. "Sportsmen stood for some of the permanent things in our national life," declared one. It just wasn't true that field sports were degrading, said another. "When the field sportsman returned home at the end of the day, he was not only a stronger and healthier man, he was a better man."[24]

There were other campaign groups on both sides of the divide, but by the end of World War II the BFSS had established itself as the main opposition to the "communistic vegetarians" of the League for the Prohibition of Cruel Sports, which was renamed the League Against Cruel Sports in 1938.[25] These two organisations squared up against each other in a fairly genteel way throughout the late 1940s and 1950s, with the RSPCA hovering awkwardly on the sidelines, refusing to support moves to ban foxhunting because its opponents "have yet to find a satisfactory way of dealing with foxes, which must be kept down because of the damage they do in destroying poultry and lambs."[26] Attlee's Labour government failed to launch the expected attack on foxhunting, and when in 1949 two Labour MPs put forward private members' bills to make hunting with dogs illegal, the Labour minister of agriculture, Tom Williams, formally opposed them on the grounds that a ban "would alienate the support of the rural population to our food production programme, which is vital in the national interest."[27] As part of its campaign the BFSS issued a countryman's and sportsman's pledge, which attracted 1.2 million signatures and led to the so-called Piccadilly Hunt, in which pro-hunters staged a mounted protest through the West End of London in 1949, with hunting horns blowing and hunting songs broadcast from loudspeakers. "We know how to treat animals," said one of the organisers, "and we are not going to be told how to do so by the townspeople."[28]

The League Against Cruel Sports was the public face of opposition to hunting throughout the 1950s. It tended to promote its case through political lobbying and focused on the evils of stag hunting, acquiring land in strategic locations to provide sanctuaries for hunted animals around Exmoor in a coordinated effort to thwart the Devon and Somerset Staghounds. The league was also swift to condemn public figures for participating in hunting of any sort: in 1955 its executive committee issued a statement deploring the fact that Prince Charles and Princess Anne had been taken to a meet of the West Norfolk Foxhounds, a few miles from Sandringham. "Neither the Queen nor those whose duty it is to advise her can have any conception of the loathing and contempt which at least half the people of Britain have for foxhunting, which they consider a cruel and degrading relic of a barbarous age, nor of the sorrow which they feel on reading of the royal family's association with it."[29]

Some of the league's activists engaged in more direct action, laying false scents and sometimes trying to disrupt a hunt. In January 1960, for example, a former professional huntsman who had gone over to the other side and now devoted his time to aiding the league, turned up at a meet of the Quorn and did his best to confuse the hounds by blowing a hunting horn. Two years later a league militant named Gwen Barter brought the Norwich Staghounds to a halt by climbing onto the front of the deer cart and holding up a placard declaring that "the cruel barbaric ritual of carted deer hunting must stop now." (Carted deer were kept in captivity, released, hunted with hounds, and recaptured when they were at bay so that they could be hunted again.) A few months later Barter prevented the East Kent Foxhounds from digging out when she sat in a foxhole. "There was nothing we could do," confessed a nonplussed huntsman. "We just stopped digging out the fox and went away."[30] And sometimes the opposition came not from animal welfare activists but from farmers who were fed up with the damage done to their fields and fences by the hunt. In April 1962 a Gloucestershire farmer saw the Beaufort on his land, grabbed his gun, and shot the fox they were chasing. Then, he explained to the press, "I told the hunt to leave and led the Duke of Beaufort's horse off onto the road."[31] But in general both sides preferred to engage in a war of mutual and public recrimination, with truth the first casualty in most of the arguments.

That all changed on Boxing Day 1963, when a meeting of the South Devon Foxhounds was disrupted by a group of young activists blowing hunting horns and feeding the hounds fifty pounds of meat donated by a local butcher. The hunt was cancelled.

This was the first outing of the Hunt Saboteurs Association, founded eleven days earlier by John Prestige, a twenty-one-year-old journalist from Brixham in Devon who, having witnessed the end of a deer hunt, was so appalled by the sight that he resolved to bring together "all young people who hate cruelty and are prepared to do something to stop it."[32] Unlike the League Against Cruel Sports, the HSA adopted a strategy of disruption and direct action, and it tapped into a mood of teenage rebellion in the early 1960s which fitted neatly with the rejection of conservative values. One hundred members were enrolled in the first week for a fee of 2s. 6d. each, and Prestige received around a thousand letters of support in the first ten days. The HSA's first secretary was Joyce Greenaway, helpfully described in the press as a blonde twenty-five-year-old dancer who had just finished a show with Bruce Forsyth. "We are hoping the Beatles will set a lead for all the other youngsters by accepting life membership," she said.[33] They didn't.

The movement grew rapidly, but its tactics quickly led to violent confrontation. At the beginning of February 1964 thirty teenagers from the HSA disrupted a meet of the Cowdray Hunt in Sussex, throwing scraps of meat to the hounds and spraying aniseed. They blew horns, fired off signal rockets, blocked lanes with cars, let the air out of the tyres of all the travelling horse boxes, and, according to hunt members, dumped dead foxes in the surrounding fields to confuse the hounds still further. Hunt members were sworn at and several were hit with sticks.

A couple of weeks later huntsmen charged a group of saboteurs at Ewhurst in Surrey, lashing out with whips. And in May, nine saboteurs who attempted to disrupt a meet of the Culmstock Otterhounds in Devon were attacked by hunt supporters in what the prosecuting counsel in the resulting court case described as a scene "reminiscent of a student riot in South America."[34] One of their cars was blocked in and, Prestige said, "about twenty followers came at us with brass-tipped otter poles and whips. They bashed and dented the car roof and bonnet, let down the tyres and even tried to turn it over and set it on fire with matches while some of us were still inside."[35] The driver of the car was punched in the face and had his jaw broken. Four hunt followers were fined for assault.

In a separate case, seven of the saboteurs were found guilty of disturbing the peace and bound over to be on good behaviour for twelve months. The object of bringing the case against the saboteurs, explained the prosecutor, was "to ensure that the overburdened police would not have to go to hunts of all descriptions to prevent possible clashes between people of opposing views."[36]

That was a forlorn hope. Prestige lost heart after his conviction and took no further part in the HSA's activities, but the movement he had founded continued in various forms, some more palatable than others, and the presence of hunt saboteurs became a regular fixture at meets all over the country. So did the fistfights and intimidation, on both sides.

Ironically, the growing public opposition to hunting with dogs—which would culminate in the early twenty-first century in the outlawing of the practice in Scotland, England, and Wales (but not Northern Ireland)—did more than anything else to bolster its supporters' determination to continue it, and by the early 1970s hunting had come to symbolise a cluster of oppositional values in British society—left and right, town and country, progressive and traditional. That still holds true today.

12

BALLS

THE COUNTRY HOUSE—*EVERY* country house—was built for large-scale entertaining. All over Britain the gawky sons and daughters of the landowning classes stood embarrassed in baronial halls and elegant drawing rooms, ready to receive guests at coming-of-age parties and coming-out dances. Brides blushed in marquees under drumming rain as proud fathers made awkward speeches welcoming grooms into long-lineaged families. That staple of Victorian and Edwardian country house life, the tenants' ball, may have been in decline after the Second World War, along with the tenants, but it still surfaced here and there. In 1959, the Packe-Drury-Lowes of Prestwold Hall in Leicestershire held a coming-of-age party for their son, with everyone on the estate invited. The villagers weren't used to champagne: "As soon as they got into the fresh air outside they fell down dead drunk," remembered the Packe-Drury-Lowes' butler, whose job it was to help the local vicar sling them into the back of his car.[1]

One social event which certainly did hold its own in the country was the annual hunt ball. Like the coming-out dance, this mainstay of the social calendar in many counties, part dance, part fundraiser, wasn't exclusively a country house affair. Some hunt balls were held in hotels or country clubs and a few in schools and town halls. Occasionally the army's premises were requisitioned. In 1953 the Wylye Valley Hunt Ball was held at the mess at the School of Infantry in Warminster. And the Royal Armoured Corps, whose officers sometimes rode with the South Dorset Hunt, regularly used to lend the hunt its mess at Bovington Camp for the night. One hunt held its annual ball in the local hospital—no bad idea considering the number of broken bones that hunts attracted.

The balls weren't sedate affairs. The Croome Hunt was banned from using the Worcester Guildhall in 1960, after "incidents" were brought to the attention of the city council. Apparently towards the end of the night there was a pitched battle between two groups of middle-aged men who hurled food at each other. A waitress was hit in the eye with some cheese, and an oil painting of an ex-mayor of Worcester was torn when a bread roll missed its target. "They were aiming at each other," wailed the hunt secretary. "It is not as if they had anything against the old boy."[2] Fiona MacCarthy has left a memorable description of the Irish hunt balls she attended in and around Dublin Horse Show week in 1958. The men wore hunting pink, and this brought "a touch of latent violence" to the evening. As the night wore on, she recalled, "the scene became semi-orgiastic."[3] People danced on the tables; men and women in full evening dress hurled bread rolls and champagne corks at each other. Lemon and orange peels were thrown on the dance floor and splashed with champagne, so that the dancers slipped and fell. When a waiter dared to remonstrate with guests at the Meath Hunt Ball at the Gresham Hotel, a group of drunks marched him outside and tried to throw him in a fountain. He was saved from a soaking by a young woman who ordered them to stop. "Society Girl Defies the Debs' Delights" ran the headline the next day.[4]

Perhaps that is why so many hunt balls took place in country houses, where there was no risk of officialdom complaining about noise and rowdy behaviour, and where the rules of hospitality militated against flinging food at the old masters. At Cowdray House in West Sussex, the turreted and battlemented Victorian home of Viscount Cowdray, guests danced around the baronial Buck Hall as generations of Cowdray ancestors gazed down from the walls, and on a tapestry-backed dais at the upper end of the hall the evening was presided over, not by the lord of the place, but by bandleader Tommy Kinsman and his orchestra. Guests at the Bicester and Warden Hill Hunt Ball at Kirtlington Park in Oxfordshire sat between dances in the Monkey Room, its ceiling painted in 1745 by the French artist J. F. Clermont, who thoughtfully depicted monkeys dressed as huntsmen frolicking among landscapes and flowers. In 1954 the Warwickshire Hunt was lent the magnificent eighteenth-century Compton Verney, then empty and unused: curtains and chandeliers were brought out of storage for the occasion, and the house was filled with scarlet poinsettias and boughs of holly. The *Tatler* singled out the car parking arrangements, of all things, for special praise: "There were a dozen or more trained chauffeurs ready to give you a ticket, take your car to its parking place, and at the end of the evening fetch it for you."[5]

Three years later the Warwickshire Hunt Ball went to the National Trust's Coughton Court, described as "the lovely home of Sir Robert and Lady Isabel Throckmorton, who very kindly lent it for the occasion. . . . Beautiful tapestries hung in the supper room, and more magnificent pictures on the finely panelled walls of the first-floor dining room, where a bar had been arranged all along one wall."[6] In the 1950s and 1960s the Chiddingfold and Leconfield Hunt often held its ball at Petworth House, even though Petworth had been handed over to the National Trust on the death of the 5th Lord Leconfield in 1947. (As at Coughton Court, the family still lived in the house.) More than seven hundred people attended the 1969 hunt ball, which was a good deal more successful than the meet the following day. "After the ball" meets rarely produced memorable sport, which is hardly surprising considering the quantities of drink consumed on such occasions.

Society held its breath at the Pytchley Hunt Ball at Holdenby House, Northamptonshire, in 1950, when the twenty-three-year-old Marquess of Blandford danced into the small hours with nineteen-year-old Lady Rose Fane, sister of the Earl of Westmoreland, and then shared a buffet breakfast with her at 3 a.m. The gossips noted that the heir to the Blenheim Palace estate had also hosted a birthday party for Lady Rose a few days earlier, at which he'd given her a gold powder case, and speculated that their engagement would soon be announced. The gossips were half right: the couple was soon to be married, only not to each other.

IN FEBRUARY 1958, the *Tatler* published its debutante issue, "to help those who are bringing out daughters this year."[7] There were articles on "fashions for her first season"; pages and pages of photographs of teenage girls looking variously confident, shy, or sullen; and an endless calendar of cocktail parties, buffet luncheons, and coming-out dances. "The social season of 1958 looks like being an exceptionally full one," wrote the *Tatler*'s social diarist, "Jennifer." "To begin with, there are three afternoon Presentation parties at Buckingham Palace instead of the usual two."[8]

These royal parties had once been the entire raison d'être of the London Season, that period between April and August when the elite and would-be elite came together at a glittering array of social and sporting occasions from opera to Ascot. A debutante's presentation at court—the queuing, the nerves, the sovereign acknowledging the practised curtsey with a glimmer of a smile before the deb was quickly moved on so that the performance could be repeated with the next girl, and the next, and the next—this was what marked a young woman's coming out into Society with a capital S, her arrival on the marriage market, her transition to adulthood, and her admission to a privileged elite.

After social norms had been inconveniently interrupted by the Second World War, presentations at court were revived by George VI in 1947. But the business was less exclusive, less glamorous than before. And it felt uncomfortably anachronistic in a postwar Britain which was struggling with rationing and bomb damage. The presentation party went into a slow decline until finally, in November 1957, the lord chamberlain's office announced that there would be no more presentations after the following year's Season. "The present time is one of transition in the sense that the traditional barriers of class have been broken down," admitted the author of a rueful leading article in the *Times* the following day. "It has long ceased to be true to say that the Court is the centre of an aristocracy, the members of which form a clearly recognisable section of the community."[9] Princess Margaret was more succinct: "We had to put a stop to it," she said. "Every tart in London was getting in."[10]

So 1958 was to be the last royal Season, and anxious social commentators predicted that its demise heralded the end of the Season altogether. In fact, the hectic round of social activities continued into the 1960s, with the overlapping worlds of aristocracy and plutocracy simply getting on with the business of bringing out their daughters and advertising their availability for marriage. Traditional fixtures were maintained—Queen Charlotte's Ball, the Royal Caledonian Ball, both held at the Grosvenor House Hotel in Mayfair—as were the great sporting occasions—Royal Ascot, Henley Royal Regatta, Wimbledon, and the Royal International Horse Show at White City Stadium. There were also the private events, the cocktail parties, the "small dance" in Holland Park or Hampstead, perhaps shared between two or three debutantes, the grand ball with royal guests. There were around a hundred private dances each year well into the 1960s. Mothers whose own debuts had taken place in prewar days went for familiar venues—stalwarts like the Hyde Park Hotel and Claridge's, the Ritz, the Dorchester. Others, with impressive addresses in Mayfair or Belgravia or Chelsea, opted for their own town houses.

But around half of the coming-out dances held both before and after the end of presentations at court didn't take place in London at all. In 1956, for instance, Lady Cynthia Asquith gave a ball for her granddaughter at Stanway House in Gloucestershire, the Jacobean country home of her nephew Francis, Earl of Wemyss and March. Also in Gloucestershire, Mrs J. H. Dent-Brocklehurst gave a ball for her daughter Catharine at the family's fifteenth-century seat of Sudeley Castle. The Marchioness of Abergavenny brought out her daughter, Lady Anne Nevill, at Eridge Park in Sussex; Mrs Bromley-Davenport did the same for her daughter at Capesthorne Hall in Cheshire, which had belonged to the Davenport family since the mid-eighteenth century.

The country house was coming to rival the traditional hotel and the Mayfair mansion as a fashionable venue for a coming-out ball, as indeed it had been for years both in Ireland, where the season revolved around the Dublin Horse Show in August, and in Scotland, where the best of the Northern Season's autumnal entertainments had always taken place in private homes. And while the country house made for a very different experience—guests were more likely to meet with country doctors, inebriated clergymen, and horse-mad matrons rather than the determinedly sophisticated types that might be found at the big London dances—it was usually a pleasant one. "The best dances were in the country, in some castle or huge house," remembered Angela Huth, who came out in 1956.[11] Fiona MacCarthy, who came out two years after Angela and who, like Angela, went on to forge a distinguished career as a writer, reckoned that "the Season only came alive out in the country." People dressed less formally and were generally more relaxed. "In the last hour or two of a good party in the country, as dawn rose on dancing partners sleepily entwined on the dance floor in the garden, even girls who had their reservations about the Season felt fortunate indeed."[12] Angela Huth agreed: "The unforgettable part of the country dances was the return to the house at which we were staying to find the brilliance of the previous evening veiled in early mist, melancholy wisteria drooping more heavily, mourning doves cooing—all so uniquely English that tears came to tired eyes."[13]

There was the added frisson that the early mist and melancholy wisteria veiled a house and a family that were completely unfamiliar to the debutante. A modest country house might be perfectly capable of accommodating three hundred, five hundred, eight hundred guests at a ball, but even the grandest of mansions, with vast expanses of state rooms and acres of attics, didn't have beds for them all. The usual thing was to farm out guests to obliging neighbours who might own an old rectory, a moated manor house, or a full-scale, featured-in-*Country Life* stately home. The day of the dance, the local railway station would be thronged with country squires and their drivers, all there to meet people they didn't know. "The train arrives and disgorges its cargo of beauty which the ladies and gentlemen of the County then attempt to sort out," observed Anglo-Irish writer and historian Mark Bence-Jones in 1961. "It must be quite easy to go to the wrong house."[14] And sometimes the right house turned out to be the wrong house. Fiona Mac-Carthy recalled the story of two debs who, having been put up at Highclere Castle in Hampshire, decided to share the state bed "as mutual protection against the attentions of the marauding earl [of Carnarvon] known to tramp his corridors in search of succulent young girls."[15] Others, though, had nothing but gratitude for the hosts who put themselves out to entertain strangers. "We came to understand," said Huth, "that there are innumerable English country houses of grey stone covered in wisteria, porches cluttered with gum boots, dogs of all sizes lumbering about—and hosts who made an extraordinary effort to ensure the enjoyment of the strange young things they had been asked to accommodate for a night."[16]

ONE ADVANTAGE OF having a coming-out dance in the country was that it kept down the costs, especially if, as was often the case, parents could spread those costs by sharing the event with another couple. In the 1950s the minimum outlay for a coming-out dance was around £1,000, around £25,000 in today's money. A ball in one of the big London hotels could easily cost four times that amount, sometimes much, much more. But against that, there were formidable logistics involved in using one's own country house or borrowing someone else's for the night. It wasn't only the need to arrange accommodation: there was also the struggle involved in luring guests to a remote location. Textile magnate Miki Sekers had a large and attractive Georgian country house of his own, Rosehill, which would have been perfect for his daughter's dance: it even had its own theatre with an interior designed by family friend Oliver Messel. But Rosehill was in Cumberland, and Cumberland, Sekers decided, was "too far away for the young."[17] For his daughter Christine's coming out in 1961, he and his wife, Agota, made use of the Pavilion at Syon Park in Middlesex, lent by the Duke and Duchess of Northumberland. Less than ten miles from central London, it was a happy compromise between town and country.

Then there were marquees to rent, waiters and waitresses to hire, reliable caterers to find. One young woman who ran a freelance catering business in the early 1960s recalled her first job, a ball at an Elizabethan country house in Leicestershire. "The kitchen, we reckoned, was half a mile in length, and two of us were supposed to cook for three hundred people on a stove that hadn't been lit for twenty-two years."[18] A local photographer would be needed on the night to record the fun, at around twenty-five guineas. One, two, or even three dance bands were required, and they had to be up to the almost impossible task of keeping several generations happy at the same time. Despite the advent of rock and roll, Bert Ambrose and His Orchestra was still going strong after a career which began during the First World War; Edmundo Ros and his Latin American sound were popular after Ros was invited to play at Windsor Castle by George VI; Bobby Harvey and his orchestra were known to make any dance a lively affair, perhaps because of their habit of helping themselves liberally to the free drinks.

Top of the private dance pops, though, was Tommy Kinsman and His Orchestra, famed as the "Deb's Delight Band." Kinsman charged at least £100, and perhaps several times that amount, depending on the distance his band had to travel and the number of musicians involved. He was said to have asked for more than £1,000 to bring his band from London to play at a twenty-first birthday party at Powerscourt House in County Wicklow in 1962. Local dance bands were much cheaper, of course. But there was often a reason for that.

Then there were the decorations. At the very least, there must be flowers for the hall and the drawing room and the long gallery, enough flowers to exhaust the resources of several florists' shops. The marquee on the lawn must be disguised as something else—a jungle, a Parisian street scene, a South Sea island, or a Neapolitan nightclub. There should be a fountain, and at a country house the younger guests expected a pool—falling, jumping, or being shoved into its icy waters in the early hours was a necessary part of the fun. House and pool should be floodlit. Trees and shrubs should be festooned with coloured lights to give a glimmering effect to a summer evening that everyone prayed was going to be mild and dry.

These were the basics. Those with the money and ambition to make a more memorable evening didn't stop there. Instead, they called on the services of a professional designer. Most decorators were happy enough to dabble in this most ephemeral of art forms if the money was right, happy to provide an off-the-peg theme for the night and artful swathes of material as a backdrop for floral displays. But the better designers revelled in the opportunity offered by wealthy and socially ambitious hostesses to create a night to remember.

The doyen of postwar dance decorators was undoubtedly the designer Felix Harbord, whom we last saw decorating Aileen Plunket's Luttrellstown Castle. In fact, Harbord was better known in his lifetime for his party decor than for his country house interiors. He worked with clients in the haut monde, people who expected—or hoped—to see royalty, diplomats, and A-list film stars at their dances. In 1961, for example, he was brought in by Miki and Agota Sekers for their daughter's coming out, and for three days and three nights he laboured to turn Syon's Pavilion into fairyland. A covered way lit by flickering candles in red and blue glass holders led the way to a "nightclub," the castellated facade of which was covered in moss, as were the life-size statues of musicians in alcoves flanking the entrance. The Pavilion itself was decorated in "authentic eighteenth-century" blues and pinks. Harbord put the finishing touches on his masterpiece only half an hour before the party started and vanished discreetly as the first guests arrived, then reappeared at 1:30 a.m. and surveyed with satisfaction the effect his handiwork was having on guests who included Princess Margaret, Vivian Leigh, the Duchess of Buccleuch, and John Profumo.

Harbord's best customers were Aileen Plunket and her sister Maureen, Marchioness of Dufferin and Ava. Maureen and Aileen had both lost their husbands in the war, although Aileen had managed to divorce hers beforehand. In July 1952, Maureen hosted a ball at the exclusive Hurlingham Club in Fulham for her daughters Caroline and Perdita Blackwood, and Harbord's decorations stole the show. He hung tapestries on the walls of the supper rooms and draped them round the usually-bare pillars; he lit the chandeliers with hundreds of red candles, while in the main ballroom (one of four dance floors in use on the night) mermaids made of fresh flowers hovered on the walls, holding bouquets of pale-mauve gladioli. "A ball which will perhaps primarily be remembered for its wonderful decor," said the *Tatler* (which was perhaps not how the marchioness would have liked it to be remembered, having forked out a small fortune to entertain her six hundred guests). "Mr Felix Harbord . . . is one of our cleverest interior decorators."[19]

Harbord's working relationship with the marchioness's sister, Aileen Plunket, was even closer. As we've seen, he devoted a quarter of a century to decorating her Irish house, Luttrellstown Castle, and he was the natural choice when it came to creating lavish settings for her parties, both in London and in Ireland. In 1949, when Aileen gave a dance in Knightsbridge for her younger daughter, Doon, there were topiary birds, floodlit statues, swathes of yellow gauze, and pyramid-shaped trees made of blue laurel and baby's breath. When she was in London for a short stay in December 1953 and wanted to give a supper party, she held it in Harbord's Knightsbridge house, 1 Trevor Square. He set up a ballroom in the garden for the occasion, the walls of which were covered with real oranges and lemons on branches, and vines drooping with muscats and black grapes. Dancers would pause every now and then to pick a grape or two.

This kind of decorating was an ephemeral art. The stardust and elaborate floral displays sparkled for a few hours and then vanished almost as soon as the party was over. The marquees were dismantled, the chains of fairy lights were removed from the trees, and while host and hostess discreetly examined the floor of the long gallery for cigarette burns and stiletto marks, the decorator was largely forgotten—until his bill came in, anyway. Adam Pollock, one of Swinging London's most innovative young interior designers, was casually dismissive of the craft: "It is architecture and the people in the houses that are important," he said in 1967, shortly before he dropped out and went to live in a ruined monastery in Tuscany. "What is on the walls is only a background."[20]

That background could cost Pollock's customers anywhere from £750 to £15,000 for a private dance, and even then there was sometimes a tussle over what the client wanted and what Pollock thought they ought to want. "Dances are interesting to do but the fun depends on what the demands are," he said. "The ideal decoration for me would be abstract and mad but unfortunately, most people won't spend money on something abstract."[21] They may not have wanted abstract, but they sometimes wanted mad. At Dropmore, an eighteenth-century country house in Buckinghamshire which he decorated for the coming out of Tana Alexander in 1963, Pollock covered everything in gold foil and diamanté. There were twenty-four jewelled chandeliers, and in the corners of the main room were grottos of the elements—Air, Earth, Fire, and Water—each supported by four ten-foot-high statues.

"Only slightly camp," said Pollock.[22]

At the coming-out ball which Lord and Lady Brocket gave at Brocket Hall in Hertfordshire for their only daughter, Elizabeth Nall-Cain, in May 1956, the lake and the trees in the park were floodlit, and two marquees were set up to provide a supper room and a buffet and bar for the eight hundred guests who danced the night away in Brocket Hall's ornate ballroom, where 150 years before Lady Caroline Lamb is said to have surprised her lover Lord Byron by having herself served naked in a large soup tureen during her husband's birthday dinner. It was a lovely scene, gushed the *Tatler*'s Jennifer (referring to the dance, not the sight of a naked Caroline Lamb). "Every woman seemed to have put on her prettiest dress. All those who possessed a tiara wore one, and most of the older women wore other magnificent jewellery as well."[23]

The conspicuous display of wealth played an important part in balls like this, even if some of the magnificent jewellery might be paste, the originals having been discreetly hocked several generations ago. And if the appearance of naked women in soup tureens was a relatively rare occurrence, a certain amount of horseplay was also compulsory, and the older people were expected to show some good-natured tolerance. When the Earl of Lanesborough and Mrs John King gave a joint party for their daughters at Friar's Well, Mrs King's country house near Melton Mowbray, attention centred on a second ballroom in a marquee erected round a fountain in the grounds, next to a swimming pool. By 3 a.m. Mrs King was overheard saying to a girl in a dripping evening dress, "There are a couple of my old dresses in a cupboard upstairs—help your-self." The girl came back in a blue satin number sparkling with diamanté and sequins, having ransacked the wrong cupboard. As dawn was breaking, Simon George Robert Monckton-Arundell, 9th Viscount Galway, abruptly stopped playing backgammon in one of the downstairs rooms and went out to make up a four at croquet. Shortly afterwards one of the older guests, keen to be on the move, was heard desperately saying, "I can't remember what the debs we have to stay look like. They're in the pool and they all look different now." Around 6 a.m., as a man wearing an Italian suntan, an evening coat, and a pair of wet red shorts clambered into his car and roared off down the drive, some of the night's younger survivors decided to go riding, while the older guests staggered off to their beds.[24] Balls were a tiring business.

The problem for hostesses and chaperones was to ensure that the young people enjoyed themselves while at the same time not letting things get out of hand. Debs' mothers had a code for young men, who were SIT (safe in taxis), NST (not safe in taxis), or VSPQ (very safe, probably queer). But until the sixties began to filter down to the shires, there was remarkably little in the way of serious sexual transgression, apart from the expected inexpert fumbling in the shrubbery. "Most of the debutantes had been co-piously kissed—in taxis, parked cars, moonlit gardens, darkened dance floors," remembered Angela Huth. "But we doubted that more than two or three had 'gone all the way.' 'You can always tell which ones have,' people said, with a sagacity based on nothing but surmise and vague scrutiny."[25]

13

HOW TO RUN A STATELY HOME

T HE EARL OF Rhyall was broke. The responsibility of hanging on to his Hampshire stately home, with all its treasures and its beauty and its history, weighed heavily on him. His butler confessed to being bored to death with buttling; in any case, a butler was a luxury he couldn't afford. His beautiful young countess, tired of growing mushrooms to make a little extra money, had begun an affair with an American oil tycoon who took her to nightclubs and bought her a mink coat. Worst of all, this distinguished and long-lineaged English nobleman had somehow acquired a distressingly mid-Atlantic accent.

Because the Earl of Rhyall was Cary Grant. His wandering countess was Deborah Kerr, her oil tycoon lover was Robert Mitchum, and the Hampshire country house was a film set that looked remarkably like Osterley Park in Middlesex. They all appeared together in the 1960 romantic comedy *The Grass Is Greener*. "He comes to peer and remains to leer at the Kerr in the garage" was one reviewer's magnificent description of Mitchum's millionaire.[1]

Cary Grant's Earl of Rhyall was part of a great British literary, theatrical, and cinematic tradition. The impoverished aristocrat trying to make ends meet in his crumbling stately home had become a staple of stage and screen. He (or, more rarely, she) featured regularly in films, from the eccentric Lord Wilcot (Alistair Sim) in the satirical comedy *Left Right and Centre* to Lord Whitebait (Naunton Wayne) in *Nothing Barred*, who tried to save Whitebait Manor by having a friendly cat burglar steal his most valuable painting, a work by "Vincent Van Gogough."

The near-bankrupt 19th Earl of Locharne (David Tomlinson) had to wrestle with postwar bureaucracy in the shape of an official from the coal board determined to requisition his decrepit Scottish castle—"The moat is overgrown and the earl is overdrawn"—as a holiday home for miners in the 1952 film *Castle in the Air*. Dame Edith Evans played the eccentric Lady Sophie Fitzmore in *Crooks and Coronets* (1969), a bizarre transatlantic crime comedy in which two American ex-cons, played by Telly Savalas and Warren Oates, arrived in England to rob Lady Sophie's stately home but decided instead to turn it into a tourist attraction. And eccentricity toppled over into madness with Peter O'Toole's 14th Earl of Gurney, the leading character in *The Ruling Class* (1972), who believed he was first Jesus Christ and then Jack the Ripper, and whose relatives—those he didn't murder—went to great lengths to have him committed so that they could get their hands on his vast country house, played in the film by the vast Harlaxton Manor in Lincolnshire.

Real-life country house owners rarely resorted to theft or murder to keep the towers from tottering and the bailiffs from banging on the nailed portals, although almost anything else was considered. Desperate to find half a million pounds to pay the death duties on his ancestral seat of Inveraray Castle, the 11th Duke of Argyll sold his name in the 1950s to the American Burlington Hosiery Company, who advertised their tartan socks as "styled for Bur-Mil by the Duke of Argyll." A photograph of the debonair duke appeared next to pictures of the socks in question, which were apparently "filled with the very flavor of Scotland."[2]

Others rented out their country houses to film companies. In 1966 the Duke of Rutland rented Belvoir Castle in Leicestershire to an Italian company for £2,000 for ten days. The company was making *Matchless*, an unmemorable post-Bond spy thriller starring Ira von Furstenberg. "When they rang me up and asked me if they could rent the place, I was quite frank," said the duke. "I told them it was just a matter of L. S. D." (by which he meant pounds, shillings, and pence, of course, rather than the then-fashionable hallucinogenic drug).[3] He was careful to charge extra every time the director wanted to borrow any of the family heirlooms as props. "We need every penny we can get for the upkeep. [Belvoir] is like a bottomless pit."[4]

Others were less well-equipped to deal with film companies. When Major Benjamin Hervey-Bathurst rented Eastnor Castle in Herefordshire to MGM in 1969 for a crime caper called *One More Time*, he had no idea what he was letting himself in for. Sammy Davis Jr., Peter Lawford, and director Jerry Lewis bounced around the grounds on mopeds "to save their legs between takes," while an increasingly uneasy Major Hervey-Bathurst surveyed Eastnor's forecourt, littered with lighting equipment, cameras, and film

Sammy Davis Jr. (centre), Peter Lawford (left), and Jerry Lewis (right) at Eastnor Castle

company trucks, and admitted that he hadn't realised the filming would be such a major operation. "It's a bit frightening," he told a local reporter. Worse, he had a niggling feeling that he hadn't asked for enough money, although he refused to say how much the company was paying him. "It's a rather sore point now that we have seen just what is involved," he said. "I am beginning to think they have got it rather cheaply for what they are doing to the place."[5]

The Earl of Rhyall managed to solve his marital problems in *The Grass Is Greener* by challenging his rival to a duel in the long gallery and ensuring that he, the earl, was wounded. (Both pistols were loaded with blanks, and he persuaded his butler to shoot him in the arm.) His wife's resulting flood of sympathy was enough to put an end to her affair. His financial problems remained at the end of the film, but he was doing his best to alleviate them by opening his stately home to the public for a half-crown admission fee. So were the 19th Earl of Locharne in *Castle in the Air* and Lord Wilcot in *Left Right and Centre* and Lord Whitebait in *Nothing Barred*. In fact, almost every fictional country house owner stood smiling at the door of their ancestral seat with their hand out to welcome charabancs full of bank holiday trippers, each with their half crown at the ready.

And Art was simply holding up a mirror to Life. "Dukes, earls, barons, viscounts, baronets, knights and honourables are all climbing aboard the gilt-edged wagon," declared an awestruck American journalist in 1955. "And the plain John and Jane Does are walking up in their thousands to peep into ancestral halls, corridors, bedrooms and boudoirs."[6] The stately home business was booming.

COUNTRY HOUSES HAD been opening their doors to the public for centuries, and many had charged for admission before the war, although the proceeds had gone to charity—the Red Cross, or the Queen's Institute of District Nursing, or the Gardeners'

Evelyn, Dowager
Duchess of Devonshire,
at Hardwick in 1950

Rex Whistler, *The Letter*

The Duchess of Devonshire in the Gold Drawing Room at Chatsworth in 1952

Luggala, Oonagh Oranmore and Browne's retreat in the Wicklow mountains

Luggala at Christmas, 1959

Callernish

Oldany House by Felix Kelly, as featured in a Shell-Mex
advertisement in *Country Life*

John Fowler's Gothic bedroom for Nancy Lancaster at Haseley Court

Patrick Lichfield in front of Shugborough Hall, his ancestral seat, in 1973

Midford Castle in Somerset, rescued and restored by Michael and Isabel Briggs in the 1960s

John Lennon and Yoko Ono at Tittenhurst Park

The Rolling Stones performing at Longleat House in 1964

Rex Whistler, jacket illustration for *The Last of Uptake*, 1942

Benevolent Institution. Dukes of Devonshire opened both Chatsworth and Hardwick in the 1930s; the Earl of Exeter opened Burghley House; and the Duke of Norfolk opened Arundel Castle.

Before the war, the idea of the owner of a great mansion throwing it open to the public for any reason other than charity seemed distinctly vulgar. Now, though, an increasing number of owners faced up to the fact that charity begins at home and began to join the tourism industry, installing car parks and cafeterias and souvenir shops. In 1951, the year of the Festival of Britain, around a million people paid their half crowns to visit stately homes whose owners, in the words of one journalist, "have decided the only way to weather the blizzard of death duties, supertax, soaring repair costs and high wages is with public assistance."[7] Blenheim Palace, home of the Dukes of Marlborough, played host to 126,000 visitors that summer; 90,000 tramped through the state rooms at Longleat. Chatsworth, which before the war might have attracted a few hundred visitors, welcomed 205,000 cash customers in 1954. By 1972, Britain's privately owned stately homes admitted 6.5 million customers—more, probably, since some owners, like the Duke of Bedford at Woburn Abbey in Bedfordshire, steadfastly refused to divulge their visitor figures. When asked, a receptionist at Woburn said, "In all the years we have been open, we have never divulged these figures. Ever. His Grace says that if the press phones we're to say, 'Lots and lots.'"[8]

The man usually credited with launching the stately home business is Henry Thynne, 6th Marquess of Bath. Selling off the village of Corsley and other chunks of the Longleat estate weren't enough to meet the death duties that resulted from his father's untimely death in 1946, and the new marquess and his agent began to discuss Cheddar Caves in Somerset, two caves on the edge of the Longleat estate which had been opened to the public before the war at a charge of one shilling a head. Looking for ways to hang on to Longleat House itself, he said, "I had the brainwave—why not open it like Cheddar Caves to the public?"[9]

So on April 1, 1949, Longleat House opened its doors for the first time as a commercial concern, and it remained open from 10:00 a.m. to 4:30 p.m. every day until the end of September, at a charge of half a crown for adults and a shilling for children. Lord and Lady Bath were featured on the front cover of the *Tatler*, which praised the opening as "an event of great cultural importance, and a high tribute to the public spirit of the Marquess and Marchioness."[10] Using slightly more measured tones, the *Times* predicted Longleat was "likely to prove a 'show-place' of very wide appeal, a memorial to a way and scale of living no longer possible."[11]

Lord Bath always claimed that Longleat was "the first house ever to be opened to the public on a thorough-going commercial basis."[12] The truth was slightly more complicated. The state rooms at Warwick Castle, closed during the war when the castle was occupied by the Ministry of Supply, had reopened at Easter 1946, drawing record crowds and leading to gridlock in the town. "At times the traffic island outside the Castle gates was covered with bicycles parked in heaps," said a reporter for the *Warwick and Warwickshire Advertiser*.[13] Chatsworth opened its doors to the public in the same month as Longleat for the first time since the outbreak of war. In 1950, when petrol rationing was finally abolished (May 26, 1950, was known at the time as "VP Day"), the *Times* began to publish an annual list of country houses open to the public. It included thirty-nine private houses, plus another twenty-eight belonging to the National Trust. By 1956, around 250 of Britain's finest homes were throwing open their doors. And now there was no mention of half crowns going to the Red Cross or the Queen's Institute of District Nursing.

If Longleat wasn't exactly the first into the field, it was the most successful, with 134,000 paying visitors in its first year of operation. Lord and Lady Bath were photographed leaning nonchalantly against the parapet on the roof with their dogs, standing with their dogs on the steps to welcome visitors, posing (with their dogs) against the monumental marble chimneypiece in the great hall. By deliberately courting publicity rather than shying away from it, Lord Bath was the first of a generation of showmen-peers.

Not unnaturally, other hard-up owners began to wonder if they might be able to follow his lead and turn a liability into an asset. At Palace House on the edge of the New Forest in Hampshire, a young Lord Montagu was pondering the future and looking to Longleat for inspiration. Palace House was neither big nor beautiful: it had started life as the gatehouse to Beaulieu Abbey, founded by the Cistercians at the beginning of the thirteenth century, before being converted into a private house at the dissolution of the monasteries and extended by Arthur Blomfield in 1872, in a curiously Scotch Baronial episode which left it looking oddly out of place in Hampshire. Montagu had inherited the title and the estate back in 1929, when he was two years old; everything was held in trust until his twenty-fifth birthday in 1951, but as that grew closer he began to think about what to do with Palace House. He refused to sell up—"Whereas most people possess their belongings," he wrote later, "I, paradoxically, belonged to my possessions"—so he tried to find a tenant, with the idea that he could maintain the family connection by keeping an apartment in a corner of the house.[14] For a time it looked like the Bishop of Winchester might take it as a home for distressed clergymen. When that fell through Montagu tasked his agent with finding a school or college to move in, without success. His sister suggested turning it into a hotel, but he didn't like the idea of being a permanent guest in his own home.

Like the Marquess of Bath, Montagu could look to a precedent when it came to charging for admission. Since the 1890s visitors had paid a shilling a head to wander round the ruins of the Cistercian abbey at Beaulieu, and at the height of their popularity in the 1920s the ruins attracted forty thousand visitors a year. "I reckoned that if 40,000 people paid a shilling each to look round some monastic ruins then most of them would be prepared to pay 2s. 6d. to be allowed inside an historic home full of family heirlooms," wrote Montagu.[15]

Montagu had been working in public relations in London after being sent down from Oxford in 1949 when the Bullingdon Club smashed up his rooms during a boisterous Christmas party. He also had some experience in opening a stately home to the public: while he was staying with the Earl and Countess of Pembroke early in 1951 they told him they were opening Wilton House that year and asked him to help with the PR. His hand can be seen in the preemptive statement issued by the Pembrokes at the opening, which stressed that it cost £15,000 a year to heat, clean, and maintain the house and grounds, and pointed out that although the house had eighty-seven rooms, the family kept only seven of them for their own use.

Lord Montagu asked advice, not from the Marquess of Bath, but from Lord St Levan's agent at St Michael's Mount in Cornwall, which had been open since soon after the war. (The agent advised coconut matting in the state rooms and a route which enabled the public to see as much as possible "without interference with Lord Montagu's privacy."[16]) He decided to live in an upstairs flat, feeling that "this ancient home is a greater asset if it is lived in." His presence would prevent it from becoming "a hollow museum like the chateaux of France," he said.[17] And, realising that Palace House and its contents—chiefly a motley collection of family portraits—could never compete with some of the big showplaces like Longleat and Chatsworth, Montagu, a motoring enthusiast, hit on the brilliant idea of adding value to a visit by creating a motor museum, the first of its kind in the country.

There was a drawback. He only possessed one historic car, a 1903 De Dion-Bouton given to his father by a tenant in lieu of a bad debt. That didn't stop him: he begged and borrowed until, when the time came to open Beaulieu in April 1952, the hall at Palace House was filled with veteran cars and motoring memorabilia, including a summons issued to his father, the 2nd Lord Montagu,

Lord Montagu at Beaulieu

in 1902 for exceeding the 12 mph speed limit.* He brought down a few press photographers before the opening and posed for them, not in front of the house or surrounded by aristocratic dogs, but trundling through the grounds in the De Dion-Bouton, and polishing the pewter, and scrubbing the floor. "It's enough to bring a peer to his knees," declared the *Sunday Pictorial*.[18]

The half-crown sightseers loved this. Schadenfreude was mingled with a voyeuristic interest in how the nobility lived, coupled with a secret satisfaction on finding that they were Just Like Us. Which of course they weren't. On the first day of opening, Lord Montagu promised his houseguests that there would be

---

*The 2nd Lord Montagu's enthusiasm for motoring extended into his personal life. His secretary and mistress was Eleanor Thornton, the model for the *Spirit of Ecstasy*, the famous Rolls-Royce bonnet ornament.

champagne with dinner if they had more than a hundred visitors by the time Palace House closed to the public that evening. The doors opened at 11:00 a.m., and the hundredth visitor had arrived by 12:30. There was champagne for lunch. The following weekend was the Easter bank holiday, and seven thousand people turned up, immediately putting Beaulieu third in the league table of stately homes open to the public, after Chatsworth and Blenheim.

THE THIRD, AND arguably the greatest, showman-peer of the post-war years was Ian Russell, 13th Duke of Bedford. Like the Marquess of Bath and the Duke of Devonshire, Bedford had to contend with an untimely death and punitive death duties. Whether by accident or design, his father, the 12th Duke, shot himself in October 1953, less than two months before the arrangements he had made to avoid death duties were due to come into play. As a result, his son was faced with an unexpected tax bill of £4.5 million. The 13th Duke had not liked his father, and his father had not liked him, so his grief was directed at the prospect of losing the family seat of Woburn Abbey in Bedfordshire. "If Woburn was sold or otherwise disposed of to the National Trust or some institution," he said, "something would have gone out of the family, and indeed the history of England, which could never possibly be replaced."[19] He didn't want to be the one to let it go.

Thirty-six years old, with five young children—three of his own and two stepchildren—Ian Russell was farming in South Africa when he heard the news of his father's death. He returned to find Woburn in chaos: the gilding was black with dirt, all the pictures the family owned were stacked twelve deep against the walls of the long gallery, and there was no kitchen. Sir Albert Richardson's work for the 12th Duke had included demolishing the kitchen block, and since no one was living at the Abbey, Ian's father had seen no need for a replacement. The new duke and duchess camped out in one of the bedrooms, taking their meals at the local pub—the Bedford Arms—while they took stock. (They also bought themselves a house in the Channel Islands after the duke's mother-in-law enthused about the tax savings.) Within a very short time the duke decided, as he recalled later, that "the only way of financing the reopening of the house would be to follow the tentative example of other families in our position, and allow the public to see it in return for an entrance fee."[20] His wife, Lydia, arranged the main state rooms so that they artfully suggested that the family lived at Woburn, which they didn't, at least not in the early years of opening. She also discarded most of the heavy Victorian and Edwardian furniture that had been installed by previous dukes and concentrated instead on French and Georgian pieces. "In doing so she completely transformed the house," said her husband. "The heavy, dead atmosphere I recalled from my first visits to the house in the thirties had completely gone. It was as if someone had waved a magic wand."[21] They bought linoleum for visitors to walk on and miles of rope to keep them to the designated route.

Woburn Abbey opened to the public on Good Friday 1955. Bedford brought down friends and relations to act as room guides, assigning each one to a particular room and giving them a thorough briefing about the history of the house and the contents of the room where they were to be. After lunch, the doors opened and everyone went to their stations and waited nervously to see what would happen. Eventually someone saw two cars and a bicycle coming up the drive, recalled Bedford, "and we all rushed to the windows to look at our first visitors."[22]

Like Longleat and Beaulieu, Woburn was a tremendous success. With 181,000 visitors in its first year and a staggering 37,000 on a single bank holiday Monday, it tapped into—what? A voyeuristic desire to see how the former ruling class lived? A rage for self-improvement? A wish for gilded glamour after grim years of war and austerity? The Duke of Bedford put it down to a need to escape. Visitors come, he wrote, "because they are trying to escape into a different world. They lead a humdrum life and they invest the Stately Home with an air of romance which their own homes do not possess. Such a visitor wishes to spend some hours in a make-believe world and to become a lord for a day. He chooses the right length of time. I wonder if he would like it if it lasted any longer."[23]

All of these things were true, at different times and for different people. Add to that a general sense that such places had had their day and that before long they would be gone, and one has an inkling of the reasons behind the phenomenal success of the stately home business, which meant that by 1972, *seven million* visits a year were made to privately owned country houses.

That success didn't extend to solving the problems faced by destitute dukes and broke barons. By 1959, six years after his father's death, the Duke of Bedford's trustees still owed £3 million in death duties, and in spite of Woburn's popularity with the public, they were trying their hardest to persuade the National Trust to take it on. (Under the terms of a settlement put in place by his father and grandfather, the duke himself neither owned Woburn nor had any say in decisions about its future.) It was only the absence of a suitably large endowment that enabled Bedford to hang on to his ancestral seat. But ticket sales and teas at least contributed towards the upkeep of houses that would otherwise have fallen into terminal decline.

OPENING A COUNTRY house to the public in the early 1950s wasn't the science it is today, with marketing consultants and interpretive specialists hammering on the door and experts in everything from heritage catering to inclusive visitor experience queuing up to offer their services. In those days it was rather more ad hoc. When the Earl and Countess of Pembroke opened Wilton in April 1951, they didn't have any guides: instead the earl and members of the family showed visitors round the house while they tried to recruit a team of local people to take over. Lord Bath's wife, Daphne, wrote the guidebook to Longleat, really a short history of the family.

"We thought Women's Institutes, British Legions, etc., like to be told funny anecdotes about the family," said Lord Bath. "Quite frankly, I don't think that Rembrandts or Van Dycks interest them very much."[24] Car parks turned into mud baths. Lavatories were always a problem. The Duke of Bedford was once trying to cross a busy London street when he was harangued by a woman who complained, "I came down to Woburn with my Women's Institute and I had to queue up fifteen minutes for the toilet. It's not good enough."[25]

It took time to establish the best route round a house, especially if an owner decided not to opt for guided tours. What worked perfectly on a wet Wednesday at the end of the season could be disastrous on the August bank holiday Monday. Dead ends caused horrible congestion on busy days as visitors tried to double back against the prevailing traffic. Lord Montagu quickly found that it was a mistake to allow visitors to climb one particularly narrow staircase at Palace House and made it off-limits. Otherwise, he said, "we might have fat ladies stuck there for hours and hours before they could be extricated."[26]

The stately home business was a cottage industry in which the cottage was a castle or a palace. And that's how it stayed for some—the Under Eleven, as Lord Montagu called them, owners whose country houses were never going to draw visitors in the tens of thousands because they were too far off the beaten track, or too small, or just too unexciting. For some, that didn't matter at all, because attracting hordes of tourists wasn't their reason for opening. When Historic Buildings Councils were set up in 1953 in the wake of the Gowers report, they quickly established a policy of public money for public benefit: in order to obtain a grant from one of the HBCs, an owner had to agree to open their house for a stipulated period, usually one day a week between Easter and the end of September. That led to many smaller houses opening their doors without exactly welcoming visitors. Wolterton Hall in Norfolk was open on Thursday afternoons from June to September, and members of the public had to give twenty-four hours' notice of their intention to visit. In 1965 a total of forty-six people managed to breach its defences: "This house is very remote and not easy to find," said Lord Walpole, with a mixture of pride and relief.[27]

As well as a distinction between the big show houses like Chatsworth, Woburn, and Longleat and Lord Montagu's Under Eleven, by the 1960s there was also a clear difference between showmen-peers like Bedford and Montagu and those country house owners who felt there was something not quite nice about self-promotion and commercialisation, in much the same way that their parents and grandparents might have felt about going into "trade." As the octogenarian Ivo Murray Twisleton-Wykeham-Fiennes, 20th Lord Saye and Sele, put it, referring to his ancestral seat of Broughton Castle in Oxfordshire, "Souvenirs and catering are not worthwhile and turn the place into a shop instead of a home."[28] The showmen, led by the Duke of Bedford, Lord Montagu, and the Marquess of Bath, would do anything to attract visitors, in spite of frequent gibes from the press and fellow peers for their vulgarisation of a great British institution. In Woburn's second year of opening Bedford, he turned the stables into a milk bar and covered the walls with sky-blue tiles, each decorated with a ducal coronet. The following year he held scooter rallies and traction-engine rallies, and installed espresso machines and a jukebox in the milk bar. He appeared on television playing the washboard in a skiffle group. He publicly invited Marilyn Monroe to spend the night in the bed slept in by Queen Victoria when she visited Woburn in 1841. (She declined the invitation.) He hosted the Sixth International Congress of Naturists in 1958 and put up his butler, James Boyd, as prize in an American magazine competition to have a butler for a weekend. "I have been accused of being undignified," he wrote in 1959. "That is quite true, I am. If you take your dignity to the pawnbroker he won't give you much for it."[29] Two years later he had a cameo role in the stately home caper comedy *Nothing Barred*—not as a stately home owner but as a convict sewing mailbags.

At Beaulieu, Lord Montagu (who accused Woburn of being a mere nudist camp, after Bedford called Palace House a "garage") ran a series of jazz concerts. They began in a small way in 1956 when a group of young jazz fans from Southampton asked if they could stage a concert on the front lawn one evening. About four hundred people turned up to hear the now-forgotten Avon City Jazz Band, and the youngsters split the receipts with Montagu. Everyone was well behaved, not least because there was no bar, and Montagu resolved to turn it into an annual event, the Beaulieu Jazz Festival. By 1960 it was huge, taking place over three days and catering to more than ten thousand fans, with a lineup that included the best of British jazz, from Johnny Dankworth and Cleo Laine to Acker Bilk, Humphrey Lyttelton, and Ronnie Scott. The BBC agreed to broadcast live from the festival.

Unfortunately the 1960 festival ended in a riot when fans of modern jazz began fighting with fans of trad, the scaffolding holding the BBC's outside broadcasting equipment collapsed under the weight of youths who had climbed up to get a better view of the proceedings, and the crowd invaded the stage, flinging bottles right, left, and centre. The BBC producer stopped the transmission—"thus blacking out what would have been one of the Corporation's most dramatic live broadcasts," said Montagu afterwards—and eventually police, ambulances, and fire engines arrived to bring a halt to proceedings.[30]

Undeterred by the damage both to Beaulieu and to his reputation, in 1961 Lord Montagu went ahead with one more jazz festival. But although it was better organised and better policed than ever before, and the twenty thousand fans were well behaved when they were in the grounds, the same couldn't be said for those who wandered around the village. "They fought in the streets, copulated in front gardens, disrupted the traffic, defecated in garages and urinated in gutters," recalled Montagu. "The situation was intolerable, and I knew I could never risk a repeat."[31] Accordingly, at midnight on the last night, he brought the seven top names onstage together, asked them to play "When the Saints Go Marching In," and announced that there would be no more jazz festivals at Beaulieu.

When asked what he feared most, Prime Minister Harold Macmillan is supposed to have replied, "Events, dear boy, events." Perhaps the showmen-peers should have heeded his advice. In May 1964 Longleat hosted an event starring Billy J. Kramer and the Dakotas. Upward of ten thousand people turned up, but in an echo of the Beaulieu riot of 1960, the fans stormed the stage in front of the house when the group launched into their current hit, "Little Children." Billy J., the Dakotas, and Lord Bath were forced to run inside and barricade the doors of the mansion as screaming girls hammered on the windows with umbrellas and handbags. Fans fainted and had to be carried into the house, where Lord Bath's daughter-in-law tried to administer first aid. "One girl had just recovered from a faint when Billy J. walked through the hall," she said. "She promptly fainted off again. After that I gave up."[32]

Lord Bath, who only just managed to run inside before the crowd trampled him, said it was "hell." Nevertheless, twenty thousand people watched the Rolling Stones perform at Longleat that August, when there were two hundred casualties. "So few hospital cases out of 20,000 is not a bad record," he told the press, with aristocratic insouciance.[33]

More successful was Woburn Abbey's 1967 Festival of the Flower Children, which attracted twenty-five thousand hippies, complete with bells, beads, and bangles—and a vast amount of national publicity for Woburn and the Bedfords. It went off without a hitch, apart from a bomb hoax, which the Bedfords refused to lay at the door of the flower children. "We drove over with the children," said the duchess, "and as I left the car, a girl ran up to me and offered me some flowers. I was very touched."[34] Desperate journalists did their best to find trouble. One reporter from a German magazine, unable to find any evidence of excess, suggested he might go down to the village to find some empty bottles and

Festival of the Flower Children, Woburn, 1967

other rubbish, throw it on the lawn, and photograph a suitably ap-palled duchess surveying the damage. When she refused, furious, he offered her twenty pounds. In the end, the only thing that the press could find to complain about was an incident where a group of hippies invaded a swimming pool in a neighbouring village. "After splashing about for nearly half an hour, they left quietly."[35] "While the 'flower children' gathered at Woburn at the week-end, Amersham flower people got on with the real thing—the Amer-sham Horticultural Association autumn show," declared a defiant *Buckinghamshire Examiner*.[36]

STORIES ABOUT THE behaviour of visitors are legion, although they sometimes say rather more about the owner than about his or her public. Everard Radcliffe of Rudding Park in Yorkshire used to complain that the great disadvantage of opening his house to the public was "the very special horrid smell left in the house after-wards."[37] Harry Margary, who bought Lympne Castle in Kent in 1962 and opened it a couple of years later, thought that visitors only came to Lympne to get a nice tea, and because they couldn't think of anything better to do. "Coach parties," he maintained, "are only interested in the lavatories, a first-rate cheap tea and a sit down—in that order."[38] At Kedleston in Derbyshire, Viscount Scarsdale voiced a paranoid suspicion shared by many owners: "Opening provides an obvious opportunity for potential thieves to get a lay-out of the house."[39] For the same reason, many of the Under Eleven refused to include floor plans in their guide-books, or even to allow Christopher Hussey or John Cornforth over the threshold to write up their homes for *Country Life*. There was certainly a good deal of truth in the Duke of Bedford's obser-vation, made after a few incognito visits to stately homes open to the public when he was trying to get a feel for how Woburn might operate, that "they were all doing it rather on the theory that the sooner the visitors were in the sooner they would be gone and the quicker you got the money the better and goodbye."[40]

In an age which still regarded the aristocracy with awe, even if that awe was mingled with pity and occasional contempt, a sighting of a real-life peer of the realm was something to be cherished. "I found, somewhat to my embarrassment, that one of the principal attractions of the house was myself," said Bedford, who developed a routine of making a couple of circuit tours of Woburn every day, besides doing a stint in the gift shop, signing autographs, and selling guidebooks: he found that sales went up dramatically whenever he was there.[41] Someone once told a guide at Chatsworth that they had caught a glimpse of the Duchess of Devonshire in the gardens: "She looked quite normal, really."[42] The Marquess of Bath confessed to feeling a sense of satisfaction whenever he heard someone at Longleat exclaim, "That's Lord Bath!" The public adored that, he said in 1967. "But how long it is going to last I don't know."[43]

There's no question but that the public could be trying. On the day that Woburn opened for the first time, a woman was caught cutting a piece from a brocade curtain as a souvenir, while some-one else decided they wanted something more substantial to remember Woburn by and stole the Bedfords' dog. It was never seen again. The Duchess of Devonshire received a letter of complaint about the state of the park at Chatsworth, which was free to visitors all year round. The writer was "disgusted by the animal faeces on the grass" and said the sheep droppings made it impossible for her to play ball games with her grandchildren.[44] At Wilton House the 16th Earl of Pembroke's private wing, which included its own garden and swimming pool, was occasionally invaded by tourists who always apologised for having lost their way, even as they were training their movie camera on the earl as he lazed by the pool.

Deference wasn't in it. Michael Saunders Watson was summoned by one of the Rockingham Castle guides because a visitor with a bristling moustache was demanding to know more about a particular crest on an iron-bound chest in the hall. When Saunders Watson confessed he had no idea whose crest it was, the man snapped at him, "You would get a great deal more from this house if you knew more about it."[45] Saunders Watson found out later that the irate visitor was the politician Enoch Powell.

But these were nothing compared to an encounter which the Duke of Bedford had at Woburn. It began when he received a letter from a woman which said, "Your Grace, I was sitting on the Via Veneto facing you and I opened my legs. I know you looked, so I am prepared to be your mistress." A second letter followed, demanding a meeting, and then a third, which ran, "I notice that you have not got rid of Nicole [his new wife] yet, so I will come and get rid of her myself."[46] The Bedfords laughed off the threat. At least, the duke did; his duchess was less amused. Then one day, while Woburn was open to the public and he was doing his usual stint in the souvenir kiosk, the woman suddenly appeared and grabbed him with one hand while trying to undo his trousers with the other. The police were called, and she was eventually admitted to a psychiatric hospital.

The impact of public opening was usually less dramatic than this. But it was real. One or two or six afternoons a week, a country house ceased to be a home and became public property, with guides and ropes and hundreds, even thousands of half-crown trippers strolling through the state rooms. Some owners, like the Duke of Bedford and the Duchess of Devonshire, revelled in their new role. Others maintained a tactful distance. Lord Bath hadn't lived at Longleat since 1927, and he saw no reason to move in when the house was opened to the public. The 7th Earl of Warwick split his time between Switzerland, Italy, and France, leaving the running of Warwick Castle to others. The Duke of Norfolk soared majestically above the day-to-day details of operating Arundel Castle as a tourist attraction, leaving them to his castle opening manager: "I have never taken part in any of the details of the opening of this place," he said.[47]

Most owners were stoic, resigned to changing circumstances. If they didn't exactly embrace the stately home business with the same enthusiasm as Montagu or Bedford, they accepted it as inevitable and made the best of things. Lord Lichfield, who shared Shugborough Hall with the Staffordshire County Council, which opened Shugborough on behalf of the National Trust, spoke for many when he was asked, "Do you mind the hordes descending on the house from Easter onwards?" "A bit, but not desperately," he replied. "After all, they help to keep me here."[48]

14

U MEETS NON-U

I N 1954, THE Finnish philological journal *Neuphilologische mit-teilungen* published an article by a British professor of linguistics, Alan Ross. In "Linguistic Class-Indicators in Present-Day English," Ross argued that in mid-twentieth-century Britain, most of the traditional behaviours and attributes which once set the upper classes apart from the rest of society—wealth, education, participation in public affairs—were no longer their sole preserve. There were still a few points which set them apart, but they were minor: the playing of real tennis and piquet, having one's card engraved rather than printed, not playing tennis in braces, and a dislike of modern inventions like the telephone and the cinema. Ross also held that "when drunk, gentlemen often become amorous or maudlin or vomit in public, but they never become truculent."[1] His experience of gentlemen was clearly rather limited.

Ross argued that language was now the chief means of separating the upper classes, which he abbreviated to "U," from the rest, the "non-U." The ideal U address, for example, took the form of P Q R, where P was a place name, Q a describer, and R the name of a county or its abbreviation, as in Shinwell Hall, Salop. (Although it was non-U to use place name and describer in conversation, as in "I'm going to Shinwell Hall for the weekend"; the U usage would be "I'm going to Shinwell.") In spoken language, always something of a minefield, the *a* as in "cahstle" or "bahth" was U. But it was non-U to "take" a bahth, U to "have" a bahth. The omission of the final *g*, as in "huntin', shootin', and fishin'," was once a U indicator, but it was fast disappearing. "It still survives," maintained Ross, "among a few very elderly U-speakers; among younger ones, it seems, today, to be altogether dead."[2] U speakers ate lunch in the middle of the day and dinner in the evening; non-U speakers had their dinner in the middle of the day, as did U children and U dogs. "Serviette" was non-U, as against the U "table-napkin." "Lounge" was a name given by non-U speakers to a room in their houses. U speakers might use "hall" or "dining room."

Professor Ross's article might never have had much effect outside the somewhat limited readership of *Neuphilologische mitteilungen* if his distinction between U and non-U hadn't been taken up the following year by Nancy Mitford in an article she published in the September 1955 issue of *Encounter*. "The English Aristocracy" argued that there was a definite border between the aristocracy and their close relatives, the upper middle classes, and the rest—a border which was easily recognisable "by hundreds of small but significant landmarks."[3] She proceeded to use Ross's ideas to demonstrate her argument, adding to his lists of U and non-U usage. "Phone" was non-U. "Sweet" was non-U for "pudding." "Dentures" was non-U for "false teeth," and "glasses" for "spectacles."

"I shrieked over your article about the aristocracy," wrote Nancy's sister Debo, who as the Duchess of Devonshire was about as U as it was possible to be. The article proved to be an unexpected sensation, and "U and non-U" became a public parlour game, with the phrase entering into the vocabulary of the nation as everyone, from judges on the bench to comedians on the halls, vied with each other to come up with the most amusing examples. Shakespeare's Richard II was brought in by the *Observer* to contradict Mitford's assertion that "mirror" was non-U and "looking-glass" U: "An if my word be sterling yet in England, / Let it command a mirror hither straight." To which Mitford replied, "It is probable that Richard II, like many monarchs, was non-U."[4] *Punch* devoted a whole issue to the topic, with a cover showing a spoof coat of arms and the motto "Snoblesse Oblige," and an agony column, "Aunt Nancy's Casebook," with questions like this one:

My mother forbids me to use the word "Tuesday": she says it is common.

Your mother is quite right. Tuesday is a very non-U word, indicating the day people who stay on after a Friday to Monday fail to leave.[5]

There was another flurry of interest in 1956 when Mitford's article was republished as the lead piece in a little collection called *Noblesse Oblige: An Enquiry into the Identifiable Characteristics of the English Aristocracy* (known among the Mitford sisters as "the U-book"). Other contributors included Ross, who produced a simplified version of "Linguistic Class-Indicators," and Evelyn Waugh, who declared that "impotence and sodomy are socially O.K. but birth control is flagrantly middle-class."[6] (He and his wife had seven children.)

Peter Fleming, brother of Ian, contributed a thoughtful piece on the nuancing of linguistic usage within and between social groups, and Christopher Sykes, no stranger himself to landed society, made much the same point whilst admiring the fact that one of the features of the upper classes has always been the delusion that their personal foibles were met with approval by the rest of humanity: "There are secluded lords who maintain that in gentle usage the word 'wood' has no meaning in the English language except in connection with port, bowls, and fire, and a Gloucestershire landowner believes that persons of family always refer to the wines of Bordeaux as 'clart' to rhyme with 'cart.'"[7]

The collection closed with John Betjeman's great hymn to non-U usage, "How to Get On in Society."

The notion that language still marked out the upper classes as special was an attractive one to a group that was grappling with insecurities and facing an uncertain future in a world which saw it as something of an anachronism. (The rest of the country revelled in the fun, at the same time doing its best to avoid mentioning dentures and serviettes.) Before the war it had still been possible to rise above these things. One evening in the 1920s, during Evelyn Waugh's first visit to Renishaw Hall in Derbyshire, Sir George Sitwell took his houseguests out to the terrace before dinner to enjoy the beauty of the setting sun lighting up the distant hills: "In the valley at our feet," recalled Waugh, "still half hidden in mist, lay farms, cottages, villas, the railway, the colliery and the densely teeming streets of the men who worked there. They lay in shadow; the heights beyond were golden. . . . [Sir George] turned and spoke in the wistful, nostalgic tones of a castaway, yet of a castaway who was reconciled to his solitude. 'You see,' he said, 'there is *no one* between us and the Locker-Lampsons.'"[8]

Now, though, the barbarians were at the gate, and they were impossible to ignore. Sir Giles Tanroy, one of the characters in Francis Vivian's 1947 novel, *The Threefold Cord*, spoke for many of his class when, having been forced to sell his family mansion to a brash furniture manufacturer, he burst out that "an aristocracy of birth and manners has given place to one of money and dictatorial power. . . . These people . . . have been yelping at our heels for hundreds of years—they weren't sturdy enough to bark—and now they have turfed us out of our homes, and collared our heritages."[9] When the furniture manufacturer is found in the garden of his newly acquired stately home with his head chopped off, no one is sorry, least of all Sir Giles, who is thus able to buy back his ancestral seat.

Behind all the jokes, Nancy Mitford posed some serious questions about class and status. She argued that the aristocracy—a class to which she belonged, incidentally, as the eldest daughter of the 2nd Baron Redesdale—still led landed society in the 1950s.

Everyone assumed they were impoverished, "a view carefully fostered by the lords themselves."[10] Yet in spite of death duties and frighteningly high rates of income tax, many of them were still able to run establishments with servants. They still held on to their ancestral seats and the treasures they contained. They were able to augment their income in ways which would appear shameful to the middle classes: a sense of shame was definitely non-U. Peers not only let strangers into their houses for money; "they throw themselves into the sad commerce with rapture, and compete as to who among them can draw the greatest crowds," Mitford pointed out. "It is the first topic of conversation in noble circles today, the tourists being referred to in terms of sport rather than of cash—a sweepstake on the day's run, or the bag counted after the shoot."[11]

The argument that the famous stately homes of Britain were in a much better state than their owners would have us believe was a familiar one, a consequence of the burgeoning stately homes industry. (No one gave much thought to the country houses that were not famous.) In 1958 Winston Churchill's son Randolph Churchill asked in an article for *House and Garden* "Are the Stately Homes Really in Decline?" and concluded that a combination of initiatives ranging from half-crown opening to institutional ownership by schools, government departments, and the National Trust were enabling the houses, if not their owners, to hold their own in challenging times.* Evelyn Waugh took violent exception to Nancy Mitford's claim that all was well, both privately and in print, but even Waugh was forced to admit a few years later, in his preface to the 1960 edition of *Brideshead Revisited*, that the cult of the country house meant "the ancestral seats which were our chief national artistic achievement" were not in fact doomed to decay

---

*Randolph, whose appetite for strong drink was even greater than his father's, once dressed up as Father Christmas for a children's party at Chartwell and harangued the bewildered children on the iniquities of Anthony Eden's government. Kenneth Rose, *Who's In, Who's Out* (Weidenfeld & Nicolson, 2018), 107.

and spoliation, as he had thought when writing *Brideshead* back in 1944, and that the book was therefore "a panegyric preached over an empty coffin."[12]

More interesting perhaps was the question raised by Alan Ross and Nancy Mitford about membership of an elite which was no longer elite, about who was in and who was out. When peerages were awarded for party political reasons or acts of philanthropy or success in business, what constituted belonging to the upper classes? Could *anybody* join if they had the money and the traditional accoutrements, a title and a country estate?

Professor Ross suggested that it was impossible for non-U speakers to become U: there were too many pitfalls, and all it needed was a single pronunciation for an apparent U speaker to be found out as a charlatan. And this was the point. Membership of an exclusive group necessarily involves exclusion, and assimilation into the upper reaches of British society had always been problematic, as Victorian railway kings and Vanderbilt heiresses had found out in the past. Wealth was not enough. A big house and a couple of thousand acres were not enough. Only pedigrees counted, a view applauded by those with pedigrees.

Take the Dockers. Sir Bernard and Lady Docker were one of the richest couples in Britain. Born in 1896, Sir Bernard was an old Harrovian and an immensely successful businessman, a director of the Midland Bank and chairman of the family firm, the Birmingham Small Arms Company, a vast industrial combine involved in armaments, iron and steel, machine tools, BSA motorcycles, and Daimler cars. He was knighted in 1939 for services to Westminster Hospital, where he was chair for several years. He owned a Mayfair town house, a 210-foot oceangoing motor yacht, the *Shemara*, and a 2,215-acre shooting estate at Stockbridge in Hampshire, at the heart of which was Heath House, a pleasant if undistinguished Edwardian house with an indoor heated swimming pool and a squash court.

In 1933 Docker had married a young actress, Jeanne Stuart, much against his family's wishes. His father hired private detectives to gather evidence of Ms Stuart's adultery, something they did with astonishing swiftness, and the marriage came to an abrupt end after only five months. From then until he was fifty-two Docker remained single, and just about as U as it was possible to be.

But in 1948 he met Norah Collins, and in February 1949 he married her. And Norah was non-U. Born over a Derby butcher's shop in 1906, she had worked as a dance hostess at the Café de Paris in the 1930s, where she had a number of affairs with older men, including a High Court judge and Sunny Spencer-Churchill, 9th Duke of Marlborough. After having at least one abortion she married Clement Callingham, the wealthy chairman of wine and spirit merchant Henekeys. Fifteen months after Callingham's death in July 1945, Norah married the even-wealthier Sir William Collins, the seventy-three-year-old chairman of a string of companies including Fortnum & Mason. And when Collins died after a year of marriage, leaving her a wealthy woman in her own right, she took Sir Bernard as her third husband—"Millionaire Number Three," in her own words.[13]

Lady Docker loved being in the headlines. She loved to spend money, and she loved to remind people that no matter how rich the Dockers were—and they were really very rich indeed, with a combined fortune of some £16 million—her roots were in the working class. She might wear mink and Chanel, but she deliberately allowed herself to be photographed eating fish and chips out of newspaper as she sat in the back of her Rolls-Royce. Christened "the Sensational Dockers" by the press, she and Sir Bernard threw a "nonausterity" party for two hundred show business friends at Claridge's in 1954; guests included film stars Michael Redgrave, Jane Russell, and Jack Hawkins, comedians Norman Wisdom and Benny Hill, TV personalities Gilbert Harding and Isobel, Lady

Lady Docker dances the night away

Barnett. What was a nonausterity party? asked reporters. "Some of these parties can become stuffy, but we want ours to be absolutely free from formalities," replied Norah Docker. "We hope our stage friends will come along and have fun."[14] Caviar and oysters were on the menu, washed down with magnums of champagne. Norah jived the night away in uninhibited fashion. At one point she was photographed crawling between a guest's legs while an indulgent Sir Bernard looked on.

Nonausterity characterised most features of their lives. Sir Bernard brought his wife onto the board of BSA and several of its daughter companies, which meant she could put down her expenditures on furs and pink champagne as business expenses and have the firm fund her lifestyle. In 1951 Daimler began to produce a series of yearly one-off show cars, with coachwork and interior detailing designed in part by Lady Docker herself. The first, which was covered in golden stars and gold leaf, made the cover of *Picture Post*, along with Norah. The fifth and last, a Daimler DK400 coupe, was known as the "Golden Zebra." It was fitted out in cream and gold, with an ivory dashboard cocktail cabinet, solid gold accessories, and zebra skin upholstery, which extended to the camping stools in the boot. The doors had Norah's initials engraved on them in gold. "Why zebra skin?" she was asked. "Because mink is too hot to sit on," she replied.[15]

With taste like that and Lady Docker's hunger for the limelight, there was no question of the Dockers moving in the social circles that a captain of industry like Sir Bernard might have expected. They were not invited to the right parties. The county did not ask them to stay for the weekend. They did not belong.

Norah tried not to mind. "They are not interested in me and I am not interested in their outdated pretentious rubbish," she said. "They can stuff their coronets. I've seen three balls over a pawnbroker's shop, that's reality. And as for *Burke's Peerage*, give me the *News of the World* any time."[16] Sir Bernard, who had once harboured an ambition to follow up his knighthood with a baronetcy or better, was quieter.

In other ways, though, the Dockers' lives followed a conventional pattern of weekdays in town and weekends down at Heath House, where Sir Bernard, who had previously used the place primarily as a shooting lodge, took up farming. (He won prizes for his herd of Jerseys.) They took the *Shemara* down to the South of France, where they wined and dined in Cannes and played the tables in the Casino de Monte Carlo. They thought of following the trend and buying somewhere in the Caribbean. In fact they bought Wyndways, composer Ivor Novello's house on

Montego Bay in Jamaica, for £19,000; but they never even saw it before selling up a couple of years later and buying Cottonwood, a colonial-style mansion on the beach. "I've seen ten photographs of [Cottonwood], and the place looks lovely," Norah told the press, "but I know it is difficult to judge things from photographs—for instance, the swimming pool looks huge from aerial pictures, but from the measurements we know that is only three-quarters the size of our swimming pool at Stockbridge." She then managed to slip in a reference to their enormous yacht, laughingly adding, "If we don't like the house, the *Shemara* will be there."[17]

In about 1952 the Dockers bought themselves another country house—or rather, BSA bought one for them. Glandyfi Castle, a Regency Gothic mansion in the style of John Nash built in around 1818, stands in a breathtaking setting on a hillside looking out over the Dovey estuary to the mountains of Snowdonia. Battlements and buttresses and a high octagonal tower provided a suitably picturesque composition, while inside there were some attractive imported fireplaces and old oak panelling, although it isn't clear whether these were in place when the Dockers took on Glandyfi or they formed part of a typically extravagant scheme of renovation, said to cost BSA £17,500 on top of the £12,500 purchase price.

The ostensible reason for the acquisition of Glandyfi was that BSA needed somewhere to keep their records and a meeting place for management, but just why that should require a lofty panelled hall, an octagonal Gothic library with an ornate plaster ceiling and stained glass windows, ten bedrooms, and extensive servants' accommodation, might not have been clear to the board of BSA—which is perhaps why Sir Bernard didn't tell them about it. Instead, he and Lady Docker installed a state-of-the-art kitchen and some flamboyant furnishings and used the home as a base for entertaining friends and business clients.

Both Dockers were heavy drinkers, and quite early on in their marriage they began to appear in the press for the wrong reasons, confirming Society's impression of them as non-U even before the term gained currency. In 1951, Norah publicly harangued the president of Monte Carlo's Sporting Club and Casino, Prince Jean-Louis de Faucigny-Lucinge, over the poor quality of the cabaret at a Red Cross charity ball the Dockers were attending. The prince told Sir Bernard to take his wife home, security men were called, and the evening ended with the Dockers being banned from the casino and Norah hitting a casino official in the face. That was the first of several embarrassing incidents in Monte Carlo over the years, culminating in a night when a drunken Norah climbed on the stage at the casino nightclub and used the microphone to insult Prince Rainier and his film star wife, Princess Grace—"the Irish navvy's daughter"—before ripping up a paper Monegasque flag. The Dockers were permanently barred from entering Monaco after that.

In 1953 Sir Bernard was removed from the board of the Midland Bank because of, in his words, "the character and extent of the publicity which I have been receiving of late."[18] Three years later the Dockers suffered a more serious blow to their prestige when Sir Bernard was ousted as chairman and managing director of BSA in a boardroom coup. There were a number of reasons, but they boiled down to the fact that he and his wife had been using BSA and its daughter companies as their own private fiefdom, using the outrageous Daimler show cars as their own, putting Norah's dress bills through the business, and, as Sir Bernard's successor as chairman pointed out, "failing to report to the board the purchase of a country house in Wales at a cost of £32,000."[19] Glandyfi Castle was sold a few months later. The Heath House estate went in 1966, and the couple retreated to the Channel Islands, where they propped up bars and reminisced and acted as if there were no such thing as class.

"I WANT TO be part of a swinging new England," said the 13th Duke of Bedford in 1966. "Just because I'm a duke I don't see why I should be relegated to some museum morgue."[20] True to his word, he took to wearing exuberantly frilly shirts and performing the twist on television.

He wasn't the only country house owner to welcome the sixties as a liberation from the stuffy formality of the previous decade. All over Britain, stately Tory matrons and red-faced majors did the watusi and the mashed potato at the annual hunt ball while their sons and daughters were embracing the sexual revolution down by the lake and tripping out on the terrace. As were some of their parents, of course, only a little more discreetly.

But the Duke of Bedford's "swinging new England" belonged primarily to the younger generation, as someone should perhaps have told him. In June 1966 a new nightclub opened just off Piccadilly Circus. Sibylla's, which was named after Scottish baronet's daughter Anna Sibylla Edmonstone, aimed to bring two worlds together. The opening night guest list included the Beatles, three Rolling Stones, Michael Caine and Julie Christie, David Bailey and Mary Quant. Kevin Macdonald, its twenty-eight-year-old cofounder and a great-nephew of Lord Northcliffe, described Sibylla's inclusive ethos:

> Man, I felt so deeply about class that I started this club to throw off all the old frustrations that I inherited. . . . This is Psychedelphia man, it's all happening. Can you read me? No, well I'll try and explain. You see, it's dreamland, and to enjoy it you have to be dreaming. Everyone here's in touch. . . . We've married up the hairy brigade—that's the East End kids like photographers and artists—with the smooth brigade, the debs, the aristos, the Guards officers. The result is just fantastic. It's the greatest, happiest, most swinging ball of the century.[21]

The idea that Sibylla's "smooth brigade" of debs and aristos and Guards officers could mix as social equals with artists from a different class wasn't new. In the 1950s Lady Oranmore and Browne entertained Brendan Behan and friends at Luggala; the Duchess of Devonshire dined with Francis Bacon and Lucian Freud at Ann Fleming's Westminster home; Freud was briefly married to Lady Caroline Blackwood. But things changed "between the end of the 'Chatterley' ban and the Beatles' first LP," as Philip Larkin put it.[22] There was something new in the air in the 1960s. Anthony Sampson, in his classic 1962 exploration of the ruling classes, *Anatomy of Britain*, pointed out that "interacting with the traditional Society of old families is the new Society of the self-made rich, the entertainers, the communicators, and the urban hurly-burly sometimes called café society."[23]

The interaction didn't mean an end to social barriers. New and old Society were never so united as when they were keeping out the hoi polloi, and snobbery and inverted snobbery fought each other for supremacy at social gatherings. Jonathan Aitken, whose 1967 survey of Swinging Londoners, *The Young Meteors*, swung between adulation and contempt, wrote that "if they come together at all, scions of ancient families consort self-consciously with former barrow boys, their conversation often turning into a competition as to who can out-condescend whom."[24]

Aitken made that remark in the course of a bitchy description of Patrick Lichfield, 5th Earl of Lichfield, old Harrovian, ex-Guards officer, cousin to the Queen, and a Society photographer whose name was mentioned in the same breath as David Bailey, Terence Donovan, and Antony Armstrong-Jones. Aitken poured scorn on Lichfield's attempts to move between the two worlds, one minute a handsome, trend-setting photographer, "equipped with an ample supply of Mayfair-boy-makes-good charm, dressing with the flashiness of the Carnaby Street extremist, speeding round the metropolis in Aston Martin, motor-bike or Mini-Moke"; the next, a country squire lording it over his Staffordshire estates, chairing local charities, always "acutely conscious of the trust and duty he owes to his family to keep up the respected good name amongst royal and titled friends."[25]

Lichfield took up photography—that quintessentially sixties art form—when he came out of the Guards in 1962, entering "a world I barely knew existed."[26] An aristocratic relative told him at the time that his choice of career was far worse than being an interior decorator and only marginally better than hairdressing. It turned out to be considerably more prestigious: his portraits included just about every member of the royal family (the fact that he was cousin to the Queen did him no harm); a nude Marsha Hunt, star of the rock musical *Hair*; Joanna Lumley, whom he photographed in a bathing costume in the Serpentine in March, "a pose which demonstrated her professional fortitude if nothing else"; and the iconic 1967 "Swinging London" portrait of fifteen Beautiful People, including David Hockney, the Kinks' Dave Davies, designer David Hicks, Roman Polanski, actress Susannah York, and, bizarrely, Conservative politician Reginald Maudling and the assistant bishop of Exeter.

But there was no getting round the fact that as well as being a fixture in Swinging London, Lichfield was a landed proprietor and a peer of the realm. At the end of the war his grandfather, the 4th Earl of Lichfield, owned three country houses, all in Staffordshire: Ranton Abbey, Orgreave Hall, and Shugborough Hall. Ranton was a ruin, having been gutted by fire during the war, and the earl sold off the Orgreave estate in 1953. But that still left Shugborough, which had been in the family since 1624 and which was by general agreement one of the grandest country houses in Britain, heavily remodelled by Samuel Wyatt in the 1790s and early 1800s and set in an astonishing classical landscape filled with temples and monuments.

Born in 1883, the 4th Earl kept up Shugborough on an Edwardian scale. In the 1930s there were thirty-eight indoor staff, a number that didn't decline appreciably during the war. Shugborough had its own railway station; when that closed in 1939 the earl used to pull the communication cord at just the right moment, hand the guard a five-pound note to cover the fine, clamber down from his carriage, and stroll across the park to the house. (Years later, when he was late for a tenants' ball, Patrick Lichfield tried the same trick only to disappear into a six-foot snowdrift.) The 4th Earl's eccentricities became more pronounced in the 1950s, and he took to jotting down on slips of paper things that he wanted to remember. One of the last things he did was to make a note to himself to reprimand the staff: "Beans cold. Butler farted."[27]

He took all the right steps to secure the future of Shugborough, making over a large portion of the estate to his son, Patrick Lichfield's father. But as so often happened to landed families in the 1950s, Death refused to play the game, and Patrick's father, Viscount Anson, died suddenly from a beesting in 1958, aged only forty-four. The 4th Earl mothballed Shugborough and decamped to Bournemouth, but he followed his son to the grave two years later, leaving twenty-one-year-old Patrick Lichfield the earldom, the house and its contents, and a double set of death duties he couldn't pay.

The solution, brokered by his grandmother, was to hand over Shugborough to the Treasury and hence to the National Trust. Lichfield and his sister Liz leased apartments in the house and brought in fashionable young designer David Mlinaric to decorate them in browns and fawns, while the trust used John Fowler for "its" parts of the house. The pair maintained that family presence which the trust was beginning to value as a selling point with visitors, and when his globe-trotting work for *Vogue* and other magazines allowed, Lichfield would drive up to Staffordshire on weekends.

"I regret nothing about Shugborough's old way of life," he said in 1968. "I much prefer my own."[28] And of course that old way of life wasn't exactly lost, since he still had the use of the south wing. "I do find . . . that on weekends I mentally change as I drive up the M1 from being a photographer to being a landowner. One has to, because one has to see things rather differently."[29] A vérité television documentary from the early 1970s shows him presiding, ruffed and frilled, over dinner for twelve at Shugborough while his butler, Arthur Brearley, hovers at his shoulder in white tie and tails, in command of a small army of footmen. This was not how most people in Britain lived. The guests included Britt Ekland, Joanna Lumley, and a long-haired and gold-jacketed David Bailey, who relentlessly patronised his dinner companions, determined to emphasise the social gulf between him, a working-class boy from Leytonstone, and his aristocratic host. The dinner party had an edge, a slight uneasiness that showed itself whenever the two worlds collided.

"THE MODERN RICH man will have a house in London and one or two in the country," declared the Duke of Bedford in 1971. "He will have a flat in Paris; one in Rome; a place in the mountains; another on the sea. He will need a skiing place; he will need a yacht or two—otherwise how can he show his face?"[30]

If Bedford had his tongue firmly in his cheek, there was still truth in his characterisation of the new rich—the jet set, as postwar society had learned to call them. There was a restless urgency to high life for these globe-trotters: skiing in Gstaad one moment, powerboat racing in Miami the next; twisting the night away at Manhattan's Peppermint Lounge before hopping on a plane to lose at baccarat in the Casino de Monte Carlo. Being one of the Beautiful People was an exhausting business.

Anglo-American Olive Baillie, who in the 1950s and 1960s still maintained a staff of fifty at her country house, Leeds Castle in Kent, behaved as if the war and austerity Britain had never happened. (As though the twentieth century had never happened, come to that.) She spent the spring and early summer in England, staying during the week at Lowndes House, her London mansion, and travelling down to Leeds Castle each weekend. Late July, August, and early September were spent in the South of France, where she had a villa in Cap Ferrat, and where she passed her time shopping, drinking, gambling in the casinos of Monte Carlo, and entertaining friends like David Niven and Noël Coward. Then it was back to Lowndes House and Leeds Castle for the autumn before a three-month stay at Harbourside, the house on Paradise Island in the Bahamas which had been decorated for her by Stéphane Boudin. She took her entourage with her—friends and hangers-on, relations, her English butler Borrett. Two Black footmen were recruited for the duration of her stay. She never appeared until lunch. Afternoons were given over to canasta and bridge, and evenings to entertaining or being entertained in the homes of other members of the transient community of Brits and Americans who gathered in this particular corner of the Bahamas. She returned to Leeds in the spring, an annual progress on a scale to rival those of Edwardian industrialists and medieval magnates. Those who thought the country house–owning classes were on the verge of extinction clearly didn't know Olive Baillie.

IN 1964, *VOGUE* carried a long feature on twenty-six-year-old Alistair Vane-Tempest-Stewart, 9th Marquess of Londonderry, and the twenty-three-year-old marchioness, Nico. Alistair and Nico were the embodiment of Cool Britannia, decades before the term was invented. The marquess, grandson of the great society hostess Edith, Lady Londonderry, was photographed in the drawing room at his colossal family seat, Wynyard Park in County Durham, wearing dark glasses, dressed all in black corduroy, and lounging on a sofa. The Beatles' latest album, *With the Beatles*, was prominently displayed on a table in the foreground. Nico, sultry and wearing heavy Biba-esque eyeshadow, posed beneath a Thomas Lawrence portrait of her husband's ancestor, the 3rd Marquess.

The *Vogue* article made much of the ways in which this glamorous young couple ignored the boundaries between the traditional country house world and the youth culture of the Swinging Sixties. While they were careful to fulfil their obligations to the county, opening fetes and holding traditional pheasant shoots, they happily brought together country gentry and fashionable figures from London. "Last year," said *Vogue*, "a celebrated jazz musician missed all his birds but bagged a very fair brace of colonels."[31] The Londonderrys' Hampstead town house was transformed by Nico and David Hicks. Between them, gushed the *Vogue* article in a cultural reference that would have surprised Le Corbusier, the designer and the noblewoman had produced "a bright civility of design and pattern that makes the intricate old house a machine for modern living."[32] Photos showed paisley curtains and wallpaper; the marchioness played with her two little daughters, Cosima and Sophia, on a tile-patterned rug loomed by Hicks. There were typically Hicksian juxtapositions between old and new: a huge abstract painting by Kenneth Noland hung over a Louis XV chest signed by the king's *ébéniste*, Pierre Macret.

Nico drove an Alfa Romeo which was fitted with a gramophone. (Not as unusual as it sounds: Keith Richards's Bentley had a little Philips car record player which took 45s. But then the suspension on a Bentley was rather smoother than that on an Alfa Romeo.) She and Alastair were seen at the newest nightclubs, at film premieres. With a penchant for popular culture which seems less odd today than it did half a century ago, they made no secret of the fact that they were addicted to Hammer horror movies. And Nico in particular loved pop music: "A surprised Hampstead record shop, that usually does brisk business in Shostakovich, has a standing order to deliver to her the newcomers to the British and American Top Twenties every week: she thinks of backing a pop group from across the river, and auditions them in the drawing room."[33]

She also loved musicians. Quite early on in her marriage, she had an affair with Robin Douglas-Home, jazz pianist and nephew of British prime minister Sir Alec Douglas-Home, who would embark on an affair with Princess Margaret before committing suicide in 1968.

One evening in January 1965, the marquess's sister Annabel, whose husband, Mark Birley, had just named a nightclub after her, was at home watching *Top of the Pops* on television when she was so struck by the good looks of one of the performers that she telephoned Nico and told her sister-in-law to watch the programme. The man's name was Georgie Fame, and with his band, the Blue Flames, he had just reached number one in the British charts for the first time with a song called "Yeh Yeh."

Nico was just as intrigued as Annabel. A few years later, when the Blue Flames were touring in the north of England on a double bill with the Supremes, she and Alastair invited them all to stay at Wynyard, where she began an affair with Georgie Fame that ended in a humiliating series of court cases. In 1970 the Marquess of Londonderry divorced her, citing her adultery with the pop singer, and demanded that blood tests be carried out on the couple's baby son and heir presumptive to the Londonderry titles. They proved that the marquess wasn't the biological father.*

The symbiotic fascination which the county set and Swinging London had for each other, and which both felt for those who were a little dangerous, those whose lives were lived on the edge of things, could lead to some curious social occasions. In 1971 septuagenarian Frances Partridge, who in her Bloomsbury youth had been no stranger to curious social occasions, was staying for the weekend with the Marquess and Marchioness of Bath at their home, the "romantically lovely" Job's Mill near Warminster.[34] She found the Baths nice but boring, which is perhaps why the marchioness's daughter Georgia took her out to dine with a neighbour on Saturday night. He was Michael Caborn-Waterfield, known as "Dandy Kim," a charming crook who had been involved in gunrunning for Batista in 1950s Cuba, who had spent time in a French jail for theft, and who was friendly with the Kray twins. Caborn-Waterfield had bought the early nineteenth-century

---

* Nico married Georgie Fame in 1972 and the couple had a second son together.

Sedgehill Grange in Wiltshire in the early 1960s and led a double life, riding to hounds with the South and West Wilts when he was in the country and haunting the Chelsea social scene when he was in town, when his party guests might include Lucky Lucan and, before the Profumo affair hit the headlines in 1963, the society osteopath Stephen Ward and his young friends Mandy Rice-Davies and Christine Keeler. When Frances met him, he had just opened a sex shop near Marble Arch, called after a former girlfriend who was working as the manager of the Sedgehill estate. Her name was Ann Summers.

There were seventeen for dinner that night. Many of them, according to Frances Partridge, were attractive girls in hot pants. There were also a gay actor and his boyfriend, who laughed so loudly and incessantly that she was sure he was stoned. And there was a collection of the not-quite-famous and not-quite-aristocratic, including Marjorie Portman, the aunt of Viscount Portman and the mother of society hostess Synove Portman; Gerard Campbell, the son of the director of the Arts Council; and Georgia and Frances. The evening wasn't a success. Sedgehill was practically devoid of furniture, pictures, and books; there were a log fire and some huge Labradors in one room, and a table with two long benches in another. "A procession of servants brought in a not very good dinner and worse wine."[35] Frances was placed next to her host, but he had no conversation and kept jumping up and rushing out of the room for no apparent reason. "It was strange, but not quite strange enough to be interesting" was Frances's verdict on the evening.[36]

Each world saw the other as glamorous. Sampson talked in *Anatomy of Britain* of the "aristocratic embrace," in which noblemen and women were "hugging angry radicals, poets, or working-class radicals into their cosy world."[37] That became more pronounced as the sixties wore on. When Gavin and Lady Irene Astor moved into Hever Castle in 1964, the press noted in astonishment that their three young daughters had foot-high photographs of the Beatles on their bedroom doors. Houseguests at Chatsworth would sit down to watch the Fab Four on television. On one such occasion the Duke of Devonshire was surprised to hear the Earl of Sefton exclaim, "Nobody has ever accused me of being a bugger, but I do think the third boy from the left is rather fetching."[38] Cecil Beaton ran into Mick Jagger, Brian Jones, and Keith Richards in the lobby of a Marrakesh hotel in 1967; they were there on holiday with Jones's girlfriend, Anita Pallenberg, and the art dealer Robert Fraser, a.k.a. "Groovy Bob." Beaton fell hopelessly for Jagger, and his many subsequent photographs of the singer drip with homoerotic yearning. "His skin is chicken-breast white," the photographer confided to his diary. "He is beautiful and ugly, feminine and masculine." Jagger responded to the attention by urging him to take LSD: "It would mean so much to you; you'd never forget the colours."[39]

"The Beatles are beat. The Stones are hip. A world of difference separates the two," wrote cultural commentator Charles Hamblett in 1966, going on to stretch a point by announcing that it was the difference between Sartre and Genet, Cocteau and Cellini (what?), Dalí and Francis Bacon.[40] But Hamblett, who was attempting to analyse the Stones' celebrity, was quite right to say that "people who a few months ago were asking 'Would you let your daughter marry a Rolling Stone?' would now gladly forfeit a weekend of golf to have Mick Jagger at Penelope's coming-out dance—even at the risk of inducing her nineteenth nervous breakdown."[41] Pop stars were celebrities, they were dangerous, and they were desirable.

When the country house set invited bohemia into their homes in the 1950s, it was as pets, performing monkeys, and bohemia was happy to perform as long as there was free food and drink. Now these new bohemians had become essential fashion accessories. Photographer Tony Sanchez, who used to buy Keith Richards's drugs for him, could have been talking about any number of sixties rock stars when he said of Brian Jones and Anita Pallenberg that they were "the reigning Beautiful Couple of Europe and they took full advantage of the power they possessed over the young dukes, lords and other highborn friends and admirers who flocked to pay homage."[42] A house party without a Beatle or a Rolling Stone was no party at all.

In some cases, the cultural crossover went much further as pop stars and the landed classes became friends and lovers. Lord Montagu of Beaulieu got stoned with the Stones. Alice Ormsby-Gore, sixteen-year-old daughter of the 5th Baron Harlech, moved into Hurtwood Edge with Eric Clapton for a time, although the relationship was a stormy one, and she would decamp to Glyn Cywarch, her father's Jacobean manor house in North Wales. Clapton later said that this aristocratic milieu wasn't for him, although the reasons he gave were not what one might expect. "You'd go up to stay at the house [Glyn Cywarch]," he wrote in his autobiography, "and the whole place would be full of people who just seemed to sit around all day smoking dope." His reluctance to follow Alice to Wales may also have been affected by the fact that at the time he was sleeping with Paula Boyd and desperately courting Paula's sister Pattie. The 5th Earl of Gainsborough's daughter, Lady Maria Noel, married The Who's sound engineer, Bob Pridden, in 1971. The wedding, announced in the *Times*, took place in the private family chapel at Exton Park, the Gainsboroughs' Rutland estate, with a reception afterwards in the mansion.

THE ROCK AND roll party to end them all took place at Luggala in 1966. Just as Oonagh Oranmore and Browne had watched worlds collide in the 1950s when she brought the Anglo-Irish aristocracy together with the likes of Brendan Behan, Lucian Freud, and Cyril Connolly, so in 1966 she repeated the experiment with a different cast at the twenty-first birthday party she held for her son

Tara. It took place on the grounds in a marquee which had been decorated by David Mlinaric, one of the invitees, and Irish high society was there in force, actors and artists and aristocrats. There were traditional touches to the evening's entertainment, too: in a nod to feudal times, Oonagh's estate manager made a speech on behalf of the estate workers.

In other ways Tara Browne's party was not so traditional. The band was his favourite, the Lovin' Spoonful, then riding high in the charts on both sides of the Atlantic with hits like "Do You Believe in Magic" and "Daydream." The band's drummer, Joe Butler, remembered being overawed by his first sight of Luggala's grandeur, although he relaxed a little when Tara himself met them at the door with some cannabis and a pipe for each of them. Guests from Tara's London set included the antique dealer Christopher Gibbs, Mick Jagger and his girlfriend Chrissie Shrimpton, Brian Jones and Anita Pallenberg. Paul McCartney, who took his first LSD trip with Tara, had to send his apologies—the Beatles were stuck at Abbey Road recording *Revolver*. But Paul's brother Mike McCartney was there, and John Paul Getty Jr., and boutique owner Rupert Lycett Green with his pregnant wife, Candida, daughter of John Betjeman. Brian Jones brought his sitar. Someone else brought LSD. Joe Butler made love in a field to a girl he'd just met, both of them high as kites. "Then we rode on horseback to some other castle to have breakfast or lunch. . . . We saw two rainbows together at Luggala."[43]

Tara, his wife Nicki, Brian, and Anita all dropped acid. Nicki recalled that she and Anita got it into their heads that Mick Jagger was the devil, so they locked him in a courtyard at the back of the house and fled into the woods, clutching walkie-talkies which had been a birthday present to Tara. "A dangerous number of irresponsible, young people in the grandeur of this old castle in the middle of the Irish countryside," recalled the Spoonful's John Sebastian. "It was extraordinary."[44]

Eight months later, just after midnight on December 18, 1966, Tara Browne drove his Lotus Elan at speed into a parked van in South Kensington. He was pronounced dead two hours later. "We thought we were indestructible," said Anita Pallenberg, who gave Tara's name to a short-lived son she had with Jones. "But then Tara died [and] the Sixties weren't the Sixties anymore."[45]

15

ALMOST A FAIRY STORY

I T RAINED, BUT no one let that spoil the day. The bride looked stunning in white lace appliqued on white tulle, with a veil held in place by a circlet of orange blossoms. Her young bridesmaids—all eight of them—behaved themselves surprisingly well in the packed church, and the service was kept commendably brief, with no mass—the groom didn't share his bride's Catholic faith. After-wards, everyone piled into their cars and decamped to the reception at Faircourt, the bride's parents' Sussex country house, where they milled around admiring the art on the walls and the wedding presents on the tables until finally, the speeches over, the newly-weds set off for a honeymoon in Rome.

It was March 20, 1954. The bride was a bewitchingly beautiful twenty-year-old, Camilla Grinling; her groom, nine years older, was an inventor and entrepreneur from Bristol, Jeremy Fry. For a few years Jeremy and Camilla Fry were the golden couple of their time, at the heart of a social set which included industrialists, so-cialites, and royalty and which centred on the home they bought together on the outskirts of Bath, Widcombe Manor, a house as bewitchingly beautiful as Camilla. A number of the young friends who were there to witness their marriage that day—best man Peter Saunders, usher Andy Garnett, guests Michael and Isabel Briggs—would also buy themselves country houses around Bath,

Jeremy and Camilla Fry, 1954

moving in and out of each other's lives in a dance to the music of time. They were perfect examples of a different kind of country house owner who came to prominence in the 1950s—ambitious, entrepreneurial, not tied to the land and its traditions but revelling in their acquaintance with the past and in command of the future.

THE FRYS AND their friends came from a privileged world where country house life was taken for granted. Andy Garnett went to Eton (apparently the only boy ever to have converted to Catholicism while there). Jeremy Fry and Peter Saunders met at Gordonstoun. Camilla's parents had made a habit of buying, restoring, and selling picturesque Sussex mansions since well before the war, so that by the time of her marriage Camilla had already lived in three or four, including Faircourt and a beautiful Jacobean house outside Tunbridge Wells, Haremere Hall. Jeremy Fry was born at

Grove House near Bristol, not exactly a country house but certainly a substantial Georgian villa. Isabel Briggs, then a literary agent but now better known as the novelist Isabel Colegate, grew up at her father's family home, the early eighteenth-century Redbourne Hall in Lincolnshire, and then with her mother's family at Hovingham Hall in Yorkshire. Andy Garnett spent school holidays with one of his mother's friends, the Countess of Shrewsbury, at the Jacobean Ingestre Hall in Staffordshire. Only the Jewish and German Peter Saunders had a more complicated past: his father, a well-known equestrian, had brought the family to England in the early 1930s.

But none of the group was traditional gentry. They were all raised to be part of a world where people had jobs and carved out careers and made money of their own. Andy Garnett's mother, a widow, ran a successful home-decorating shop near Harrods. (She was almost overcome with excitement one day when the Queen came in to discuss wallpapers.) Jeremy Fry came from a dynasty of Quaker chocolate manufacturers; it was J. S. Fry & Sons who made the first solid chocolate bar in 1847 and the chocolate Easter egg in 1873. The family had merged with Cadbury's after the First World War, but Jeremy's father served as chair of the firm from 1924 until his death in 1952.

As a circle of friends, the Frys, the Briggses, Garnett, and Saunders were all intent on making their way in the 1950s. The fact that they all ended up living in country houses of their own suggests not only that they succeeded but also that the acquisition of a country house and the lifestyle that went with it was still seen as a potent symbol of that success. Even better, with demolitions having reached their peak and the estate market in free fall, country houses were cheaper to buy in real terms than at any time in their history—an attractive proposition for monied but business-minded young people.

Widcombe Manor, built in the late seventeenth century and given an attractively baroque facade in the 1720s, had been on the market for three years when Jeremy and Camilla Fry bought it in 1955. It had belonged to Horace Annesley Vachell, a prolific novelist and playwright whose works are now largely forgotten, with good reason. Vachell put "the Golden House," as he called the thirteen-bedroomed manor, on the market at the end of 1952, when he was in his late eighties, saying that staff difficulties and increasing taxation were forcing him to sell. But in spite of interest from American buyers, who were attracted by agents' unfounded claims that Widcombe was designed by Inigo Jones, there were no takers, and Vachell took up residence in a converted coach house while the main house was mothballed.

Vachell died in January 1955, and soon afterwards the Golden House finally found new owners in the Frys. It was tired, and guests formed working parties on weekends, Camilla sewing curtains, Jeremy holding up the drawing room floor with jack posts while he replaced a sagging beam, and friends clearing the weeds in the garden with a flamethrower.

Jeremy Fry wanted more than a fine historic house. After the war, he and his brother David had acquired a small engineering workshop in Bristol called Rotork, and in 1952 he steered Rotork towards the production of motorised valve actuators, mechanisms for automatically opening and closing valves used in pipelines, refineries, power plants, and a host of other industrial contexts. Rotork began to prosper, and in 1957 Fry decided to move the Rotork Engineering Company Ltd workshop and its twelve staff to Widcombe Manor.

Two years later, he recruited his old friend Andy Garnett as foreign sales director, and shortly after that Michael Briggs, who had a commercial background in the City, joined Rotork, becoming its managing director. Garnett, who led a hectic social life, showed no signs of settling down, but in 1961 Michael Briggs bought Midford Castle, a fifteen-minute drive from Bath.

The hills and valleys around Bath are peppered with architectural oddities, most of them put up by bored Georgians who were tired of taking the waters, but Midford is both the oddest and the most attractive, a bizarre little make-believe castle consisting of a cluster of battlemented turrets perched on a platform, with a subterranean labyrinth of offices and stables and passageways beneath it. It was based on a 1774 design by John Carter for "A Gothic Mansion to be Erected on an Eminence that Commands an Extensive Prospect," and it was said locally to be an architectural interpretation of the ace of clubs, commemorating a spectacular win at cards by its owner, Henry Disney Roebuck. The story "may be true," wrote Christopher Hussey in 1944, before going on to debunk it so comprehensively that he confessed he was worried at being such "a pedantic spoilsport."[1] That doesn't matter. The oddly shaped interiors were filled with spidery rococo plasterwork, and the castle came with its own rustic hermitage, a Gothic conservatory, a chapel, and a ruined priory lurking in the woods, folly piled upon delicious folly.

By 1961 Midford Castle had been on the market for several years, at an asking price of £4,000 with six acres. Most of the land had been sold off separately. The current occupant was a local hairdresser who was, Isabel Briggs recalled, "in the course of putting up some fairly amazing flock wallpaper and had picked out the plasterwork in pastel shades, like a wedding cake."[2] The Briggses bought the castle, restored it, retrieved some of the surrounding land, and lived there for nearly fifty years while Michael combined his work for Jeremy Fry with leading the emerging preservation movement in Bath and Isabel wrote her brilliant novels of country house life. "I am not at the centre of such life," she said. "It is much easier to see things if you are on the periphery, but I do know the smells and the sounds."[3] Their rescue of Midford Castle reminds one of another motive for buying an old country house at a time of crisis in the market, a growing feeling in the 1960s: a happily altruistic desire to preserve something of the past before it vanishes.

And then there was the sheer romance of history. In 1957, Fry's best man Peter Saunders married Didi Potter, an enterprising

American he'd met on a Swiss ski slope, and the couple worked hard together to develop a business Saunders had set up in Aberdeen after the war. Peter Saunders Tweeds was a made-to-measure tweed and knitwear firm which operated by mail order, initially from an old coach house using an even older handloom. The firm's typical client, Saunders said later, was "a special kind of Englishwoman: one who loves English country, and English country colours; one who prefers the gentler, more timeless fashions." One newspaper put it less kindly but more accurately: Peter Saunders Tweeds produced "tailored clothes for the not so young, not so modern, not so perfectly shaped middle-class woman."[4]

The business did well. It expanded steadily, and in 1959, persuaded by Didi that they should move their operations closer to London, Peter began to hunt for a country house, someplace which could accommodate both their young family and their business. Their aim, he said, was to marry the old with the new, to let a modern, efficient, twentieth-century business support an otherwise unsustainable historic house, rather as Fry was doing at Widcombe.

On a motoring holiday in the Cotswolds in the summer of 1959 the Saunderses found Easton Grey, a late eighteenth-century house in an absurdly attractive setting overlooking the long valley of the Avon. There was a "To Be Sold" sign. "Anyone who loves old English manors will understand how we felt," wrote Saunders. "It was so empty. And somehow, it had the feel of a house that has been empty for a long time. It was a little sad—and quite astonishingly beautiful. *A sleeping beauty.*"[5] They wandered round the deserted house, peering in the windows. There was a stable block with twenty loose boxes (like his father, Saunders was a keen horseman) and a courtyard with all the usual domestic offices. This was what clinched it for them. "I like to think I had a glimpse, even then, of the changes that were to come. All that cobweb-y emptiness, lit only by gaslight, was to be transformed into modern offices, a Peter Saunders boutique, with oil-fired central heating throughout. It was to be filled with employees."[6] And there would be a coat of arms over the door—not their own, but one which celebrated their commercial success in the form of a recently acquired royal warrant: "By appointment to His Royal Highness, the Duke of Edinburgh, Makers of Peter Saunders Tweeds."

The Saunderses took to life in the English country house with gusto, perhaps because neither *was* English. They rode with the Beaufort Hunt, entertained, and researched the history of Easton Grey, which stretched back to a mention in the Domesday Book. They were enchanted to find that in the fourteenth century the rent for the manor consisted of agreeing to "keep one of the king's falcons until the time of flight"; intrigued to learn that around the turn of the century, when it belonged to the sister-in-law of Prime Minister H. H. Asquith, it was a regular rendezvous for fashionable Society; delighted to discover that in the 1920s the Prince of Wales, later Edward VIII, rented it when hunting with the Beaufort.

They drove about with their three children and two dogs in a pony and trap, like a Victorian country squire and his family. And they lovingly restored the house, mixing old and new. Eighteenth-century Chinese wallpaper and Georgian furniture sat side by side with modern paintings and sculptures. Tom Parr decorated their drawing room, covering the walls in a bright yellow faux-Regency stripe; David Hicks designed their bathrooms, Didi's an opulent boudoir and Peter's a combined study/dressing room with bath. "Both are done in clear, modern, brilliant colour schemes." There was a swimming pool, and an orangery that functioned as changing rooms, and, in keeping with the times, a "bar-cum-barbecue."[7]

Eventually the Saunderses opened Easton Grey to the public as an element in their Peter Saunders Boutique, along with courtyard showrooms, a restaurant, and a "bargain bazaar": "While your

Didi Saunders in her Hicks-designed bathroom at Easton Grey

escort is free to relax with a cup of tea or coffee and the daily papers (or he can browse through the new men's collection) you are at liberty to wander unhurried through the spacious showrooms and try on your choice of classical clothes in comfort and at your leisure. In fact, why don't you both make a day of discovering Easton Grey and the Peter Saunders style for living?"[8]

Crass commercialism? It pales beside the pop concerts and adventure playgrounds and safari parks that were springing up in the grounds of stately homes all over Britain at the time. The Saunderses managed to set up their business in a country house and make that business support a way of life which would otherwise have been difficult, if not impossible. The old house, the quiet gardens, the Avon meandering by, belonged not to the past, thought Peter, nor to the present, nor to the future, but to all three. Their discovery of it, he said, was "almost a fairy story."[9]

THE FOURTH MEMBER of the group, Andy Garnett, left it late to find his country house—his English country house, anyway. In the early 1960s he went halves with Michael and Isabel Briggs on a ruined farmhouse at Castellina in the Tuscan hills. That was for holidays: the rest of the time he lived out of suitcases or in a succession of apartments in London and Paris.

Then in the summer of 1967, when he was thirty-seven, Garnett married twenty-three-year-old Irish journalist Polly Devlin. They had a civil ceremony in England, followed by a "a marvellous magical party" at Midford Castle; then they went off to Castellina for a second ceremony in the little oratory there.[10] Seamus Heaney, Polly's brother-in-law, gave the bride away, and Michael Briggs was best man. After the honeymoon the couple lived for a time in New York, where Polly wrote for *Vogue* and Andy set up Rotork's American sales office. Two years later they were back, Polly was expecting their first child, and they were living in a flat in Bath while looking for a place in the country. "I dreamed of an eighteenth-century farmhouse with a few acres of land," said Garnett.[11]

What he found was something rather more. Bradley Court in Gloucestershire dates from the middle of the sixteenth century, when it was built for members of the Berkeley family of Berkeley Castle, seven miles to the northwest. By the early 1700s, when a bird's-eye view by Jan Kip appeared in Sir Robert Atkyns's *Ancient and Present State of Gloucestershire*, it belonged to a cloth merchant named Thomas Dawes, who laid out the formal gardens. Atkyns described Dawes as "the present owner of the Manor of Bradley, where he has a large, ancient seat and a great estate adjoining it which he has gained by his own industry and let off his employment because he knew he had enough."[12] In the 1780s or 1790s a two-storey wing was added to the mansion, creating a fourteen-foot-high drawing room with a bedroom above.

And apart from the usual Victorian tinkering with domestic offices, that was pretty much that. The house changed hands frequently in the twentieth century, with successive owners installing mains water and electricity, oil-fired central heating, bathrooms, and all the other necessities of modern life; but no one did anything much to damage Bradley's intrinsic charm.

The Garnetts came across Bradley Court between Christmas and New Year of 1970. The then owner had panicked when permission was given for a caravan park in the field opposite, and he was offering the house and nine acres at a giveaway price. It was bigger, more unusual, and more spectacular than what they had been looking for, but it was in commuting distance of Bath, and the M4 motorway was about to open, giving them better access to London. Ten days after viewing the house they exchanged contracts, without even waiting for a survey, and they moved in immediately. Polly redecorated in a late-sixties taste which her mother-in-law found hard to take. The Garnetts' bedroom was given dark brown wallpaper with a gold pattern, "a bit like the inside of a box of expensive chocolates," said Andy. When his mother came to stay after the birth of their first child, she took one look at the room and went out, whispering to the nurse, "I can imagine your feelings if you see a baby being tortured or abused. Well, you can imagine my feelings after seeing the way this handsome room has been desecrated. . . . I'm not sure I can face going back into it."[13]

The Garnetts quickly established a circle of friends. There were the Briggses down in Somerset, and Peter and Didi Saunders lived nearby at Easton Grey: Andy was godfather to one of their children. The irascible and sensitive travel writer Bruce Chatwin lived in the next village with his wife, Elizabeth. Chatwin got on all right with the Garnetts, but he didn't like Saunders, sneering at his "beastly collection of modern pictures" and his house "tarted up by David Hicks."[14]

James and Alvilde Lees-Milne lived ten minutes from Bradley Court at Alderley Grange, on the Duke of Beaufort's Badminton estate; and the Garnetts lunched with them every few months. A couple of miles away, Texan architect and antique dealer Bob

Parsons was just taking on the tenancy and restoration of Newark Park, a Tudor hunting lodge in Georgian costume in a spectacular setting which the National Trust had acquired in 1949 without any clear idea of what to do with it.

WITHIN A FRAMEWORK which was quite rigorously defined by wealth and social prestige, there was an overlap between the business worlds of the Garnetts, the Saunderses, the Frys, and the Briggses, and the more traditional gentry and aristocratic networks. Peter and Didi Saunders were on the fringes of ducal society in Gloucestershire through their possession of Easton Grey and their enthusiasm for the Beaufort Hunt. The Garnetts were friendly with art dealer David Somerset, heir to dukedom of Beaufort, and his wife, Caroline, daughter of the 6th Marquess of Bath, who lived at the Dower House on the duke's fifty-two-thousand-acre Badminton estate. So was James Lees-Milne, who loved a lord. One evening in 1972, while the Somersets and Jeremy Fry were dining with him, the talk turned to drugs, and Caroline Somerset described an occasion when she and her husband smoked a joint each. It had no effect on her, she recalled, except that when David said, "Take off all your clothes," she did. Then he was sick.[15]

Cecil Beaton drifted in and out of the circle throughout the 1960s, spending a weekend with the Somersets, having lunch with the Frys. So did Frances Partridge, who liked Jeremy and Camilla Fry—"both had a good deal of charm"—and enjoyed weekends at Alderley with the Lees-Milnes, although to begin with, she didn't really like their corner of the Cotswolds.[16] "It's too sad and full of superstitions and ghost stories," she wrote after a visit in January 1967. "Jim told me Lord Methuen [artist Paul Methuen, owner of Corsham Court in Wiltshire] was in constant communication with his dead wife."[17] But there were interesting fellow guests to entertain her. She was amused when James Pope-Hennessy, whom she first noticed on the train down from London trying to pick up a handsome guardsman, suddenly declared at dinner that class was the root of all evil and it was high time Britain got rid of the royal family. Lees-Milne was so appalled that he stormed off to bed. "Jim minds so terribly about all kinds of traditions being kept up," explained Alvilde.[18] By the time of Frances's next visit to the Lees-Milnes a few years later, she had warmed towards "the beauty of grey stone and green countryside," perhaps because this time she was there in June rather than in the depths of winter. And it felt as though a way of life which was supposed to have disappeared half a lifetime ago was alive and well at Alderley. "Tea on the lawn as in a past age," she wrote, "silver kettles, swooping white doves . . . sweet, drowsy bumblebee weather."[19]

NOBLE FAMILIES AND hazy historic Cotswolds summers were attractive. And let no one claim that the people who moved in these circles were immune to the glamour. But down in Bath, Jeremy and Camilla Fry had something more. They had royalty.

The royal connection began in a roundabout way with Andy Garnett, who, in his last year at Eton, became friendly with a boy who was recovering from an attack of polio—Antony Armstrong-Jones, the son of a barrister, Ronald Armstrong-Jones, and his wife Anne, who was the sister of designer Oliver Messel. Andy and Tony remained friends after the war. They dated the same girls, drank in the same clubs and bars in Chelsea and Whitechapel, roared round London on sunny summer evenings on Andy's Triumph Tiger. Peter Saunders was another friend of Tony's, and it was through Saunders that Tony met Jeremy Fry. The two men hit it off immediately and became best friends. "They were so close that their voices eventually began to sound alike," said Tony's biographer, Anne de Courcy.[20] When Fry married Camilla Grinling in 1954, Tony, who was beginning to make a name for himself as a photographer, took the wedding pictures. When the society papers published a photograph of the Frys' eldest child, three-year-old Francis, sitting on a step at Widcombe Manor, the credit line read

"Photograph by Tony Armstrong Jones."[21] And when Tony began seeing Princess Margaret in 1958, after meeting her at a dinner party held by Lady Elizabeth Cavendish, Margaret's lady-in-waiting, the Frys were delighted to entertain the lovers at Widcombe Manor, demonstrating their membership of that bohemian elite to which Tony introduced his uncertain but intrigued princess. "Was the second weekend you stayed much easier than the first?" Camilla asked Tony. "I am sure PM enjoyed it more this time. She seemed so much easier to talk to."[22] It was during one of their visits to Widcombe that Tony and Margaret became engaged.

The couple's engagement was announced in February 1960, after a delay requested by the Queen, who was expecting Prince Andrew and asked them to wait until after the birth.* The wedding was set for Westminster Abbey on May 6. Peter Saunders was dead set against the idea of Tony marrying Margaret, warning his friend that the royal family would chew him up and spit him out. "I know it's a physical thing at the moment, but at the end of the day for goodness sake don't do it."[23] Reporters called Andy Garnett, who was in Paris for Rotork at the time, suggesting that he was going to be best man. But Tony and Margaret were at Widcombe Manor again that March—when they left to drive back to London the Frys' staff lined the drive to give them a rousing send-off—and when the press announcement came on March 19,

---

*While they waited, Tony decided to stay out of the public gaze and went to visit his sister Susan, Viscountess de Vesci, at her husband's country house in County Laois. While there he photographed Brendan Behan, who took brother and sister to a Dublin bar after the shoot. Seeing a priest of his acquaintance, Behan turned to Susan and said, "Do you know what that feckin' priest said to me the other feckin' day? He said, 'I want to feck my feckin' sister-in-law.' So I said to him, 'Well, it's a lot better than feckin' your feckin' brother-in-law.'" Susan, who hardly ever drank, asked for a large gin and tonic. Anne de Courcy, *Snowdon: The Biography* (Phoenix, 2012), ebook, chapter 5.

1960, no one who knew the two couples was surprised to hear that the best man was to be Jeremy Fry. He and Camilla drove straight down to Royal Lodge Windsor to spend the weekend with Tony, the Princess, and the Queen Mother.

Two weeks later, a *Daily Mirror* front-page headline screamed, "I Can't Be Best Man, Says Jeremy."[24] After a week of press speculation and two days of talks with royal advisers, Fry had announced he was having to withdraw from the ceremony on doctor's advice. Camilla, who was expecting their third child in a few weeks' time, told reporters who called at Widcombe Manor, "My husband cannot be certain that he will be fully recovered from his jaundice before the wedding."[25]

Jaundice? The real reason was that the palace had discovered Fry had an unacceptable past—unacceptable to the establishment, at least. Eight years earlier, in 1952, he had appeared at Marlborough Street magistrates' court, pleading guilty to male importuning and receiving a fine of two pounds, and it appeared that at least one newspaper had got hold of the story.

In 1960 the Sexual Offences Act, which decriminalised homosexual acts in private between consenting men, was still seven years away: men were still going to jail for being gay and homophobia was perfectly acceptable, with references in the press to "unrepentant perverts" and to homosexuality as "a contagious moral disease."[26] No whiff of scandal could attach to the wedding of the year.

What the palace and the press did not know, or chose to ignore, was that the bridegroom, too, was bisexual. "If it moves, he'll have it" was how one friend summed up Tony Armstrong-Jones's attitude to sex, and he certainly had many lovers of both sexes throughout the 1950s. Designer Nicky Haslam had an affair with him. So did David Hicks's ex-partner Tom Parr. Three days before his engagement to Princess Margaret was announced, Tony arrived at Parr's flat, ostensibly for a drink but asking casually if, while he was there, he could look at his ex-lover's photo albums.

He went through them all, examining each picture carefully, and only afterwards did Parr realise he was checking to make sure there was no compromising material which might find its way into the newspapers. He never forgave Tony for his lack of trust.

To complicate matters much, much further, Tony was also having an affair with Camilla Fry. "Friends didn't just like Camilla," wrote Andy Garnett. "They loved her."[27] Sixty years after their first meeting, he was still fascinated by the memory of her beauty and what he described as her animal attraction. She had been Peter Saunders's girlfriend as a teenager, and she went out with Tony for a while before she started seeing Jeremy Fry. The relationship—or relationships, plural—with the Frys resumed during Tony's visits to Widcombe Manor in the late 1950s. "It was a pretty good free-for-all there," said one friend, with drink and drugs leading to some intriguingly uninhibited behaviour.[28] Three weeks after Tony's wedding to Princess Margaret, Camilla gave birth to his child, a daughter named Polly.

None of this dampened the friendship. Nor did the wedding. Tony chose another best man, a blameless neurologist named Roger Gilliatt, and around twenty million people watched the ceremony on television, the first-ever televised royal wedding. Margaret and Tony, now the Earl of Snowdon, stayed at Widcombe again that November, causing a minor stir when they drove with the Frys to nearby Bradford-on-Avon to do some Christmas shopping and the Princess sat down at an old organ she saw in an antique shop and belted out selections from *South Pacific*, with Tony, Jeremy, and Camilla joining in with the choruses. "I left the party to it," said the bemused shop owner. "They seemed to have a thoroughly enjoyable time."[29]

The royal couple weekended at Widcombe a couple of times a year throughout the early 1960s, sometimes combining official duties with their private visit. In June 1962 they visited the Bath Festival, posing with jazzmen Johnny Dankworth and Chris Barber: Princess Margaret joined in the foot-stamping and hand-clapping for tunes like "When the Saints Go Marching In." That night Dankworth and Barber were putting on another royal command performance, this time at Widcombe Manor itself, as guests of the Frys. "The group was swinging again," said the *Daily Mirror*.[30]

Jeremy and Camilla's marriage broke down in 1964, after Fry was cited in a divorce case brought by sculptor Lynn Chadwick against his young wife Frances, with whom he had bought Lypiatt Park in the Cotswolds. Frances committed suicide before the case came to court and the Frys later reconciled, but they divorced in 1967, the judge giving them both a good telling-off: "It is quite obvious that this husband and wife have totally disregarded the obligations of matrimony."[31] It meant the end of official royal visits, although Tony continued to come. Widcombe Manor went on the market with an asking price of £50,000—"landscaped grounds of outstanding beauty maintainable by one gardener," announced the agent's particulars—but it took years to sell.

In the summer of 1974, Jeremy Fry dined at Alderley Grange with the Lees-Milnes. Their other guest was the Duchess of Devonshire, and the four of them gossiped familiarly about Tony and Margaret, and the increasingly public breakdown of their marriage. Fry confessed to Jim Lees-Milne that he hated leaving Widcombe, "but the relief of being free from the burden of the house was now immense."[32]

When Lees-Milne came out to see his guest off at the end of the evening, Fry kissed him full on the mouth. Then he climbed into his car and drove away, to another future, another dance.

16

IMAGINE

O N FRIDAY, AUGUST 22, 1969, the Beatles came together for a photo shoot. They were already far advanced on the long and winding road to dissolution, and even without the benefit of hindsight, one could sense the tension in the pictures that were taken that day. George Harrison looked angry. John Lennon looked bored. Paul McCartney looked worried. Only Ringo Starr smiled a lot, and even he seemed anxious. As if in acknowledgment of the strained atmosphere, the photographers, Ethan Russell and Monte Fresco, had the boys pose repeatedly with space between them, simultaneously together and alone. Two days earlier the group had put the finishing touches to their eleventh album, named *Abbey Road* after the EMI studio in St John's Wood. That would be the last time they were all in a recording studio at the same time, and although they didn't know it, this would be their last photo shoot.

The setting was Tittenhurst Park, an early Georgian country house near Windsor Great Park set in seventy-two acres. John Lennon and Yoko Ono had bought "one of the finest small residential estates within twenty-five miles of London" (in the estate agent's estimation, anyway) three months earlier; the couple had moved in eleven days before the shoot.[1] Tittenhurst was a fine house, with two big curving bays, a picture gallery, a long colonnaded terrace, beautiful gardens famous for their collection of weeping trees, and a half-timbered "Tudor" tea pavilion tucked away in the shrubbery.

On this particular Friday it was still quite bare, with hardly any furniture. The group—if they could still be called a group—posed in the long grass of Tittenhurst's overgrown cricket pitch, and by a fountain with a statue of Diana, and on the lawn with the house as a backdrop. As they strolled down the long drive, a heavily pregnant Linda McCartney clung possessively to her husband's arm while John Lennon and Yoko Ono lagged far behind, as if they had already said goodbye to their guests. Which, in a way, they had.

IN THE 1960s rock stars and stately homes went together like cannabis and cookies or Rolls-Royces and swimming pools. But the idea of successful performers splashing out on a mansion was nothing new: actor-manager David Garrick had bought himself a villa on the Thames in 1754, and he certainly wasn't the first. As a means for performers of all sorts to celebrate and confirm newfound prosperity and professional success, the acquisition of a country house was a well-established tradition. And in the twentieth century, when the film industry gave a boost to the acting profession, it offered a measure of privacy, an escape from over-enthusiastic fans who were eager for a glimpse of their heroes and heroines.

In the 1920s and 1930s, for example, a new generation of movie stars took advantage of the collapsing property market to acquire houses in the country. Merle Oberon and her husband, the director Alexander Korda, lived in the late seventeenth-century Hills House in the pretty Buckinghamshire village of Denham until their divorce in 1945; Korda had bought a 165-acre estate there, which was designed by Walter Gropius and Maxwell Fry, in order to found his own film studio. After the war, David Niven and his second wife, the Swedish model Hjördis Tersmeden, bought Wilcot Manor, a ten-bedroomed house with its own lake in seventy-two acres just outside Marlborough, although the purchase wasn't a success. Niven left his new wife alone there, next door to his first wife's grave and the home of his former in-laws, while he went off to Hollywood. Hjördis drank a lot of gin and complained that ghostly nuns floated across the lake.

Buckinghamshire was popular with the British film industry, partly because it was within easy reach of London, but mainly because Pinewood and Denham Studios were both in the county, and there was also a cluster of film studios at Borehamwood in neighbouring Hertfordshire. Heatherden Hall, an opulent early twentieth-century country house in the grounds of Pinewood Studios, doubled as a country club for staff and a convenient set for any number of films, from *Those Magnificent Men in Their Flying Machines* and *Chitty Chitty Bang Bang* to *Carry On up the Khyber*. Denham Mount, an elegant Regency villa designed by architect Robert Lugar which stood just outside Denham Studios, became the principal setting for David Lean's 1945 classic *Blithe Spirit*: this was where Margaret Rutherford's Madame Arcati conducted the séance which disturbed the ghost of Charles Condomine's first wife, Elvira. Stoke Park, an enormous domed Georgian house partly designed by James Wyatt, with grounds by Capability Brown and Humphry Repton, has been featured in films as varied as the creepy country house thriller *Dead of Night* and the third outing for James Bond, *Goldfinger*.

For a time, Buckinghamshire was also a favourite haunt of some of Britain's biggest celebrities. At the end of the war Laurence Olivier and Vivien Leigh bought Notley Abbey, a house built around the ruins of a medieval Augustinian monastery. They kept it for sixteen years. "At Notley I had an affair with the past," said Olivier. "I could not leave it alone, I was a child lost in its history." When the couple came to sell up in 1960, Leigh was distraught. "I walk from place to precious place and gaze at the beloved views with tears pouring down my face," she wrote.[2] Michael Denison and Dulcie Gray lived in a wing of Shardeloes near Amersham, a magnificent early work by Robert Adam. Peter Sellers, who bought sixteenth-century Chipperfield Manor in Hertfordshire in 1959 for £17,500, said he was looking for a "civilised exile" while announcing to the press that he was "trying to build a legend that I'm a mad actor who rides a black mare across the fields at night."[3] Better than ghostly nuns on a lake—or perhaps not.

Sellers later moved with his wife, Britt Ekland, to the fifteenth-century Brookfield House in Surrey, installing a home cinema and importing a new front door from Italy at vast expense. In 1968 he sold Brookfield to Ringo Starr, who, according to legend, cut a pet flap in that door so that his Siamese cats could come and go.

PRIVACY, PROSPERITY, AND an element of theatrical mythmaking came together in the series of country houses that Dirk Bogarde owned at the height of his fame as a film star. Gay and living with his partner, Tony Forwood, Bogarde certainly required privacy: although the circles in which he moved didn't care about his sexuality, Rank, the studio to which he was contracted, most certainly did. Nothing must mar the image of a handsome heterosexual heartthrob.

In 1954, Bogarde was living at Bendrose House near Amersham, a rambling place with oak beams and panelling which had been Forwood's family home, when he heard that Beel House next door was for sale. Beel was much grander than Bendrose, an odd mixture of gables, tall chimneys, Regency bows, and colonnades, with an Edwardian conservatory equipped with Doric columns. But it was in a poor state. "Too many rooms," Bogarde recalled, "nothing facing the right way, poor lighting and water systems, badly proportioned rooms and too much land."[4] He bought it for £4,000, knocked down "a wing of eleven ugly rooms," and gutted the place, adding a swimming pool and a croquet lawn, filling the enormous conservatory with palms and tropical birds, and playing the part of a landed gentleman. Every September he hosted the local gymkhana in the park and presented the cups dressed in a tweed cap and cavalry twill. "The Country Squire was fast in danger of believing his own image and changing to Lord of the Manor," he said ruefully. "It is an insidious business."[5]

Like most movie stars who bought themselves big places in the country, Bogarde loved to entertain friends and celebrities from the world of films. Kay Kendall was a regular guest until her death from leukaemia in 1959. (She christened Beel's conservatory "the Out-Patients' Department.") Capucine, the glamorous French model and actress whom the studios tried hard to link romantically with Bogarde, used to come for extended visits. One weekend Judy Garland turned up unexpectedly, and she and Bogarde drove into the Cotswolds, walked the dogs, and sat around in the Out-Patients' Department drinking Blue Nun with ice.

In 1960 Bogarde sold Beel to Basil Dearden, who was to direct him the following year in *Victim*, one of the actor's best films, in which he played Melville Farr, a married barrister who is blackmailed over his sexuality. (*Victim* was apparently the first film to use the word "homosexual.") Bogarde and Tony Forwood stayed in Buckinghamshire, moving to Birchens Spring, a large house near Beaconsfield, which they christened "the Palace." A strangely austere building on the outside, it had been built in 1937 for a South African diamond merchant named Rissik, who was evidently not content for that austerity to continue inside.[6] The main staircase had colourful marble inlay in the risers of each stair, and the circular dining room, which rested in the angle of the L-shaped plan, boasted curious murals on an Indian theme painted by a Rissik cousin who was drawing master at Uppingham School, and a circular burr-ash dining table with a glass centre which was lit from below. By the 1950s the murals had gone and Birchens Spring had become a home for children who had a parent suffering from tuberculosis. Bogarde claimed that he got it cheap—it cost £12,000—because "no one knew what to do with all the partitioning, frosted glass, and red crosses everywhere."[7]

The couple only stayed at the Palace, which they renamed Drummers Yard after a lead statue of a drummer boy which stood in the grounds, for a couple of years, moving in 1962 to a ten-bedroomed, eight-bathroomed, six-reception-roomed yeoman's house in Surrey, with two cottages in the grounds and a gay past: it had once belonged to poet and aesthete Brian Howard, and Howard's old friend Daphne Fielding, a frequent visitor to Dirk and Tony's new home, used to say his presence lingered there. (The asking price was £35,000, but the owners raised it to £40,000 when they realised who was buying it.) But until their move the couple entertained at the Palace on a grand scale, having celebrity guests for weekends and Sunday luncheons, and hosting extravagant theatrical parties. Sylvia Syms remembered a particularly star-studded occasion one Sunday in June 1961 when Bogarde threw a party for Judy Garland, who was then making what would be her last film, *I Could Go On Singing*, with Bogarde as her romantic male lead. Noël Coward was there with the actress Joyce Carey: everyone gathered round the piano while Garland and Coward sang duets. Apparently Garland knew all of Coward's lyrics by heart. When they sang "If Love Were All," "it brought the packed room roaring to its feet."[8]

Writers Keith Waterhouse and Willis Hall once enjoyed a memorable Sunday lunch at the Palace. They went down to discuss the possibility of Bogarde's appearing in an adaptation of a John Osborne play, *Epitaph for George Dillon*, although they were also intrigued to see the film star at home: they thought Capucine might be there and they wanted to check a rumour that she was, in fact, a man. Bogarde's sexuality was no secret in the film world.

The first hint that this wasn't going to be a conventional lunch party came as their chauffeur-driven car cruised up the drive and they saw Tony Forwood wearing an apron and walking up and down the lawn. He was vacuuming it with a Hoover on a long cord. Once inside, Bogarde was there to welcome them and Forwood appeared, sans apron and sans Hoover, to pour them some champagne. Then more. And more. The house, recalled Willis Hall, was "enormous, luxurious and immaculate," but there was no sign of any staff, and no sign of any lunch. Every now and then Bogarde would disappear into the nether regions of the house and they would hear raised voices. Then he would reappear, charming and urbane, and offer them another drink. They moved into the circular dining room, where the table was set and where champagne gave way to Chablis. But there was still no sign of lunch. "We moved on to a second bottle of Chablis," said Hall, "and the elegant French clock on the dining-room's elegant marble mantlepiece ticked on towards 2.30."[9]

Suddenly the dining room door opened and Capucine swept in, carrying a large silver salver. She slammed it down on the table, said, "There you are, cunt," and walked out again. The four men looked at the salver for a moment; then Bogarde lifted the cover to reveal a mound of tinned spaghetti in tomato sauce. *Cold* tinned spaghetti in tomato sauce.

Hall and Waterhouse never did discover the story behind that lunch. No one mentioned the food or the service. Everyone simply carried on as if nothing unusual had happened. Hall remembered asking for seconds. Then the pair stood up from the table, politely thanked their hosts, and went back to London.

ROCK AND ROLL was still young in the early 1960s, and as a breed, rock and roll rebels were more impetuous, more self-indulgent than the average British film star. Once they had the white Rolls-Royce and the house in Esher or St George's Hill, the next step was a more substantial place in the country. And here, as with so much else, they could look across the Atlantic for their role model. Early in 1957 Elvis Presley realised he could no longer go on living in the $40,000 house in Memphis that he had bought the previous year. It was in a residential neighbourhood, fans and journalists were camping out at the door, and the neighbours were complaining. He gave his parents a budget of $100,000 and asked them to find a farmhouse-type property out of town, where he could have a little privacy when he wasn't on tour. The result was that in March 1957 he bought Graceland, a small Colonial Revival mansion built on farmland in 1939.

Graceland was at once a status symbol, a home, a playground, and a retreat for Presley and his entourage. (In the 1990s the joke in Memphis was that it was hard to find local women of a certain age who *didn't* claim to have been entertained there by the King.) And Graceland set the standard for the British stars of the Swinging Sixties, although it took them a while to come round to the idea. In one of the earlier and more unlikely examples, Socknersh Manor, a beautiful Tudor ironmaster's house in a remote corner of Sussex, was bought jointly in the early 1960s by Tom Jones and Engelbert Humperdinck. Neither of them ever lived there, but they used it as a party house, entertaining the likes of Janis Joplin and Jean Shrimpton, before quarrelling and selling up.

Between 1966 and 1971 Keith Richards, Bill Wyman, Eric Clapton, John Lennon, George Harrison, Mick Jagger, and Roger Daltrey all bought listed historic country houses. Although hardly qualifying as a statistically significant sample, they do show a wide range of architectural tastes, from timber-framed Sussex thatch (Richards) and early Tudor (Wyman) to High Victorian Gothic (Harrison) and Italianate Edwardian (Clapton). They also show a surprising staying power: only two of the seven mansions, Lennon's Georgian Tittenhurst Park and Mick Jagger's flamboyant French château-style Stargrove, were sold on. Fifty years later, the other five houses still belong to the musicians who bought them (or in the case of George Harrison's Friar Park, to his widow).

Keith Richards was first to sample the delights of living in an historic country house. One day in 1966 he was in West Sussex and, in his own words, "poncing around in my Bentley" with a couple of estate agents' brochures, having decided it might be fun to buy a country house.[10] He took a wrong turn and asked for directions at Redlands, a sixteenth-century timber-framed house with a thatched roof and a moat. He was entranced, and the owner, sensing a good thing, offered to sell the house on the spot. "I said, if I bring you down twenty grand, can we do the deal?" recalled Richards. "So I zoomed up to London, just got to the bank in time, got the bread—twenty grand in a brown paper bag—and by evening I was back down at Redlands, in front of the fireplace, and we signed the deal."[11]

Redlands became something of a base for the Stones and the setting for a string of bizarre stories about their behaviour. At one point Richards took up archery, but he was so bad at it that he was constantly missing the target and losing his arrows in the moat. Eventually he bought a single-seater hovercraft, "so I can zip straight across the lawn, into the moat, pick up my arrows and skim out again."[12] Another time, Mick Jagger and Brian Jones had a furious argument in the house over Jones's impending court case for drugs offences. Richards, Anita Pallenberg, and Tony Sanchez, who was once described by Marianne Faithfull as "dealer by appointment to the Rolling Stones," were lolling around on the lawn outside when they heard Jones scream, "I'm going to kill myself! I'm going to kill myself!" and watched in horror as he dashed out of the house and threw himself into the moat, which Richards had always claimed to be at least twenty feet deep. As he disappeared beneath the waters Jagger leaped in to save him (having paused for a moment so that Richards could tie a rope round his waist), only to discover the moat was in fact only a few feet deep. Furious, he dragged Jones out by his hair and slapped him. "Look at these velvet trousers. They cost me fifty quid, and you've ruined them!"[13] Everyone thought it was hilarious—although in retrospect it was not so funny, prefiguring Jones's death by drowning a couple of years later in the swimming pool of his own country home, a sixteenth-century farmhouse in Sussex which had once belonged to A. A. Milne.

In 1967 Redlands made the national headlines. That February, in an elaborate sting operation orchestrated (so the Stones believed) by the *News of the World*, police raided the house in search of drugs, which they duly found. Much was made during the ensuing court case of the fact that Richards burned incense at Redland—practically an admission of guilt—and of the fact that the police found Marianne Faithfull on a sofa in the drawing room wearing nothing but a fur rug, something which interested the media even more than the drugs. "Girl in Fur Rug at Stones' Party," screamed one headline, while a po-faced prosecuting counsel went into detail about how "from time to time, she let it fall disclosing her nude body," adding that "when the police arrived,

Mick Jagger and Keith Richards leaving for court, 1967

she remained unperturbed, apparently enjoying the situation."[14] Richards was given a twelve-month gaol sentence for allowing his house to be used for the smoking of cannabis; Mick Jagger was sentenced to three months for possessing amphetamines; and art dealer Robert Fraser, "Groovy Bob," was sentenced to six months for possessing twenty-four heroin tablets. Richards and Jagger had their sentences quashed on appeal. Groovy Bob had to serve his time, and Faithfull became an icon of sixties pop culture.

When fellow band member Bill Wyman decided to buy a country house, he went for something rather more ambitious than Redlands. In the summer of 1968, he and his girlfriend Astrid Lundstrom were searching for a place in the country when their agent suggested they look at Gedding Hall in Suffolk. Gedding is a superbly romantic house, a moated fragment of a much larger mansion built around 1480, with picturesque late-Victorian additions, all set in fourteen acres. The owner, Geoffrey Allen, was away that day and they couldn't see inside, but all the same they fell in love with it—"I always wanted to own a castle," said Wyman later—and the next week they went back and offered Allen £41,000. He accepted, assuring them that although a member of the royal household had offered more, he would rather sell to Wyman, who was "a self-made man like him."[15] Allen was certainly self-made: he was a gangster who later served seven years for fraud. As they chatted, Wyman was surprised to notice a large photograph in pride of place on top of the television set. It was of the Kray twins. Allen cheerfully told him they were great friends of his and regular visitors to the hall. By the time Wyman moved in, on October 30, 1968, there was no chance of his striking up an acquaintance with them, since they were in custody on murder charges which would see them jailed for the rest of their lives.

In 1970 Mick Jagger bought the Stargrove estate in Hampshire, which in 1644 had entertained no less a person than Oliver Cromwell, after the Second Battle of Newbury; although he embarked on a costly renovation scheme, Stargrove was primarily an investment. Jagger rarely spent time at the castellated seventeenth-century mansion. But for Wyman, a Lewisham bricklayer's son, Gedding was home. In his autobiography he talked proudly of officially becoming lord of the manor, of spotting a pheasant one New Year's Day, of taking photographs of the moon from the top of Gedding's tower.

The Who's Roger Daltrey felt something similar. In the spring of 1971 Daltrey and his partner, Heather Taylor, were looking in a half-hearted way for a house in the country. (What was it about the years to either side of 1970 that sent so many rock and roll rebels in search of rural grandeur—apart, of course, from their accountants, who saw the tax benefits?) They had a friend who was an estate agent, and he used to take them with him when he was checking the houses on his books. One day he took them to Pashley Manor, a big Tudor house with early Georgian additions, standing in sixty acres outside Tunbridge Wells. Daltrey took against it. "I didn't like the vibe," he remembered later. "If I don't like the vibe, that's it. I'm very susceptible to ground energy."[16] On the way back they stopped at Holmshurst, a Jacobean house in Burwash, East Sussex, not far from Rudyard Kipling's Bateman's. It had been extended—in about 1650—but the interiors still contained early seventeenth-century fireplaces, overmantels, and panelling. There were spectacular views over the Weald. "You can see for miles and miles and miles, no drug required," wrote Daltrey.[17]

He paid the asking price of £39,500, and on June 26, 1971, the couple moved into what would be their home for the next half a century. It took ten years to remove the heavy Victorian staining which had turned all the timbers black—"We were there in rubber gloves and boiler suits, sweating our bollocks off"—but eventually Holmshurst was quietly and modestly restored to its former honey-coloured state.[18] Daltrey acquired more land, so that the original 35 acres grew to 420; he kept cattle, and over the years he created a series of lakes which he turned into a full-scale trout fishery. And, as he later argued, Holmshurst saved his life. In 1975, he was trying to move a large stone ball which had been perched on top of a plinth when he dropped it on his foot. "It's one of the hazards of buying a rather grand home." A couple of years later he began to suffer from gout in the damaged toe, and that was what led him to give up alcohol. "By my mid-thirties, I was the exact opposite of the hedonistic rocker," he wrote.[19] And all because of that stone ball at Holmshurst.

ERIC CLAPTON, WHO saw an advertisement for Hurtwood Edge in Surrey in a copy of *Country Life* in 1969, shared something of the domestic pride shown by Wyman and Daltrey. Hurtwood, a nine-bedroomed Italianate villa in eleven acres with terraced gardens and spectacular views stretching down to the south coast, was much newer than Gedding or Holmshurst. Described in the agent's particulars as an "Attractive Modern House in Continental Style," it was built in 1910 and was rumoured to be by Sir Edwin Lutyens, although it turned out to be the work of the distinguished architectural historian Arthur T. Bolton, an authority on the buildings of Sir John Soane and the Adam brothers. Hurtwood had been empty and on the market for years when Clapton found it—when he went back for a second look, he surprised the agent, who had become accustomed to using the place as his private hideaway and was sunbathing nude on the terrace with a girlfriend. Clapton bought it for £30,000, the first house he had ever owned, and installed a bed, his guitars, a 1912 Douglas motorcycle which stood in the middle of the drawing room like a piece of sculpture, and two six-foot-high cinema loudspeakers.

This relaxed approach to interior decoration soon palled, and Clapton began buying furniture and other bits and pieces in the overpriced antique shops of Chelsea and Fulham. However, he realised what else was possible when he was taken to the Baghdad House, a fashionable Arabic restaurant on Fulham Road with a basement decked out like an oriental bazaar, where he was introduced to young David Mlinaric. Mlinaric brought in Christopher

Gibbs, the old Etonian antique dealer and friend of the Rolling Stones, and together they turned Hurtwood Edge into "something nice," in Clapton's words, with an old four-poster in the principal bedroom and Persian and Moroccan hangings all over the place. (Bill Wyman also used Mlinaric at Gedding Hall, having decided that David Hicks's estimate of £6,000 just for curtains and carpets was more than he could afford.)

Pattie Boyd, who moved in with Clapton five years later, painted a less tasteful picture of the Hurtwood interiors. The six-foot-high speakers were still in situ in the drawing room. The kitchen was a health hazard, all lino and Formica, with an ancient gas cooker. Clapton had a big ginger cat called Fast Eddy and a Weimaraner called Willow, but there was also other resident animal life at Hurtwood: rats in the chicken run, bats in the bedroom, and a mouse in the kitchen. There may have been more, but it was hard to tell: almost every room in the house was cluttered with dirty clothes, shoes, piles of papers, books, and records out of their sleeves. "Eric, I discovered, was not a naturally tidy man," said Pattie.[20]

Pattie Boyd and Eric Clapton were two corners of what was perhaps the most famous love triangle in rock and roll. The third was George Harrison, who had married Pattie in 1966. ("They both wore coats by Mary Quant," noted the *Tatler*.[21]) Harrison and Clapton were close friends: the Beatle composed "Here Comes the Sun" while sitting in the garden at Hurtwood one morning and jamming with his friend. Pattie and Harrison spent most of their married life together at Kinfauns, a large bungalow at Esher which Harrison bought for £20,000 in the summer of 1964, after the Beatles' accountant advised them all to invest their money in property. The same week John Lennon bought Kenwood, a big piece of stockbroker Tudor on the exclusive St George's Hill estate in Weybridge, Surrey. From 1965 to 1968 Ringo Starr and his wife, Maureen, lived nearby, at a house called

Sunny Heights on the same estate, before buying Brookfield House from Peter Sellers.

In 1969 Harrison decided to sell Kinfauns. According to Pattie Boyd, he was tripping in the landscaped grounds of the school next door one afternoon when a watchman told him to "get out and go away," despite his protestations that all he wanted to do was look at the trees. The incident hurt Harrison's feelings so much that he determined to have a park of his own. He and Pattie tried to buy Plumpton Place in Sussex, a stunningly beautiful Elizabethan country house remodelled in the 1920s by Lutyens for Edward Hudson, proprietor of *Country Life*. They put in an offer but the woman who owned it turned them down, saying she didn't want to sell to a rock and roll musician. A few years later Plumpton was bought by Jimmy Page.

Then they found Friar Park.

The authors of *A History of the County of Oxford* described Friar Park as "a colourful and eccentric mélange of French Flamboyant Gothic in brick, stone and terracotta," and colourful and eccentric it certainly is.[22] Standing just outside Henley-on-Thames, it is a vast leviathan of a house, much grander than any of the other mansions bought by Harrison's fellow rock stars, with turrets and towers, twenty-five bedrooms, ballroom, dining room, drawing room, library, and all the usual offices one would expect to find in a big Victorian country house. Dubbed "Crackerbox Palace" by Harrison (it features in an odd promotional video made to accompany his song of the same name), it was designed in about 1889 by a little-known Victorian architect named Robert Clarke Edwards, for a lawyer and amateur scientist named Sir Frank Crisp. The hall chimneypiece was twenty feet high, with painted panels showing the Tree of Life and the Tree of Destiny. A billiard room had an ornately carved chimneypiece and oak panelling; the dining room walls were covered with embossed leather and its windows were filled with Morris & Co. stained glass. Crisp had a childlike love of puns and visual jokes: Pattie Boyd remembered that the light switches were friars' faces, their noses turning the lights on and off, and just outside the dining room was a painted plaster roundel depicting a friar devouring two boys and the motto "Eton boys—a Harrowing sight."

Then there were the grounds, which formed a remarkable labyrinth of lakes, bridges, and giant stepping-stones; an Elizabethan herb garden, a pinetum, a Japanese garden; and best of all, a network of strange caves and underground waterways. These caves were a trip in themselves. The Harrisons discovered them still hung with their original distorting funhouse mirrors. One was filled with glass vines, and another with gnomes and fairies, which should have been enough to put anyone off LSD for life. Some were accessible only by boat, including a replica of the Blue Grotto at Capri and a cavern walled in mica that glistened and glimmered in torchlight. Back on the surface, Crisp's "Great Rock Garden," all twenty thousand tons of it, was described by an awed *Country Life* reporter in 1961 as a "millionaire's garden on the most lavish scale. [It] culminated in a miniature Matterhorn on which were perched model chamois that one could pick out through a telescope far below."[23] The "Matterhorn" was capped with a large chunk of rock which had been removed at some stage in the nineteenth century from its big brother in the Alps.

When George Harrison first saw Friar Park, the house had been used as a school for more than fifteen years by a Catholic teaching order, the Salesian Sisters of St John Bosco, who were preparing to have it demolished if they couldn't find a buyer. He paid £140,000 for the house, two lodges, and a gatehouse, in thirty-two acres. He and Pattie spend the next four years restoring and decorating it. They brought in David Mlinaric, who was fast overtaking John Fowler and David Hicks as interior designer to the stars and whom Pattie had met at Glyn Cywarch, Lord Harlech's Jacobean manor house in North Wales. The renowned garden designer Beth Chatto advised on replanting the gardens, and Pattie scoured the country for suitable pieces of furniture. Their bed was by the great art nouveau furniture designer Louis Majorelle, and on one occasion Pattie flew to Hollywood solely because MGM was holding an auction in which there were some art nouveau chandeliers she wanted. "I had great plans for the house," she wrote in her autobiography. "I imagined we would host wonderful charity parties with music and ballet for hundreds of people on balmy summer evenings and our friends would visit. But gradually I realised that George didn't think like me."[24]

With the Beatles gone—John Lennon announced he was leaving the band in September of 1969, and Paul McCartney filed a suit for dissolution of their contractual partnership the following year—Harrison withdrew into the Eastern mysticism which had attracted him ever since he and Pattie had travelled to India in 1966. He meditated and chanted for hours in a room high up in the house, and he filled the place with members of the International Society for Krishna Consciousness, founded a few years earlier by the Indian mystic Abhay Charanaravinda Bhaktivedanta Swami. "We could chant together and there would be good vibes in the house," remembered Pattie.[25]

But there weren't good vibes. When Eric Clapton wasn't chasing the dragon, something which was taking up an increasingly large part of his life at Hurtwood Edge, he was chasing Pattie Harrison. He sent her love notes. He wrote songs to her: "Layla" is the best known. And he told anyone who would listen, George Harrison included, that he was in love with her. Harrison responded by spending more and more time in the recording studio he'd built at Friar Park, by adding cocaine to his list of drugs of choice, and by embarking on an affair with Ringo Starr's wife, Maureen, and hardly bothering to conceal it. Pattie once discovered Harrison and Maureen locked in a bedroom. She went straight up to the top of the house, lowered the pennant with the sacred Sanskrit symbol "om" that her husband liked to fly from the flagpole, and raised a skull and crossbones instead. "That made me feel much better."[26] In 1974 she left Harrison and Friar Park for Clapton and Hurtwood Edge.

BY THEN, JOHN Lennon and Yoko Ono had left for America, selling Tittenhurst Park to Ringo and Maureen Starr. Their two years at Tittenhurst, 1969–1971, had been both productive and destructive: destructive in that this was where they both began using heroin in earnest; productive because Tittenhurst was where Lennon recorded his finest solo work, *Imagine*. Tittenhurst formed the backdrop for the official video accompanying "Jealous Guy," in which, clad all in black, Lennon rowed Yoko Ono out to an island in the middle of the huge lake he'd created in the park (without obtaining the necessary permissions).

And Tittenhurst played a central role in one of the most memorable pop videos of the twentieth century. As the opening chords of *Imagine*'s title song roll out, John and Yoko walk up to the front of the mansion and vanish on the doorstep, to reappear in the long bow-windowed drawing room, which is all white—white window shutters, white floor, white walls and ceiling. Lennon sings at a white grand piano in a corner of the room while Yoko—in a long, flowing white dress and a golden circlet—methodically opens the shutters one by one, letting more and more light into the room, before taking her place beside Lennon at the piano.

As "Imagine" ends, they smile at each other and kiss, oblivious to the cameras and the lights and the crew, obviously so much in love that one feels anxious at intruding on such intimacy. Andy Garnett's journalist wife, Polly Devlin, who was there at Tittenhurst Park during the filming and watched while Lennon played, remembered Yoko saying that day that she worried about which of them would die first. "Because that's the one thing we can't control."[27]

17

BAD BEHAVIOUR

O N MARCH 17, 1954, Frances Partridge wrote in her diary that her husband, Ralph, had spent the past couple of days in the public gallery at Winchester assizes. The attraction, if "attraction" is quite the right word, was "the trial of Lord Montagu and others for buggery," which sounds like some half-forgotten event from the eighteenth century instead of a court case which took place within living memory.[1]

The 1950s and 1960s saw a series of notorious sex scandals play out in the bedrooms of the stately homes of England, on their manicured lawns, by their swimming pools, and occasionally in their lovingly tended shrubberies. The huge public appetite for these aristocratic dramas was driven by a mixture of schadenfreude, class envy, bourgeois outrage, and good old-fashioned prurience. But there was also a general feeling that, as the *Washington Post* commented about the Profumo affair in June 1963, "a picture of widespread decadence beneath the glitter of a large segment of stiff-lipped society is emerging."[2]

The narrative of events which brought the twenty-seven-year-old 3rd Baron Montagu of Beaulieu to be in the dock at Winchester in March 1954 with his two codefendants—his cousin, a Dorset gentleman-farmer named Michael Pitt-Rivers, and a friend, journalist Peter Wildeblood—reveals a lot about postwar attitudes to homosexuality. Bisexual and recently engaged to a society beauty named Anne Gage, Edward Montagu was typical of a new generation of aristocratic country house owners who cheerfully disregarded traditional social boundaries—as witnessed by the flamboyant and highly effective way in which he had opened Beaulieu to the public in 1952. Working in public relations as he did (he was an executive with Voice and Vision, a subsidiary of the advertising firm of Colman Prentis and Varley), Montagu mixed with the internationally rich and famous, including the likes of Gianni Agnelli, later the head of the Fiat empire; the Queen's dressmaker Norman Hartnell; the producers of the musical *South Pacific* ("My most glamourous theatrical experience," he recalled years later); and the new Tarzan, Lex Barker, who confided that he enjoyed being Tarzan except that he had to shave his chest, "which made it permanently itchy."[3] Tony Armstrong-Jones was a friend—"an up-and-coming society photographer," he recalled, "who was once debagged at a deb dance and thrown into the Thames."[4] Montagu's friend Peter Wildeblood declared that the peer's social circle formed an extraordinary assortment of conflicting types: "businessmen and writers, duchesses and model girls, restaurateurs and politicians and musical comedy actresses and Guards officers and Americans wearing hand-painted ties."[5]

In August 1953 Montagu held a house party at Beaulieu. Guests included the gay film director Kenneth Hume, who would go on to surprise his friends and hers by marrying Shirley Bassey—not once but twice. It was a bank holiday weekend; Beaulieu, in its second season of public opening, was busy; and a troop of Boy Scouts who were camping on the estate volunteered to help out as guides.

One afternoon, Montagu invited two of the scouts for a swim, and they wandered down with Hume to a beach hut on the Solent. Afterwards, when Montagu found that an expensive camera was missing and reported it to the police along with his suspicions that one of the scouts had swiped it, they responded by telling him that the boys had made counterallegations against him and Hume, claiming the two men had sexually assaulted them.

Montagu always insisted that he did nothing untoward, although he later admitted that when he and Scout A walked into the hut after their swim, they disturbed Hume "behaving mildly indecently" with Scout B.[6] The boys were aged fourteen and fifteen. Whatever the truth of the matter, the two adults were charged with indecent assault and committed for trial at Winchester, where, in December 1953, the teenage scouts gave contradictory and inconsistent testimony. Montagu was acquitted of one charge, although the jury failed to agree on a second or on the charges against Hume, and a retrial was ordered. In April 1954, the case against them was quietly dropped. By then, however, Montagu was in more trouble.

Lord Montagu arriving for a hearing at Lymington magistrates' court, November 1953

In fact, he was in jail.

As Lord Montagu's first trial was coming to its inconclusive end, the Royal Air Force Special Investigation Branch arrested two young airmen, John Reynolds and Edward McNally, who were orderlies at an RAF hospital in Ely. Both were gay—"perverts," the prosecuting counsel would later allege, "men of the lowest possible moral character"—and they were accused of committing offences with several men in Cambridgeshire and London after incriminating letters were found in McNally's kit. Under questioning they named twenty-four men, none of whom was ever prosecuted.

But among McNally's letters the RAF police found one from Peter Wildeblood, who had picked up McNally at the Piccadilly tube station and taken him back to his flat. The letter mentioned Beaulieu, and under rigorous questioning the airmen revealed that in 1952 they had spent time at the Beaulieu beach hut with Montagu and Wildeblood, and later with Wildeblood and Michael Pitt-Rivers at a house in Dorset.

The mention of Edward Montagu was enough to bring in the Hampshire police, who had been in charge of the investigation into the Boy Scouts' accusations against him and Kenneth Hume and who were determined to catch their peer. Reynolds and McNally were promised immunity from prosecution if they turned Queen's evidence against Montagu, Wildeblood, and Pitt-Rivers.

At 8 a.m. on January 9, 1954, a month after Montagu's first trial, police arrived at Beaulieu Palace House. Let in by the butler, they insisted on going straight up to Montagu's bedroom, where they told him to get dressed because he was being arrested. Wildeblood and Pitt-Rivers were arrested at the same time, and that evening the three men were charged with, at various times and places, "conspir[ing] to incite certain male persons—namely John Reynolds and Edward McNally—to commit serious offences with male persons."[7] They were committed for trial at the Winchester assizes and released on bail to appear at court in March.

This was the Montagu case. Or at least that was how the press referred to it, and that was how the public saw it. The other two defendants were bit players, a supporting cast in a drama that was as much about class and the abuse of power as it was about the law. The *Daily Mirror* wrote in shocked tones about a "beer party" at the beach hut, "an all-male affair at which the men danced with each other."[8] G. D. Roberts, QC, who appeared for the prosecution, portrayed the defendants as posh seducers, plying the two working-class boys with champagne and visits to West End theatres. "Under the seductive influence of lavish hospitality, loaded upon them by these persons, who were so infinitely the social superiors of these aircraftmen, Reynolds and this Corporal McNally responded perfectly cheerfully to the advances that were made, and were perfectly ready to gratify the desires of the three defendants."[9] That rather ordinary beach hut had become, wrote Wildeblood later, "a gilded den of vice in which all-male orgies went on till dawn."[10]

At the end of the eight-day trial the jury found all three men guilty. Mr Justice Ormerod sentenced Montagu to twelve months in prison and Wildeblood and Pitt-Rivers to eighteen months each. The difference in sentences was because Montagu had only committed gross indecency, while the other two were found to have committed "serious offences," by which was meant sodomy.

Much was made in court of the legal distinction between sodomy and other kinds of sexual contact, and of the difference between "inverts," who were mentally ill, and "perverts," who were moral degenerates. Before sentencing, Peter Wildeblood's barrister called a Dr Hobson, of the department of psychological medicine at Middlesex Hospital, who said he thought suitable treatment could "effect a cure" for Wildeblood's "sexual abnormality."[11] Wildeblood himself wrote in *Against the Law*, his 1955 account of the trial and its aftermath, that as he sat in the dock looking at the jury and the people on the public benches, all sitting with pinched mouths and clasped hands, he "wanted to get up and shout: 'It was not I who made "love" into a dirty word—it is you!'"[12]

"I do not suppose," said Wildeblood, "[that] it ever occurred to Edward Montagu that there were certain dangers in rejecting the class-system which so many of his friends and neighbours held sacred."[13] Montagu himself always believed that his prosecution was an act of vengeance by the establishment for the way he ignored social divisions. Half a century later he maintained that Mr Justice Ormerod steered the jury towards a guilty verdict because of the class difference between the three defendants and the two chief witnesses for the prosecution, "the dreadful social impropriety—as he saw it—of 'upper-class' people like us consorting with 'lower-class' men such as McNally and Reynolds."[14]

Certainly, it was Montagu's face that dominated the front pages, Montagu's reaction to the verdict which made the headlines. (He "swayed slightly."[15]) As the three were committed to prison to begin their sentences, reporters didn't rush round to Wildeblood's London flat or to Pitt-Rivers's Dorset farm, but they did rush down to Beaulieu. The *Daily Mirror* described the scene (bold in the original):

> Tate, the butler, drew the heavy velvet curtains as dusk came down over stately Palace House, near Beaulieu, Hants, last night.
>
> Walking slowly through the mansion's spacious rooms, he carried out all the nightly duties which have been his for many years—except one.
>
> For there was no need for him to turn back the coverlet of his master's bed.
>
> **Lord Montagu of Beaulieu was not at home.**[16]

It was the first time that a peer of the realm had been found guilty in a criminal court since the 1948 abolition of their right to trial by their fellow peers in the House of Lords. Other gay and bisexual members of the landed classes had been exposed in the past, of course, and occasionally prosecuted, but without the kind of publicity that attended the Montagu case. When Nancy Astor's son from her first marriage, Robert Gould Shaw III, was picked up by police in 1931 and sentenced to four months in jail for soliciting, Nancy used all her influence to keep the story out of the newspapers. Since her husband owned the *Observer* and her brother-in-law owned the *Times*, she had something of a head start. She also made a personal appeal to Lord Beaverbrook, owner of the *Daily Express* group. News of Shaw's conviction didn't appear in print.

The Montagu case had an unintended consequence. In the early 1950s there were already demands for a more humane approach to homosexuality, with letters to the *Times* calling for the home secretary to review the current punitive laws. "No man ought to be penalised by the law for a condition for which he is not to blame," wrote one correspondent from the Church of England Moral Welfare Council.[17]

Now those demands grew louder. The left-wing columnist Hannen Swaffer urged compassion for Montagu, Wildeblood, and Pitt-Rivers, and more generally for gay men. (Sexual acts between women were not and had never been illegal.) "Shutting up a nervous, highly strung individual is mere brutality," he wrote in the *People*. "Society must realise that imprisonment is not a cure for abnormality."[18] Within weeks there were debates in both the Lords and the Commons on whether or not the law should be changed. Robert Boothby argued in the Commons that "what consenting adults do in privacy may be a moral issue between them and their Maker, [but] it is not a legal issue between them and the State." Lord Hailsham, a future lord high chancellor of Great Britain and a man who could be relied on as a reactionary voice, took the opposite view. All gay men were promiscuous, unbalanced, and unhappy, he claimed. This was "inherent in the nature of an activity which seeks a satisfaction for which the bodily organs employed are physically unsuited."[19]

In August 1954 the government set up a Committee on Homosexual Offences and Prostitution, chaired by an educationalist and ex-headmaster, Sir John Wolfenden. Peter Wildeblood was one of those who gave evidence to the committee. (Another was the director of public prosecutions, Sir Theobald Mathew, who testified that "young men should be taught that these habits are dirty, degrading and harmful, and the negation of decent manhood."[20]) In 1957 the committee recommended decriminalising homosexual acts between consenting adults, and ten years later, the Wolfenden report's principal recommendations passed into law. Nearly half a century after his conviction, Lord Montagu broke down in tears when it was suggested to him that the reform of the law on homosexuality would be his monument. "I am proud," he said in a speech to mark the fiftieth anniversary of the publication of Wolfenden. "I am proud that the so-called Montagu Case had more effect on changing the laws than any other factor."[21]

NEITHER OF THE main protagonists in the second great aristocratic scandal of the postwar period had much to be proud of. In 1963 Ian Douglas Campbell, 11th Duke of Argyll and chief of Clan Campbell, and his third duchess, Margaret, found themselves embroiled in a notorious divorce case involving jet-set infidelities that took place not in a ramshackle beach hut on the Solent but in New York, Paris, Mayfair, and the duke's eighty-four-room ancestral seat, Inveraray Castle on the shores of Loch Fyne in Scotland.

It was the duchess's second marriage and the duke's third, in itself a pointer to the fact that, as Prime Minister Harold Macmillan put it in 1958, "now people marry for a year or two and then pass to the next period of what is really licensed concubinage."[22] They married in 1951 and spent their honeymoon at Inveraray, where their arrival was heralded by Ian's personal piper playing "The Campbells Are Coming."

The castle is an imposing mixture of clunky eighteenth-century Gothic Revivalism and elegant Adamesque interiors, all turrets and battlements on the outside and neoclassical detailing on the inside. James Lees-Milne saw it in 1943 when the 11th Duke's predecessor, a scholarly eccentric who spoke to fairies and greeted visitors with recitals from Italian opera, was still alive: Lees-Milne was not impressed with the architecture, calling the castle "grim and forbidding like some hydropathic hotel," but he found some good Georgian furniture; and he was intrigued by the 10th Duke, who would rush without warning from the room to play a Gregorian chant on a harmonium, and who had a cuckoo whistle "which he likes to blow in the woods in order to bewilder the soldiers."[23]

The daughter of a self-made millionaire, Argyll's new duchess was wealthy and socially ambitious, and if Margaret Whigham's not-altogether-reliable memoirs are to be believed, it was her

The Duchess and Duke of Argyll in fancy dress, circa 1955

wealth which attracted her to the impoverished Duke of Argyll, who was struggling to pay death duties of around half a million pounds. She knew the value of money. Staying in Seville early on in their marriage, the duke started throwing his weight about and demanding a better hotel room: "After all, I am the Duke of Argyll." Margaret pointed out to her new husband that "in this town dukes are two-a-penny" and advised him, "If you want to get results just start crackling a few crisp dollars."[24]

Back in Scotland, Margaret found that she was expected to crackle more than a few crisp dollars. She and her father poured money into Inveraray Castle, as well as settling her husband's other debts, which included £4,000 he still owed to the House of Worth for a mink coat he had bought his previous wife to celebrate inheriting the dukedom in 1949. Outlying farms were sold off, along with some of the choicest pieces of furniture, and Margaret persuaded her husband and his trustees that Inveraray should open to the public at half a crown a head, which it did on Saturday, April 25, 1953. "Guests were able to appreciate the duke's skill and taste shown in the task of transforming an ancient and decaying building into a home of rare distinction and beauty," gushed the *Tatler*, with scant regard for the pivotal role played by the duchess.[25]

Margaret enjoyed being a duchess, and she enjoyed having a ducal seat. She was happiest, she said, when she was at Inveraray, although she never quite forgot that appearances should always trump reality: On one occasion when society photographer Brodrick Haldane decided to photograph the castle from a little bridge beside the loch, Margaret's daughter stopped him. "Mummy says it doesn't look large enough from there."[26]

But the marriage was soon in trouble. Margaret's new husband was an alcoholic and an inveterate gambler who was given to wild mood swings, something she ascribed to his regular use of Drinamyl, a cocktail of amphetamine and barbiturate. He stole from her and was violent towards her. And he was frequently unfaithful during their stormy marriage. But she was also unfaithful, and it was the duchess's sexual exploits rather than the duke's which scandalised British society.

Margaret had a powerful sexual appetite. "Sometimes I feel I need a man so desperately that my body aches," she once told a friend, and stories of her sexual exploits are legion.[27] The journalist Michael Thornton claimed that in the hot summer of 1958, when he was a seventeen-year-old schoolboy, she picked him up on the street in Oban, drove him back to Inveraray Castle, and, after suggesting he might like to go up and cool off in her pink seashell of a bath, strolled into the bathroom stark naked. "'I thought I would come and join you,' she said in a charming and normal manner, as if sharing her bath with a naked stranger were an everyday occurrence."[28] Her friends attributed her enthusiastic and sometimes predatory sexual behaviour to the fact that she had fallen down a lift shaft during the war. Others were less charitable. The celebrity fortune-teller Eva Petulengro, whom Margaret once consulted, said later that she was like "a cross between a high-class whore and the wicked witch who gave Snow White the apple."[29] Ian claimed, ungallantly, that he had put a bolt on his bedroom door to prevent his duchess getting into his room and into his bed.

As the ducal marriage collapsed, both sides sought to gain the upper hand by resorting to underhand methods. Margaret forged letters which suggested that Ian's sons by his second marriage weren't his, and she padded her stomach to indicate she was pregnant while hatching a wild plan to buy a baby in Poland and pass him off as the legitimate heir to the dukedom. Ian took out an injunction to prevent his wife from visiting Inveraray: she was allowed one day from dawn till dusk to gather all her personal possessions, something she did with remarkable aplomb, due in part to the Benzedrine she was taking to keep her spirits up. He broke into her bedroom at her London house on Upper Grosvenor Street when she was sleeping and, while his daughter from a previous marriage held her down, stole her diary from her bedside table, desperate to find hard evidence of her infidelity. On another occasion he broke into a locked cupboard at Upper Grosvenor Street and stole incriminating letters.

He also found a manila envelope addressed to his wife containing thirteen Polaroid photographs. Two of them showed a woman performing sex acts on a man—or possibly two different men; the head was cut off in the images. The woman, whose back was to the camera, wore three strands of pearls in a necklace with a diamond clasp. Margaret habitually wore just such a necklace, bought at Asprey.

Ian brought divorce proceedings against Margaret, initially accusing her of adultery with eighty-eight men, although this was eventually whittled down to three: Peter Combe, a young man who had worked as a press officer at the Savoy Hotel; Sigismund von Braun, brother of the rocket scientist Wernher von Braun; and John Cohane, a man she met at a party in New York in 1956, whose letters to her were quoted by the judge: "I have thought of a number of new, highly intriguing things that we might do, or I might do to you."[30] There was also the unnamed man or men in the Polaroids.

Margaret contested the divorce and countersued, accusing the duke of adultery with her own stepmother, who was a year younger than she: theirs were complicated lives. It did no good. When the duke's case was heard in the Court of Session at Edinburgh in May 1963, the fact that young Peter Combe had taken her home after a visit to a nightclub and remained with her at Upper Grosvenor Street for several hours was quite enough for the judge, Lord Wheatley, to grant a divorce on the assumption that they must have slept together. He accepted that, while the duchess had been sexually involved with von Braun and Cohane, defence counsel's plea of condonation—that the duke had previously forgiven or condoned acts of which he now accused her—was reasonable because her husband had known of these affairs and had continued to live with her.

But it was the Polaroids which captured the world's attention. Margaret's counsel argued that the woman wasn't her—until the evidence of the necklace was produced. Then he claimed that the "headless man" was her husband, who was known to have a fondness for pornographic photographs. But, as the *Times* delicately put it, "an expert had made an examination of the Duke and a comparison of the photographs and had come to the conclusion that the male in the photographs was the same in each case and that the male in the photographs was not the pursuer [the Scottish term for the plaintiff]."[31] Margaret always claimed the expert had realised her husband's penis was much smaller than that of the headless man.

If these details seem absurd now, they did not seem absurd to Lord Wheatley, who didn't confine himself to granting the Duke of Argyll his divorce. Deciding that the photographs seemed, from their contents, to be more likely to appeal to "a woman with a sex perversion than by a man with a sex perversion," he launched a savage attack on the duchess, who was, he said, "a completely promiscuous woman whose sexual appetite could only be satisfied by a number of men, and whose attitude to the sanctity of marriage was what moderns would call enlightened, but in plain language could only be described as wholly immoral."[32] And at dinner tables and in bars across the country, people speculated on the identity of the headless man. It was Sigismund von Braun. It was a member of the royal family. It was a film star. Douglas Fairbanks Jr was in the frame, so to speak, for years. He had been sexually involved with the duchess, and Christine Keeler, with whom he was also involved, maintained that everyone in her circle knew it was him. Duncan Sandys, minister of defence in Macmillan's government, was another name that was bandied about. But Sandys clearly wasn't the man, since his legs and feet were badly scarred as a result of a wartime car crash, unlike the headless man's; although, like so many others, he did have a fling with the duchess.

Neither side came out of the divorce with reputation intact. While the judge reserved his harshest condemnation for the duchess, he also criticised the duke's evidence as unconvincing and said of his habit of keeping pornographic photographs (and showing them to male and female acquaintances at parties), "I do not commend his standard of tastes and habits."[33] The duke, who successfully pursued his ex-wife for court costs and attorney fees, was asked to resign from his club. He retreated to Inveraray and married his fourth wife, the American Mathilda Coster Mortimer, a few weeks after his divorce came through. She was a sensible, thoughtful woman who ran Inveraray with the help of a butler, a cook, and a daily cleaning woman, and who drove round the estate in an old Mercedes-Benz she had bought when she lived in Paris and which now had the Argyll arms enamelled on its doors. Margaret, devastated at Wheatley's harsh and very public condemnation of her, retreated from the British social scene and waited for memories to fade. Thank God for the Profumo affair, she wrote to a friend: it gave people something else to think about.[34]

EVEN TODAY, NEARLY sixty years later, the scandal that brought down a prime minister lives on in the public consciousness. The Profumo affair had everything: sex, lies, and espionage; an establishment cover-up and a mysterious death; a cast of call girls and cabinet ministers and pimps. "Above all there was Cliveden, stateliest of stately homes," as the critic and intellectual John Gross put it at the time. "It would have taken a recklessly melodramatic novelist to link such an Establishment stronghold with the sleazy, near-gangster world of some of Christine Keeler's friends."[35]

The sequence of events is well known but so convoluted that it bears a brief retelling.[36] On the weekend of July 8–10, 1961, William Waldorf Astor II, 3rd Viscount Astor, and his wife, Bronwen, hosted a house party at Cliveden, a magnificent Italianate mansion overlooking the Thames in Buckinghamshire. Viscount Astor's parents had given Cliveden to the National Trust in 1942 along with a very large endowment, but the gift came with the proviso that the family could continue to live there for as long as they liked, and it was still used regularly by the viscount and viscountess. On this occasion the Astors had assembled a glittering crowd to meet the guest of honour, Ayub Khan, president of Pakistan. Lord Mountbatten came to lunch on Saturday with his daughter Lady Pamela and her husband, designer David Hicks. Interior decorator Derek Patmore and artist Felix Kelly were also there, along with an assortment of friends and relations of the Astors. Some left in the afternoon, to be replaced at dinner by the satirical cartoonist Sir Osbert Lancaster and his wife, Karen, and Sir Roy and Billa Harrod. Roy Harrod was Macmillan's economic adviser, and the couple were regulars at Cliveden.

Another couple made up the house party: John Profumo, Macmillan's secretary of state for war, and his film star wife, Valerie Hobson. It was their first visit to Cliveden.

After dinner Astor took his guests out into the summer evening and they wandered down to a walled garden which held a tennis court and an open-air swimming pool. Astor and Profumo were a little ahead of the others, and they found a rather different kind of party going on in the pool. Stephen Ward, an osteopath friend of the Astors, was allowed the use of Spring Cottage, a substantial nineteenth-century Tudor Revival house on the estate, and he often came down for the weekend and brought guests of his own. This particular evening, they included an Iranian friend, Leo Norell; a pretty young hitchhiker known to history only as Joy, whom Ward had picked up on the drive down from London; and Christine Keeler, a twenty-year-old exotic dancer and model.

According to Keeler, whose memory of events was often at odds with the facts, she was swimming naked in the pool when Astor and Profumo appeared. Ward greeted them and at the same time picked up Keeler's swimsuit from the edge of the pool and threw it into the bushes, leaving her to try unsuccessfully to cover herself with a very small towel. At which point—again, according to her unreliable memory—Bill Astor and John Profumo chased her round the pool trying to whip the towel away. "I was giggling and enjoying the game. The towel would slip or I would let it slip a bit and there were schoolboy shrieks from the two of them." Then the rest of the party arrived. "The women were in stark contrast to me in their evening gowns and jewellery," Keeler said.[37] No doubt they were.

Ward and his guests were invited up to the big house for after-dinner drinks, and the next day, Sunday, July 9, the Astors' party went down to splash around in the pool, where they joined up with Ward, Keeler, and several others—including Eugene Ivanov, a naval attaché at the Soviet embassy in London. Ivanov and Ward had been introduced over lunch at the Garrick by one of Ward's patients, the *Daily Telegraph* editor Sir Colin Coote. They began seeing each other socially with the knowledge of MI5, and it seems probable that both men were tasked by their respective intelligence

Eugene Ivanov, Christine Keeler, and friends at Cliveden, 1961

services with passing on fake news and tidbits of information they wished the other side to have.

The upshot of the Cliveden weekend was that Profumo, who like rather a lot of male politicians at the time didn't take his marriage vows too seriously, asked Keeler for her phone number.* She told him to get it from Ward, with whom she was living in a platonic relationship at the time, and went back to Ward's London flat with Ivanov and slept with him. "He wanted good, old-fashioned sex without any fuss or trimmings," she said. "He was a Soviet warrior."[38] Within days she had also started an affair with John Profumo.

"He thought he could get away with it," Valerie Profumo told their son. "After all, most of his friends did."[39] And he might have done, if it weren't for a low-life Antiguan jazz promoter and drug dealer named Johnny Edgecombe. In December 1962, long after Keeler's brief affair with Jack Profumo had fizzled out, Keeler was with her friend, Mandy Rice-Davies, at Stephen Ward's flat when Edgecombe, who was or had been Keeler's lover, turned up and demanded to be let in. He was a violent man who had recently slashed yet another of Keeler's lovers, a Jamaican jazz singer called Lucky Gordon, leaving him needing seventeen stitches in his face. Now Edgecombe refused to believe Rice-Davies when she lied that Keeler wasn't in the flat. He produced a revolver and fired, first at the lock of the front door and then at Rice-Davies, who was leaning out of a first-floor window. Having tried and failed to get into the flat by climbing up a drainpipe, he dropped the gun and ran off, but police picked him up and he was charged with attempted murder.

---

*Valerie Profumo was only too aware of her husband's roving eye, complaining that he flirted in front of her and was always on the lookout for his next conquest, even when they were dancing together. She also complained about his tight trousers: "Surely there must be *some* way of concealing your penis." Richard Davenport-Hines, *An English Affair: Sex, Class and Power in the Age of Profumo* (HarperPress, 2013), 61.

Over Christmas 1962 Keeler began to gossip at parties about her various relationships—her friendship with Ward, her affair with Profumo, her narrow escape from Johnny Edgecombe. The world in which she moved was a curious one in which drug dealers and jazz singers mixed with MPs and journalists, and as her stories grew wilder with each telling, rumours began to circulate, and Fleet Street started to take an interest, especially when she implied that Ward was in league with Ivanov, saying that the osteopath had urged her to find out from Profumo if and when America might give atomic weapons to West Germany. (Apparently, as it came out later, Ward really did say this, but only as a joke.) She tried to sell her story to the press only for Ward to say that he, Profumo, and Astor would sue if any newspaper dared to publish it. Ivanov was recalled to Moscow.

When, at the end of January 1963, a detective paid a routine visitor to Keeler and Rice-Davies to remind them they would be called as prosecution witnesses at Edgecombe's coming trial, the girls told him rather more than he expected. They were both angry with Stephen Ward: Keeler because he had wrecked her chance of selling her story and Rice-Davies because after the shooting he had moved to a flat in Bryanston Mews that she believed had been given to her by her late lover, the notorious slumlord Peter Rachman. They told the policeman about Ward, whom they accused of being a pimp, and Keeler described her affair with Profumo, said that Ward had asked her to find out about Germany and American atomic weapons, and mentioned that Ward had introduced her to Ivanov.

The police decided to take no action, but by the following week the tales of goings-on at Cliveden had reached the prime minister's office. Macmillan's private secretary, John Wyndham, was told privately that the secretary of state for war had compromised himself with a girl who was involved in a criminal court case. In a memo for his boss, Wyndham stated that according to his informant, Mark Chapman-Walker—once a Conservative

Party press officer but now managing director of the *News of the World*—Profumo had met Keeler through Lord Astor at Cliveden, where they had chased her naked round the pool. The memo noted Ward's involvement, saying that he had brought Keeler and Profumo together, and also claimed that Profumo, visiting Keeler at Ward's house, passed Ivanov on his way out. Profumo flatly denied any sexual relationship with Keeler, both to political friends and to the prime minister's office. And they believed him, because they wanted to believe him.

When Johnny Edgecombe's trial opened at the Old Bailey on March 14, the prosecution's star witness was missing. Christine Keeler had fled to Spain. People said Profumo had packed her off out of the way in case she blurted out something about him and Ivanov under cross-examination. In fact, she had been driven down there by Paul Mann, an ex–racing driver who was trying to negotiate a lucrative exclusive for her—and presumably for himself—with Fleet Street, and who realised that by keeping her out of the witness box he was making her more valuable. (Because she wasn't there to testify, Edgecombe was acquitted on the more serious charges, but he was still sentenced to seven years for possessing a firearm with intent to endanger life.)

The trial was the trigger for an explosion of press interest and innuendo in Profumo and Keeler. The *Daily Express* ran a front-page story about Keeler's disappearance with a revealing photograph of her. It was next to another story headlined "War Minister Shock," which claimed that Profumo had offered to resign for personal reasons but Macmillan had refused to accept his resignation. Labour politicians, sensing an opportunity to damage the government, asked questions in the House under parliamentary privilege, while Profumo continued to deny everything. Mandy Rice-Davies, eager to cash in on the notoriety engulfing her friend, claimed to have slept with Viscount Astor. Journalists burgled Astor's London house and stole letters; they ransacked Spring Cottage; they even broke into lockers at his eleven-year-old son's school.

Lord and Lady Astor were in America while the affair was playing out in the press. When they arrived home Lord Astor was astonished to find himself invited to a police interview, where he was asked the names of women he had had sex with. It emerged during questioning that he had once given Keeler a cheque for the rent of a flat in Barons Court she shared with Mandy Rice-Davies—rather an awkward admission for him. Because they believed the two girls had brought men back to that flat, the police briefly toyed with the idea of charging Astor with keeping a brothel. They followed up the interview a few months later by arriving at Cliveden just as the Astors' houseguests were leaving and saying they were there to collect evidence that he had allowed a brothel at Spring Cottage. He was snubbed in public and pilloried by the press. "Today, Cliveden has plenty of sightseers, but very few visitors," reported a gleeful *Daily Express*.[40]

Astor's embarrassment pales beside the fates of the leading players in the Profumo affair. John Profumo, having been persuaded by senior colleagues in the Conservative Party to stand up in the House of Commons and state categorically that there had been no impropriety in his relationship with Christine Keeler, was then persuaded by his wife to come clean. He resigned from the government on June 5, 1963, and the *Daily Mirror* screamed, "What the Hell Is Going On in This Country?" in a front-page editorial attacking the government. "Mr Macmillan has told Mr Profumo that this is a great tragedy for Mr Profumo, his family and his friends. All that is sadly true. But the greatest tragedy, surely, is for Mr Macmillan, HIS family (most of them are in the Government) and HIS friends. And HIS political party."[41] The *Mirror* was right: four months later Macmillan resigned as prime minister.

Three days after the announcement of Profumo's resignation was made public, Stephen Ward was arrested and charged with living on immoral earnings, in an act of revenge by the establishment for causing it so much trouble. On July 31, 1963, the jury found him guilty of living on the immoral earnings of Christine

Keeler and Mandy Rice-Davies. He wasn't in court to hear the verdict, having taken an overdose of barbiturates in the early hours of that morning. He died without regaining consciousness on August 3.

The following day, eager for another sacrificial victim, the editor of the *Sunday Express*, John Gordon, launched a spiteful attack on Viscount Astor, claiming that his father had given Cliveden to the National Trust "to evade death duties in the normal way some of the abnormally rich evade them." (The day after Ward's overdose the trust had issued a statement distancing itself rather anxiously from the Astors: "The Trust lets Cliveden House with its grounds and cottages direct to Lord Astor, for a substantial rent."[42]) Declaring that the trust must be disturbed about the disrepute brought on an estate which it owned, Gordon went on: "What if it decided to cancel the arrangement and return the estate to Lord Astor bringing the shadow of future death duties back upon his family? That would certainly be a popular retribution."[43] A curious notion. Give the Astors back their vast mansion with its equally vast endowment—that'll teach them. Needless to say, the National Trust did not oblige.

The public's taste for scandal and its capacity for moral outrage wasn't confined to aristocratic targets in the 1950s and 1960s. Countless scout leaders and choirmasters and pop stars could testify to that. But a country house setting provided an additional frisson of schadenfreude at the tragicomic fall from grace of a class that had once ruled the country and that now provided headlines of a different kind. The suggestion that promiscuity and perversion were rife in landed society offered confirmation that the owners of country houses were not only no better than us—they were worse. And the public rather liked that idea.

18

LIONS RAMPANT

I N THE SUMMER of 1964 James Seaton Methuen Chipperfield had a bright idea.

Lions.

That idea was to make him an awful lot of money, and for a brief time it caused a revolution in the stately home business.

Jimmy Chipperfield, as he was better known, was born in 1912 into one of the oldest circus families in Britain. He was actually born in a mahogany caravan parked up on the 3rd Lord Methuen's Corsham estate in Wiltshire, where Chipperfield's Circus was performing at the time—hence the middle name. As a boy he learned clowning and the trapeze, but his real interest lay in performing animals. He trained lions and tigers, and he married the daughter of another circus proprietor and lion tamer whose lions had clearly been insufficiently tame, since they killed him. Jimmy and his brother Dick built up the family business until by the early 1950s Chipperfield's Circus and Menagerie was the largest travelling show in Britain, with a big top that could seat four thousand people and a show which offered more than two hundred animals, including performing lions, Bengal tigers, grizzly bears, and zebras.

In 1955, restless and bored with managing the business side of the circus, Jimmy left the family firm and went out on his own, training animals for films. He also set up his own zoo and, in a less regulated age, made a number of trips to Kenya and Uganda on animal-catching expeditions, coming back with elephants, giraffes, and other beasts. It was while he was watching animals in the wild in Africa (and chasing them, lassoing them, and putting them into crates) that he first thought of enabling the British public to see them at close quarters, not in cages in the zoo but roaming free (or free-ish) in the landscape. A safari park, in other words: a drive-through reserve, with tourists watching big game from the safety of their cars.

Right from the start, Chipperfield was sure he wanted to concentrate on lions. His basic conviction, he said later, was that "to be able to drive about among lions would be a tremendous attraction for the public, because lions are killers, and danger is a very strong attraction. Everyone likes to court death a little, without getting too near it."[1]

A country house estate would be ideal for the park and, since he wasn't in a position to buy one and provide all the start-up costs himself, he looked around for a landed partner. His first choice for the new venture was Hale Park in the New Forest, where the baroque architect Thomas Archer had built himself a handsome house back in 1715. The current owner, David Booth-Jones, invited the showman down to Hale in the summer of 1964 to discuss ideas for attracting more visitors to the house and grounds; seizing the opportunity, Chipperfield broached the idea of lions. Booth-Jones was keen, but his octogenarian mother, who lived with him, was not. "I know what you're like," she told her son. "You'd go off, and I'd be left to feed the lions myself."[2] Both men realised that the plan wouldn't work at Hale—Booth-Jones went for concerts by the King's Singers instead, and the estate was sold ten years later—but as Chipperfield was leaving, Booth-Jones offered to give him an introduction to Henry Thynne, the Marquess of Bath. Their sons knew each other.

Chipperfield met Bath at Longleat for the first time in November 1964. To begin with, Lord Bath was slow to grasp the idea. "The cages will have to be awfully big if the cars are going to get into them at the same time as the lions," he said.[3] But as Chipperfield outlined his scheme to allow up to forty lions to roam free in the Capability Brown park, Bath's enthusiasm grew. Longleat had been open to the public as a commercial concern for twenty-five years. It was attracting around 135,000 visitors a year, placing it in the top five commercial stately homes, but behind Woburn, Chatsworth, Blenheim, and Beaulieu.

As far as Lord Bath was concerned, there was room for improvement, and he was constantly on the lookout for new ways of boosting Longleat's visitor figures. When Chipperfield warned him that if the safari park proved as popular as he thought it might, there could be "millions" of people, and said, "I wouldn't want you to blame me for bringing them all in," all the marquess did was to repeat over and over again that there could never be too many visitors.[4]

It was a partnership, with Lord Bath supplying the fences and roads through the park, and Chipperfield finding, paying for, and managing the forty or so lions that were needed. Once the safari park was established, they would split both the costs and the profits fifty-fifty. While Chipperfield looked for lions, Lord Bath obtained planning permission from the local council to put up a fence "to contain animals."[5] The chain-link fencing for the main perimeter came from government surplus: it had originally been ordered to defend military bases in Kenya during the Mau Mau uprising of the 1950s.

The lions were more difficult to find. Chipperfield acquired almost all of them from zoos and circuses—none came from the wild. As word went round, a film company cabled to say they had ten lions in Nairobi, left over from filming *Born Free*, the British drama about a couple raising an orphaned lion cub in Kenya: they didn't know what to do with them. Chipperfield offered £100 for the lot, and the offer was accepted. They ended up costing more like £300 each, once transportation costs had been factored in. The infrastructure in the park at Longleat—new roads, inner and outer perimeter fences—were reckoned at about £75,000.

The partners were anxious to keep their plans quiet for as long as possible, but by early 1965 the story had leaked out. According to Chipperfield, it was Lord Bath's fault: he got drunk at the annual Bristol Press Club dinner and suddenly announced to the assembled journalists, "I'm going to have fifty lions at Longleat."[6] And all hell broke loose. Outraged that planning permission had been given for the project, the *Times* urged the government to step in and put a stop to it. "Cattle, sheep and deer ought to be good enough for a Wiltshire man," it roared. "The proper place for lions in an island that is spared them in the wild state is in heraldry."[7] Questions were asked in Parliament. The local Conservative MP prophesied that the lions would escape and start ravaging the sheep population of the West Country. Local Labour councillors lobbied Richard Crossman, minister of housing and local government, to prevent the safari park from going ahead; Crossman declined to become involved, passing the buck back to the local council. Joy Adamson, author of *Born Free*, and Bill Travers, who played her husband in the film version, both weighed in to criticise the scheme, saying it was dangerous and amateurish.

There were so many protests that Lord Bath had to issue a statement making it clear that the wardens would all be carrying big-game rifles, he would have a horse patrol circling the perimeter fence at all times, and there would be watchdogs. His public relations officer claimed (with some truth) that "most of the neighbours would rather face lions than the 15,000 screaming teenagers at pop concerts here last year."[8]

But everyone's fears looked to be confirmed in April 1966, shortly before what was billed as the first safari park outside Africa opened to the public. A rumour flew round that some lions had escaped. So they had: two cubs squeezed under the inner fence into the no-man's-land between it and the fourteen-feet-high electrified outer fence. They were swiftly apprehended. Then three young lions on their way from Frankfurt to Longleat by air broke out of their crates somewhere over the North Sea, and the pilots had to keep them out of the cockpit by brandishing a hatchet at them. The plane landed at Brussels to be met by riot police with machine guns, but the day was saved by a female zoologist who turned up and shooed the ferocious beasts out of the aircraft and into new crates. With a broomstick.

ALTHOUGH YOU WOULDN'T think it from the shrill tone of the protests, the lions of Longleat had a long and historic pedigree. One of the safari park's earliest ancestors in England was the menagerie at the Tower of London, started in 1235 when the Holy Roman Emperor Frederick II sent three live leopards to Henry III, an allusion to the three leopards on the king's arms. They were followed by a polar bear from Norway, and an elephant which was a present from Louis IX of France. Cages were built for them around a baiting pit. By the fourteenth century a lion and a lioness had been added to the royal collection, and lions continued to feature prominently in the Tower menagerie, along with wolves, monkeys, other big cats, and the occasional elephant. At the end of the sixteenth century there were also an eagle and a porcupine. There were six lions there during the Commonwealth, and in 1731 lions were successfully bred at the Tower. That same year the governor recorded that the visiting Duke of Lorraine was shown a young male lion "and took him up in his arms, stroked, kissed and pulled him by the whiskers."[9]

By this time the public was paying sixpence for the privilege of seeing the animals at the Tower, but its fortunes declined until in 1822 there was only a grizzly bear, an elephant, and one or two birds. However, it gained a new lease of life under the watchful eye of Alfred Cops, who became keeper that year and who seems to have known more than his predecessors about animal welfare. Within less than ten years, Cops had built up the collection to fifty-nine specimens. There were three different kinds of lions, five other big cats, a wolf, a jackal, several hyenas, monkeys and baboons, and all manner of exotic birds. All were kept clean and well fed, so that a contemporary noted that not a single death had occurred from disease and only one from accident: the secretary bird had rashly poked its neck into the hyenas' den and "was deprived of it and of its head in one bite."[10]

Unfortunately, there was another accident in 1835, when one of Cops's lions mauled two soldiers. As soon as he heard of it the Duke of Wellington, then constable of the Tower, said they had to go. "The King is determined that wild beasts shall not be kept there," he told the resident governor. "Mr Cops had better dispose of his."[11] So he did. The animals all went to the newly formed Zoological Gardens in Regent's Park, and that was the end of the royal menagerie.

But the Tower was far from being the only place where wild animals were kept for the entertainment and education of the public. In the eighteenth century especially, a menagerie was, if not exactly a common adjunct to a country house, then at least not a rarity, and distinguished architects turned their hand to producing buildings which were part folly, part cage, and part observation post. William Chambers designed a menagerie and an aviary for the banker Robert Child at Osterley Park; Capability Brown designed the same at Castle Ashby; and the menagerie that Thomas Wright designed for Lord Halifax at Horton in Northamptonshire was an elaborate affair with rococo plasterwork by Thomas Roberts of Oxford. Horace Walpole, who visited Horton in 1763, was impressed:

In the Menagerie which is [in] a little wood, very prettily disposed with many basins of gold fish, are several curious beasts.

Storks; raccoons that breed there much, and I believe the first that have bred here; a very large strong eagle, another with a white head; two hogs from the Havannah with navels on their backs; two young tigers; two uncommon martins; doves from Guadaloupe, brown with blue heads, and a milk white streak crossing their cheeks; a kind of ermine, sandy with many spots all over the body and tail.[12]

Ironically enough, Longleat also had wild animals in the eighteenth century. Leopards, wolves, a bear, and various eagles and vultures were housed in dens in the woods, although they seem to have been a youthful fad, because in 1734, only a year after two local carpenters were paid for building the dens, twenty-four-year-old Lord Weymouth decided to get rid of them all. His son and heir was born that year: perhaps fears for the child's safety influenced Weymouth's decision.

By the twentieth century, lions and tigers were more likely to be found gazing down from the walls of the great hall, or spread-eagled and glass-eyed in front of the fireplace in the library. There were exceptions. A herd of wallabies roamed the Peak District National Park in the 1960s and 1970s, escapees from a private zoo on Sir Philip Brocklehurst's Swythamley Park estate in Staffordshire. Sir Garrard Tyrwhitt-Drake, a wealthy Kent businessman with a passion for the circus (at one time he toured the country with Garrard's Royal Circus and Menagerie), kept his animals in ten acres of cages and paddocks in the grounds of Cobtree Manor, his country house outside Maidstone. Between 1934 and 1959 the collection was regularly open to the public, and Tyrwhitt-Drake showed dozens of different species: bears, lions, wolves, and zebras, two elephants called Gert and Daisy, and a tiger called Tiger Tim.

But when Jimmy Chipperfield and Lord Bath were planning the Lions of Longleat, the most intriguing country house menagerie belonged to a professional gambler.

TO BE MORE precise, John Aspinall—Aspers to his friends—facilitated gambling. In the 1950s, when gaming was still illegal in Britain, Aspers ran high-class private poker and chemin de fer parties at his Belgravia flat and elsewhere, varying the location in an effort to escape the attention of the police. His mother, Lady Osborne, joined in the fun: she used to serve the food and drink, and sometimes the gambling parties were held at her flat in Hyde Park Street, Paddington. Players included Ian Fleming, Lucian Freud, the Earl of Derby, and the Duke of Devonshire. According to John Burke, Aspinall's accountant and partner in crime, Derby once lost £300,000 in a single night, which was a great deal more than the cost of his new and very grand country house, Knowsley Hall in Lancashire.

At 1 a.m. on January 10, 1958, police raided Lady Osborne's flat and found twenty-four people round a green baize table, with bowls of counters and a dealer's shoe equipped with six packs of cards, the number used in chemin de fer.* Aspinall, his mother, and John Burke were charged with keeping a common gaming house. According to legend, Lady Osborne said to the police officer, "Young man, there was nothing common here until *you* walked in."[13] She had a point: among the men and women arrested with them were the son and daughter of the Earl of Ancaster, the son of the Duke of Portland, and the son of the Earl of Yarborough. Most of the others had aristocratic pedigrees, less direct but there nonetheless. Aspinall claimed they were all his intimate friends.

Those intimate friends were all ordered not to frequent gaming houses and to be on good behaviour for twelve months when they appeared at Marylebone magistrates' court later that day. Aspinall, Burke, and Lady Osborne were remanded for trial, but the case was dismissed when it came to court that March.

---

* It was later claimed that the raid took place because Lady Osborne had forgotten to pay off the local police.

Nevertheless, it made national headlines, and it contributed to the passing of the 1960 Betting and Gaming Act, which legalised members-only casinos under licence from the Gaming Board for Great Britain. Aspinall was quick to see the potential, and in 1962 he took advantage of the change in the law to found a casino at 44 Berkeley Square in Mayfair. The Clermont Club was named after a well-known Georgian gambler, the 1st Earl of Clermont, who had owned 44 Berkeley Square in the eighteenth century.

Aspinall and his friends were a fast set: hard-drinking aristocrats and wheeler-dealers who lived by their wits and moved on the fringes of high society. The 7th Earl of Lucan, "Lucky" Lucan, was employed by Aspinall at the Clermont Club to encourage the punters. Mark Birley, a nightclub entrepreneur, was married to Annabel, the daughter of the 8th Marquess of Londonderry and sister of the 9th. Annabel's, Mark Birley's members-only nightclub, opened in the basement of Aspinall's casino in 1963. Another member of the set was James Goldsmith, a bullying business tycoon whose affair with Annabel Birley, begun in 1964, culminated in their marriage fourteen years later, although the augurs were not promising—as Goldsmith famously said at the time of this, his third marriage, "When you marry your mistress, you create a job vacancy."[14]

When Aspers and his mother won their court case in 1958, the press was invited into his Eaton Place flat to watch the celebrations. A white-coated manservant served champagne as Aspinall spoke to journalists, his "glamorous ex-model wife" Jayne at his side.[15] (Jayne Aspinall had an entire centre spread to herself in the *Daily Mirror* that day: it was devoted entirely to the clothes she wore to the trial.) As the champagne flowed Aspers declared defiantly, "I have always been a gambler and I always will be."[16] And, almost as an aside, a reporter noted that "Aspinall's two pet black Himalayan bears looked through the window from their centrally-heated cages in the roof garden, which is part of the flat."[17]

Pet bears in Belgravia? Centrally heated cages on the roof? John Aspinall had been keeping creatures of one sort or another since he was a child, befriending half-wild ferrets and young jackdaws. During a short-lived school career at Rugby he took his pet jackdaw with him. In the spring of 1957, he noticed a sorry-looking capuchin monkey in a London pet store and bought it. Dheddi was the first in what was to be a long line of exotic purchases. The following year he bought Tara, a nine-week-old tigress that cost £200 from a pet shop near Regent's Park, and the two black bears. They were all installed in the Eaton Place flat, but neighbours' pets began to disappear mysteriously, and the neighbours began to complain.

After moving his small menagerie to a rented country house near Abingdon for a couple of months, Aspinall bought a small country estate of his own in Kent with the proceeds of a good win on the Cesarewitch. Built for an East India Company nabob in 1787, Howletts was an attractive classical house with an imposing portico and fifty acres, just outside Canterbury. In the early 1960s John Fowler, who worked on the Clermont Club, was commissioned to decorate the interiors. His work was occasionally interrupted by Siberian tiger cubs who wandered round the house like Persian cats, "only rather more troublesome."[18]

The purpose behind the purchase of Howletts was to provide space for Aspinall's growing collection of animals. His first gorillas, a male and female called Gugis and Shamba, came in 1958. The next year he bought his first chimpanzee, Yonkus, in Henry Trefflich's animal store in Manhattan, after winning a few thousand dollars at Yonkers Raceway (he and his wife had to smuggle the chimp back to England disguised as their baby). Wolves followed, and elephants, and panthers, and snow leopards.

Aspinall's zoo was run on professional lines, with a highly successful breeding programme. It wasn't open to the public. Like some Georgian squire's menagerie, it was there for his own amusement, although, unlike a Georgian squire, he maintained a close personal relationship with the animals. His approach was unorthodox: when the pair of Himalayan bears, Ayesha and Esau, escaped into the walled garden at Howletts, he lured them into an empty chimpanzee cage with a bucket of green Chartreuse and left them to sleep it off.

But more than that, he believed in engaging directly with the animals. "Most high mammals," he maintained, "are responsive to affection and return it in good measure."[19] So he would play with his tigers and hug his gorillas, regularly going into their enclosures and encouraging others to do the same. His animals were never trained in the way that a circus animal was trained, but he regularly played with them, even when games with one of his tigers involved him pretending to be its prey. "This involves the tiger

John Aspinall and friends at Howletts, 1971

stalking you, preferably when your back is turned, pouncing on you, knocking you down and taking your neck between its teeth."[20]

That approach was fraught with risk. "It is quite possible that I shall be killed by a wild animal," Aspinall wrote in 1976.[21] He wasn't. The killer would be cancer of the jaw, twenty-four years later. But there were other casualties. One Sunday in 1965 a neighbour, Michael Tree, the son of Ronald Tree and Nancy Lancaster, asked if he could bring his house party over to see the animals. He arrived with his wife, Anne, who was the sister of the Duke of Devonshire, Michael Astor, and Lady Diana Cooper, who was then in her seventies. "She appeared to me to be somewhat frail for a gorilla ramble," said Aspers afterwards.[22] But she insisted on accompanying the others, and when he suggested that she should at least remove the cloche hat she was wearing, because one of the gorillas was going through a phase of stealing hats, she refused, saying, "I can't believe that these delightful gorillas . . . have not the most perfect manners."[23] She was mistaken: one of them crept up behind her when no one was looking, knocked her to the ground, and stole her hat. She was unhurt, and she behaved as if nothing had happened in spite of the fact that the theft revealed her hair to be in curlers.

A much more serious incident occurred five years later. On Easter Monday 1970 Annabel Birley took her three children, Rupert, Robin, and India Jane, down to Howletts for the day to see the animals. They played with the little gorillas and watched Aspers as he wrestled with one of the big males. Then he took them into another enclosure to see Zorra, a young female tiger. Without warning, Zorra launched herself at twelve-year-old Robin, pulling him to the ground and taking his head into her mouth. Aspinall managed to prise her jaws apart while his wife held on to the tiger's legs and they got the boy out, but his jaw was badly damaged. "There was just a hole where one side of his face had been," remembered his mother.[24] A nine-hour operation, a spell in intensive care, and years of plastic surgery were the result. When he went to Eton he was known as Tiger Birley.

Aspinall, whose fortunes depended heavily on his luck at the tables, succumbed to financial pressure and opened Howletts to the public in 1971, and two years later he expanded his activities to take in a second country house: the 273-acre Port Lympne estate near Hythe in Kent, made famous in the 1920s and 1930s as one of the homes of connoisseur, politician, and legendary party-giver Sir Philip Sassoon. That, too, was opened to the public. Aspinall was a pioneering ecowarrior, a man who believed in animal rights and advocated swift action to save the planet. Unfortunately, he combined this with a Nietzschean belief in his own superiority and that of his class. The result was that he believed that, faced with an "Armageddon on a raped planet gutted of most of its resources," we must limit the human population by any means necessary. "The billions blown on medicare are monies ill-spent and worse than wasted," he wrote. The world's problems were caused by humanity's growing ability to sidestep the process of natural selection. So medical research funds should be reallocated for abortion, infanticide, euthanasia, and birth control. "A population readjustment on a planetary scale . . . would be the only possible solution for the survival of our own species and of the eco-system or systems that nurtured us."[25] He looked for the survival of the fittest. And richest.

THE LIONS OF Longleat enterprise had no such high-minded and dubious motives behind it. It was there to make money for Jimmy Chipperfield and the Marquess of Bath, and make money it did. "Nobody was eaten here today," reported the man from the *Times* at the inaugural press day on April 3, 1966, with just a hint of disappointment, although he did note how the forty-six lions paced up and down inside the perimeter fence, "eyeing meaty cows in the parkland beyond."[26] Two days later, on Tuesday, April 5, the park opened to the public. Lord Bath stood at the gate to take the first motorist's pound note.

There wasn't much interest to begin with. A hundred and sixty-four cars cruised through the park on that first day, and numbers were similarly unimpressive on Wednesday and Thursday. But the next day, Good Friday, was a public holiday. And on Good Friday three thousand cars turned up. The roads leading to Longleat were gridlocked, with drivers waiting five or six hours to see the lions. The park was closed down at seven that evening, while there was still a half-mile queue waiting to get in. And the pattern was repeated on Saturday, Sunday, and Monday. Altogether, about fifty thousand people saw the Lions of Longleat that first weekend. Over the first season, 106,000 cars and nearly 2,000 coaches visited the new attraction.

Lord Bath knew he was on to a winner. Admissions to the house went up by 80 per cent. "When people leave the lion reserve," he said, "they have to pass the house, so they pop in and see it"—at half a crown each.[27] He was quite sanguine about the impact that lions might have on his historic house. "When does a stately home become unstately?" he asked. "To my mind the lions definitely have not reduced the stateliness of Longleat—I think the lion is a very stately animal." But in the end, it all came down to money. "The whole object is to make the thing pay."[28] The next year chimps and sea lions joined the lions; the year after that, a new section opened with giraffes, zebras, and antelopes; and the year after that saw the arrival of baboons, whose ways with wing mirrors and car aerials are now part of the Longleat legend.

Jimmy Chipperfield knew he was on to a winner, too. One day in 1966, the year the Lions of Longleat opened, Rex Harrison arrived on the Wiltshire set of his new film, *Doctor Doolittle*, and posed for photos. The animals used in the film were trained by Jimmy Chipperfield's daughter Mary: it was no coincidence that the cute little lion cub that Harrison held in his arms was named

Mr Merrett, after the council surveyor who granted planning permission for the lion park.

Suddenly everyone wanted safari parks, and Chipperfield was bombarded with requests from the owners of run-down country houses to come and rejuvenate their estates with an electric fence and a few dozen wild animals. But for his second safari park, he chose the most successful stately home business in Britain. A year or so after Longleat became such an enormous triumph, the Duke and Duchess of Bedford invited him and Lord Bath to lunch. Woburn already had its fair share of exotic fauna: the duke's grandfather, a president of the Zoological Society, had stocked the park with rare animals including European bison, Père David's deer, and a herd of wild horses from the Gobi Desert. Bedford wanted something more, though, and the result of the lunch was that Jimmy Chipperfield entered into the same agreement he had with Lord Bath: a fifty-fifty split, with his team having full control of the animals.

The process was more complicated this time because Chipperfield now had competition from other circus men who were looking to diversify, and as a result the price of lions went through the roof. In 1968 Jimmy's brother Dick, who had his own lion reserve in Natal, went into partnership with the 2nd Lord Gretton, who had already begun to broaden the appeal of his Leicestershire country house, Stapleford Park, by installing a two-mile-long miniature steam railway and a miniature liner, the *Northern Star*, which cruised up and down the lake with Gretton at the helm. The following year the Smart brothers opened the Royal Windsor Safari Park on the 144-acre St Leonard's Hill estate near Windsor which their father, the showman and circus owner Billy Smart Sr., had bought shortly before his death in 1966. It had a motley assortment of animals—pumas, leopards, llamas, fallow deer, giraffes and zebras, monkeys and elephants, dolphins—and "magnificent views of Windsor Castle."[29] The brothers also offered

£5,000 to anyone who could catch the legendary Loch Morar Monster, a cousin of the more famous Loch Ness Monster, saying they wanted to make it a top attraction at the new park.

The ethics of obtaining and importing wild animals sits rather uncomfortably with modern sensibilities. While Lord Gretton's daughter claimed that "the lions at Stapleford will breed and then several will be sent back to Africa," adding that "the blood will probably save the African lion from extinction," her father told a different story.[30] The lions, most of which came from Dick Chipperfield's Natal reserve in the first place, were to be used to breed for zoos and circuses, he said. The Smart brothers' pre-opening publicity campaign for Windsor had a British Overseas Airway Corporation air hostess posing with three baby elephants that had been recently caught in the jungles outside Calcutta. "They were caught specially for us," said a Windsor Safari Park spokesman. "We have someone getting us another nine. They surround the herd and catch the babies."[31]

After a massive capital investment, variously reported to be £400,000, £1 million, or £2 million, Woburn Safari Park was opened—by Lord Bath—on May 19, 1970. There were lions, but there were also white rhinos, elephants, cheetahs, herds of giraffe, and plenty of monkeys. Just as Lord Bath cut the ribbon, the baby elephant which had been produced for the benefit of photographers trod on his foot. His shout of "Hell!" echoed through the PA system.

That proved to be a foretaste of things to come. Apart from the agonised cries of Lord Bath, the opening met with a deafening silence. The press failed to report on it. The public didn't seem interested in spending one pound a car to see what was billed as "the largest drive-through safari park outside Africa."[32] They didn't care about the white rhinos. ("When they arrived I was bitterly disappointed by their lack of whiteness," confessed Bedford.[33]) Chipperfield was inclined to blame the poor start on the fact that, while the paying public continued to pour into Longleat, after all the

Jimmy Chipperfield, the Duke of Bedford, and the Marquess of Bath at Woburn's opening

Duke of Bedford's publicity stunts, people no longer took Woburn seriously. Whatever the reason, the new safari park looked like a resounding flop.

Salvation came in the shape of a five-year-old girl called Sian Symons-Jones. At the end of August 1970, three months after Woburn Safari Park opened, Sian arrived with her mother and two friends for their first visit to the game reserve. They were warned to keep the car windows rolled up, but it was a hot day, and as they drove through the lion enclosure Sian hung out of one of the rear windows until a warden told her off. She climbed back inside, but the window was left open, with predictable but disastrous results. A lioness called Twiggy got her paw through the window and then sank her teeth into Sian's leg. A woman following behind saw what was happening and aimed her car at Twiggy, forcing her to let go and pushing her away while Sian's mother drove to the edge of the compound.

Surgeons managed to save the girl's leg, although she required a series of skin grafts. A spokesman for the duke placed the blame squarely on her mother for disregarding the warnings. So did Chipperfield. "It was very hot," her mother explained.[34] The incident might have spelled the end for Woburn.

But the following Sunday a record thirty-three thousand people drove nose-to-tail through the safari park in stifling temperatures, most of them with windows open, all of them eager to see Twiggy, who had in fact been moved to another reserve. Woburn never looked back, and by 1974 there were 350,000 cars driving through its grounds every year. "The game park solved all my problems," said the duke. "I was able to settle my debts and for the first time my bank balance is comfortably in the black."[35]

Now country house owners queued up to turn their historic landscape parks into miniature versions of the Serengeti. In Ireland, the Marquess of Sligo went into partnership with Fossetts Circus to bring lions and monkeys to the walled kitchen garden of his eighteenth-century seat, the magnificent Westport House in County Mayo. Jimmy Chipperfield opened a third game reserve at Blair Drummond near Stirling at the same time as Woburn, and another at the Earl of Derby's Knowsley Hall on the outskirts of Liverpool in 1971. (Perhaps the earl was still trying to recoup his losses at Aspinall's gaming tables.) Although never a success on the scale of Longleat or Woburn, Knowsley Safari Park was reasonably profitable, in spite of Liverpool police warning them to expect the most appalling vandalism and to count the lions carefully. (There was never any trouble.) A fifth safari park opened at Lambton Castle in County Durham in 1972: Lambton Lion Park was the most short-lived of the five, lasting only eight years. Most of the others were still going strong in the twenty-first century. In each case the model was the same: begin with lions, add other animals as the safari park establishes itself to refresh the offer, and then diversify, with pets' corners, garden centres, boating lakes, and, in Woburn's case, a cable railway running over the lake.

Owners seem to have taken the presence of wild animals in the park in stride. (Easy to do, of course, when they were a happy reminder of one's healthy bank balance.) Weekend houseguests at Lord Bath's house, Job's Mill, were taken to see the animals at Longleat. Frances Partridge, who was invited down in April 1971 by Georgia Tennant, Lord Bath's stepdaughter, was entranced when "one giraffe bent benignly over our stationary car and licked the windscreen with its huge tongue."[36] She was less impressed with "the mouldy old lions with their hopelessly cross expressions."[37]

There were incidents. Monkeys escaped and ended up in back gardens, sending householders into panic. The West Midland Safari Park, a sixth game reserve that was set up after Chipperfield, in a departure from his established practice, bought a 270-acre estate near Birmingham called Spring Grove complete with a rather nice late eighteenth-century mansion, was the scene of the legendary Great Baboon Escape of 1974, when eighty-four baboons made a break for it after a keeper accidentally left a gate open. Police were deluged with complaints from local residents, who said the escapees were throwing things at their windows, and one group colonised trees in the grounds of a nearby maternity hospital before they were all lured back by a carpet of oranges and bananas spread on the ground in their compound.

The West Midland Park was particularly prone to these escapes. They lost a tiger at one stage, and a sea lion escaped onto a main road, where it was accidentally run over by a local police constable on patrol. And some incidents were more serious than others. In 1972 a keeper was mauled by a young lion at Knowsley, and his colleagues had to shoot the lion to save him. Lions also managed to break into the cheetah enclosure at Knowsley, killing three cheetahs before they were restrained—a disaster, said Chipperfield, "for we had lost three animals worth twelve hundred pounds apiece."[38] A lioness called Spitfire leaped over the eight-feet-high inner fence at Woburn one night and then burrowed under the outer fence; she was spotted early the next morning near the public road through the estate and the Duke of Bedford's head deer keeper shot her dead.

The craze for lions in the landscape was brief. No new parks were established in Britain after Jimmy Chipperfield's West Midland Safari Park opened in 1973, and Lambton, Stapleford, and Windsor subsequently failed. But the others are still thriving, as are Howletts and Port Lympne, the latter now describing itself as a safari park, wild animal reserve, and hotel. And for a time, they managed to eclipse the other elements of the stately home business, the miniature steam trains and boating lakes and carousels. Even today, advertisements for Longleat exhort the visitor to "enter a land of adventure. Where lions roam. Tigers stalk. And monkeys swing."

And almost as an afterthought: "Travel through time in a grand stately home."[39]

19

HOW DO YOU KEEP IT CLEAN?

"THERE WAS ALWAYS somebody to bring more," said the 7th Earl of Harewood, speaking in 1969 about life at his family home, Harewood House in Yorkshire. "Alfred Blades, my butler, remembers an indoor staff of twenty-seven and house parties with forty for dinner in the Big Dining Room and nine serving at table, and gold and silver services in use. Things are a good deal different now, as you might imagine, but Blades is still here."[1]

Aside from the dreamy nostalgia for a cosseted past in which servants figured prominently, on which more later, the most interesting point about the Earl of Harewood's remarks is that in 1969 Blades was still there, still "my butler," still polishing what was left of the family silver, still dedicating himself like a latter-day Jeeves to easing the earl's path through life. And it is interesting because, like the narrative which maintains that the period 1945–1974 saw the destruction of the country house and the way of life it epitomised, the conviction that a golden age of domestic service came to an abrupt end with the Second World War is a powerful feature of postwar British social history. Yet pretty much every owner of a country house continued to employ servants. There were just fewer of them, and they no longer conformed to the structured prewar belowstairs hierarchies.

Domestic service had been declining steadily since the beginning of the twentieth century, when servants formed the largest occupational group in Britain; when an astonishing 1.5 million women (and domestic service was overwhelmingly a female occupation) were working as private domestic servants; and when so many British households employed staff that whether they did or didn't was taken as a demarcation line between middle-class and working-class homes. And the reasons for that decline are well known: an increase in alternative employment opportunities for women in factories and offices; a perception that being a servant was degrading; a reluctance to commit to wearing a uniform, to having no autonomy and little free time. Equally well known is the fact that very few made domestic service their career. The vast majority of servants were girls who entered service on leaving school at fourteen or fifteen and moved from one place to another until they married in their midtwenties and left to set up households of their own.

The servant shortage hit the smaller households first, the one- or two-servant homes with perhaps a cook-housekeeper and a skivvy who had to do all the heavy work. In contrast, even in the 1920s and 1930s a big country house with a full complement of twenty or thirty indoor servants (and perhaps as many men working outside in the gardens, the stables, the garage, and elsewhere on the estate) had a certain glamour, with opportunities for travel and, most importantly, clear lines of demarcation between departments, and up until 1939 plenty of grand households were still being run on an Edwardian scale. Even after the war there were a few. Staying at Birr Castle in County Offaly with the Earl and Countess of Rosse in 1948, James Lees-Milne counted a butler, a footman, four housemaids, a cook, and an unknown number of kitchen maids; and when the Earl of Derby's Knowsley Hall made the headlines in 1952 after the trainee footman Harold Winstanley ran amok with a submachine gun, the press noted that in addition to Winstanley, the Derbys employed a butler, an under-butler, a valet, a footman, a housekeeper and an assistant housekeeper, a French chef, several housemaids, and a lady's maid. But households on this scale were increasingly rare. The Marquess of Bath, whose father had kept forty-three liveried servants, was now looked after by a butler, a cook, and a part-time cleaner. In a 1958 article on stately homes for *House and Garden*, Randolph Churchill, the journalist son of Winston, mentioned one unnamed country house where the owners kept twenty-seven indoor servants in the 1930s. Now they kept nine, but expenses had trebled, and the nine cost as much as the twenty-seven did before the war. Two years later, the *Financial Times* estimated the cost of service in a "well-appointed household":[2]

Butler	£500
Two footmen at £350	£700
Odd man	£250
Head housemaid	£300
Two housemaids at £250	£500
Cook	£400
Kitchenmaid	£250
Lady's maid	£300
Chauffeur (non-resident)	£650
Three daily helps at £150	£450
	£4300
Keep (residents only)	£2,000
Total	£6,300

For all but the wealthiest, an annual bill of £6,300 was out of the question.

But a life without servants was unthinkable and, if not impossible, then at least jolly difficult in a rambling country house, and it was taken for granted that a family would need paid help to run it. When Quentin Crewe and Angela Huth bought Wootton House in 1965, they didn't think of managing it alone. "Help,

Butler Michael Bentley polishing the silver, 1955

obviously, was needed in such a large house," recalled Huth; it had twelve bedrooms and stood in twelve acres of grounds. They employed a gardener who lived in the attic, a driver and general helper for Crewe (who suffered from muscular dystrophy), a cook-housekeeper, and a cleaning woman who came in from the village.[3]

Servants didn't only cook and clean; they were evidence of status, reassuring symbols of U, holding out against the barbarian hordes of non-U hammering at the portals. "I don't like the proletariat at all," wrote Ann Fleming, wife of Ian, "and only believe in oligarchy, a ruling class employing contented craftsmen, cooks, charcoal burners, ladies' maids and laundry maids, all bobbing and curtseying and taking pride in their work."[4] In a 1968 study of Britain's aristocrats and their way of life, Roy Perrott recounted the case of one owner who told the butler to have a talk with the three footmen and come back with a list of economies, since the house was costing so much to run. "It just didn't occur to him that three footmen was going it a bit. When the butler came back, the first thing he had on his list was, 'No cooked breakfast.'"[5]

So when a shortage of servants became apparent, it was seen as more than a threat to the outmoded lifestyle of a privileged elite. "The future of the home, that cornerstone of the national life, is at stake," declared the authors of a Ministry of Labour report, *Post-War Organisation of Private Domestic Employment*, in June 1945, when it still seemed possible that the answer to the servant problem lay in an alliance between home and state.[6] "Is the home with its many and varied traditions, its individuality and the flame of ancient sanctities still alight beneath the surface of a mechanised age, to give place to the drab uniformity of the apartment house or residential hotel? It is for those who value family life to find the right answer to that question." The report's authors, Violet Markham and Florence Hancock, advocated a National Institute of Home-makers to provide training facilities for domestic servants, to issue qualifications, and to set fair wages and conditions. Others suggested more radical steps, such as the establishment of a state-controlled community service scheme, Help for House-wives, administered by local officials. "On marriage, when most workers seek a one-family house with a garden, the family would take out a new policy in the State social security scheme, the husband paying a shilling a week, and the wife while remaining at work two shillings."[7] This would entitle the new housewife to eight hours' help a week, and if and when the couple had children, they could depend on full-time help for a short period.

Very much the product of an age which was seeing the emergence of a welfare state in Britain, such proposals didn't grapple with the essential problem, which was that people just did not *want* to be servants anymore. It was degrading. Employment agencies placed desperate advertisements for cook-generals, housekeepers, "mother's helps," nursery governesses, gardeners, and chauffeurs.

Married couples as servants, something of a rarity before the First World War, were welcomed now. An advertisement for a "really expert head gardener of five" for St Osyth's Priory in Essex announced that preference would be given to an "applicant with wife available for cooking or other domestic service."[8] Property adverts stressed that this country house or that was easily maintained, skilfully modernised, fitted with every up-to-date amenity.

The postwar debate on the servant problem took it for granted that for women of the middle classes and above, it was unthinkable to run a home without servants. And for country house owners, the notion that a house was not a home without help blurred into a more practical question. Most country houses—*all* country houses built before the 1930s—were specifically designed to be run by an army of cheap labour, and as things stood, it was jolly hard to imagine how they would work without them. Who would cook in the vast and inconvenient kitchen and carry the food through the labyrinthine maze of passageways and corridors until it finally reached the dining room? When it got there, who would serve it up? Who would do the washing up and make the beds and sort the laundry?

In a letter to her sister Diana Mosley, Debo Devonshire noted that at Lismore, the Devonshires' Irish country house, "there are no servants . . . except some blissful dailies all aged about eighty." The employment of "blissful dailies," local women who lived out and came in part-time to cook, clean, and occasionally wait at table, was without doubt the most widely adopted solution to the problem, and there were very few country houses whose owners did not make use of them.

At Ham Spray just after the war, Ralph and Frances Partridge relied on the services of Mrs Chant, who regaled them with tales of how her soldier brother-in-law had looted his way round Germany—"They just go into shops and houses and take things"—before her erratic attendance record forced Frances to look for a replacement, even though her good liberal conscience was racked with guilt at the idea that "'our class' should depend on those less fortunate to hoist us bodily through our physical lives as well as managing this feat for themselves."[9] She went to the local labour exchange in search of daily help and found herself immediately caught up in the bureaucratic machine as an official demanded to know if her husband was disabled or if they suffered any special hardship. In the end Frances said she had a contract to write a book, and if she had to do all the work of the house it would be impossible to finish it. The official relented, and shortly afterwards Mrs Chant gave way as cook-housekeeper to Mrs Hoare, while the Partridges also employed a man for the garden, Wilde. A few years later Frances was able to salve her conscience over employing domestics by installing Mrs Hoare and her family in the nursery wing at Ham Spray after they had been turned out of their house.

For those who weren't content with a woman who came in to help, and who perhaps had a husband prepared to wrestle with acres of flower borders and lawns which once kept a dozen gardeners busy, there were basically three courses of action: look abroad for men and women who were prepared to work as servants, and prepared to do it for less money than their British counterparts; reduce the *need* for servants; or make do and mend.

Ireland was already a source of foreign workers, with the added benefit that Irish servants already spoke the language, and agencies regularly offered jobs in England to Irish nationals looking for work as cooks, housemaids, butlers, manservants, and gardeners. In the years immediately after the war there were also various schemes to find work for the thousands of Poles who had fought with the Allies, and to make use of the thousands of German and Italian prisoners of war who were awaiting repatriation to their own countries. But since the vast majority of these were of course men, and private domestic service remained predominantly female, they didn't have much impact on the servant shortage. In any case, it was government policy to return POWs to their home countries as soon as possible.

However, there were calls for the government to recruit German women as domestics to help hard-pressed British housewives, and under the various European Voluntary Workers (EVW) schemes of the late 1940s, displaced women from the British Zone of Germany, Austria, Italy, Poland, Ukraine, and the Balkan states began to appear in British households, as well as in the textile industries, hospitals, and the hospitality industry. All of these schemes were subject to strict government supervision—one scheme was almost halted amid bureaucratic concerns that Communists were infiltrating British society in the guise of Italian women EVWs—and a great deal was made of the need for them to assimilate. Requests by Austrian workers living in hostels to have an Austrian cook were turned down on the grounds that they would integrate more quickly if they had to eat British food. For the same reason, workers had to be white. A 1949 royal commission report on population made it very clear that "immigration on a large scale into a fully established society like ours could only be welcomed without reserve if the immigrants were of good human stock and were not prevented by their religion or race from intermarrying with the host population and becoming merged in it."[10]

In 1950 a new initiative was introduced, matching British employment agencies with their German counterparts to find German servants for British households. The Private Domestic Worker scheme, as it was known, was quickly extended to include Austria, in spite of concerns by British officials that private agencies were receiving government support just so that "Mrs X . . . can be free to attend a bridge party."[11] Advertisements appeared assuring country house owners, "Your servant problem [is] solved. Austrian maids are willing workers, clean, honest, reliable"; "The servant problem! Why not import a German domestic?"[12]

Foreign servants became a country house staple, with Italians, Maltese, Portuguese, and Spaniards joining Germans and Austrians. Chatsworth was run by two Hungarian sisters, Ilona and Elizabeth Solymossy, who had come to England as refugees before

the war and had worked as cook and housemaid for Debo Devonshire's sister-in-law "Kick" Hartington until her death in a plane
crash in 1948. The sisters kept the house clean with the help of an
eastern European staff. "No English people would do such work
at that time," said Debo. Interestingly, Afro-Caribbean domestics
were almost unknown, as were servants from India and Pakistan,
in spite of large-scale immigrations from both parts of the world:
it isn't clear whether this was a result of racial prejudice on the
part of employers, or because Black and Asian immigrants shared
the distaste for private domestic work shown by their native counterparts. But Black or Asian domestic servants in country houses
were a rarity. In the early 1970s the thriller writer Evelyn Anthony
and her husband, Michael Ward Thomas, employed an "African
butler" at Horham Hall, their Elizabethan mansion in Essex; and
the Brownlows are said to have had a Black housekeeper at Belton
House in Lincolnshire around the same time. But it was much
more common to see southern or eastern Europeans as butlers
and cook-housekeepers, and they expected terms and conditions
which would never have occurred to a prewar servant. At Prestwold Hall in Leicestershire, the Packe-Drury-Lowes kept an elderly English butler, Herbert Parker, until in 1966 the widowed
Penelope Packe-Drury-Lowe married again. Her new husband
brought his own servants, a Spanish couple, and Parker was retired, only to be brought back into service for several months each
year because the Spaniards demanded extended holidays in Spain.

The difficulty of finding good servants, and the upheaval caused
by their departure, meant that a renewed emphasis was placed on
behaving well towards them. They were allowed to receive their
own friends, and in larger houses they had their own sitting room
in which to receive them. Employers were urged to respect off-
duty hours and not try to change them at short notice, and to give
time off in lieu if the staff had been asked to work particularly
long hours at a dinner party or a dance. "A lady must remember,"
declared the author of a 1964 etiquette manual, "that rudeness

towards those paid to serve her, or anything which deliberately emphasises their relative positions as employer and employee, is not a ladylike trait."[13] Where there was still a reasonably large staff, employers should keep up prewar traditions by laying on a Christmas party for them, with good food, prizes, and music, advised the manual. It was essential that the family join in the fun and games, and desirable that they should look as though they enjoyed it.

The royal family set the standard here. Every December the Royal Household Social Club organised a staff dance at Buckingham Palace or in the Waterloo Chamber at Windsor Castle. At the palace, Joe Loss and His Orchestra were regulars, providing the accompaniment to a fairly traditional dance programme which included sambas, tangos, and cha-chas along with waltzes and foxtrots. The Queen, the Duke of Edinburgh, the Queen Mother, and Princess Margaret usually attended for part of the evening and made a point of dancing with members of staff. Things were livelier at Windsor, with much more of an emphasis on A-list entertainers. The cabaret was hosted by Peter Brough and Archie Andrews, surely the only ventriloquist and dummy to make their names on the wireless. In 1956, music was provided by Billy Cotton and his band, with appearances by Max Bygraves and Bob Monkhouse; and in 1964, the lineup consisted of Diana Dors, Tommy Cooper, and Morecambe and Wise.

The scarcity of servants meant that eccentricities which would have been unthinkable in an Edwardian household were often tolerated. When Ronald Pearson turned Baynton House in Wiltshire into a country club after the war in an attempt to keep it in the family, he trawled the Polish Resettlement Corps camps on Salisbury Plain to find an all-Polish staff of cook, waiter, handyman, chauffeur-porter, and two housemaids. The fact that one of the housemaids, Marya, had a disconcerting habit—disconcerting for the guests, anyway—of singing songs of exile in the moonlight while prowling on the roof did not deter him from employing her.

But one could only take so much. Lady Elizabeth Basset and her husband, Ronald, who lived in a sixteenth-century house on Lord Salisbury's Hatfield estate, were surprised one day to hear their gardener, who hated foreigners, threatening to knife their Spanish butler. She rushed out, grabbed the gardener by his collar, and told the unfortunate butler to run for it. But he only got as far as shutting himself in the dining room before the gardener broke away and put his fist through the dining room window. "I felt I had to sack him," said Lady Elizabeth. She felt sorry for his wife and children, but her guilt was lessened when a local psychiatric hospital employed him, "which I thought just right as he was definitely unbalanced. . . . He used to give in his notice regularly, but his wife told me to ignore this as it was always at the time when his football team had been defeated."[14]

The *Tatler* lamented that the shortage of servants meant that "less silver is displayed on our tables than at any time in the country's history."[15] One observer suggested that foreign servants were responsible for an upheaval in domestic cuisine, with pizzas and pasta and pepperoni making their appearance on the dinner table. "This revolution has been caused by the elimination from the native scene of the native domestic servant. Parker the butler, Hoskins the maid, Mrs Browning the cook, and Nanny are no longer with us. They have been replaced by the Pepitas, the Perditas, the Giovannis, the Marios and the Marias." That wasn't all: just as influential was a succession of Ginas and Trudies, "those enchanting *au pairs* (Baby Walking in the Morning, Political Economy in the afternoon and Baby Sitting at Night) who are not very strong, and not very domesticated actually, but such sweet girls to have around the house."[16]

The au pair, a servant who wasn't on any account to be called a servant, whose grasp of the English language was tenuous, and who spent her afternoons and evenings off sitting in milk bars with long-haired boyfriends who were invariably unsuitable, was a new arrival on the domestic scene after the war. Although the au pair scheme had been founded after the First World War as an exchange programme intended to foster greater understanding of different cultures, it really took off after the Second World War, and by 1964 around twenty thousand young au pairs were being brought to Britain every year.[17] Staying for anywhere from a few months to a year, the au pair was cheap, expecting a weekly allowance which was between a quarter and a fifth of the wages paid to the lowliest kitchen maid. In return she was expected to help around the house and take over a lot of the childcare, acting as a nanny, although with varying degrees of success. "Sometimes it seems as if it's quite incidental that they're looking after children," said one kindergarten headmistress. "Shall we say, it is not their first love."[18]

For her part, the au pair often found that British food was disgusting, British children were revolting, and British manners, particularly the habit of the host family to condescend and patronise, were insulting. As for the avoidance tactics required to escape the predatory attentions of fathers and occasionally teenage sons . . . Even so, the au pair became a fixture in many country houses, a substitute nanny.

"Is an 'au pair' really worthwhile?" asked the headline of a 1963 advertisement feature. "No," was the answer. There was an alternative which was cheaper, more reliable, ready to work at any hour of the day with never an afternoon or an evening off. It was the "all-electric, fully automatic New Colston Mark IV Dishwasher. A blessing in even the best-staffed households."[19]

The Colston Mark IV and its counterparts exemplified the other solution to the postwar shortage of servants: a house equipped with all modern conveniences, a house where, having demolished the servants' wing so there was nowhere to put the staff anymore, an owner could spend the wages they couldn't afford on creating that utopian ideal of the postwar period—a country house that didn't *need* servants.

Making a virtue of necessity, *Complete Etiquette for Ladies and Gentleman* declared in 1964 that a "shortage of domestic staff . . . plus the many new items of labour-saving equipment now available, have revolutionised the business of running a house and most families, if they have any choice, prefer to manage with the minimum of staff and the maximum of mechanical equipment."[20] It was noticeable that country houses on the market were increasingly advertised as having "every labour-saving device" or being "completely modernised on labour saving lines."[21] Albert Richardson built a small country house near Basingstoke in Hampshire in the late 1950s for a retired major. It was Regency in character, but "as labour-saving as possible, and for this reason electric heating [was] used throughout, supplemented by open fires in the study and drawing-room." Underfloor, thermostatically controlled heating elements were buried in concrete. There was no staff accommodation.[22]

The labour-saving nature of central heating was obvious. Shell-Mex proclaimed the success of oil-fired central heating installed in the sixteenth-century Avebury Manor in Wiltshire by its owner, Sir Francis Knowles, "a scientist."[23] And plenty of country squires and long-lineaged lords were driven by the shortage of domestic staff after the war to seek out the latest labour-saving devices. Kitchens were moved closer to dining rooms: "a comparatively inexpensive and easy matter," noted one commentator in 1950. "Any little room with a good light and access to a flue and a drain can be made into an admirable working kitchen."[24] The serving hatch was another popular introduction, although it wasn't popular with everyone: "I could not, for the life of me, stand this system of having food poked at me through a hole in a wall, as though I was a political prisoner."[25] The vacuum cleaner, which first made its appearance in the early years of the century, was hailed as a godsend: "It is only by the use of this supremely effective method that the householder of today can hope to equal the standard of cleanliness attained in former times by bevies of housemaids."[26] Wall-to-wall carpets were another labour-saving feature: it was well known that one parquet floor or one staircase with bare side-treads involved more work than running a vacuum cleaner through a whole house. In the garden, electric hedge trimmers and an electric lawn mower—"one of the greatest labour-saving devices yet invented for the gardener"—were already being advocated for country houses in the early 1950s.[27]

The third option for the owners of a small-to-medium-size country house was simply to make do, although very few indeed made do without any help at all. But even with a daily cleaning woman (or two) it was impractical to keep up a house with, say, ten bedrooms, three or four large reception rooms (excluding the great hall), and an unknown number of little panelled and tapes-tried parlours which had once had a purpose that no one could now remember. So families retreated. They lived in the kitchen and watched television in one of those little parlours and slept in what had once been a governess's bedroom. The state rooms were shuttered; the furniture was swathed in dust sheets; the family portraits gazed down on emptiness, only coming to brilliant, can-dlelit life a couple of times a year when the county came to dine.

It was perfectly permissible now for a hostess to disappear into the kitchen before dinner, for houseguests to bring their own soap and make their own beds. It was all right to pay the children to polish the silver or lay the table. All members of the household should turn back the bedclothes to air before leaving their rooms, advised Lady Lamb in *Country Life*, "and on Monday mornings they should bring down with them their laundry bags with the soiled clothes, and put them in the kitchen"; although even she urged a wife to employ a maid three mornings a week to help out with the cleaning.[28] Where there was no manservant, the eti-quette manuals advised guests coming for a weekend not to bring heavy luggage. "Two light suitcases are better than one heavy one, where there are stairs to be negotiated."[29] But if one were faced with the dreadful prospect of carrying one's own bags, there were nonetheless benefits to visiting a country house which operated on modern lines:

> Remember with gratitude the big advantage of the new kind of week-end as opposed to the old. There will be no butler to hold the Chicken Marengo just a fraction too high for you to help yourself without scattering some of it on the table; no house-maid to unpack your clothes and gossip about them in the ser-vants' hall, and best of all no valet to wonder about whether a pound will be enough.[30]

A slightly more romantic consequence of the decline of do-mestic service was a flood of nostalgia for a mythical golden age when the big house was populated with faithful old retainers who had willingly devoted their lives to this family or that. The line ran from *Brideshead Revisited*'s Nanny Hawkins—"long hours of work in her youth, authority in middle life, repose and security in her age, had set their stamp on her lined and serene face"—to Se-bastian Beach, the faithful and all-knowing butler in P. G. Wode-house's Blandings Castle stories, taking in Jeeves, Mary Poppins, and the entire cast of *Upstairs, Downstairs* along the way.[31] One tends to forget that the country house world which Wodehouse's characters inhabit is in part a postwar construct. Twenty-nine of his novels were written after 1945; his last, which he was still writ-ing as he lay dying in 1975, was *Sunset at Blandings.* For Wode-house's golden world of goofy younger sons and bewildered earls in monumental mansions, the sun never did set.

Margaret Powell's memoir of her life as a kitchen maid on the south coast in the 1920s, *Below Stairs*, was a bestseller and turned her into a media star. Rosina Harrison's *Rose: My Life in Service* introduced readers to life behind the scenes at Cliveden and to

Harrison's tempestuous relationship with her mistress, Nancy Astor. By the 1970s visitors to country houses, weary of an endless parade of Gainsboroughs and Van Dycks, began to ask to see the kitchens and to know why the servants' bedrooms in the attics weren't on display. The domestic servant was just as potent a symbol of a world we had lost as the stately home that he or she once inhabited.

In 1956 Lord John Manners, who was living at Haddon Hall in Derbyshire, took on Arthur Wootton as his butler, not knowing that Wootton had a long criminal record for theft or that he had only recently been released from prison. All went well for about a year. Then the butler received a phone call from a blackmailer who threatened to tell Lord John about his record unless he came up with a substantial sum of money. He didn't want to hurt his employer by taking anything dear to him, he said later, "so I decided to take old stuff from the storeroom."[32] Four carloads of old stuff, in fact, including a sixteenth-century Mortlake tapestry, a fifteenth-century stool, and two seventeenth-century chests. The stolen items were valued at more than £1,600, but the hapless butler sold them to a Chesterfield antique dealer for £71, only for another dealer, who had carried out an inventory of the contents of Haddon before the war, to recognise them in the shop window and inform the police. Wootton hastily left Haddon Hall and ran for Scotland, where he was arrested and committed for trial at Derbyshire quarter sessions. He was sent to prison for six years.

While all-knowing butlers shimmered through popular culture, extricating their masters from trouble, butlers with criminal records were a surprisingly regular feature of country house life. They staged fake burglaries; they deliberately left windows open and doors unlocked for accomplices; they succumbed to temptation and pocketed jewels and money. In 1973 Anthony Collingwood, a butler at Borde Hill in Sussex, stole thirteen oil paintings, porcelain figures, and silverware worth £277,517 from his employer, although one can't help wondering if this really came as such a surprise, since Collingwood already had twenty-two previous convictions for theft. John Marsh held down a dual career as a thief and a butler for years: he went into service in 1946 and worked—at both jobs—in many famous houses for the next decade. Described as "absolutely first-class at his work as a butler," he received excellent references in spite of frequently stealing from his employers and occasionally being caught. He finally met his match when he stole an £18,000 stamp collection from Colonel D'Arcy Hall of Ewelme Park House in Oxfordshire. In spite of flamboyantly producing his chequebook in the dock and writing out a cheque to the chief constable of Oxfordshire for £138 15s "to recompense as far as possible those who had lost money," he still got ten years.[33] Forty-three-year-old Patrick Dempsey, who had eighteen previous convictions for theft, housebreaking, and burglary, worked as a butler to Lord St Aldwyn at Coln St Aldwyn in Gloucestershire in 1954. The night after he left his job he popped back and stole all Lady St Aldwyn's jewels before burgling two more country houses. None of the stolen goods were ever recovered, and police believed Dempsey was working with a large gang of receivers. He got twelve years.

Even the most devoted old retainer wasn't immune from temptation. Thomas Gaskin served as a butler to a Derbyshire family, the Ratcliffs, for thirty years, before stealing two watches, a brooch, and some diamond rings. When Mrs Ratcliff visited his house and noticed that his wife was somewhat indiscreetly wearing one of the rings, the penny dropped. Others were more sophisticated. Rodwell Patience was butler and valet to Captain Noel Thornhill of Diddington Hall in Cambridgeshire for twenty-five years, during which time he assiduously cheated his invalid employer, forging cheques and stealing china and jewellery. In 1954, when Captain Thornhill was close to death, Patience flew three paintings over to Antwerp in search of a dealer and then, frightened that the disappearance of so many items would be discovered, he attempted to stage a fake burglary at Diddington, but his accomplice turned Queen's evidence and he was sentenced to six years at Norfolk assizes.

WHAT DID THE typical country house household look like without a butler (who may or may not have been enjoying a stretch in jail for fraud or theft), without a pair of liveried footmen and an army of housemaids and kitchen staff? How did it function now there was only a terrace where the domestic wing once stood and a kitchenette off a small private dining room?

In 1966 the personal columns of the *Tatler* carried an advertisement for a cook-housekeeper required by a family living in rural surroundings at Gerrards Cross in Buckinghamshire. The house wasn't identified; the family consisted of husband, wife, and five children, only one of whom was away at school. Their existing staff, said the advert, included a family chauffeur, two cleaning women who came in daily, and an au pair, who must have had her hands full looking after the four resident children. "A person is also employed to cope with the ironing." The cook-housekeeper's duties, on a fixed one-year contract of employment with the possibility to renew, involved the general running of the household and cooking for the family. "Applicants must be fond of children and able to control other staff."[34]

Leave aside the fact that the four resident children and the phrase "able to control other staff" should have set alarm bells ringing in the ears of most applicants, this is a typical example of how the country house was maintained by the late 1960s. The au pair might be from Spain or Sweden; the dailies might refuse to work weekends; the "family chauffeur" would live out and might in fact be the gardener, prepared to leave off pruning the roses for an hour or two to drive his mistress into town. The family still employed half a dozen servants.

Only no one called them that any more.

20

THE LAST OF UPTAKE?

SIMON AND ROSAMOND Harcourt-Smith drift through the history of the middle years of the twentieth century, hovering on the edge of other people's memories, shadows glimpsed in passing. Rosamond, the daughter of a prominent lawyer, might roar into the gossip columns in her sleek blue sports car or make an entrance at fashionable cocktail parties "in one of the ultra-simple frocks and gardenish hats that suit her so well."[1] She wrote sophisticated romantic fiction about country house life: her novel *Fever of Love* was praised by the *New Statesman* as "the quintessence of top-drawer chi-chi [in] 1952."[2] Her husband, Simon, whose father had been director of the Victoria and Albert Museum and surveyor of the royal works of art, started out as a career diplomat but turned to literary journalism when the Second World War broke out and spent the rest of his long life producing thoughtful reviews, elegant monographs on Babylonian art and Chinese horology, biographies, novels, and film scripts.

The couple had married in 1930, when Simon was twenty-four and Rosamond six years his senior. True to the spirit of her age, the bride had a penchant for interior decoration. The Harcourt-Smiths' house in Chelsea was described in the society pages as charming "in a very 'Oliver Messel-ish' way: a colour scheme of turquoise and petunia, stiff striped silks, flowers and birds under glass covers."[3] They also had a place in Sussex, not a country house but a rather lovely seventeenth-century farmhouse just north of Eastbourne.

The Harcourt-Smiths earn their place in these pages because in the spring of 1942, Simon wrote a country house novella called *The Last of Uptake, or The Estranged Sisters*.

Exquisitely illustrated by Rex Whistler, *Uptake* started life as a distraction for Rosamond when she was laid up in plaster during the Blitz. Dedicated to her and described by Simon's publisher as "a fantastic concoction based on legends of his family and of those of certain friends," it tells the strange story of two elderly spinster sisters, Tryphena and Deborah Caudle, and their anxieties about the future of Uptake, their palatial Palladian family seat by the sea.[4]

Vast and sinister, Uptake was the creation of Tryphena and Deborah's great-grandfather, Lord Winterbourne, a Georgian profligate who almost ruined the family with his extravagant building schemes. His son rescued the family fortunes, first by accidentally conquering Rak, an Indian state two-thirds the size of France, a move which earned him a peerage as Marquess of Indus, and then by marrying an heiress he met in Calcutta, "the admirable if slightly vulgar Miss Bouncer."[5] In later life he retreated to Uptake, where he avoided the tantrums of his marchioness and consoled himself in the arms of his Creole mistress. The mansion became his world, his sanctuary. For Tryphena and Deborah, it became a prison.

AT PRECISELY 3:14 on the afternoon of Wednesday, June 26, 1974, the 11th Duke of Grafton rose to his feet in the House of Lords to address his fellow peers. He was opening a debate on the proposal by Harold Wilson's new minority Labour government to introduce a wealth tax, and specifically, on the impact this could have on the nation's country houses. Grafton was well qualified to speak on such matters, as he reminded his audience. He was, he said, chairman of the Society for the Protection of Ancient Buildings, a long-standing member of the Historic Buildings Council for England, and, before he inherited his dukedom in 1970, the National Trust's historic buildings representative for the East of England. And as Lord Shepherd, the Labour Leader of the House of Lords, was equally quick to remind everyone, Grafton was also the owner of Euston Hall, a vast mansion in Suffolk which he had opened to the public. Although it was less vast than it had been because Grafton's father had pulled down the south wing and most of the west wing in 1952.

The duke spoke eloquently about all the good work that had been done to help country house owners in the twenty-four years since the publication of the Gowers report—the grants awarded, the houses saved, the public-private partnerships which had blossomed since then. All this good work would be undone, he argued, if the new Labour government carried out its pledge to introduce a wealth tax on an individual's assets and, on top of that, to replace death duties with a new tax on the transfer of those assets. Estates would be broken up, he said; mansions would be sold; collections would be dispersed. Labour's plans to use taxation as a tool to redistribute wealth spelled disaster for the country house. Grafton ended by saying: "I should like to ask your Lordships whether, by envisaging taxation such as this, we are really prepared to jeopardise the whole future of our surviving houses and their collections, which I believe to be the envy of the world, and to condone what one critic has described as possibly the greatest act of sacrilege since the Dissolution of the Monasteries."[6]

Lord Shepherd's response, after reminding the House that it was Labour which set up the Gowers committee and trotting out the expected statistics on government funding for stately homes, was to say that the government would listen carefully to what was said. With that he left the chamber, thereby avoiding having to listen—carefully or otherwise—to an impressive array of peers who were queuing to plead for tax exemptions for the country house, from Beaulieu's Lord Montagu and Burghley's Marquess of Exeter to Stratfield Saye's Duke of Wellington and Blenheim's Duke of Marlborough. The prize for the best quote of the day, however, went to one of the lords spiritual—Ronald Williams, bishop of Leicester, who ended his speech with a new version of the hymn "All Things Bright and Beautiful":

> *The poor man in his castle,*
> *The tourist at his gate,*
> *The Chancellor with his wealth tax*
> *Broke up the whole estate.*[7]

If the new government thought that the stately homes of Britain would be a popular target as elitist bastions of privilege and inherited wealth, it had chosen a bad time for its assault. *Country Life* waved its shooting stick in the air, claiming, "We face not only attack on a central part of our artistic patrimony, but the most serious assault on the face of the countryside since the Industrial Revolution."[8] Roy Strong, the young new director of the Victoria and Albert Museum, declared that the new taxes meant "the end of a thousand years of English history and culture. . . . I can't tell you the horrors looming unless one fights and intrigues at every level behind the scenes."[9] A lengthy *Times* editorial was devoted to tax and the country house, making the familiar point that the most sensible solution to the country house problem was to make it possible for private owners to remain in charge of their own homes, and arguing that substantial relaxations in the wealth tax were vital. Country house owners had just formed their own lobby group, the Historic Houses Association. It was chaired by Lord Montagu, whose experience in PR and in promoting Beaulieu made him a formidable adversary. Montagu argued the economic benefits of country house tourism before the select committee on the wealth tax and organised a petition which attracted 1.25 million signatures, one of the largest ever presented to Parliament.

The government's timing was bad for another reason. In 1972 the Council of Europe had declared that 1975 was to be European Architectural Heritage Year. It would also be the twenty-fifth anniversary of the Gowers report, and to mark the two events the British Tourist Authority commissioned John Cornforth, architectural editor of *Country Life*, to write a report examining what had been achieved and what was still to be done. *Country Houses in Britain—Can They Survive?* was published on October 3, 1974, although it was more or less complete before the Wilson government came to power, and it had been circulating in typescript among interested parties for months: the Duke of Grafton quoted from it during his speech in the Lords on June 26.

It was an astonishing piece of work, wide ranging, well informed, impassioned, and occasionally rather odd, as when, in the middle of a welter of statistics relating to maintenance backlogs, HBC grants, and landscape planning, Cornforth introduced a chapter called "The Role of the Wife." ("In many cases it is she who has to take on the day-to-day management of the opening arrangements, if her husband has a career or has to be away a great deal."[10])

Using Cornforth's own subjective definition of country houses which he considered "notable" rather than those which were "listable," in the sense that they warranted inclusion on a statutory list of buildings considered to be of special architectural or historic interest and so protected from demolition, *Country Houses in Britain* nonetheless provided a remarkable snapshot of the state of the stately home in the early 1970s. He reckoned there were around 950 "notable" houses, of which 430 were privately owned and not open to the public. Around 270 notable houses in England and Wales had been lost since the war, and a further 70 in Scotland. New uses had been found for some as schools and university outstations: Wroxton and Cliveden were both occupied by American colleges. Local authorities managed others. The Mutual Households Association, a small charity founded in 1955 to save country houses and turn them into apartments for retired or semiretired people, owned or leased ten houses, "of which all but one are historically and architecturally notable."[11] (That word "notable" again—Cornforth listed the MHA's ten houses but didn't say which one was the dud.) The National Trust and the National Trust for Scotland had done good work, but they had limited resources. Country house tourism had helped—by 1972, when he began his report, there were eight hundred historic houses and ancient monuments open to the public, and forty-three million visits to them. But tourism simply wasn't a viable commercial answer for most houses.

Cornforth's predictions for the future were gloomy. Although the situation had improved vastly over the past decade—there had only been four demolitions in England since 1964, from a peak of one every five days in 1955—he confessed, without explanation, to having already felt in 1972 a vague sense "that we were about to enter a new period of crisis for country houses."[12] Then the 1973 oil crisis hit country house tourism, a sliding stock market hit incomes, and a Labour government came to power intent on introducing a wealth tax and a capital gains tax. The only hope for the country house was a combination of government aid, exemption from estate duty, and tax relief on repairs. Otherwise, "owners now holding country houses and keeping them up at considerable sacrifice will be forced to sell up," he declared. "It will be a heart-breaking end for them."[13]

Smaller houses and new owners both got short shrift in Cornforth's report: "In some cases a house may command quite a high price when it is put onto the market . . . but there is no guarantee that the purchaser will use it as his own house: he may wish to adapt it for an hotel, club or institution, which almost invariably means a loss of character."[14] In general the report was heavily skewed towards the interests of established private country house owners, and towards the biggest and best country houses, the "notable" ones. He was careful not to pry too far into the long-term intentions of those owners—the Earl of March was one of very few to admit that the collection at Goodwood House "in economic terms represented the family's final reserve."[15] And he skirted round the issue of personal wealth and its relation to the upkeep of a house, taking it as a given that the erosion of family collections in the past had been due to the elderly baronet's desperate attempts to hang on to his crumbling ancestral seat, never to his penchant for chorus girls or the tables at the Casino de Monte Carlo.

Cornforth's report was well received by everyone with an interest in such matters, from owners and conservationists to politicians from both camps. For the Conservatives, Airey Neave paid tribute to Cornforth for warning the country "of the danger that is coming."[16] On the left, Labour's Tam Dalyell praised the report for showing how impossible it would be for the state or the National Trust to take on a large number of country houses. It was left to the *Burlington Magazine* to take Cornforth to task, albeit very gently, for his uncritical approach and his portrayal of country house owners as victims, struggling custodians of the nation's heritage. The *Burlington* pointed out that the 8th Duke of Buccleuch, who had died the previous year, had managed to live at a prewar level in three large country houses. "He was of course entirely free to live as he chose; but the slow, steady erosion of that great family collection must have been due, in part at least, to a need to subsidize a high standard of living."[17] And this went to the heart of the problem which underlay so much thinking about saving the country house. What exactly was Cornforth asking the state to subsidize: a cultural artefact or a way of life?

UPTAKE WAS IN trouble, both as a cultural artefact and as a way of life. It was supposed to be a show house, but few visitors came to gape at its decline. That decline was accelerating, as Lady Tryphena noted when a large piece of plaster fell at her feet one day. "At this rate of disintegration it was a mystery how Uptake had stood so long."[18] Various elderly servants staggered and waddled through its marble halls: Hake, the senile butler, who tried to snuff the gas lamps in the Chinese saloon with a gigantic pair of rusty candle snuffers; Plummett and Drax, the sisters' two maids; Titmarsh, the gardener, who lived for his monstrous tropical blooms, which evoked "the spices and music of islands he would never see."[19]

The future was becoming ever more uncertain. Tryphena and Deborah were the only members of the family still in residence at Uptake. Their two brothers, who should have secured the Caudles' dynastic ambitions, were dead. Matthew, the eldest, had been killed in Spain, fighting for a cause he didn't understand; while Adolphus, to whom Tryphena had been devoted—so devoted, in fact, that according to Deborah she had acted the "incestuous strumpet . . . corrupting him with [her] harlotries"—had fallen off a cliff in Greece while searching for the tomb of Alexander the Great.[20]

Matthew's son Henry, Tryphena and Deborah's young nephew, was the current Marquess of Indus, but, cashiered from his regiment after stealing the family jewels, he had been packed off to "hawk his nobility before the curious riff-raff in the outlandish mining camps, the tinsel cities of Mexico and Western America."[21]

What was to become of Uptake, the fantastic Firbankian creation of the sisters' wicked great-grandpapa? The galleries and halls and endless state apartments were filled with curiosities: a complete malachite staircase—"not a main staircase, but an important one"—given as a New Year's gift by Aunt Lavinia, who had married into the Russian nobility; the Chinese state bed that Tryphena could never see without a feeling of awe and pleasure, "a contrivance of such exceptional nobility and imagination, with posts fashioned like tropic trees and a whole menagerie of hoopoes and devilish dragons on the top."[22] A German prince staying at Uptake once woke in this bed to see one of these dragons gazing down at him and let out a wild shriek, having mistaken it for his wife, "a consort of renowned ugliness."[23]

The grounds of Uptake were littered with strange temples and pavilions, all installed in the eighteenth century by Lord Winterbourne. There was a precarious stone bridge, a wilderness, a maze, a Chinese carousel with cars resembling phoenixes and dragons. The moss that grew over the carefully crumbled stonework of a replica of some well-known ruins in the Forum had been imported specially from an Alpine valley in southeastern Switzerland. A vast shell grotto dripped with remembered sins and was equipped with useful sofas placed discreetly in half-hidden alcoves. And there were life-size clockwork dolls: a woodcutter who at the tug of a string would split logs for you; a pair of dancers who waltzed through a rococo pavilion with a glass floor and mirrored walls, like a giant music box; a philosopher who lived in a cave by the lake and who "would rise from his apparent meditations and strike you gently with his stick, in token of your own worthlessness."[24] There were others, but Tryphena's mother had deemed them unsuitable, and they had been moved to a locked storeroom which no one dared to enter, although Tryphena "had often caught herself wondering about their exact nature and, ashamed, had turned her mind elsewhere."[25]

THE PROSPECT OF country houses going under the hammer, their collections being broken up and sold abroad, their history being trampled on by a socialist government, harked back to the arrival of Attlee's Labour government in 1945 and the flood of demolitions in the 1950s. But things were different now. The conservation movement was more coherent than it had been when the Marchioness of Exeter predicted the end of Burghley if she couldn't find any decent servants. The stately home business was a significant part of the economy: forty-three million visits a year were ample proof of that. And now that so many had gone, people *liked* country houses; they regarded mansions and manor houses—and their owners, come to that—with affection, as an endearing part of the nation's heritage. Blandings Castle belonged to all of us. So did Lord Emsworth.

So with the government's proposals on the wealth tax still unpublished, leading figures in the country house world came together to get their retaliation in first. Without doubt the most telling piece of polemic was unveiled in October 1974, when the Victoria and Albert Museum staged what is still remembered today as one of its greatest exhibitions. Timed to coincide with the publication of John Cornforth's report and heralding the start of European Architectural Heritage Year, *The Destruction of the Country House* was the brainchild of architectural historian John Harris, pioneering conservationist Marcus Binney, and the V&A's new director, Roy Strong. The organisers, said Strong, "have been enthusiastically concerned with an utterly objective presentation."[26] This was disingenuous, to put it mildly: the exhibition was a brilliant piece of polemic aimed squarely at mobilising public opinion in the face of Chancellor Denis Healey's threatened tax changes. Its goal was to show how many country houses had been lost over the past hundred years, devastation which could only be likened, said Harris, "to that inflicted by war," and to suggest that destruction on such a scale might happen again if the government were to go ahead with its tax reforms.[27]

The exhibition contained lavish displays of past country house glories, and two case studies in loss: the Deepdene, a Regency masterpiece in Surrey, which was demolished in 1969 to make way for an office block; and the monumental Hamilton Palace in Lanarkshire, which went in 1921 with the sale and dispersal of its contents. But the room that everyone remembered was the Hall of Lost Houses, created by designer Robin Wade as the vast tumbling facade of a country house, with each block of masonry a photograph of one of the thousand country houses which had been lost since 1875. Against a background soundtrack of burning timbers and falling stonework, John Harris's voice intoned the name of every house. "The impact on the public was overwhelming," recalled Roy Strong. "Many was the time I stood in that exhibition watching the tears stream down the visitors' faces as they battled to come to terms with all that had gone."[28]

The collection of essays which accompanied the exhibition was in many ways more extraordinary than the show itself, linking the country house and the life that was lived in it to a mythical past in a startlingly reactionary way. "Is it purely fortuitous that the decline of our civilisation and the collapse of the country house way of life are coincidental?" asked James Lees-Milne.[29] Roy Strong suggested that a love for the country house was nothing less than patriotic duty: at the merest glimpse of some noble pile "the ravished eyes stir the heart to emotion, for in a sense the historic houses of this country belong to everybody, or at least everybody who cares about this country and its traditions."[30] John Harris harked back to a halcyon past when everyone knew their place and the Labour Party was a twinkle in Keir Hardie's eye, when the country house epitomised a way of life "that at its most enlightened was perhaps one of the happiest social structures that Western man has ever achieved."[31] Marcus Binney restored a note of quiet, understated sanity. "Of course it is a good thing that people are no longer doomed to lifetimes of domestic service with no practical alternative," he admitted. "But on the whole I think the destruction is regrettable."[32]

The Destruction of the Country House was a massive success. Until it opened, very few people had realised the extent of the losses that had occurred over the past hundred years, and as those losses were revealed, there was an outraged clamour for something to be done to save what was left of old England. "It may even be a trifle premature for the Maoists to throw their stevedores' caps in the air," wrote one reviewer.[33] It was left to Caroline Tisdall in the *Guardian* to point out that the exhibition polarised the problem and left visitors with a disagreeable choice: either to sympathise with those who lived in great houses, or to be identified "with the pitiless vandalism of the demolition man's ball."[34]

The Labour government did back down over the wealth tax, rather to everyone's surprise; although the fact that Harold Wilson had managed only a three-seat majority when he went to the country for a second time in October 1974 was probably a factor in Denis Healey's decision not to try to push through such contentious legislation. Healey later confessed, "You should never commit yourself in Opposition to new taxes unless you have a very good idea how they will operate in practice."[35] In five years of government he never found it possible to draft a wealth tax that would yield enough revenue to be worth the administrative cost and political hassle.

But the country house lobby regarded the government's retreat as their victory, and theirs alone, and it would be churlish to let hindsight take that away from them. There is no question that the V&A exhibition caught the public's imagination, gave birth to a powerful conservation movement, and paved the way for the cult of the country house, a new renaissance which included the phenomenal success of Mark Girouard's bestselling *Life in the English Country House* in 1978, and Granada Television's dramatization of *Brideshead Revisited* three years later. An awareness of what had been lost led to a determination to save what survived.

Yet by highlighting the dangers and confining itself to discussing the "notable" stately homes, the showplaces, the Uptakes, *The Destruction of the Country House* also confirmed that the country house belonged to the past. It was heritage. It was an exhibit in a museum, a threatened species rather than a living, breathing social construct; its custodians were victims, martyrs who deserved our pity and the government's generosity. Yes, some of that was true. But it was only part of the story.

UPTAKE WAS LOCKED in the past, a sinful, strange, eccentric past when the wicked Lord Winterbourne used to drive his shell-shaped carriage through the local towns, drawn by plumed circus horses with monkeys dressed as postillions riding on their backs like jockeys. Tryphena and Deborah and their ancient and decrepit staff couldn't adapt to a changing world, so they soldiered on, struggling to keep things together with dwindling resources because, as Tryphena said, "It's our duty, our trust to keep everything in perfect order for those who come after. That we must do with all the poor means we possess."[36]

At the end of the novella, the sisters heard some terrible news. Their dissolute young nephew Henry, Marquess of Indus, was dead, having drowned after a night in a waterfront gambling den in San Francisco. That meant the extinction of the line: their nearest relation was a "slimy parson from the Colonies" who had no claim on the title or the mansion.[37] Now Uptake no longer had any reason to exist except its dilapidated beauty. And beauty wasn't enough. Tormented by uncertainty, raging at each other because they had no one else to blame, Tryphena and Deborah decided they would be the ones to let Uptake go.

One moonlit night, the sisters' luggage was loaded onto two carriages, and they left Uptake for the last time. Their little cortege trundled down a drive flanked by sphinxes and caryatids, past pools "where doddering old carp still smacked their lips at the thought of the rich morsels that had come to them in great-grandfather's day," through the gates and up to a high ridge overlooking the park. And there the sisters waited, watching in an agony of suspense. After what seemed like an age, Tryphena noticed a bright glow in the one of the windows: Titmarsh the gardener had obeyed her orders. "Suddenly a flame blossomed out of it like a lovely flower, was joined by another, and yet more, till there was a bed of great petunias."[38] With a roar, the whole of Uptake cracked and fell into the flames.

HOW TYPICAL WAS Uptake, in all its glorious desolation and despair? In 1939, with help from *Country Life*, the National Trust took up the call for a survey of significant country houses and compiled a list of houses considered to be "of first importance."

It named 313 houses in England and 7 in Wales. (Scotland and Northern Ireland didn't get a mention.) And as one would expect, the great showplaces were all there: Castle Howard and Blenheim Palace, Chatsworth and Woburn Abbey. So were the mansions of old romance, Haddon Hall and Penshurst Place and Baddesley Clinton. But in what was a geographically very uneven survey— only one house in Cambridgeshire (Wimpole Hall) against sixteen in Gloucestershire and twenty-one in Northamptonshire—there were some less-expected examples. Rothamsted in Hertfordshire, seventeenth-century with some later additions, made the list, although since 1934 it had been part of an agricultural research station; so, too, did the magnificent Broome Park in Kent, though it had already been turned into a hotel, and Stanwick Park in Yorkshire, which had in fact been demolished back in 1923.

When one looks at the subsequent histories of these "houses of first importance," some intriguing patterns emerge. By 1974, 12 of the 320 houses had gone. Shavington Hall, built in 1685 and undoubtedly the finest mansion of its period in Shropshire, was demolished in 1959. Two years later Rushbrooke Hall, an Elizabethan moated mansion and one of the biggest houses in Suffolk, was destroyed by fire weeks after the demolition contractors moved in. Coleshill in Berkshire, arguably the finest seventeenth-century gentry house in the country, was saved by the octogenarian philanthropist Ernest Cook only to catch fire during restoration work in September 1952, "molten lead pouring from the roof like silver rain," reported a journalist with literary aspirations in the *Swindon Evening Advertiser*. "Mr Cook was said to be too distraught today to make any comment."[39]

These were grave losses. But that still left 308 houses "of first importance" standing thirty-five years after the prophets of doom had predicted the end of the country house. By 1974, 41 had been taken on by the National Trust, and one, Audley End, had been acquired by the state; but even excluding these, a surprisingly high number of houses on the list—122, in fact—had changed hands since 1939, sometimes more than once. There was the expected spate of private schools, but there were also other institutional uses: Northwick Park in Gloucestershire became a drug rehabilitation centre; Bramshill in Hampshire was turned into the National Police College; Allington Castle in Kent was a Carmelite friary; and Staunton Harold Hall in Leicestershire, the home of the Shirley family for over five centuries, was sold for scrap in 1954 before being rescued by philanthropist Leonard Cheshire and turned into a "home for the relief of suffering." A spokesman for Cheshire's charity said that "Group Captain Cheshire and his trustees hope to move patients in there very quickly. They may be incurable T.B. patients or very old people."[40]

But more than five in six remained private homes, even if the families that owned them in 1939 had gone. And while there were more casualties among the thousands of smaller country houses of Britain, the ones which didn't pass John Cornforth's test of what was notable and what was not, even here the vast majority survived, preserved by a listing system which increasingly in the 1960s gave a measure of protection to historic buildings.

The truth was that country houses continued to change hands, as they had for centuries. They were remodelled and rebuilt and refurnished, and the families that loved them sometimes lost them—as they had for centuries. In 1974 there might be a television in the drawing room and the sound of pop music coming from the gramophone in the housekeeper's room. There might be an au pair in the nursery, a turnstile at the gate, and a housing estate on the horizon. These things were part of life, too. The country house wasn't dying. It was just adapting to a changing world.

And in spite of the casualties, it was doing so rather well.

ACKNOWLEDGMENTS

So many people have been extraordinarily generous with their time and expertise while I have been writing this book, responding to my frequent cries for help with patience and wisdom.

I would particularly like to thank the following: Sophie Andreae; Edward Bayntun-Coward; Matthew Beckett; Marcus Binney; Robert and Charlotte Brudenell; the Country Houses of the UK and Ireland Facebook Group; Ben Cowell; Dan Franklin; Norman Hudson; the Marquis of Huntly; Lord and Lady Hylton; Anne-Marie Jordan; Nicholas Kingsley; Patricia Lankester; the Marquis of Lansdowne; Anthony Mould; Jeremy Musson; Patrick Newberry; John Orna-Ornstein; Mitch Owens; Rachel Ring; Susan Ronald; Louise and Mike Seabrook Scrase; David Sekers; Cathryn Spence; and Chris Wynne-Davis.

And last, first, always, Helen. I have her to thank for everything.

ILLUSTRATION CREDITS

Illustration Credits

BLACK-AND-WHITE ILLUSTRATIONS WITHIN TEXT

NOTES

FOREWORD

1. Neil Lyon, *"Useless Anachronisms?": A Study of the Country Houses and Landed Estates of Northamptonshire Since 1880* (Northamptonshire Record Society, 2018), 25.

2. Evelyn Waugh, preface to *Brideshead Revisited: The Sacred and Profane Memories of Captain Charles Ryder* (Chapman & Hall, 1960), 10.

CHAPTER 1: This Is Why

1. "Show and Sports Again at Corsley," *Western Daily Press*, August 9, 1945, 2.

2. James Lees-Milne, *Caves of Ice* (Faber and Faber, 1984), 164.

3. Robert Harling, *Historic Houses: Conversations in Stately Homes* (Condé Nast Publications, 1969), 65.

4. "Lord Bath to Sell Big Estates," *Western Daily Press*, August 6, 1946, 4.

5. "Lord Bath to Sell Big Estates," 4.

6. "Lord Bath to Sell Big Estates," 4.

7. "Lord Bath to Sell Big Estates," 4.

8. *An Act to Incorporate and Confer Powers upon the National Trust for Places of Historic Interest or Natural Beauty 1907*, c. 136, https://nt.global .ssl.fastly.net/documents/download-national-trust-acts-1907-1971-post -order-2005.pdf (accessed December 13, 2020).

9. "A Stronger National Trust," *Times*, October 20, 1936, 17.

10. Adrian Tinniswood, "Guidebooks and Historic Buildings," *Bulletin of Local History: East Midland Region* 17 (1982): 6.

11. "Peer Hits Back in Trust Row," *Observer*, November 13, 1966, 1.

12. Advertisement, *Northampton Mercury*, January 31, 1947, 4.

13. Advertisement, *Wiltshire Times and Trowbridge Advertiser*, July 5, 1947, 6.

14. Daphne Fielding, *Mercury Presides* (Eyre & Spottiswoode, 1954), 191.

CHAPTER 2: The Terrors That Had Broken Loose

1. Daphne Fielding, *Mercury Presides* (Eyre & Spottiswoode, 1954), 193.

2. Fielding, *Mercury Presides*, 194.

3. Fielding, *Mercury Presides*, 199.

4. Fielding, *Mercury Presides*, 199.

5. Maud Russell, *A Constant Heart: The War Diaries of Maud Russell 1938–1945*, edited by Emily Russell (Dovecote Press, 2017), 131.

6. Russell, *Constant Heart*, 120.

7. Russell, *Constant Heart*, 131.

8. Cecil Beaton, *The Years Between: Diaries 1939–44* (Weidenfeld & Nicolson, 1965), 21.

9. John Summerson, "Houses of Twenty Years," *Country Life*, October 12, 1940, 332.

10. "Homes After the War: A Project for a Country House," *Country Life*, October 19, 1940, 342.

11. "Country Houses After the War—III: A Family Home with Differences," *Country Life*, March 29, 1941, 282.

12. "Houses After the War—II: For a Site on the Welsh Coast," *Country Life*, January 4, 1941, 17.

13. "Country Houses After the War—IV: A Small Country House," *Country Life*, August 15, 1941, 284.

14. "Country Houses After the War—VI: What Will Be Wanted?," *Country Life*, July 21, 1944, 112.

15. "Country Houses After the War—VI," 112.

16. "Country Houses After the War—VI," 113.

17. "Country Houses After the War—VI," 113.

18. Osbert Sitwell, foreword to *The English Country House* by Ralph Dutton (B. T. Batsford, 1935), vi.

19. Oliver Sylvain Baliol Brett, 3rd Viscount Esher, "Youth and Reconstruction," *Fortnightly Review*, July–December 1941, 230.

20. W. A. Forsyth and Christopher Hussey, "The Future of Country Houses," *Country Life*, October 17, 1941, 730.

21. Forsyth and Hussey, "The Future of Country Houses," 731.

22. Dorothy Roddick, "A Future for Great Houses," *Country Life*, November 30, 1945, 964.

23. John Martin Robinson, *Requisitioned: The British Country House in the Second World War* (Aurum Press, 2014), 74.

24. Julie Summers, *Our Uninvited Guests: The Secret Lives of Britain's Country Houses 1939–1945* (Simon & Schuster, 2018), 210.

25. Robinson, *Requisitioned*, 53.

26. "Longleat—'Jewel of the West,'" *Bath Chronicle and Weekly Gazette*, April 2, 1949, 10.

27. "Proposed Aerodrome at Stourhead," *Wiltshire Times and Trowbridge Advertiser*, June 17, 1939, 5.

28. "Stourhead Saved for the Nation," *Western Daily Press*, June 29, 1939, 7.

29. James Lees-Milne, *Prophesying Peace* (Faber and Faber, 1984), 236.

30. James Lees-Milne, *Ancestral Voices* (Faber and Faber, 1984), 142.

31. I owe this account of Wilton's troubles to Robinson's excellent *Requisitioned*.

32. Robinson, *Requisitioned*, 191.

33. Robinson, *Requisitioned*, 192.

34. Robinson, *Requisitioned*, 192.

35. Deborah Devonshire, *Wait for Me! Memoirs of the Youngest Mitford Sister* (John Murray, 2011), 130.

36. Deborah Devonshire, *Counting My Chickens, and Other Home Thoughts* (Long Barn Books, 2001), 89.

37. Longleat MSS, quoted in Peter Mandler, "Thynne, Henry Frederick, Sixth Marquess of Bath," *Oxford Dictionary of National Biography*, September 23, 2004, https://doi.org/10.1093/ref:odnb/50818.

38. Fielding, *Mercury Presides*, 225.

CHAPTER 3: "I Don't Want to Be the One to Let It Go"

1. "'The Old Order Changeth . . .': Some of the Stately Homes of England That Have Passed to Other Hands," *Illustrated London News*, February 18, 1950, 262–263.

2. "'The Old Order Changeth,'" 263.

3. "He Tears Down Castles," *Birmingham Daily Post*, February 4, 1959, 22.

4. Roy Strong, Marcus Binney, and John Harris, *The Destruction of the Country House 1875–1975* (Thames and Hudson, 1974), 97.

5. Evelyn Waugh, *The Diaries of Evelyn Waugh* (Weidenfeld & Nicolson, 1976), 629.

6. Maud Russell, *A Constant Heart: The War Diaries of Maud Russell 1938–1945*, edited by Emily Russell (Dovecote Press, 2017), 293.

7. Russell, *A Constant Heart*, 294.

8. Quoted in Mark Amory, *Lord Berners: The Last Eccentric* (Faber and Faber, 2012), ebook, chapter 17.

9. Labour Party Executive Committee, *Let Us Face the Future: A Declaration of Labour Policy for the Consideration of the Nation* (1945), 8.

10. Labour Party Executive Committee, *Let Us Face the Future*, 5.

11. Marchioness of Exeter, "The Future of Great Country Houses—I," *Country Life*, November 9, 1945, 810.

12. Marchioness of Exeter, "Future of Great Country Houses," 814.

13. Vita Sackville-West, *English Country Houses*, Britain in Pictures series (Collins, 1941), 46.

14. Marchioness of Exeter, "Future of Great Country Houses," 814.

15. Lord Methuen, "The Future of Great Country Houses—II: The Preservation of Historical Monuments," *Country Life*, November 16, 1945, 860.

16. H. D. Walston, "The Future of Great Country Houses—III: The Country House as a Centre," *Country Life*, November 23, 1945, 904.

17. Walston, "The Future of Great Country Houses," 904.

18. Walston, "The Future of Great Country Houses," 905.

19. Walston, "The Future of Great Country Houses," 905.

20. "Reliefs in Taxation This Year," *Times*, April 10, 1946, 4.

21. *Finance Act 1946*, c. 64, part IV, section 50, paragraph 3, https://www.legislation.gov.uk/ukpga/Geo6/9-10/64/contents (accessed December 15, 2020).

22. "Mr. Dalton Announces Budget Changes," *Times*, April 16, 1947, 4.

23. *Finance Act 1953*, c. 34, part IV, section 30, paragraph 1, https://www.legislation.gov.uk/ukpga/Eliz2/1-2/34/contents/enacted (accessed December 15, 2020).

24. James Lees-Milne, *Midway on the Waves* (Faber and Faber, 1987), 60.

25. Lees-Milne, *Midway on the Waves*, 196.

26. "Historic Houses: Planning a Policy for Preservation," *Manchester Guardian*, December 11, 1948, 3.

27. "Sir Ernest Gowers," *Guardian*, April 18, 1966, 5.

28. Lees-Milne, *Midway on the Waves*, 189.

29. Sir Ernest Gowers, *Report of the Committee on Houses of Outstanding Historic or Architectural Interest* (HMSO, 1950), 3.

30. Gowers, *Report of the Committee*, 3.

31. Gowers, *Report of the Committee*, 30.

32. Peter Mandler, *The Fall and Rise of the Stately Home* (Yale University Press, 1997), 341. I owe much of the following account of the reception of the Gowers report to Mandler's groundbreaking study.

33. Gowers, *Report of the Committee*, 3.

34. Gowers, *Report of the Committee*, 5.

35. Gowers, *Report of the Committee*, 5.

36. Gowers, *Report of the Committee*, 6.

37. Gowers, *Report of the Committee*, 50.

38. Mandler, *Fall and Rise*, 344.

39. Mandler, *Fall and Rise*, 344.

40. Mandler, *Fall and Rise*, 344.

41. Mandler, *Fall and Rise*, 346.

42. Mandler, *Fall and Rise*, 346.

43. "Many Historic Houses Falling to Ruin," *Manchester Guardian*, September 20, 1952, 3.

44. Mandler, *Fall and Rise*, 347.

45. *Birmingham Daily Post*, June 26, 1964, 1.

46. John Cornforth, *The Country Houses of England 1948–1998* (Constable, 1998), 35.

47. Lord Montagu of Beaulieu, *The Gilt and the Gingerbread, or How to Live in a Stately Home and Make Money* (Michael Joseph, 1967), 106.

48. Deborah Devonshire, *Wait for Me! Memoirs of the Youngest Mitford Sister* (John Murray, 2011), 189.

49. Evelyn, Dowager Duchess of Devonshire, to Francis Thompson, December 30, 1950, in David Adshead and David A. H. B. Taylor (eds.), *Hardwick Hall: A Great Old Castle of Romance* (Yale University Press, 2016), 305.

50. "National Chatsworth," *Manchester Guardian*, June 26, 1954, 3.

51. "Future of Chatsworth," *Country Life*, June 24, 1954, 2080.

52. "But the Taxman Laughs Last," *Daily Herald*, June 19, 1954, 4.

53. Deborah Devonshire, *Counting My Chickens, and Other Home Thoughts* (Long Barn Books, 2001), 87.

54. March 16, 1953, in Adshead and Taylor, *Hardwick Hall: A Great Old Castle of Romance*, 302.

55. Andrew Devonshire, *Accidents of Fortune* (Michael Russell, 2004), 48.

56. Kenneth Rose, *Who's In, Who's Out: The Journals of Kenneth Rose 1944–1979* (Weidenfeld & Nicolson, 2018), 76.

57. D. Devonshire, *Wait for Me!*, 191.

58. A. Devonshire, *Accidents of Fortune*, 49.

59. Curtiss Hamilton, "Stately Homes," *Britannia and Eve*, January 1, 1952, 56.

60. D. Devonshire, *Wait for Me!*, 192.

61. D. Devonshire, *Wait for Me!*, 194.

62. D. Devonshire, *Wait for Me!*, 194.

63. "Duke Returns to Chatsworth House," *Birmingham Daily Post*, November 28, 1959, 5.

64. D. Devonshire, *Wait for Me!*, 195.

CHAPTER 4: Keeping Up Appearances

1. James Lees-Milne, *Ancestral Voices* (Faber and Faber, 1984), 73.

2. Lees-Milne, *Ancestral Voices*, 209.

3. John Cornforth, "Clandon Revisited I," *Country Life*, December 4, 1969, 1456.

4. Cornforth, "Clandon Revisited I," 1456.

5. Earl of Onslow, "Lord Onslow and Food Supply," *Surrey Advertiser*, August 3, 1940, 5.

6. Advertisement, *West Sussex Gazette*, February 13, 1947, 11.

7. Notices, *Surrey Mirror*, April 4, 1947, 6.

8. James Lees-Milne, *Midway on the Waves* (Faber and Faber, 1987), 235.

9. Ronald Hooke Pearson, *Baynton House* (Putnam, 1955), 14.

10. Advertisement, *Western Gazette*, January 25, 1946, 5.

11. Advertisement, *Wiltshire Times and Trowbridge Advertiser*, November 29, 1947, 4.

12. Pearson, *Baynton House*, 187.

13. Sackville-West to Nicolson, Sissinghurst, April 10, 1958, in *Vita and Harold: The Letters of Vita Sackville-West and Harold Nicolson 1910–1962*, ed. Nigel Nicolson (Weidenfeld & Nicolson, 1992), 425.

14. James Lees-Milne, *Caves of Ice* (Faber and Faber, 1984), 127.

15. Frances Partridge, *Everything to Lose: Diaries, 1945–1960* (Victor Gollancz, 1985), 342.

16. Partridge, *Everything to Lose*, 343.

17. Advertisement, *Country Life*, January 4, 1924.

18. Partridge, *Everything to Lose*, 57.

19. Partridge, *Everything to Lose*, 197.

20. Partridge, *Everything to Lose*, 259.

21. Partridge, *Everything to Lose*, 259.

22. Elizabeth Bowen, *Bowen's Court*, in *"Bowen's Court" and "Seven Winters"* (Vintage, 1999), ebook, chapter 1.

23. Partridge, *Everything to Lose*, 260.

24. Bowen, afterword to *Bowen's Court*.

25. Antonia Fraser, *My History: A Memoir of Growing Up* (Weidenfeld & Nicolson, 2015), 139.

26. Fraser, *My History*, 148.

27. Robert O'Byrne, *Luggala Days: The Story of a Guinness House* (CICO Books, 2012), 120.

28. O'Byrne, *Luggala Days*, 142.

29. Michael Luke, "Obituary: Oonagh Oranmore," *Independent*, August 12, 1995, https://www.independent.co.uk/news/obituaries/obituary-oonagh-oranmore-1595833.html.

30. Both quotes from O'Byrne, *Luggala Days*, 127.

31. Luke, "Obituary: Oonagh Oranmore."

32. Partridge, *Everything to Lose*, 163.

33. Partridge, *Everything to Lose*, 163.

34. "A Gay Week in Eire," *Tatler*, August 20, 1952, 324.

35. Partridge, *Everything to Lose*, 164.

36. Partridge, *Everything to Lose*, 164.

37. Partridge, *Everything to Lose*, 166.

38. Partridge, *Everything to Lose*, 164.

39. Lord Kilbracken, "Tea at Luggala," *Tatler*, February 3, 1960, 200.

40. O'Byrne, *Luggala Days*, 156.

41. O'Byrne, *Luggala Days*, 159.

42. Kilbracken, "Tea at Luggala," 200.

43. Kilbracken, "Tea at Luggala," 200.

CHAPTER 5: Reducing Mansions

1. "Reducing Mansions," *Country Life*, March 27, 1953, 894.

2. "Leyswood House," Savills, February 2016, https://media.onthe market.com/properties/2462996/doc_1_4.pdf.

3. "Mulgrave Castle, Yorkshire," *Handed On* (blog), September 26, 2019, https://handedon.wordpress.com/2019/09/26/mulgrave-castle-yorkshire.

4. Sofka Zinovieff, *The Mad Boy, Lord Berners, My Grandmother and Me* (Jonathan Cape, 2014), 51.

5. Duke of Bedford, *A Personal Statement* (privately printed, no date), 7.

6. House of Lords debate on postwar settlement, HL Deb (June 2, 1942), vol. 123, col. 1–68, https://api.parliament.uk/historic-hansard/lords /1942/jun/02/post-war-settlement (accessed February 13, 2021).

7. House of Commons debate on building operations (control), HC Deb (July 31, 1951), vol. 491, col. 1400–1409, https://api.parliament .uk/historic-hansard/commons/1951/jul/31/building-operations-control (accessed February 13, 2021).

8. John Martin Robinson, *Latest Country Houses* (Bodley Head, 1984), 15.

9. "'Tell Us' Poster to Stay," *Daily Herald*, July 1, 1948, 3.

10. "'Tell Us' Poster to Stay," 3.

11. "Foreman in Charge," *Staffordshire Sentinel*, October 20, 1949, 5.

12. "Charges Against Lord Peel," *Scotsman*, October 31, 1950, 5.

13. "Building on the Woburn Estate," *Times*, May 7, 1953, 5.

14. "Fallen Officers," *Times*, January 4, 1945, 7. The *Times* got his rank wrong—he was a major.

15. John Britton, *Beauties of Wiltshire*, vol. 2 (J. D. Dewick, 1801), 220.

16. "Bowood, Wiltshire: The Seat of the Marquess of Lansdowne," *Country Life*, May 21, 1904, 738.

17. 8th Marquis of Lansdowne to James Bettley, September 11, 1985, Bowood Archive.

18. John, Duke of Bedford, *A Silver-Plated Spoon* (Cassell, 1959), 193.

19. 8th Marquis of Lansdowne to James Bettley, September 11, 1985, Bowood Archive.

20. Lord Rosse, "Bowood," *Times*, July 9, 1955, 7.

21. The Marquis of Lansdowne, "Bowood," *Times*, June 28, 1955, 9.

22. "The Case of Bowood," *Country Life*, July 7, 1955, 4.

23. "A Famous English Home Is Demolished," *Sphere*, July 9, 1955, 55.

24. "£18,000 Bowood Sale," *Times*, July 1, 1955, 12.

25. Marquis of Lansdowne, "Bowood," 9.

26. James Lees-Milne, "Bowood," *Times*, June 29, 1955, 11.

27. Lees-Milne, "Bowood," 11.

28. Lees-Milne, "Bowood," 11.

29. John Cornforth, "Bowood, Wiltshire Revisited—II," *Country Life*, June 15, 1972, 1550.

30. J. Mordaunt Crook, "The Fate of Neo-Classical Houses," *Country Life*, June 1, 1972, 1383.

31. "Controversy and a Beautiful Home for £100,000," *Reading Evening Post*, October 5, 1977, 9.

32. Michael Webb, "Looking at Design: A House That Integrates Old and New," *Country Life*, January 12, 1967, 80.

33. Webb, "Looking at Design," 80.

34. Webb, "Looking at Design," 80.

CHAPTER 6: Fit for a Queen

1. "A Home for the Princess," *Times*, August 15, 1947, 4.

2. "Royal Bridal Home," *Lancashire Evening Post*, September 1, 1947, 6.

3. "This Is How the Princess Will Await Her Baby," *The People*, June 13, 1948, 4.

4. Robert Lacey, *Royal: Her Majesty Queen Elizabeth II* (Time Warner, 2002), 162.

5. William Shawcross, *Queen Elizabeth: The Queen Mother* (Macmillan, 2009), 668.

6. Shawcross, *Queen Elizabeth*, 669.

7. Elizabeth Basset, *Moments of Vision: A Memoir* (Ledburn, 2004), 137.

8. Christopher Warwick, *Princess Margaret: A Life of Contrasts* (André Deutsch, 2002), ebook, chapter 9.

9. "Sandbeck House Party to Meet Princess Margaret," *Yorkshire Post and Leeds Intelligencer*, April 17, 1953, 5.

10. Audrey Whiting, "I Visited the Mountbattens at Home," *Daily Mirror*, February 22, 1960, 11.

11. Kenneth Rose, *Who's In, Who's Out: The Journals of Kenneth Rose 1944–1979* (Weidenfeld & Nicolson, 2018), 27.

12. Lacey, *Royal*, 162.

13. Anne de Courcy, *Snowdon: The Biography* (Phoenix, 2012), ebook, chapter 7.

14. Jane Ridley, *Bertie: A Life of Edward VII* (Vintage, 2013), ebook, chapter 8.

15. "The Queen Watches Polo-Playing Duke," *Western Mail*, July 5, 1954, 1.

16. Warwick, *Princess Margaret*, chapter 10.

17. Peter Townsend, *Time and Chance: An Autobiography* (Collins, 1978), 237–238.

18. "Crowds Besiege Country House to See Princess," *Birmingham Daily Gazette*, October 31, 1955, 1.

CHAPTER 7: Ideal Homes

1. "The Estate Market," *Country Life*, January 5, 1951, 63; January 18, 1952, 171; January 16, 1953, 170.

2. Advertisement, *Country Life*, October 21, 1954, 1331.

3. Advertisement, *Country Life*, January 9, 1958, 79.

4. "The Estate Market," *Country Life*, January 5, 1951, 63.

5. Frances Partridge, *Hanging On: Diaries December 1960–August 1963* (Phoenix Giant, 1998), 46.

6. Partridge, *Hanging On*, 48.

7. Advertisement, *Country Life*, December 6, 1946, 1034.

8. Advertisement, *Country Life*, January 12, 1956, supplement, 1.

9. John Martin Robinson, *The Latest Country Houses* (Bodley Head, 1984), 74.

10. Ralph Dutton, *Hinton Ampner: A Hampshire Manor* (National Trust, 2010), 94.

11. Lewis Mumford, "From Crotchet Castle to Arthur's Seat," in *The Highway and the City* (Harcourt, Brace and World, 1963), 90, 91.

12. Clough Williams-Ellis, *On Trust for the Nation* (Paul Elek, 1947), 8.

13. Williams-Ellis, *On Trust*, 23.

14. Williams-Ellis, *On Trust*, 22.

15. Clough Williams-Ellis, *Architect Errant* (Constable, 1971), 260.

16. Williams-Ellis, *Architect Errant*, 260.

17. Williams-Ellis, *Architect Errant*, 261.

18. Williams-Ellis, *Architect Errant*, 262.

19. Clough Williams-Ellis, *Around the World in Ninety Years* (Golden Dragon Books, 1978), 45.

20. Williams-Ellis, *Around the World*, 47.

21. Williams-Ellis, *Around the World*, 50.

22. Williams-Ellis, *Around the World*, 51.

23. Williams-Ellis, *Around the World*, 53.

24. "Sir Martin Beckett, Bt," *Telegraph*, August 6, 2001, https://www
.telegraph.co.uk/news/obituaries/1336490/Sir-Martyn-Beckett-Bt.html.

25. "A Design That Alarms the Neighbours," *Country Life*, May 19, 1960, 1139.

26. Robinson, *Latest Country Houses*, 121.

27. John Cornforth, "A Classicist from the Heart," *Country Life*, January 4, 1996, 38.

28. "Driffield Mansion Gutted by Fire," *Driffield Times*, November 23, 1940, 3.

29. "Sunderlandwick House," Historic England, https://historicengland
.org.uk/listing/the-list/list-entry/1375668 (accessed December 13, 2020).

30. John Cornforth, "Space, Light and Movement: The Country Houses of Francis Johnson," *Country Life*, October 25, 1984, 1186.

31. Christopher Hussey, "A Castle's Substitute: Belsay House, Northumberland," *Country Life*, April 2, 1959, 724.

32. "Footman Alleged to Have Said Panic Caused Shooting," *Manchester Guardian*, November 7, 1952, 4.

33. "Knowsley's New Look for Easter," *Liverpool Echo*, April 17, 1954, 3.

34. *Liverpool Echo*, April 17, 1954, 3.

35. Robinson, *Latest Country Houses*, 127.

36. *Liverpool Echo*, October 19, 1963, 3.

37. Lucy Archer, *Raymond Erith: Progressive Classicist 1904–1973* (Soane Gallery, 2004), 11.

38. Lucy Archer, *Raymond Erith, Architect* (Cygnet, 1985), 31.

39. Archer, *Raymond Erith, Architect*, 31.

40. Archer, *Raymond Erith, Architect*, 76.

41. Archer, *Raymond Erith, Architect*, 141.

42. Archer, *Progressive Classicist*, 49.

43. Archer, *Raymond Erith, Architect*, 76.

44. Mark Bence-Jones, "A Palladian Villa in Modern Terms: Wivenhoe New Park, Essex," *Country Life*, July 22, 1965, 218, 220.

45. John Cornforth, "Kings Walden Bury, Hertfordshire—I," *Country Life*, September 27, 1973, 858.

46. Cornforth, "Kings Walden Bury," 859.

CHAPTER 8: Modern Movements

1. John Martin Robinson, *The Latest Country Houses* (Bodley Head, 1984), 141.
2. Nikolaus Pevsner and Edward Hubbard, *The Buildings of England: Cheshire* (Penguin Books, 2001), 208.
3. Christopher Hussey, "Joldwynds, Surrey," *Country Life*, September 15, 1934, 277.
4. *Architects' Journal* 79 (February 15, 1934): 244.
5. H. Dalton Clifford, "A House with Glass Walls," *Country Life*, March 16, 1961, 600.
6. H. Dalton Clifford, *The Country Life Book of Houses for Today* (Country Life, 1963), 82. This book contains an expanded version of Clifford's original *Country Life* article.
7. Advertisement, *Country Life*, September 12, 1957, 503.
8. Clifford, *The Country Life Book of Houses for Today*, 37–38.
9. "Whittaker Wright," *West Gippsland Gazette* (Victoria, Australia), August 11, 1903, 4.
10. Mark Girouard, "A Change from Neo-Georgian: Witley Park, Near Godalming," *Country Life*, December 19, 1963, 1693.
11. "Mr. John Dennys," *Times*, September 1, 1973, 14.
12. "Mansion 'Resented,'" *Guardian*, March 13, 1972, 7.
13. Hugh Pearman, "Unmodernise This Eyesore, Says the Duke," *Sunday Times*, February 7, 1988, 4.
14. Pearman, "Unmodernise This Eyesore," 4.

CHAPTER 9: The American Dream

1. *A Handbook for Travellers in Kent*, 5th edition (John Murray, 1892), 238.
2. "Ightham Mote," *Country Life*, April 17, 1897, 406.
3. Charles Robinson to Lady Colyer-Fergusson, widow of Sir Thomas, December 13, 1953, National Trust archive, Ightham Mote, Kent.
4. Advertisement, *Illustrated Sporting and Dramatic News*, September 19, 1951, 3.
5. "The Fate of Country Houses," *Country Life*, July 11, 1952, 106.
6. *Ightham Mote* (National Trust, 2016), 52.
7. C. H. Robinson, note of April 7, 1964, to letter withdrawing offer, National Trust archive, Ightham Mote, Kent.
8. *Ightham Mote*, 52.
9. Quoted in Richard Pells, *Not Like Us* (Basic Books, 1997), 138.

10. Henry James, *English Hours* (Houghton, Mifflin, 1895), 236.

11. James, *English Hours*, 84.

12. James, *English Hours*, 87.

13. Michael John Law, *Not Like Home: American Visitors to Britain in the 1950s* (McGill-Queen's University Press, 2019), 47.

14. A. McClune, letter to the editor, *Picture Post*, July 26, 1952; quoted in Law, *Not Like Home*, 20.

15. Ruth McKenney and Richard Bransten, *Here's England: A Highly Informal Guide* (Rupert Hart-Davis, 1955), 160.

16. McKenney and Bransten, *Here's England*, 155.

17. Advertisement, *Country Life*, June 6, 1957, supplement, 6.

18. Lord Montagu of Beaulieu, *The Gilt and the Gingerbread, or How to Live in a Stately Home and Make Money* (Michael Joseph, 1967), 58.

19. Introduction to *Debrett's Peerage, Baronetage, Knightage and Companionage* (Odhams Press, 1947), xxi.

20. Robert Rhodes James (ed.), *Chips: The Diaries of Sir Henry Channon* (Penguin, 1970), 155.

21. James, *Chips*, 20; Gore Vidal, *Palimpsest: A Memoir* (Random House, 1995), 195.

22. James, *Chips*, 544.

23. David Patrick Columbia, "A Classic Man of Style: John Galliher," *Quest*, March 9, 2016, https://www.questmag.com/blog/a-classic-man-of -style-john-galliher; Michael St John-McAlister, "Michael Renshaw: A Society Figure in War and Peace," *eBLJ* (2015), article 6, https://www .bl.uk/eblj/2015articles/pdf/ebljarticle62015.pdf.

24. Anthony Russell, *Outrageous Fortune: Growing Up at Leeds Castle* (Robson Press, 2013), 59.

25. J. Paul Getty, *As I See It* (Berkley Books, 1986), 207.

26. Getty, *As I See It*, 208.

27. Getty, *As I See It*, 291.

28. Betty Kenward, *Jennifer's Memoirs: Eighty-Five Years of Fun and Functions* (HarperCollins, 1992), 200.

29. Getty, *As I See It*, 214.

30. Getty, *As I See It*, 214.

31. Peter Aspden, "The Collections of Stanley J Seeger," *Financial Times*, January 24, 2014, https://www.ft.com/content/0884418e-82b9 -11e3-9d7e-00144feab7de.

CHAPTER 10: A Rich Interior Life

1. John Harris, "Designs on the Unworldly," *Country Life*, May 27, 1993, 82.

2. James Lees-Milne, *Caves of Ice* (Faber and Faber, 1984), 39.

3. "Greatest Hunt for Art Treasures," *Yorkshire Post and Leeds Mercury*, May 21, 1945, 2. To be fair, he only tweaked his name, going from Cyril Felix Harbord to Felix Paul Jerome Harbord. Presumably he didn't think "Cyril" struck the right note.

4. John Cornforth, "Luttrellstown Castle, Co. Dublin—II," *Country Life*, March 29, 1984, 824.

5. "Jennifer," "A Dress Show Before Royalty," *Tatler*, December 15, 1954, 690.

6. Cornforth, "Luttrellstown Castle—II," 826.

7. "At Home to the Sketch: Mr. Cecil Beaton," *Sketch*, October 10, 1951, 349; Christopher Hussey, "Reddish House, Broad Chalke, Wilts.—I," *Country Life*, March 21, 1957, 543.

8. Jennifer Boles, "The Felix Harbord Dining Room," *Peak of Chic* (blog), January 25, 2013, http://thepeakofchic.blogspot.com/2013/01/the-felix-harbord-dining-room.html.

9. Mark Girouard, "Oving House, Buckinghamshire—II," *Country Life*, November 27, 1958, 1235.

10. Mark Girouard, "Oving House, Buckinghamshire—I," *Country Life*, November 20, 1958, 1174.

11. "Storied Luttrellstown Castle," *Leinster Leader*, January 11, 1941, 3.

12. "Jennifer," "Social Journal," *Tatler*, September 15, 1948, 195.

13. "Jennifer," "Sir Winston Conquers the U.S.," *Tatler*, March 26, 1958, 618.

14. Cornforth, "Luttrellstown Castle—II," 822.

15. Cornforth, "Luttrellstown Castle, Co. Dublin—I," *Country Life*, March 22, 1984, 763.

16. Robert Becker, *Nancy Lancaster: Her Life, Her World, Her Art* (Alfred A. Knopf, 1996), 151.

17. Becker, *Nancy Lancaster*, 157, 156.

18. Becker, *Nancy Lancaster*, 208.

19. Becker, *Nancy Lancaster*, 308.

20. Becker, *Nancy Lancaster*, 308.

21. Quoted in Becker, *Nancy Lancaster*, 308.

22. James Lees-Milne, *Fourteen Friends* (John Murray, 1996), 163.

23. Becker, *Nancy Lancaster*, 310.

24. Becker, *Nancy Lancaster*, 333.

25. Becker, *Nancy Lancaster*, 337.

26. Becker, *Nancy Lancaster*, 347.

27. Becker, *Nancy Lancaster*, 342–343.

28. Becker, *Nancy Lancaster*, 343.

29. Quoted in Becker, *Nancy Lancaster*, 398 fn 7.

30. John Cornforth, *The Inspiration of the Past: Country House Taste in the Twentieth Century* (Viking in association with *Country Life*, 1985), 201.

31. Cornforth, *Inspiration of the Past*, 164.

32. Martin A. Wood, *John Fowler, Prince of Decorators* (Frances Lincoln, 2007), 119.

33. Cornforth, *Inspiration of the Past*, 201.

34. Wood, *John Fowler*, 123.

35. John Cornforth, "Sudbury Hall Revisited," *Country Life*, June 10, 1971, 1431.

36. Wood, *John Fowler*, 223.

37. "National Trust 'Destroying Stately Home Character,'" *Times*, August 5, 1971, 2.

38. John Cornforth, "Sudbury Hall," *Country Life*, August 12, 1971, 389.

39. Cornforth, "Sudbury Hall," 389.

40. Robin Fedden, "The Work of the Trust," *Country Life*, July 15, 1971, 166.

41. Richard Tyler, "Changes at Sudbury," *Country Life*, August 5, 1971, 341.

42. George Seymour, "Changes at Sudbury," *Country Life*, September 9, 1971, 627.

43. Seymour, "Changes at Sudbury," 627.

44. Jonathan Aitken, *The Young Meteors* (Secker & Warburg, 1967), 221.

45. Ashley Hicks, "The House and Garden Feature That Launched David Hicks' Career," *House and Garden*, October 7, 2017, https://www.houseandgarden.co.uk/article/david-hicks-scrapbooks.

46. David Hicks, *David Hicks on Living—with Taste* (Leslie Frewin, 1968), 11.

47. Aitken, *The Young Meteors* 47.

48. Gervase Jackson-Stops, "Britwell Salome, Oxfordshire—II," *Country Life*, October 12, 1972, 887.

49. Quoted in Nicholas Haslam, "Obituary: David Hicks," *Independent*, October 23, 2011, https://www.independent.co.uk/news/obituaries/obituary-david-hicks-1153956.html.

50. Hicks, *David Hicks on Living*, 112.

51. Gervase Jackson-Stops, "Baronscourt, Co. Tyrone—III," *Country Life*, July 26, 1979, 235.

52. Jackson-Stops, "Baronscourt," 235.

CHAPTER 11: Country Pursuits

1. Angela Ince, "Home Counties Escape and Evade Course," *Tatler*, December 18, 1963, 830.

2. Ince, "Home Counties Escape and Evade Course."

3. Ince, "Home Counties Escape and Evade Course."

4. Advertisement, *Country Life*, November 21, 1968, 1341.

5. J. Wentworth Day, "On Running a Shoot," *Country Life*, February 15, 1952, 426.

6. Day, "On Running a Shoot," 427.

7. Day, "On Running a Shoot," 427.

8. Johnathon Radcliffe, "Man's World," *Tatler*, September 14, 1960, 516.

9. Arthur H. Hoare, "Good Manners While Shooting," *Country Life*, January 30, 1948, 225.

10. Advertisement, *Country Life*, December 27, 1962, supplement, 9.

11. Richard Wells, "Syndicate Shoots: The Right Approach," *Country Life*, November 21, 1968, 1341.

12. Muriel Bowen, "The Hunts Move Off . . .," *Tatler*, November 11, 1959, 330.

13. Lionel Edwards, "War-Time Fox-Hunting, 1914 and Today," *Country Life*, March 2, 1940, 218.

14. Lionel Edwards, "Foxes Make Playful Pets," *Country Life*, September 19, 1941, 540.

15. "Flourishing State of Fox-Hunting," *Times*, November 19, 1960, 11.

16. Gregory Blaxland, "Fox-Hunting in a Changing World," *Country Life*, September 27, 1962, 701.

17. Anonymous, *Customs and Etiquette of the Hunting Field* (Rowlands Press, 2014), chapter 5.

18. Geoffrey Moorhouse, "The Hunt at Bay," *Guardian*, December 30, 1964, 5.

19. T. F. Dale, *The Eighth Duke of Beaufort and the Badminton Hunt* (Archibald Constable, 1901), 218.

20. M. F., "The Duke of Beaufort at Badminton," *Country Life*, August 18, 1934, 165.

21. Clive Aslet, "Chatelherault, Near Glasgow," *Country Life*, August 13, 1987, 87.

22. James Bettley and Julia Wolton, "Establishing in Pompous Style: Heyday of the Kennel," *Country Life*, February 7, 1985, 311.

23. Michael Tichelar, "'A Blow to the Men in Pink': The Royal Society for the Prevention of Cruelty to Animals and Opposition to Hunting in the Twentieth Century," *Rural History* 22 (2011): 89.

24. "Protection of Field Sports," *Times*, December 5, 1930, 21.

25. Tichelar, "'A Blow to the Men in Pink,'" 95.

26. Tichelar, "'A Blow to the Men in Pink,'" 103.

27. Tichelar, "'A Blow to the Men in Pink,'" 103.

28. "Piccadilly Hunt Big Success," *Gloucestershire Echo*, February 26, 1949, 4.

29. "Fox Hunt 'Not Suitable' Protest," *Coventry Evening Telegraph*, January 25, 1955, 11.

30. Steve Poole, "1963: Protest to Resistance," Hunt Saboteurs Association, n.d., https://www.huntsabs.org.uk/index.php/about-the-hsa/hsa-history.

31. "Beaufort Hunt Ordered Off," *Birmingham Daily Post*, April 12, 1962, 1.

32. "A Cheeky Plan to Sabotage Fox-Hunting," *The People*, December 15, 1963, 8.

33. "A Cheeky Plan to Sabotage Fox-Hunting," 8.

34. Ned Grant, "Otter Hunt Punch-Up as Saboteurs Moved In," *Daily Mirror*, September 30, 1964, 4.

35. "Saboteurs in Otter Hunt Clash," *Times*, May 4, 1964, 9.

36. "Hunt Saboteurs Bound Over," *Times*, October 1, 1964, 8.

CHAPTER 12: Balls

1. D. H. Parker, *The Story of My Life in Gentlemen's Service* (privately printed, 1978), 60.

2. "Horseplay at Hunt Ball: Bread Roll Damages Painting," *Guardian*, February 19, 1960, 4.

3. Fiona MacCarthy, *Last Curtsey: The End of the Debutante* (Faber and Faber, 2010), ebook, 175.

4. MacCarthy, *Last Curtsey*, 175.

5. "Jennifer's Social Journal," *Tatler*, January 13, 1954, 47.

6. "Jennifer," "Social Journal," *Tatler*, January 2, 1957, 5.

7. Cover caption, *Tatler*, February 19, 1958, 310.

8. "Jennifer," "Brilliant Vista of Last Royal Season," *Tatler*, February 19, 1958, 314.

9. "Presentation at Court," *Times*, November 15, 1957, 11.

10. MacCarthy, *Last Curtsey*, 14.

11. Angela Huth, *Not the Whole Story: A Memoir* (Constable, 2018), 147.

12. MacCarthy, *Last Curtsey*, 157.

13. Huth, *Not the Whole Story*, 149.

14. Mark Bence-Jones, "Staying at Second-Hand," *Tatler*, October 11, 1961, 104.

15. MacCarthy, *Last Curtsey*, 159.

16. Huth, *Not the Whole Story*, 147.

17. Muriel Bowen, "Fairyland at Syon," *Tatler*, July 5, 1961, 10.

18. Susan Lydon, "The Things London Girls Do for Money," *Tatler*, March 19, 1966, 26.

19. "Jennifer," "Mirrors and Garlands," *Tatler*, July 30, 1952, 190.

20. Jonathan Aitken, *The Young Meteors* (Secker & Warburg, 1967), 222.

21. Aitken, *Young Meteors*, 222.

22. MacCarthy, *Last Curtsey*, 208.

23. "Jennifer," "A Scintillating Début," *Tatler*, May 23, 1956, 410.

24. Muriel Bowen, "The Country Spirit," *Tatler*, August 14, 1963, 312–313.

25. Huth, *Not the Whole Story*, 153.

CHAPTER 13: How to Run a Stately Home

1. "Castle-Gawking Tourists Inspire Cary Grant Film," *Daily News* (St. John's, Newfoundland), July 25, 1960, 13.

2. Advertisement, *Daily Record* (Long Branch, New Jersey), November 29, 1956, 15.

3. David Wynne-Morgan, *Tatler*, August 6, 1966, 10.

4. Wynne-Morgan, 10.

5. "Million-Dollar Comedy Is No Joke for the Stately Home," *Birmingham Daily Post*, August 1, 1969, 1.

6. "British Blue-Bloods Find Gold in Opening Castles to Tourists," *Indianapolis Star*, July 17, 1955, 14.

7. Curtiss Hamilton, "Stately Homes," *Britannia and Eve*, January 1, 1952, 25.

8. John Windsor, "Stately League Upstaged by State," *Guardian*, October 5, 1973, 6.

9. Lord Montagu of Beaulieu, *The Gilt and the Gingerbread, or How to Live in a Stately Home and Make Money* (Michael Joseph, 1967), 104.

10. "The Marquess of Bath Opens Longleat to the Public," *Tatler*, April 6, 1949, 1, 18–19.

11. "Longleat Open to the Public," *Times*, March 31, 1949, 6.

12. Robert Harling, *Historic Houses: Conversations in Stately Homes* (Condé Nast Publications, 1969), 66.

13. "Record Crowds Easter Visit to Warwick Castle," *Warwick and Warwickshire Advertiser*, April 26, 1946, 1.

14. Lord Montagu of Beaulieu, *Wheels Within Wheels: An Unconventional Life* (Weidenfeld & Nicolson, 2000), 144.

15. Montagu, *Wheels Within Wheels*, 144.

16. Montagu, *Wheels Within Wheels*, 150.

17. "Palace House, Beaulieu," *Portsmouth Evening News*, April 7, 1952, 5.

18. Quoted in Montagu, *Wheels Within Wheels*, 151.

19. John, Duke of Bedford, *A Silver-Plated Spoon* (Cassell, 1959), 193.

20. Bedford, *Silver-Plated Spoon*, 195.

21. Bedford, *Silver-Plated Spoon*, 204.

22. Bedford, *Silver-Plated Spoon*, 213.

23. John, Duke of Bedford, with George Mikes, *How to Run a Stately Home* (Deutsch, 1971), 52.

24. Montagu, *Gilt and the Gingerbread*, 108.

25. Bedford, *Silver-Plated Spoon*, 217.

26. Montagu, *Gilt and the Gingerbread*, 186.

27. Montagu, *Gilt and the Gingerbread*, 129.

28. Montagu, *Gilt and the Gingerbread*, 130.

29. Bedford, *Silver-Plated Spoon*, 219.

30. Montagu, *Wheels Within Wheels*, 271.

31. Montagu, *Wheels Within Wheels*, 273.

32. Ned Grant, "Stately Home Stormed by Pop Fans," *Daily Mirror*, May 4, 1964, 32.

33. "200 Injured at Pop Concert," *Birmingham Daily Post*, August 3, 1964, 1.

34. Nicole, Duchess of Bedford, *Nicole Nobody: The Autobiography of the Duchess of Bedford* (W. H. Allen, 1974), 315.

35. "'Flower Children Charming,'" *Birmingham Daily Post*, August 28, 1967.

36. "Amersham Has Real Flowers and Flower People," *Buckinghamshire Examiner*, September 1, 1967, 2.

37. Montagu, *Gilt and the Gingerbread*, 120.

38. Montagu, *Gilt and the Gingerbread*, 131.

39. Montagu, *Gilt and the Gingerbread*, 131.

40. Bedford, *Silver-Plated Spoon*, 196.

41. Bedford, *Silver-Plated Spoon*, 215.

42. Deborah Devonshire, *Counting My Chickens, and Other Home Thoughts* (Long Barn Books, 2001), 99.

43. Montagu, *Gilt and the Gingerbread*, 114.

44. Devonshire, *Counting My Chickens*, 103.

45. Michael Saunders Watson, *I Am Given a Castle: The Memoirs of Michael Saunders Watson* (JJG 2008), 84.

46. Bedford, *Nicole Nobody*, 324.

47. Montagu, *Gilt and the Gingerbread*, 118.

48. Harling, *Historic Houses*, 181.

CHAPTER 14: U Meets Non-U

1. Alan S. C. Ross, "Linguistic Class-Indicators in Present-Day English," *Neuphilologische Mitteilungen* 108 (1954): 22.

2. Ross, "Linguistic Class-Indicators," 39.

3. Nancy Mitford, "The English Aristocracy," in *Noblesse Oblige: An Enquiry into the Identifiable Characteristics of the English Aristocracy*, ed. Nancy Mitford (Harper & Brothers, 1956), 25.

4. Nancy Mitford, introduction to *Noblesse Oblige*, xiii.

5. Mitford, introduction to *Noblesse Oblige*, xii.

6. Evelyn Waugh, "An Open Letter to the Honourable Mrs Peter Rodd [Nancy Mitford] on a Very Serious Subject," 103.

7. Christopher Sykes, "What U-Future?," in *Noblesse Oblige*, 149.

8. Osbert Sitwell, *Laughter in the Next Room* (Macmillan, 1949), 349.

9. Francis Vivian, *The Threefold Cord: An Inspector Knollis Mystery* (Dean Street Press, 2018), 100.

10. Mitford, "English Aristocracy," 39.

11. Mitford, "English Aristocracy," 41.

12. Evelyn Waugh, preface to *Brideshead Revisited: The Sacred and Profane Memories of Captain Charles Ryder* (Chapman & Hall, 1960), 8.

13. Tim Hogarth, *The Dazzling Lady Docker: Britain's Forgotten Reality Superstar* (Scratching Shed Publishing, 2018), 110.

14. "No Austerity," *Lancashire Evening Post*, December 1, 1954, 6.

15. Hogarth, *Dazzling Lady Docker*, 139.

16. Hogarth, *Dazzling Lady Docker*, 133.

17. "Mail-Order House," *Londonderry Sentinel*, May 24, 1956, 2.

18. "Dispute on Bank Board," *Times*, January 27, 1953, 8.

19. "Sir B. Docker's Move for Reinstatement Fails," *Times*, August 2, 1956, 8.

20. "The Duke of Bedford on Saving Our Stately Homes," *Tatler*, October 8, 1966, 38.

21. Jonathan Aitken, *The Young Meteors* (Secker & Warburg, 1967), 270–271.

22. In his poem "Annus Mirabilis," which begins with the lines, "Sexual intercourse began / In nineteen sixty-three . . ."

23. Anthony Sampson, *Anatomy of Britain* (Hodder and Stoughton, 1962), 17.

24. Aitken, *Young Meteors*, 44.

25. Aitken, *Young Meteors*, 46.

26. Harling, *Historic Houses*, 181.

27. Harling, *Historic Houses*, 179.

28. Harling, *Historic Houses*, 180.

29. Aitken, *Young Meteors*, 46.

30. John, Duke of Bedford, with George Mikes, *How to Run a Stately Home* (Deutsch, 1971), 86.

31. "The Londonderrys," *Vogue*, August 1, 1964, 121.

32. "The Londonderrys," 122.

33. "The Londonderrys," 122.

34. Frances Partridge, *Life Regained: Diaries, 1970–1972* (Weidenfeld & Nicolson, 1998), 139.

35. Partridge, *Life Regained*, 140.

36. Partridge, *Life Regained*, 140.

37. Sampson, *Anatomy of Britain*, 7.

38. Kenneth Rose, *Who's In, Who's Out: The Journals of Kenneth Rose 1944–1979* (Weidenfeld & Nicolson, 2018), 265.

39. Cecil Beaton, *The Parting Years 1963–74* (Sapere Books, 2018), ebook, part 3.

40. Charles Hamblett, "Mick Jagger: The Man and the Cult," *Tatler*, February 26, 1966, 23.

41. Hamblett, "Mick Jagger," 23.

42. Tony Sanchez, *Up and Down with the Rolling Stones: My Rollercoaster Ride with Keith Richards* (John Blake Publishing, 2010), 20.

43. Paul Howard, *I Read the News Today, Oh Boy: The Short and Gilded Life of Tara Browne, the Man Who Inspired the Beatles' Greatest Song* (Picador, 2016), 253.

44. Howard, *I Read the News*, 248.

45. Howard, *I Read the News*, 292.

CHAPTER 15: Almost a Fairy Story

1. Christopher Hussey, "Midford Castle, Somerset—I," *Country Life*, March 3, 1944, 376.

2. "Isabel Colegate Novelist," *Country Life*, June 18, 1998, 70.

3. "Isabel Colegate Novelist," 70.

4. Peter Saunders, *Almost a Fairy Story: A History of Easton Grey House* (privately printed, no date), no pagination; Ruth Weiss, "Unorthodox Ways to Success," *Guardian*, September 25, 1969, 21.

5. Saunders, *Almost a Fairy Story*.

6. Saunders, *Almost a Fairy Story*.

7. Saunders, *Almost a Fairy Story*.

8. Advertisement, *Country Life*, March 23, 1972, 740.

9. Saunders, *Almost a Fairy Story*.

10. Andy Garnett, *Memories of a Lucky Dog* (Turnham Press, 2011), ebook, 232.

11. Garnett, *Memories of a Lucky Dog*, 264.

12. Jeremy Musson, "Bradley Court, Gloucestershire," *Country Life*, September 15, 2005, 134.

13. Garnett, *Memories of a Lucky Dog*, 268.

14. Bruce Chatwin, *Under the Sun: The Letters of Bruce Chatwin* (Jonathan Cape, 2010), 93.

15. James Lees-Milne, *Diaries 1971–1983* (John Murray, 2007), 48.

16. Frances Partridge, *Hanging On: Diaries December 1960–August 1963* (Phoenix Giant, 1998), 109.

17. Frances Partridge, *Good Company: Diaries 1967–1970* (Harper Collins, 1994), 3.

18. Partridge, *Good Company*, 2.

19. Partridge, *Good Company*, 116–117.

20. Anne de Courcy, *Snowdon: The Biography* (Phoenix, 2012), ebook, chapter 3.

21. "Francis and the Duckling," *Sketch*, July 2, 1958, 3. The hyphen in "Armstrong-Jones" was something of a moveable feast in the 1950s.

22. De Courcy, *Snowdon*, chapter 5.

23. De Courcy, *Snowdon*, chapter 6.

24. "I Can't Be Best Man, Says Jeremy," *Daily Mirror*, April 7, 1960, 1.

25. "I Can't Be Best Man," 1.

26. W. S., "Homosexuality," *Birmingham Daily Post*, November 13, 1959, 6.

27. Garnett, *Memories of a Lucky Dog*, 120.

28. De Courcy, *Snowdon*, chapter 5.

29. Ned Grant, "The Princess Plays 'Pops' in a Shop," *Daily Mirror*, November 22, 1960, 7.

30. Rex North, "Princess Margaret Bows to Jazz Kings," *Daily Mirror*, June 18, 1962, 9.

31. "Divorce Degree Against Mr. Jeremy Fry," *Times*, February 21, 1967, 3.

32. Lees-Milne, *Diaries, 1971–1983*, 150.

CHAPTER 16: Imagine

1. Advertisement, *Country Life*, April 3, 1969, supplement, 14.

2. Kendra Bean, "Notley Abbey," *Vivien Leigh and Laurence Olivier* (blog), n.d., http://vivandlarry.com/the-oliviers/notley-abbey/.

3. Amanda Hodges, "Peter Sellers at Chipperfield Manor," *Hertfordshire Life*, February 20, 2013, https://www.hertfordshirelife.co.uk/people/peter-sellers-at-chipperfield-manor-1-1643261 (accessed December 13, 2020).

4. Dirk Bogarde, *Snakes and Ladders* (Bloomsbury Reader, 2014), 196.

5. Bogarde, *Snakes and Ladders*, 196.

6. For a full account of Birchens Spring and its startling interiors, see Christopher Hussey, "Birchens Spring I and II," *Country Life*, January 29 and February 5, 1938.

7. Bogarde, *Snakes and Ladders*, 259.

8. Bogarde, *Snakes and Ladders*, 275.

9. Coldstream, *Dirk Bogarde*, chapter 12.

10. Keith Richards, *Life* (Phoenix, 2012), 187.

11. Richards, *Life*, 187.

12. Tony Sanchez, *Up and Down with the Rolling Stones: My Rollercoaster Ride with Keith Richards* (John Blake Publishing, 2010), 110.

13. Sanchez, *Up and Down*, 117.

14. "Stones' Court Told of Nude Girl in Skin Rug," *Liverpool Echo*, June 28, 1967, 1.

15. Bill Wyman with Ray Coleman, *Stone Alone: The Story of a Rock 'n' Roll Band* (privately published, 2016), ebook, chapter 10.

16. Roger Daltrey, *Thanks a Lot Mr Kibblewhite: My Story* (Blink Publishing, 2019), ebook, 172.

17. Daltrey, *Thanks a Lot*, 175.

18. Daltrey, *Thanks a Lot*, 259.

19. Daltrey, *Thanks a Lot*, 259, 261.

20. Pattie Boyd, *Wonderful Today: The Autobiography* (Headline Review, 2007), 188.

21. Charlotte Bingham, "Loving London Style," *Tatler*, February 19, 1966, 28.

22. "Henley: Outlying Estates and Country Houses," in *A History of the County of Oxford*, ed. Simon Townley, vol. 16 (Boydell & Brewer for the Institute of Historical Research, 2011), 185–189, British History Online, https://www.british-history.ac.uk/vch/oxon/vol16/pp185-189#anchorn54 (accessed December 13, 2020).

23. "The Victorians as Gardeners," *Country Life*, January 1, 1961, 43.

24. Boyd, *Wonderful Today*, 155.

25. Boyd, *Wonderful Today*, 155.

26. Boyd, *Wonderful Today*, 175.

27. Julia Molony, "Polly Devlin: 'After Learning I Was Abused I Spent 14 Years in Therapy,'" *Belfast Telegraph*, May 25, 2019, https://www.belfasttelegraph.co.uk/life/polly-devlin-after-learning-i-was-abused-i-spent-14-years-in-therapy-38134174.html (accessed December 13, 2020).

CHAPTER 17: Bad Behaviour

1. Frances Partridge, *Everything to Lose: Diaries 1946–1960* (Victor Gollancz, 1985), 198.

2. "It *Is* a Moral Issue," *Times*, June 11, 1963, 13.

3. Lord Montagu of Beaulieu, *Wheels Within Wheels: An Unconventional Life* (Weidenfeld & Nicolson, 2000), 88.

4. Montagu, *Wheels Within Wheels*, 86.

5. Peter Wildeblood, *Against the Law* (Penguin Books, 1957), 37.

6. Montagu, *Wheels Within Wheels*, 135.

7. Quoted in Montagu, *Wheels Within Wheels*, 106.

8. "'Passionate' Letter Read as Peer Faces Grave Charges," *Daily Mirror*, March 16, 1954, 6.

9. Montagu, *Wheels Within Wheels*, 107–108.

10. Wildeblood, *Against the Law*, 60.

11. "Three Men Sent to Prison," *Times*, March 25, 1954, 4.

12. Wildeblood, *Against the Law*, 145.

13. Wildeblood, *Against the Law*, 36.

14. Montagu, *Wheels Within Wheels*, 114.

15. *Aberdeen Evening Express*, March 25, 1954, 9.

16. *Daily Mirror*, March 25, 1954, 9.

17. Hugh C. Warner, "Homosexuality Laws," *Times*, December 1, 1952, 5.

18. "Hannen Swaffer Says . . .," *The People*, March 28, 1954, 2.

19. Viscount Hailsham, "Homosexuality and Society," in *They Stand Apart: A Critical Survey of the Problem of Homosexuality*, ed. J. Tudor Rees and Harley V. Usill (William Heinemann, 1955), 26.

20. Richard Davenport-Hines, *An English Affair: Sex, Class and Power in the Age of Profumo* (HarperPress, 2013), 228.

21. Quoted in "Edward, Lord Montagu—In Memoriam," Beaulieu, n.d., https://www.beaulieu.co.uk/edward-lord-montagu-in-memoriam/.

22. Davenport-Hines, *English Affair*, 12.

23. James Lees-Milne, *Diaries 1942–1954* (John Murray, 2006), 110.

24. Richard Buckle (ed.), *Self Portrait with Friends: The Selected Diaries of Cecil Beaton 1926–1974* (Weidenfeld and Nicolson, 1979), 298.

25. "The Gates of Inverary Castle Were Opened to the World," *Tatler*, May 20, 1953, 26–27.

26. Lyndsy Spence, *The Grit in the Pearl: The Scandalous Life of Margaret, Duchess of Argyll* (History Press, 2019), 175.

27. Spence, *Grit in the Pearl*, 169.

28. Michael Thornton, "How I Lost My Virginity to the VERY Racy Real Life Chatelaine of Downton's Scottish Castle," *Mail Online*, December 29, 2012, https://www.dailymail.co.uk/news/article-2254473/How-I-lost-virginity-VERY-racy-real-life-chatelaine-Downtons-Scottish-castle.html.

29. Spence, *Grit in the Pearl*, 195.

30. "Duke of Argyll Is Granted a Decree of Divorce," *Times*, May 9, 1963, 9.

31. "Duke of Argyll Is Granted a Decree of Divorce," 9.

32. "Duke of Argyll Is Granted a Decree of Divorce," 9.

33. "Duke of Argyll Is Granted a Decree of Divorce," 9.

34. Spence, *Grit in the Pearl*, 210.

35. John Gross, "John Bull and John Profumo," *Commentary*, August 1963, https://www.commentarymagazine.com/articles/john-bull-and-john-profumo/.

36. Of the many accounts of the Profumo affair, the best by far is Richard Davenport-Hines's *An English Affair: Sex, Class and Power in the Age of Profumo* (HarperPress, 2013). My own description of events draws heavily on Davenport-Hines's book.

37. Christine Keeler with Douglas Thompson, *Secrets and Lies* (John Blake Publishing, 2012), 109.

38. Keeler, *Secrets and Lies*, 116.

39. Davenport-Hines, *English Affair*, 251.

40. "At the Silent House of Astor," *Daily Express*, August 3, 1963, 6.

41. "The Big Lie," *Daily Mirror*, June 6, 1963, 1–2.

42. "Ward Guilty on 2 Counts," *Birmingham Daily Post*, August 1, 1963, 1.

43. "Current Events," *Sunday Express*, August 4, 1963, 12.

CHAPTER 18: Lions Rampant

1. Jimmy Chipperfield, *My Wild Life* (Pan Books, 1976), 185.

2. Chipperfield, *My Wild Life*, 186.

3. Chipperfield, *My Wild Life*, 186.

4. Chipperfield, *My Wild Life*, 187.

5. Chipperfield, *My Wild Life*, 190.

6. Chipperfield, *My Wild Life*, 193.

7. "The Lions of Longleat," *Times*, September 2, 1965, 13.

8. *Daily Mirror*, February 16, 1965, 6.

9. Quoted in Audrey Noel Hume, "A Royal Menagerie at the Tower," *Country Life*, January 13, 1955, 103.

10. Edward Turner Bennett, *The Tower Menagerie: Comprising the Natural History of the Animals Contained in That Establishment* (Robert Jennings, 1829), xvi.

11. J. N. P. Watson, "Going to See the Lions," *Country Life*, November 16, 1978, 1638.

12. Paget Toynbee, "Horace Walpole's Journals of Visits to Country Seats," *The Volume of the Walpole Society* 16 (1927): 53.

13. Lady Annabel Goldsmith, *Annabel: An Unconventional Life* (Weidenfeld & Nicolson, 2004), 190.

14. Geoffrey Wansell, *Tycoon: The Life of James Goldsmith* (Grafton, 1987), 288.

15. "I'll Always Gamble," *Daily Mirror*, March 20, 1958, 1.

16. "I'll Always Gamble," 1.

17. "I'll Always Gamble," 1.

18. Martin A. Wood, *John Fowler, Prince of Decorators* (Frances Lincoln, 2007), 195.

19. John Aspinall, *The Best of Friends* (Macmillan, 1976), 140.

20. Aspinall, *Best of Friends*, 140.

21. Aspinall, *Best of Friends*, 117.

22. Aspinall, *Best of Friends*, 126.

23. Aspinall, *Best of Friends*, 126.

24. Goldsmith, *Annabel*, 187–188.

25. Aspinall, *Best of Friends*, 134.

26. "On Safari amid the Pride of Wiltshire," *Times*, April 4, 1966, 9.

27. Lord Montagu of Beaulieu, *The Gilt and the Gingerbread, or How to Live in a Stately Home and Make Money* (Michael Joseph, 1967), 105.

28. Montagu, *Gilt and the Gingerbread*, 105.

29. "A New Attraction for Windsor," *Coventry Evening Telegraph*, July 11, 1969, 4.

30. *The People*, February 11, 1968, 5.

31. "Bouncy Babes with Spanking Appetites," *Reading Evening Post*, June 18, 1969, 9.

32. Advertisement, *Coventry Evening Telegraph*, May 15, 1970, 2.

33. John, Duke of Bedford, with George Mikes, *How to Run a Stately Home* (Deutsch, 1971), 118.

34. Bedford, *How to Run a Stately Home*, 117.

35. Bedford, *How to Run a Stately Home*, 114.

36. Frances Partridge, *Life Regained: Diaries 1970–1972* (Weidenfeld & Nicolson, 1998), 140.

37. Partridge, *Life Regained*, 140.

38. Chipperfield, *My Wild Life*, 219.

39. Longleat Enterprises home page, https://www.longleat.co.uk (accessed August 7, 2019).

CHAPTER 19: How Do You Keep It Clean?

1. Robert Harling, *Historic Houses: Conversations in Stately Homes* (Conde Nast Publications, 1969), 158.

2. *Financial Times*, October 18, 1960, quoted in Anthony Sampson, *Anatomy of Britain* (Hodder and Stoughton, 1962), 18.

3. Angela Huth, *Not the Whole Story: A Memoir* (Constable, 2018), 235.

4. Mark Amory (ed.), *The Letters of Ann Fleming* (Collins Harvill, 1985), 43.

5. Roy Perrott, *The Aristocrats: A Portrait of Britain's Nobility and Their Way of Life Today* (Weidenfeld & Nicolson, 1968), 238.

6. Violet Markham and Florence Hancock, Report on Post-War Organisation of Private Domestic Employment, Ministry of Labour, June 1945. Quoted in United States Department of Labor, Women's Bureau, Employment of Women in the Early Postwar Period (Washington, DC: 1946), 31, https://fraser.stlouisfed.org/files/docs/publications/women/b0 211_dolwb_1946.pdf.

7. Douglas Smith, "The Reconstruction of Domestic Service in Great Britain," *Pi Lambda Theta Journal* 24, no. 2 (December 1945): 56.

8. Advertisement, *Country Life*, February 18, 1960, 359.

9. Frances Partridge, *Everything to Lose: Diaries, 1945–1960* (Victor Gollancz, 1985), 15, 44.

10. *Royal Commission on Population Report* (HMSO, 1949), 124.

11. Quoted in Joseph Behar, "'Essential Workers': British Foreign Labour Recruitment, 1945–1951," PhD thesis, University of Toronto (1998), 215.

12. Advertisement, *Western Times*, August 9, 1946, 2; advertisement, *Country Life*, February 18, 1949, 338.

13. Ann Page, *Complete Etiquette for Ladies and Gentlemen* (Ward, Lock, 1961), 87.

14. Elizabeth Basset, *Moments of Vision: A Memoir* (Ledburn, 2004), 120.

15. Ernle Bradford, "The Hall-Mark on Your Silver," *Tatler*, May 29, 1957, 467.

16. Monja Danischewsky, "A Corner in Every Foreign Field," *Tatler*, March 26, 1958, 624.

17. Lucy Lethbridge, *Servants: A Downstairs View of Twentieth-Century Britain* (Bloomsbury Publishing, 2013), 302.

18. Karen Hart, "A Good Beginning," *Tatler*, August 27, 1966, 16.

19. Advertisement, *Tatler*, July 17, 1963, 111.

20. Page, *Complete Etiquette*, 86.

21. Advertisements, *Country Life*, January 27, 1950, 195; January 13, 1950, 75.

22. H. Dalton Clifford, "Modern House in Georgian Tradition," *Country Life*, October 13, 1960, 818.

23. Advertisement, *Country Life*, April 24, 1958, supplement, 23.

24. Michael Haworth-Booth, "Saving Labour in the House," *Country Life*, February 24, 1950, 506.

25. Haworth-Booth, "Saving Labour in the House," 506.

26. Haworth-Booth, "Saving Labour in the House," 507.

27. A. G. L. Hellyer, "Easy Garden Management," *Country Life*, March 10, 1950, 652.

28. Lady Lamb, "The Art of Organising," *Country Life*, March 3, 1950, 581.

29. Page, *Complete Etiquette*, 43.

30. Angela Ince, "Home Counties Escape and Evade Course," *Tatler*, December 18, 1963, 830.

31. Evelyn Waugh, *Brideshead Revisited: The Sacred and Profane Memories of Captain Charles Ryder* (Chapman & Hall, 1960), 44.

32. "Antiques in Court," *Birmingham Daily Post*, February 27, 1958, 5.

33. "Ten-Year Sentence on Butler," *Birmingham Daily Post*, January 22, 1955, 5.

34. Advertisement, *Tatler*, September 24, 1966, 56.

CHAPTER 20: The Last of Uptake?

1. "Going Out to Goings-On," *Bystander*, July 24, 1935, 150.

2. Advertisement, *Tatler*, December 3, 1952, 551.

3. "Goings Out to Goings-On," 150.

4. Simon Harcourt-Smith, *The Last of Uptake, or The Estranged Sisters* (Solstice Productions, 1967), dust jacket.

5. Harcourt-Smith, *Last of Uptake*, 14.

6. "Wealth Tax Proposal and Historic Houses," HL Deb (June 26, 1974) vol. 352, col. 1480–1493, https://hansard.parliament.uk/Lords/1974-06-26 (accessed December 13, 2020).

7. "Wealth Tax Proposal and Historic Houses."

8. "Fighting for the Country House," *Country Life*, October 3, 1974, 920.

9. Sir Roy Strong, *The Roy Strong Diaries 1967–1987* (Weidenfeld & Nicolson, 1997), 141.

10. John Cornforth, *Country Houses in Britain—Can They Survive?* (Country Life for the British Tourist Authority, 1974), 65.

11. Cornforth, *Country Houses in Britain*, 49.

12. Cornforth, *Country Houses in Britain*, 121.

13. Cornforth, *Country Houses in Britain*, 124.

14. Cornforth, *Country Houses in Britain*, 106.

15. "Editorial: The Decline and Fall of the Country House," *Burlington Magazine*, November 1974, 633.

16. "The Arts," HC Deb (December 13, 1974), vol. 883, col. 1046–1078, https://hansard.parliament.uk/Commons/1974-12-13 (accessed December 13, 2020).

17. "Editorial: The Decline and Fall of the Country House," *Burlington Magazine*, November 1974, 633.

18. Harcourt-Smith, *Last of Uptake*, 5.

19. Harcourt-Smith, *Last of Uptake*, 12.

20. Harcourt-Smith, *Last of Uptake*, 72.

21. Harcourt-Smith, *Last of Uptake*, 25.

22. Harcourt-Smith, *Last of Uptake*, 56.

23. Harcourt-Smith, *Last of Uptake*, 56.

24. Harcourt-Smith, *Last of Uptake*, 53.

25. Harcourt-Smith, *Last of Uptake*, 32.

26. Roy Strong, Marcus Binney, and John Harris, *The Destruction of the Country House 1875–1975* (Thames and Hudson, 1974), 6.

27. John Harris, *No Voice from the Hall: Early Memories of a Country House Snooper* (ISIS, 1998), 2.

28. Strong, *Diaries 1967–1987*, 140.

29. James Lees-Milne, "The Country House in Our Heritage," in Strong, Binney, and Harris, *Destruction of the Country House*, 14.

30. Roy Strong, "The Country House Dilemma," in Strong, Binney, and Harris, *Destruction of the Country House*, 7.

31. John Harris, "Gone to Ground," in Strong, Binney, and Harris, *Destruction of the Country House*, 15.

32. Quoted in Philip Howard, "The Fall of the Houses of England," *Times*, September 30, 1974, 16.

33. Robert Harling, "Watch It All Come Down," *Sunday Times*, October 6, 1974, 31.

34. Caroline Tisdall, "Englishmen's Castles," *Guardian*, October 9, 1974, 12.

35. Denis Healey, *The Time of My Life* (Michael Joseph, 1989), 404.

36. Harcourt-Smith, *Last of Uptake*, 28.

37. Harcourt-Smith, *Last of Uptake*, 76.

38. Harcourt-Smith, *Last of Uptake*, 79.

39. "Fire Destroys Coleshill House," *Swindon Evening Advertiser*, September 24, 1952, 1.

40. "Offer for Staunton Harold Hall," *Birmingham Daily Post*, March 22, 1955, 11.

BIBLIOGRAPHY

An Act to Incorporate and Confer Powers upon the National Trust for Places of Historic Interest or Natural Beauty 1907, c. 136. https://nt.global.ssl.fastly.net/documents/download-national-trust-acts-1907-1971-post-order-2005.pdf (accessed December 13, 2020).

Adshead, David, and David A. H. B. Taylor (eds.), *Hardwick Hall: A Great Old Castle of Romance*, Yale University Press (2016).

Aitken, Jonathan, *The Young Meteors*, Secker & Warburg (1967).

Amory, Mark (ed.), *The Letters of Ann Fleming*, Collins Harvill (1985).

Amory, Mark, *Lord Berners: The Last Eccentric*, Faber and Faber, ebook (2012).

Anonymous, *Customs and Etiquette of the Hunting Field*, Rowlands Press (2014).

Archer, Lucy, *Raymond Erith, Architect*, Cygnet (1985).

———, *Raymond Erith: Progressive Classicist 1904–1973*, Soane Gallery (2004).

Architects' Journal.

Aspinall, John, *The Best of Friends*, Macmillan (1976).

Basset, Elizabeth, *Moments of Vision: A Memoir*, Ledburn (2004).

Bath Chronicle and Weekly Gazette.

Beaton, Cecil, *The Parting Years 1963–74*, Sapere Books, ebook (2018).

———, *Self Portrait with Friends: The Selected Diaries of Cecil Beaton 1926–1974*, Weidenfeld and Nicolson (1979).

———, *The Years Between: Diaries 1939–44*, Weidenfeld & Nicolson (1965).

Becker, Robert, *Nancy Lancaster: Her Life, Her World, Her Art*, Alfred A. Knopf (1996).

Bedford, Hastings, Duke of, *A Personal Statement*, privately printed (no date).

Bedford, John, Duke of, *A Silver-Plated Spoon*, Cassell (1959).

Bedford, John, Duke of, with George Mikes, *How to Run a Stately Home*, Deutsch (1971).

Bedford, Nicole, Duchess of, *Nicole Nobody: The Autobiography of the Duchess of Bedford*, W. H. Allen (1974).

Behar, Joseph, "'Essential Workers': British Foreign Labour Recruitment, 1945–1951," PhD thesis, University of Toronto (1998).

Belfast Telegraph.

Bennett, Edward Turner, *The Tower Menagerie: Comprising the Natural History of the Animals Contained in That Establishment*, Robert Jennings (1829).

Birmingham Daily Gazette.

Birmingham Daily Post.

Bogarde, Dirk, *Snakes and Ladders*, Bloomsbury Reader, ebook (2014).

Bowen, Elizabeth, *"Bowen's Court" and "Seven Winters,"* Vintage, ebook (1999).

Boyd, Pattie, *Wonderful Today: The Autobiography*, Headline Review (2007).

Britannia and Eve.

Britton, John, *The Beauties of Wiltshire*, 3 vols., J. D. Dewick (1801, 1825).

Buckinghamshire Examiner.

Burlington Magazine.

Bystander.

Channon, Henry, *Chips: The Diaries of Sir Henry Channon*, edited by Robert Rhodes James, Penguin (1970).

Chatwin, Bruce, *Under the Sun: The Letters of Bruce Chatwin*, Jonathan Cape (2010).

Chipperfield, Jimmy, *My Wild Life*, Pan Books (1976).

Clifford, H. Dalton, *The Country Life Book of Houses for Today*, Country Life (1963).

Coldstream, John, *Dirk Bogarde: The Authorised Biography*, Weidenfeld & Nicolson, ebook (2011).

Compensation (Defence) Act (1939).

Cornforth, John, *Country Houses in Britain—Can They Survive?*, Country Life for the British Tourist Authority (1974).

———, *The Country Houses of England 1948–1998*, Constable (1998).

———, *The Inspiration of the Past: Country House Taste in the Twentieth Century*, Viking in association with *Country Life* (1985).

Country Life.

Coventry Evening Telegraph.

Daily Herald.

Daily Mail.

Daily Mirror.

Daily News (St. John's, Newfoundland).

Daily Record (Long Branch, New Jersey).

Dale, T. F., *The Eighth Duke of Beaufort and the Badminton Hunt*, Archibald Constable (1901).

Daltrey, Roger, *Thanks a Lot Mr Kibblewhite: My Story*, Blink Publishing, ebook (2019).

Davenport-Hines, Richard, *An English Affair: Sex, Class and Power in the Age of Profumo*, HarperPress (2013).

De Courcy, Anne, *Snowdon: The Biography*, Phoenix, ebook (2012).

Debrett's Peerage, Baronetage, Knightage and Companionage, Odhams Press (1947).

Devonshire, Andrew, *Accidents of Fortune*, Michael Russell (2004).

Devonshire, Deborah, *Counting My Chickens, and Other Home Thoughts*, Long Barn Books (2001).

———, *Wait for Me! Memoirs of the Youngest Mitford Sister*, John Murray (2011).

Driffield Times.

Dutton, Ralph, *Hinton Ampner: A Hampshire Manor*, National Trust (2010).

———, *The English Country House*, B. T. Batsford (1935).

Fielding, Daphne, *Mercury Presides*, Eyre & Spottiswoode (1954).

Finance Act 1946, c. 64. https://www.legislation.gov.uk/ukpga/Geo6/9-10 /64/contents (accessed December 15, 2020).

Finance Act 1953, c. 34. https://www.legislation.gov.uk/ukpga/Eliz2/1-2/34 /contents/enacted (accessed December 15, 2020).

Financial Times.

Fortnightly Review.

Fraser, Antonia, *My History: A Memoir of Growing Up*, Weidenfeld & Nicolson, ebook (2015).

Garnett, Andy, *Memories of a Lucky Dog*, Turnham Press, ebook (2011).

Getty, J. Paul, *As I See It*, Berkley Books (1986).

Gloucestershire Echo.

Goldsmith, Lady Annabel, *Annabel: An Unconventional Life*, Weidenfeld & Nicolson (2004).

Gowers, Sir Ernest, *Report of the Committee on Houses of Outstanding Historic or Architectural Interest*, HMSO (1950).

Gross, John, "John Bull and John Profumo," *Commentary*, https://www .commentarymagazine.com/articles/john-bull-and-john-profumo/.

A Handbook for Travellers in Kent, 5th edition, John Murray (1892).

Hansard.

Harcourt-Smith, Simon, *The Last of Uptake, or The Estranged Sisters*, Solstice Productions (1967).

Harling, Robert, *Historic Houses: Conversations in Stately Homes*, Condé Nast Publications (1969).

Harris, John, *No Voice from the Hall: Early Memories of a Country House Snooper*, ISIS (1998).

Healey, Denis, *The Time of My Life*, Michael Joseph (1989).

Hicks, David, *David Hicks on Living—with Taste*, Leslie Frewin (1968).

Hogarth, Tim, *The Dazzling Lady Docker: Britain's Forgotten Reality Superstar*, Scratching Shed Publishing (2018).

Howard, Paul, *I Read the News Today, Oh Boy: The Short and Gilded Life of Tara Browne, the Man Who Inspired the Beatles' Greatest Song*, Picador, ebook (2016).

Hunt Saboteurs Association, https://www.huntsabs.org.uk/index.php/about-the-hsa/hsa-history (accessed January 22, 2021).

Huth, Angela, *Not the Whole Story: A Memoir*, Constable (2018).

Ightham Mote, National Trust (2016).

Illustrated London News.

Illustrated Sporting and Dramatic News.

Independent.

Indianapolis Star (IN).

James, Henry, *English Hours*, Houghton, Mifflin (1905).

Keeler, Christine, with Douglas Thompson, *Secrets and Lies*, John Blake Publishing, ebook (2012).

Kenward, Betty, *Jennifer's Memoirs: Eighty-Five Years of Fun and Functions*, HarperCollins (1992).

Labour Party Executive Committee, *Let Us Face the Future: A Declaration of Labour Policy for the Consideration of the Nation* (1945).

Lacey, Robert, *Royal: Her Majesty Queen Elizabeth II*, Time Warner (2002).

Lancashire Evening Post.

Law, Michael John, *Not Like Home: American Visitors to Britain in the 1950s*, McGill-Queen's University Press (2019).

Lees-Milne, James, *Ancestral Voices*, Faber and Faber (1984).

———, *Caves of Ice*, Faber and Faber (1984).

———, *Diaries 1942–1954*, John Murray (2006).

———, *Diaries 1971–1983*, John Murray (2007).

———, *Fourteen Friends*, John Murray (1996).

———, *Midway on the Waves*, Faber and Faber (1987).

———, *Prophesying Peace*, Faber and Faber (1984).

Leinster Leader.

Lethbridge, Lucy, *Servants: A Downstairs View of Twentieth-Century Britain*, Bloomsbury Publishing, ebook (2013).

Liverpool Echo.

Londonderry Sentinel.

Lyon, Neil, *"Useless Anachronisms?": A Study of the Country Houses and Landed Estates of Northamptonshire Since 1880*, Northamptonshire Record Society (2018).

MacCarthy, Fiona, *Last Curtsey: The End of the Debutante*, Faber and Faber, ebook (2010).

Manchester Guardian.

Mandler, Peter, *The Fall and Rise of the Stately Home*, Yale University Press (1997).

McKenney, Ruth, and Richard Bransten, *Here's England: A Highly Informal Guide*, Rupert Hart-Davis (1955).

Mitford, Nancy (ed.), *Noblesse Oblige: An Enquiry into the Identifiable Characteristics of the English Aristocracy*, Harper & Brothers (1956).

Montagu, Lord Edward, *The Gilt and the Gingerbread, or How to Live in a Stately Home and Make Money*, Michael Joseph (1967).

——, *Wheels Within Wheels: An Unconventional Life*, Weidenfeld & Nicolson (2000).

Mumford, Lewis, "From Crotchet Castle to Arthur's Seat," in *The Highway and the City*, Harcourt, Brace and World (1963).

Northampton Mercury.

O'Byrne, Robert, *Luggala Days: The Story of a Guinness House*, CICO Books (2012).

Observer.

Page, Ann, *Complete Etiquette for Ladies and Gentlemen*, Ward, Lock (1964).

Parker, D. H., *The Story of My Life in Gentlemen's Service*, privately printed (1978).

Partridge, Frances, *Everything to Lose: Diaries, 1945–1960*, Victor Gollancz (1985).

——, *Good Company: Diaries 1967–1970*, HarperCollins (1994).

——, *Hanging On: Diaries December 1960–August 1963*, Phoenix Giant (1998).

——, *Life Regained: Diaries 1970–1972*, Weidenfeld & Nicolson (1998).

Pearson, Ronald Hooke, *Baynton House*, Putnam (1955).

Pells, Richard, *Not Like Us*, Basic Books (1997).

The People.

Perrott, Roy, *The Aristocrats: A Portrait of Britain's Nobility and Their Way of Life Today*, Weidenfeld & Nicolson (1968).

Pevsner, Nikolaus, and Edward Hubbard, *The Buildings of England: Cheshire*, Penguin Books (2001).

Pidgeon, Mary Elizabeth, *Employment of Women in the Early Postwar Period*, United States Department of Labor (1947).

Portsmouth Evening News.

Reading Evening Post.

Rees, J. Tudor, and Harley V. Usill (eds.), *They Stand Apart: A Critical Survey of the Problem of Homosexuality*, William Heinemann (1955).

Richards, Keith, *Life*, Phoenix, ebook (2012).

Ridley, Jane, *Bertie: A Life of Edward VII*, Vintage, ebook (2013).

Robinson, John Martin, *Requisitioned: The British Country House in the Second World War*, Aurum Press (2014).

———, *The Latest Country Houses*, Bodley Head (1984).

Rose, Kenneth, *Who's In, Who's Out: The Journals of Kenneth Rose 1944–1979*, Weidenfeld & Nicolson (2018).

Ross, Alan S. C., "Linguistic Class-Indicators in Present-Day English," *Neuphilologische mitteilungen* 108 (1954): 20–56.

Rugby Advertiser.

Russell, Anthony, *Outrageous Fortune: Growing Up at Leeds Castle*, Robson Press (2013).

Russell, Maud, *A Constant Heart: The War Diaries of Maud Russell 1938–1945*, edited by Emily Russell, Dovecote Press (2017).

Sackville-West, Vita, *English Country Houses*, Britain in Pictures series, Collins (1941).

Sackville-West, Vita, and Harold Nicolson, *Vita and Harold: The Letters of Vita Sackville-West and Harold Nicolson 1910–1962*, edited by Nigel Nicolson, Weidenfeld & Nicolson (1992).

Sampson, Anthony, *Anatomy of Britain*, Hodder and Stoughton (1962).

Sanchez, Tony, *Up and Down with the Rolling Stones: My Rollercoaster Ride with Keith Richards*, John Blake Publishing (2010).

Saunders, Peter, *Almost a Fairy Story: A History of Easton Grey House*, privately printed (no date).

Shawcross, William, *Queen Elizabeth: The Queen Mother*, Macmillan (2009).

Sitwell, Osbert, foreword to *The English Country House* by Ralph Dutton, B. T. Batsford (1935).

———, *Laughter in the Next Room*, Macmillan (1949).

Sketch.

Smith, Douglas, "The Reconstruction of Domestic Service in Great Britain," *Pi Lambda Theta Journal* 24, no. 2 (December 1945): 54–56, 70.

Spence, Lyndsy, *The Grit in the Pearl: The Scandalous Life of Margaret, Duchess of Argyll*, History Press (2019).

Sphere.

St John-McAlister, Michael, "Michael Renshaw: A Society Figure in War and Peace," *eBLJ*, 2015, article 6, https://www.bl.uk/eblj/2015articles/pdf/ebljarticle62015.pdf.

Staffordshire Sentinel.

Strong, Roy, Marcus Binney, and John Harris, *The Destruction of the Country House 1875–1975*, Thames and Hudson (1974).

Strong, Sir Roy, *The Roy Strong Diaries 1967–1987*, Weidenfeld & Nicolson (1997).

Summers, Julie, *Our Uninvited Guests: The Secret Lives of Britain's Country Houses 1939–1945*, Simon & Schuster (2018).

Sunday Times.

Surrey Advertiser.

Swindon Evening Advertiser.

Tatler.

Telegraph.

Tichelar, Michael, "'A Blow to the Men in Pink': The Royal Society for the Prevention of Cruelty to Animals and Opposition to Hunting in the Twentieth Century," *Rural History* 22 (2011): 1, 89–113.

Times (London).

Tinniswood, Adrian, "Guidebooks and Historic Buildings," *Bulletin of Local History: East Midland Region* 17 (1982): 1–9.

———, *The Long Weekend: Life in the English Country House, 1918–1939*, Basic Books (2016).

Townley, Simon (ed.), *A History of the County of Oxford*, 18 vols., Boydell & Brewer for the Institute of Historical Research (2011).

Townsend, Peter, *Time and Chance: An Autobiography*, Collins (1978).

Vidal, Gore, *Palimpsest: A Memoir*, Random House (1995).

Vivian, Francis, *The Threefold Cord: An Inspector Knollis Mystery*, Dean Street Press (2018).

Vogue.

Walpole, Horace, "Journals of Visits to Country Seats," *The Volume of the Walpole Society* 16 (1927): 9–80.

Wansell, Geoffrey, *Tycoon: The Life of James Goldsmith*, Grafton (1987).

Warwick and Warwickshire Advertiser.

Warwick, Christopher, *Princess Margaret: A Life of Contrasts*, André Deutsch, ebook (2002).

Watson, Michael Saunders, *I Am Given a Castle: The Memoirs of Michael Saunders Watson*, JJG (2008).

Waugh, Evelyn, *Brideshead Revisited: The Sacred and Profane Memories of Captain Charles Ryder*, Chapman & Hall (1960).

———, *The Diaries of Evelyn Waugh*, Weidenfeld & Nicolson (1976).

West Gippsland Gazette (Victoria, Australia).

West Sussex Gazette.

Western Daily Press.

Western Mail.

Western Times.

Wildeblood, Peter, *Against the Law*, Penguin Books (1957).

Williams-Ellis, Clough, *Architect Errant*, Constable (1971).

———, *Around the World in Ninety Years*, Golden Dragon Books (1978).

———, *On Trust for the Nation*, Paul Elek (1947).

Wiltshire Times and Trowbridge Advertiser.

Wood, Martin A., *John Fowler, Prince of Decorators*, Frances Lincoln (2007).

Bibliography

Wyman, Bill, with Ray Coleman, *Stone Alone: The Story of a Rock 'n' Roll Band*, privately published, ebook (2016).

Yorkshire Post and Leeds Intelligencer.

Yorkshire Post and Leeds Mercury.

Zinovieff, Sofka, *The Mad Boy, Lord Berners, My Grandmother and Me*, Jonathan Cape (2014).

INDEX

Note: Locators in *italics* indicate photos.

Adrian Tinniswood is senior research fellow in history at the University of Buckingham and the author of many books on British history, including *Behind the Throne*, the *New York Times* bestseller *The Long Weekend*, and *The Verneys*. He was awarded an OBE for services to heritage by the Queen and lives in Bath, England.